OPERATION WETBACK

Contributions in Ethnic Studies
Series Editor: Leonard Doob

Nations Remembered: An Oral History of the Five Civilized Tribes, 1865-1907
Theda Perdue

OPERATION WETBACK

The Mass Deportation of Mexican Undocumented Workers in 1954

Juan Ramon García

Contributions in Ethnic Studies,
Number 2

GREENWOOD PRESS
WESTPORT, CT • LONDON, ENGLAND

Library of Congress Cataloging in Publication Data

García, Juan Ramon.
    Operation Wetback.

    (Contributions in ethnic studies; no. 2 ISSN 0196-7088)
    Bibliography: p.
    Includes index.
    1. Mexicans in the United States. 2. United States—Relations (general) with Mexico.
3. Mexico—Relations (general) with the United States. 4. United States—Emigration and
immigration. 5. Mexico—Economic conditions—1918-   6. Alien labor, Mexican—
United States. I. Title. II. Series.
E184.M5G37   325' .272'0973   79-6189
ISBN 0-313-21353-4 lib. bdg.

Library of Congress Catalog Card Number: 79-6189
ISBN: 0-313-21353-4
ISSN: 0196-7088

First published in 1980

Greenwood Press
A division of Congressional Information Service, Inc.
88 Post Road West, Westport, Connecticut 06881

Printed in the United States of America

10 9 8 7 6 5 4 3 2 1

I dedicate this book in loving
memory to Richard B. Jensen
and Betty Samora, two people
who believed in the ability of
young people.

Contents

Illustrations

Tables

Figures

Series Foreword

"Contributions in Ethnic Studies" focuses upon the problems that arise when peoples with different cultures and goals come together and interact productively or tragically. The modes of adjustment or conflict are various, but usually one group dominates or attempts to dominate the other. Eventually some accomodation is reached: the process is likely to be long and, for the weaker group, painful. No one scholarly discipline monopolizes the research necessary to comprehend these intergroup relations. The emerging analysis, consequently, inevitably is of interest to historians, social scientists, psychologists, and psychiatrists.

Operation Wetback deals with an international problem of baffling complexity. Mexican laborers (*braceros*), both before and after World War II, were unable to eke out a satisfactory existence at home and they migrated, always regretfully and usually temporarily, to Arizona, California, New Mexico, and Texas where they toiled on large farms and fruit groves. Some gained entry legally. Others— the so called illegal aliens, illegals, undocumented workers, "wetbacks"—crossed the unguarded 1600-mile border and evaded the United States Immigration Service. The migrants were gobbled up by American growers and processors of foodstuffs and were usually compelled to live under miserable conditions; in return they received substandard wages and suffered gross discrimination and humiliation.

The tale Professor García tells, therefore, is ugly and disquieting. He has searched the records and provides relevant documentation. He depicts the plight of the Mexicans, one of whom summarized their condition in five words: "Our necessity knows no law." García shows how many, but not all, American employers have been uninhibited by moral or legal restraints to safeguard their labor supply. Corruption has occurred on both sides of the border.

The emphasis in this volume is upon "Operation Wetback" in 1954-1955, the expensive and only partially successful drive by American authorities during the Eisenhower administration to roundup, often brutally, the wetbacks in the United States and to ship them back to Mexico on foot or by bus or plane. That politically confused operation is portrayed in its historical, geographical, statistical, political, and above all human context from 1941 on. Wetbacks began arriving in

large numbers because too few were able to use the legal route then in existence.
Mexican and American officials could not reach a satisfactory modus vivendi.
The Mexican authorities were "deeply embarrassed" by the indisputable fact that
so many of their countrymen, were, in Professor García's words, "broken, hungry,
and desperate"—and unemployed. They also wished to protect their citizens who
were toiling in the north. The Americans were pressured by the growers' lobbyists
so that they allowed their border guards to authorize "instant legalization" of
migrants: "The legalization process was accomplished by having Mexicans who
entered illegally run back to the official border crossing point, put one foot on
Mexican soil and then dart back so they could be legally processed."

These depressing episodes must be encompassed by sociologists and anthropol-
igists interested in migration, culture contact, and race relations; by political
scientists and specialists in international relations who would delve beneath the
formal agreements between two countries confronted with obvious human misery
and apparent economic necessity; by behavioral scientists who would observe
how persons in real life react to desperation and greed; by economists who would
view the dynamics behind the supply and demand of a labor force; and by everyone who must ever witness and who cannot ignore the frequently ignoble and
rarely noble actions of our contemporaries. Operation Wetback may have been
terminated, but the challenge of dealing with "the seemingly insatiable appetite
for cheap labor among certain groups of employers in this country" persists, like
it or not.

Leonard W. Doob
June 3, 1980

Preface

THE PURPOSE OF this book is to examine the major factors that influenced the large influx of undocumented persons from Mexico into the United States during the 1940s and the early 1950s and to provide an in-depth study of "Operation Wetback," the mass deportation of undocumented persons in 1954, and the events that led up to it. The book also attempts to discuss other issues affecting the controversy over the influx of the so-called wetback into the United States between 1941 and 1954.

The question of illegal Mexican immigration to the United States was, and continues to be, vexing and controversial in nature—vexing because it has victimized both the "illegals" and other groups in American society and controversial because of its emotional, social, political, and economic implications. Unfortunately the undocumented person was unfairly blamed for many social and economic problems extant in the United States. Few recognized that the "illegal alien" was in reality more a symptom of these problems than a major cause.

The introduction provides a brief overview of the push/pull factors in the United States and Mexico that contributed to the influx of undocumented persons. Chapter 1 examines the Bracero Program and its relation to the growing controversy over the "wetbacks" during the "Wetback Decade." Chapter 2 examines the series of conflicting policies on Mexican immigration followed by both countries and their role in policy decisions over the "wetback issue." Chapter 3 treats the issue of increased Border Patrol appropriations and the effect of politics on the efficiency of the Border Patrol. Chapter 4 deals with the exploitation of undocumented persons and the rationale and attitudes used to justify such actions by unscrupulous employers.

Opponents of the illegal influx from Mexico credited the undocumented persons with causing a myriad of social and economic ills in the United States. This group, largely made up of members of a variety of social, welfare, religious, and labor organizations, believed that the illegal influx from Mexico could be curtailed through the passage of legislation to penalize those who employed undocumented workers. Chapter 5 examines such legislative proposals.

Critics of the undocumented persons charged that they depressed wages, lowered living standards, contributed to social problems, increased the incidence of crime and disease, and disrupted labor organizing efforts. Such charges led a number of organizations to support restrictive legislation and mass roundups in an effort to curtail the influx of "illegals." Yet the efforts of such groups proved futile in the face of the need for a large pool of cheap labor.

Action against the "illegals" came only when they were no longer necessary contributors to the economy of the United States. Such action has usually manifested itself in intense repatriation and deportation drives. One such drive occurred during the early years of the Great Depression when private, local, state, and federal agencies undertook an all-out effort to rid themselves of Mexican and Mexican-American citizens who had swollen relief rolls. A mass deportation drive also occurred in 1954. The final four chapters concentrate on "Operation Wetback" itself and the motives for its implementation.

Several themes in this period are apparent. First of all, it is evident that Mexicans, whether here legally or illegally, were welcomed in the United States only as long as their labor was needed. Second, the events of the period reflect the belief on the part of most growers that they had an inherent right to the use of illegal laborers. Third, undocumented persons were generally dehumanized and depersonalized by both those who opposed their entry and those who encouraged it. "Illegal aliens" had no true champions to take up their cause, to meet their needs, or to turn to for help. Finally, most of those involved in the debate over illegal entrants and their employment viewed the "illegal" as the cause of many problems rather than a symptom. Failing to recognize this as an error, they were unable to grapple with the real issues and problems that contributed to illegal entry into the United States.

The terms "wetback(s)," "illegals," and "illegal aliens" are used here because they were in use throughout most of the period studied. Because I find them distasteful and derogatory, I have placed these in quotation marks to signify that they were used by the individuals and groups cited.

Acknowledgments

ALTHOUGH UNDOCUMENTED PERSONS have been the source of repeated concern, attention, and controversy, there are, surprisingly enough, very few good studies of their situation. I was unable to locate a study that dealt specifically with the mass repatriation effort of 1954, "Operation Wetback." Most of the material presented here was gleaned from published and unpublished government reports, hearings, and studies. I have drawn on unpublished materials located in the files of the Departments of Labor, Agriculture, Justice, and State, in collections housed in the Eisenhower Library in Abilene, Kansas, in the Notre Dame Archives, and in the National Archives in Washington, D.C. Much information specific to the drive came from once-classified documents of the operation housed in the offices of the Immigration and Naturalization Service and the Justice Department in Washington, D.C.

A great many people made this study possible. First and foremost I wish to acknowledge the help, encouragement, and insight of Dr. Frederick B. Pike. My admiration and respect for him know no bounds, and my deepest thanks go out to him for his unfailing faith and confidence in me. I also wish to thank Dr. Julian Samora, who first suggested the topic to me and who opened his personal files on Mexican immigration to me. He, too, is a man for whom I feel a great deal of respect and admiration, not only for his guidance but for the example he has set for me and other Chicanos. A special vote of thanks to Father Marvin O'Connell, who was instrumental in helping me overcome federal bureaucratic obstacles so that I could examine information important to my study; and to Mr. Harlon B. Carter. Mr. Carter, who was instrumental in the development and implementation of "Operation Wetback," proved a most congenial and cooperative host during my visits to his office. My conversations with him concerning the events of 1954 and other matters revealed to me a man of concern, compassion, intelligence, and honesty. His input was invaluable.

The archival staff at the Eisenhower Library in Abilene, Kansas, was of immense help in locating much-needed information. Heartfelt thanks to Señor y

Señora George and Helen Ulibarri at the National Archives, who took time from their busy schedules to locate and assemble materials pertinent to my study. They made my work in the archives both rewarding and enjoyable.

Special thanks to my lovely wife, Louise, for her help, guidance, and support. Her typing skills, her critical reading ability, her keen intellect, and her patience, especially during my extended absences on research excursions or writing periods, proved invaluable. And thanks to my parents, Juan and Marcía García, my family and my *raza*, for having instilled in me pride in my culture and heritage.

OPERATION WETBACK

Introduction: Factors Influencing Mexican Immigration

FRANK TANNENBAUM'S STATEMENT that Mexico is a beautiful place in which to live but a hard place to make a living[1] provides an insight into why many Mexicans came to the United States legally and illegally following the outbreak of World War II. The migration of Mexico's citizenry to the United States was not a new phenomenon. The first large-scale immigration had occurred between the early 1900s and the onset of the Depression, when thousands of Mexicans and Mexican Americans were either deported by local agencies and organizations or returned to Mexico in hope of earning some kind of living. Although the Depression of the 1930s did not halt Mexican immigration completely, it did reduce the flow to a trickle.

The beginning of World War II and the entry of the United States into the world struggle brought an end to the Depression era. The war created new demands for labor, and within a short period of time America's unemployment disappeared. People flocked to the industrial-military complexes and to large urban centers. Many who had been forced into the migrant stream because of the Depression quickly abandoned migrant work for better-paying jobs and a more stable way of life. Whereas in 1940 there were over one million domestic migrants, that number had been reduced almost to 60,000 by 1942.[2]

Mexico was not as fortunate as the United States. Although the outbreak of war did help improve the economic picture, there still remained numerous obstacles to Mexico's economic development and to an improved standard of living for many of its people. These obstacles, when combined with economic development in the United States, served to encourage or force a renewed exodus of Mexicans to the United States.

One such obstacle was Mexico's topography. Mexico is a mountainous country. Only one-third of its land area is level, and much of that is situated at comparatively high altitudes or in the unproductive Yucatan basin. The northern part of the country does not receive sufficient rainfall to make it very productive, and the lack of rivers in Mexico makes irrigation of arid areas difficult and expensive.

Mexico's mountainous terrain has hindered the development of transportation routes from east to west; and though its high plateaus and mountains give the country a much cooler climate in summer than its tropical position on the map would indicate, they also serve to isolate the rural parts of Mexico.[3]

Problems of geography were exacerbated by the dramatic increase in the population of Mexico between 1940 and 1950. In that ten-year period Mexico's population rose to over 25 million, a net increase of 30.8 percent.[4] This tremendous growth seriously overburdened Mexico's limited arable land and its capacity to provide for the people.

During the 1940s and 1950s only 7 to 10 percent of Mexico's land was arable. Estimates at that time placed the amount of land that could be arable under any conditions at about 20 percent.[5] Of the 10 percent or 49 million acres that were "tillable" in 1950, 22 million acres (or about 46 percent of the tillable land) lay fallow (see table 1).[6]

TABLE 1

Land Use in Mexico, 1950 and 1960
(millions of hectares)

	1950 Census			1960 Census		
	Total	Private and Federal Property	Ejidos	Total	Private and Federal Property	Ejidos
Tillable land	19.9	11.1	8.8	23.8	13.5	10.3
Irrigated	2.4	1.2	1.2	3.4	2.0	1.4
Irrigated with subterranean water	0.7	0.3	0.4	0.8	0.4	0.4
Temporary crops (unirrigated)	16.0	9.1	6.9	18.3	10.3	8.0
Permanent crops	0.8	0.5	0.3	1.3	0.8	0.5
Pastures	67.4	50.9	16.5	79.1	59.5	19.6
Forests	38.8	30.0	8.8	43.7	35.7	8.0
Productive lands, not under cultivation	7.8	6.1	1.7	11.2	7.3	3.9
Unproductive lands	11.6	8.5	3.1	11.3	8.7	2.6
Total[a]	145.5	106.8	38.9	169.1	124.7	44.5

[a]Area covered by census.
Source: Mexican Agriculture Census, 1950 and 1960

Of the remaining cultivatable land, about 60 percent was devoted to the growing of corn. Yet the crop yield remained far below that needed to feed the hungry masses. Figures indicate that during the 1940s Mexico yielded only 7.8 bushels per acre, compared to Canada's yield of 37.4 bushels per acre. In comparison with production in the United States the gap was even more glaring. For example, in

1943 the state of Iowa produced 605,454,000 bushels of corn, while Mexico as a whole produced only one-fifth of that.[7]

The problem of crop yield, limited land, and population increases were exacerbated in northern Mexico by a drought that struck in 1948. Lasting for almost five years, the drought intensified Mexico's poverty, causing massive unemployment and growing discontent in the rural areas.[8] In the state of Durango about 379,000 head of cattle worth 8.7 million dollars perished in 1953.[9] This drought was so intense that many reservoirs nearly dried up, making the irrigation facilities nearly useless.[10] In 1953 the drought came to an abrupt end when northern Mexico was struck by floods, leaving many farmers completely destitute. Broken, hungry, and desperate, many of these men fled to the urban areas of Mexico seeking a new start or joined the ever-increasing stream of bracero hopefuls who sought to earn money in the United States for a new start. Thus the combined factors of topography, severe climatic changes, and unprecedented increases in population provided some of the most compelling reasons for Mexican emigration to the United States.

On top of all of these troubles, Mexico experienced severe inflation and growing unemployment, both of which served to encourage legal and illegal immigration into the United States. Again, the hardest hit by these problems was the rural agrarian sector.

The government attempted to quell discontent by painting a glowing picture of its economic growth. It pointed to the fact that the Gross National Product had risen at an average of 6 percent a year between 1951 and 1954. Wages had also increased from 1,982 pesos annually in 1951 to 3,326 in 1954.[11] The Mexican government also invested over 5.2 billion pesos from 1926 to 1958 in state irrigation projects. (Table 2) Of that, over one-third was invested in northern Mexico in an effort to stimulate the economy and reduce migration to other urban areas.[12] Unfortunately, by investing in such projects and increasing agricultural output, which required a larger work force than was readily available, Mexico itself encouraged movement toward the border regions. As was often the case, more workers showed up than was required. In the end, the surplus sought employment in the United States, which served to defeat Mexico's efforts to keep large numbers of unemployed men from gravitating toward the border, where they might emigrate illegally.

In an effort to provide more jobs for the large influx of rural migrants into urban areas, the Mexican government encouraged industrialization. Although production and the per capita income did increase through such efforts, the growth of the national market progressed slowly and consumption remained low.[13] Little progress was made with regard to social security development, price supports, and the development of a strong economic infrastructure.[14]

The problem confronting the agricultural sector continued to plague Mexican officials. This sector contained the largest and most economically depressed group and had the greatest potential for causing social unrest. Agriculture continually lagged far behind industrial growth; and although Mexico's per capita income did increase, almost all of it was eaten up by inflation. For example, the average rural

TABLE 2

Federal Expenditures
for Irrigation and Water
Resources by State, 1926-1958

Entity	Percentage
Mexico	100.0
Aguascalientes	.2
Baja California	8.5
Baja Territorio	––
Campeche	––
Coahuila	.3
Colima	––
Chiapas	.4
Chihuahua	2.6
Distrito Federal	4.3
Durango	2.4
Guanajuato	2.5
Guerrero	.3
Hidalgo	.9
Jalisco	3.1
Mexico	.2
Michoacan	6.7
Morelos	––
Nayarit	1.2
Neuvo Leon	.3
Oaxaca	10.6
Puebla	5.6
Queretaro	.3
Quintana Roo	––
San Luis Potosi	.1
Sinaloa	14.7
Sonora	13.2
Tabasco	.2
Tamaulipas	12.0
Tlaxcala	––
Veracruz	8.7
Yucatan	––
Zacatecas	.7

Source: Mexico, Secretaria de Recursos Hidraulicos,
Informe . . ., 1958-59. Cited in: James W. Wilkie,
*The Mexican Revolution: Federal Expenditure
and Social Change Since 1910* (Berkeley: University of California Press, 1967), pp. 252-53.

salary increased by 540 percent between 1940 and 1960, but the cost of living increased by 800 percent.[15] These figures are given added significance when one considers that while the agricultural sector in the 1940s and 1950s constituted over 60 percent of the population, it earned only 20 percent of Mexico's income.[16] This discrepancy was due, according to Eduardo V. Venezian, to the fact that most of Mexico's growth in agricultural output was horizontal in nature. That is, more labor was applied to more land, "under an essentially constant production function, thus resulting in greater output with no great change in factor returns."[17]

Increases in wages for agricultural workers were not that significant when one takes into consideration the rate of inflation and the disparity between wages paid in Mexico and those paid in the United States. In 1949 the average per capita income in Mexico was $114.00 per year. In that same year the average per capita income in the United States was $1,453 per year.[18] At about that time the cost of living index in Mexico City was 354, as compared to 171 in the United States.[19]

Between 1951 and 1953, figures indicate that wage rates for unskilled agricultural laborers in Mexico, although increasing, nonetheless continued to vary widely, ranging from about 4.0 pesos to 20.0 pesos a day, without board (see table 3). This was equivalent to about $0.46 to $2.31 in United States currency. Wages in the central and north central regions of Mexico were lower than those paid in the coastal and northern border regions; between 1948 and 1953 the gap in wages between these regions widened significantly. The sharpest increase in wages during this five-year period occurred in the northern border region, where wages increased by some 92 percent.[20] (Table 4) After 1953 wages increased very little and in fact decreased because of the drop in production caused by the drought. That wages in the northern border region were higher is not really surprising, given that competition for labor was keener because of a sparse population and the proximity of the United States, where wages were significantly higher.[21]

During the late 1940s and early 1950s agricultural laborers in Mexico earned anywhere from $0.38 to $0.69 per day, while in the United States they could earn from $0.25 to over $0.50 per *hour*, depending upon where they worked.[22] Because of this wage differential, the purchasing power of the peso had declined dramatically, which added to Mexico's inflationary problems. Thus, while the increase in farm wages between 1948 and 1953 was more rapid in Mexico than in the United States, the gain was offset by the real purchasing power of the peso in terms of United States currency. In January of 1948 the peso was equivalent to 20.62 cents in U.S. money, but in July of that same year it declined sharply. By July of 1949 the peso was equivalent only to about 11.56 cents, where it remained until 1953. Therefore, in January of 1948 the average wage of 3.02 pesos in the north central region was equivalent to 62.3 cents in U.S. currency, while at the devalued rate the July 1953 wage of 4.80 pesos was equivalent only to 55.4 cents U.S., an actual decline.[23]

The wage differential between the two countries also produced a geographically

TABLE 3

Average Farm Wages,
per day, without board,
quarterly, 1951 to July 1953
(pesos)

North-Central Mexico

Quarter	Chihuahua	Monterrey	Torreon	San Luis Potosi	Guadalajara	N. Cen. Average
1951						
Jan.	3.31	4.50	6.00	4.00	3.00	4.16
Apr.	3.31	4.50	6.50	3.75	3.50	4.31
July	3.31	4.50	5.25	3.50	4.50	4.51
Oct.	3.31	4.50	7.00	3.25	4.50	4.51
1952						
Jan.	4.95	4.45	7.00	4.00	4.50	4.98
Apr.	5.00	4.45	5.37	4.00	4.50	4.66
July	5.00	4.45	5.25	4.00	4.50	4.64
Oct.	5.00	4.95	5.25	4.00	4.50	5.64
1953						
Jan.	4.50	4.25	6.25	4.00	4.50	4.70
Apr.	4.50	4.50	6.25	4.50	4.50	4.85
July	4.50	4.75	6.25	4.00	4.50	4.80

Coastal Areas

Quarter	Tampico	Veracruz	Mazatlan	Guaymas	Merida	Coastal Average
1951						
Jan.	5.00	6.50	5.50	6.50	9.00	6.50
Apr.	5.00	6.50	5.60	6.50	9.00	6.52
July	5.00	6.75	5.75	7.00	9.50	6.80
Oct.	5.00	6.50	6.00	7.50	10.00	7.00
1952						
Jan.	5.00	6.50	6.00	8.00	8.40	6.78
Apr.	5.00	6.50	6.50	8.00	8.00	6.80
July	5.00	6.50	7.00	8.00	7.00	6.70
Oct.	5.00	6.50	7.00	8.00	8.40	6.98
1953						
Jan.	5.00	6.75	6.00	8.50	7.50	6.71
Apr.	6.00	6.75	6.00	9.15	7.50	7.08
July	6.00	7.00	6.00	9.00	7.50	7.10

TABLE 3—Continued

Northern Border Areas

Quarter	Mata-moros	Rey-nosa	N. La-redo	P. Ne-gras	Cd. Juarez	No-gales	Mexi-cali	Tijua-na	No. Border Average
1951									
Jan.	7.50	8.00	3.55	4.50	6.70	8.00	10.00	8.00	6.99
April	6.00	8.00	5.50	5.00	5.50	8.00	12.00	9.00	7.39
July	8.90	8.00	5.50	5.00	5.50	8.00	17.00	10.00	8.49
Oct.	7.00	9.00	6.00	4.00	6.00	10.00	18.00	10.00	8.75
1952									
Jan.	7.00	8.00	7.50	4.00	7.00	8.15	14.00	10.00	8.21
April	7.00	8.00	7.50	4.50	8.50	10.00	13.00	12.00	8.81
July	7.00	9.00	7.50	4.00	8.60	10.50	15.00	14.50	9.51
Oct.	7.00	11.00	7.50	4.00	8.60	10.00	20.00	20.00	−11.01
1953									
Jan.	7.00	1	7.00	4.50	8.60	10.00	20.00	20.00	11.01
April	7.00	1	7.00	4.50	8.60	10.00	15.00	20.00	10.30
July	7.00	1	7.00	4.50	8.60	9.75	20.00	15.00	10.26

[1] Not available

Source: Estimates by U.S. Consulates

differentiated wage level, with wages declining with distance from the international border. Finally, this differential wage level tended to create geographical price differentials that contributed to a retardation in intranational trade and investments.[24] In brief, Mexico's economy increasingly became dependent upon the United States, so that by the early 1950s 81 percent of all of Mexico's imports came from the United States, while 85 percent of its exports went to the United States.[25] This deficit in the balance of payments was somewhat offset by the remittances of the bracero program, which was one of the reasons that Mexico decided to continue the program following the end of the war. Although Mexico would not openly admit it, bracero remittances came to represent its third most important source of foreign dollar exchange.[26]

It should be pointed out that wage differences were not in themselves sufficient for insuring migration, at least not on the Mexican border. A more compelling reason for illegal immigration than wage differentials was the insatiable demand for cheap labor in the United States. The fact is that "the migration of Mexican workers to the United States is directly related to the desire of U.S. agriculturalists and industrialists to attract Mexican labor."[27] According to Richard Hancock, real wages in Mexico were either stable or declining in many industries and in nearly all phases of agriculture. Thus, assuming that the relative status of the Mexican campesino was not significantly bettered in the period from 1930 to 1940 and that his socioeconomic status may be held constant since 1940, the migration potential of the Mexican peasant during the 1940s was not significant-

TABLE 4

Average Farm Wages in Mexico, per day,
without board, by Regions,
Quarterly, 1948 to July 1953
(pesos)

Quarter	North Central	Coastal	Northern Border
1948-January	3.02	4.92	5.36
April	3.04	5.12	5.22
July	2.81	5.41	5.78
October	3.07	5.40	5.91
1949-January	3.16	5.73	5.89
April	3.04	5.70	6.06
July	3.15	5.90	5.96
October	3.33	6.10	5.98
1950-January	4.01	6.00	6.40
April	4.05	6.00	6.94
July	4.06	6.05	7.03
October	3.91	6.44	7.03
1951-January	4.16	6.50	6.99
April	4.31	6.52	7.39
July	4.25	6.80	8.49
October	4.51	7.00	8.75
1952-January	4.98	6.78	8.21
April	4.66	6.80	8.81
July	4.64	6.70	9.51
October	4.64	6.98	11.01
1953-January	4.70	6.71	11.01
April	4.85	7.08	10.03
July	4.80	7.10	10.26

Source: Estimates by U.S. Consulates.

ly greater than his migration potential throughout the 1930s. Thus, though factors in Mexico did serve to "push" people out of the country in search of better opportunities, they were not sufficient in and of themselves to cause a large emigration of Mexicans from their homeland. Perhaps the stronger factor involved economic changes occurring in the United States that provided strong "pull" factors.[28] These will be discussed shortly.

Another so-called push factor was the widespread unemployment that plagued Mexico. Like agriculture, industry also failed to keep pace with the net population increase.[29] This is not to say that Mexico's economic development remained static. In fact the government, as indicated earlier, did invest a great deal of money in industrial and agricultural development in hopes of creating more jobs. At times its efforts were rewarded, as in 1949, when the area of Matamoros along the Texas-Mexican border experienced a marked agricultural expansion. In that year the cotton crop was a major one, requiring large numbers of workers to harvest it. Because of the sparse population and the exodus of many workers as braceros and "illegals," Mexican employers did everything they could to recruit people from the economically depressed southern and central regions of Mexico to take part in the harvest. Unfortunately many growers, fearful of not having a sufficient labor supply, recruited far more workers than were needed. According to officials in Matamoros some 60,000 people came to the area to fill 25,000 jobs. As a result those who were unable to find employment joined the ranks of the unemployed or sought entry to the United States either as braceros or as undocumented workers.[30] This pattern was repeated throughout the period, as Mexican growers recruited more labor than necessary in order to make sure that they had sufficient numbers on hand to harvest their crops and to replace those workers drawn north into the United States. Because there were always more workers than jobs and because wages tended to be higher across the border, many Mexicans crossed the border by whatever means they could.

Not all the people heading for the border region initially intended to enter the United States. Some had been lured to northern Mexico by reports of a boom in Baja, California, or by reports of higher wages along the northern frontier. However the expected boom did not occur, and wages suffered because of the drought that struck northern Mexico between 1948 and 1953. When the rains finally came in 1953, they came in such quantities that floods washed out many farms and industries. Rendered destitute by this catastrophe many Mexicans either flocked to overcrowded urban areas or entered the United States.

As indicated earlier, the "pull" factor on the immigrant provided by the promise of better conditions appears to have been stronger than the "push" of poverty in the homeland.[31] Generally speaking, people are reluctant to uproot themselves and leave their homes, friends, relatives, and cultural ties. Many of the Mexican people, even after leaving their homes and villages, maintained strong ties to their country.

Yet in spite of their allegiance and ties Mexicans could not overlook the expanding economic opportunities in the United States after the outbreak of World War II. Wages soared and unemployment almost disappeared. Agriculturalists and industrialists succeeded in convincing the federal government that a labor shortage existed that required setting up a contract labor program to meet their labor needs. Although the high cost of room and board served to reduce the earnings of Mexicans while in the United States, and wage levels never reached their anticipated level and were impacted upon by a myriad of factors, nonetheless many Mexicans decided to hazard the journey. And why not? When compared to Mexico, plagued by drought, tight agricultural credit, national priority given to industrial investment, overpopulation, and massive unemployment, the United States at least offered a job and a chance to get ahead.[32]

Many reasons could thus explain the renewed exodus of Mexicans that began after World War II. There was the lack of cultivatable land, the increasing financial cost of farming, low income levels, lack of credit, lack of price guarantees, and a low productivity of land caused by poor soil or poor agricultural techniques.[33] People throughout Mexico, particularly those from the central region with the largest population and the nation's lowest agricultural wage rate, found that the economy of their home area could not provide them with adequate work to support their families. That this was an important fact was borne out by interviews with those who had emigrated to the United States as braceros. When asked why they had left Mexico for the United States they generally responded that they left because they and their families were starving and that their salaries remained low while the prices for subsistence goods continued to soar. Thus of the 303 braceros interviewed by Henry Anderson in California in 1962, 184 or 60.7 percent told him that they had come in search of work, 74 or 24.4 percent to make money, 11 or 3.6 percent to support their families, and the remainder for miscellaneous other reasons not related to economic need.[34] A study in 1950 produced similar responses. Of 160 braceros interviewed who had returned from Texas 47 percent said that they had gone to the United States in search of work, while another 38 percent stated that they had been lured north by the promise of better wages. Of the 160, 75 percent were *jornaleros* or landless workers.[35] Of 139 braceros interviewed in central and northern Mexico in 1969, over 90 percent cited necessity, the need to support their families, and the desire to find work as reasons for their emigration to the United States.[36] A 1956 article in *Excelsior,* one of Mexico's major newspapers, attributed the bracero exodus to a lack of employment opportunities and to the fact that citizens were deprived of what little they did make by local bosses, leaders, moneylenders, and politicians.[37] Others held a different opinion, stating that the migration was an attempt by Mexicans to "escape from reality—a characteristic of all Mexicans."[38] Certainly this view is at best questionable. That so many Mexicans took the risk of emigrating legally and illegally tends to attest to the fact that they assessed their situation realistically and attempted to deal with it as best they could no matter how desperate their efforts might have appeared to others. Nor does there appear to be a great deal of credence to the view held by some Mexican officials that the mass exodus was simply due to the migratory spirit of the Mexican people. As one student of the bracero movement so succinctly stated in response to this view: "[I] f there was a 'migratory spirit' it was born of need not adventure."[39]

Certainly an important factor in determining the number of braceros coming to the United States, and one that is often overlooked, was the transportation system available in Mexico. Without railroad transportation or roads to carry them by bus or car to the border regions many Mexicans would have been unable to negotiate the hostile regions that separated them from jobs in the United

States.[40] In fact the lack of adequate transportation systems might have discouraged many from making the long and arduous journey to contracting stations or to the border. That they took advantage of public transportation is attested to by the fact that trains running northward had to use whatever type of cars they had available to them, which led to railroads being criticized by the press of Mexico for transporting people in overcrowded cattle cars. Would-be passengers also complained that they could not get seats on trains going north because of the tremendous number of braceros who had booked passage northward.[41]

Near the international boundary, there was little to prevent Mexicans from crossing. The imaginary boundary line of about 1600 miles that separates Mexico and the United States is largely devoid of natural obstacles that might impede movement. Yet the crossing was not devoid of dangers. As many unfortunate individuals discovered, the journey into the United States was fraught with natural and man-made hazards which at times turned the crossing into a nightmare, ending in severe injuries and death. Those who sought to enter illegally often faced torrid temperatures in the day and freezing weather at night. At times they could not carry sufficient food or water to make the journey. There was the ever-present danger of snake bites or of falling victim to the vicious gangs that operated along the border. Unknown numbers of braceros and undocumented workers were robbed and even killed for their meager earnings or personal possessions. Undocumented workers were shot at or beaten by local ruffians as they attempted to cut across private lands. The Rio Grande claimed its share of victims through drownings. In 1953 its swollen flood waters claimed between 300 and 400 victims who had attempted to cross it.[42]

Once in the United States, at least in the southwestern part, Mexicans found that the cultural, geographic, and economic characteristics differed little from those of their homeland. The regional unity provided by climate, language, diet, and architecture proved conducive to immigration and helped somewhat to cushion the cultural shock of those who had entered from Mexico.[43] The northward movement of Mexicans and their transition to braceros and "illegals" was eased by the fact that "the distinction between internal and international migration was blurred by climatic and other similarities of the areas on both sides of the border."[44]

The labor agent from the United States also served to help along the push-pull factors, and was in turn helped by them. The labor agent or contractor had come into his own during the early part of the twentieth century with the emergence of large-scale farming in the Southwest. The development of "factories in the fields" brought with it a concomitant need for large supplies of readily available labor. In the past growers and other employers had depended upon the labor sources provided by Asia and Eastern Europe. However the passage of the Chinese Exclusion Act in 1882 and the Gentlemen's Agreement of 1907, whereby Japan agreed to take measures to end Japanese emigration to the United States, pretty well dried up the flow of labor from the Orient. The onslaught of World War I and the enactment of the discriminatory Quota Acts of 1921 and 1924 served to curtail immigration from Eastern Europe. Thus growers and industrialists turned to Mexico for a new source of labor.

In their need they turned to labor agents or to private employment agencies to provide them with Mexican workers, for these sources were usually able to readily adapt their machinery for recruiting new labor groups.[45] Usually the labor agent, whether working independently or as an employee of the agencies, belonged to the group that he was attempting to recruit. These agents would go to the major distributing points for Mexican labor in the Southwest and contract workers for companies or private employers. They would then be responsible for making sure that the contracted workers reached the employer. For contractors it often proved a lucrative business, as they generally received pay for their services both from the employer and from the contracted individual. On occasion contractors became crew leaders to the men they had recruited and were thus responsible for overseeing their work, negotiating for their wages, and paying the workers in the crew. This system led to abuses on the part of unscrupulous contractors and crew leaders, who often short-changed their workers and pocketed the profits.

As competition at the distribution centers intensified, many contractors went into Mexico and directly recruited workers from the small villages. To draw them northward it was not uncommon for labor agents to mislead unsuspecting Mexicans by promising fabulous wages and good working conditions. Some even resorted to showing prospective employees pictures of beautiful houses in which they would supposedly live during the tenure of their contracts. Needless to say, the promises and pictures were more often than not only ploys to get workers to sign on.[46]

The Depression temporarily ended the activities of the labor contractor until the advent of renewed prosperity and the need for labor brought him back into the picture. Again, contractors worked either independently or as agents for a large grower or an association of growers. At times these contractors represented a grower or growers at the recruiting stations where they selected and contracted braceros, but more often than not they went into Mexico where they arranged for the illegal entry of Mexican nationals.

It was a profitable business that entailed few risks. Because growers believed the cost of contracting braceros to be high and were dissatisfied with bureaucratic red tape, they often preferred to hire undocumented workers. This was especially true for the small farmers who were not so diversified in crop production and required only a few men for relatively short periods. Because they could not maintain braceros for the full contract period they turned to the labor contractor for workers.[47]

The cost of operating for the labor contractor was at best minimal. For example, a contractor might recruit three hundred or more undocumented workers and acquire the necessary trucks and crew to supervise them. If he kept one-half cent per pound for his fee, he could gross $1.25 per day per picker, if each worker picked an average of 250 pounds of cotton a day. With a crew of 300 his earnings would total $375 per day. If captured, labor contractors had little to worry about. Penalties for smuggling in workers consisted of a fine of $500 and/or a one-year term in prison, but these penalties were seldom enforced.[48]

The potential profits to be derived from such a system and the fact that the employees of these contractors had often been brought in illegally gave rise to many abuses. Not only did labor contractors take a good portion of a crew member's pay, they also overcharged workers for housing, food, and transportation. At times they short-weighed their workers and even absconded with payrolls. Contractors also served as a buffer between the workers and the employers, thus freeing the employer even more of his responsibilities for the care and welfare of those who worked for him.[49]

Because of the growing irresponsibility of labor contractors some states attempted to impose stricter regulations on their operations. In California it was recommended that they be licensed, that they pay large bonds that would discourage them from absconding with payrolls, that they be forced to pay their crews on a weekly basis, and that transportation safeguards be increased to reduce the number of tragic truck accidents that claimed the lives of many because of overcrowding, speeding, and the operation of unsafe vehicles.[50] Few such recommendations were ever put into effect.

The factors just described as contributing to the emigration of Mexicans to the United States by no means exhausts the list. In discussing what factors forced people to leave Mexico and drew them northward, the distinctions often become blurred as to which ones were crucial in making people decide to leave their homes and relatives to seek opportunity in the United States. Once the exodus began, other factors aided and encouraged its continuation, and these will be discussed in the following chapters.

NOTES

1. Frank Tannenbaum, *The Struggle for Peace and Bread* (New York: Alfred A. Knopf, 1950), p. 8.

2. Leo Grebler, *Mexican Immigration to the United States: The Record and Its Implications,* Mexican American Study Project, Advance Report 2 (Los Angeles: University of California, 1966), p. 9.

3. Nelson G. Copp, *Wetbacks and Braceros* (San Francisco: R and E Research Associates, 1971), p. 7.

4. Direccion General de Estadistica, *Compendia Estadistica, 1953* (Mexico: Secretaria de Economica, 1954), p. 34. The growth in population was staggering over the twenty year period between 1940 and 1960, when Mexican population increased nearly 80 percent from 19.8 million to 35 million. "Mexico: The Problem of People," *Population Bulletin* 20, no. 7 (November 1964): 174.

5. Horace E. Newton, *Mexican Illegal Immigration into California, Principally Since 1945* (San Francisco: R and E Research Associates, 1973), p. 5.

6. Kathryn A. Wylie, *Mexico as a Market and Competition for United States Agricultural Products* (New York: Alfred A. Knopf, 1960), p. 10.

7. Tannenbaum, *The Struggle for Peace and Bread,* p. 183.

8. *New York Times* (6 January 1954), p. 80; Robert C. Goodwin to Secretary of Labor, "Operation and History—Mexican Farm Labor Program" (16 July 1953), in Record Group 174, Box 6, Mexican Labor Program, 1953 Agreement File, National Archives, Washington, D.C. (hereafter cited as R.G. 174, Box 6, 1953 Agreement File, N.A.).

9. U.S., House, *Congressional Record,* 83d Cong., 2d sess., 1954, 100, pt. 6: 8133.

10. Ibid.

11. Yves Maroni, "Mexico's Economic and Financial Record," Washington Federal Reserve System (October 1965), p. 3; and Banco Nacional de Mexico, *Review of the Economic Situation of Mexico* 43, no. 498 (May 1967): 11.

12. James W. Wilkie, *The Mexican Revolution: Federal Expenditure and Social Change Since 1910* (Berkeley: University of California Press, 1967), pp. 253-54.

13. *New York Times* (7 January 1953), p. 47.

14. Howard L. Campbell, "Bracero Migration and the Mexican Economy, 1951-1954" (Ph.D. diss., American University, 1972), p. 120.

15. Moises T. de la Peña, *El Pueblo y Su Tierra: Mito y Realidad de la Reforma Agraria en Mexico* (Mexico: Cuadernos Americanos, 1963), pp. 816-23. In his study of the state of Chihuahua, Hancock found that wages increased 350 percent between 1943 and 1958. However, the average price of eighteen commodities increased 380 percent. Staples such as beans, coffee, maize, flour, and potatoes rose in price by 570 percent. Richard Hancock, *The Role of the Bracero in the Economic and Cultural Dynamics of Mexico: A Case Study of Chihuahua* (Stanford, Calif.: Hispanic American Society, 1959), p. 97.

16. *Congressional Record,* 83d Cong., 2d sess., 1954, p. 8133; Nathen Whetten, "Population Growth in Mexico" in *Report of the Select Commission on Western Hemisphere Immigration* (Washington, D.C.: G.P.O., 1968), p. 175.

17. Eduardo V. Venezian, "The Agricultural Development of Mexico," quoted in Campbell, "Bracero Migration," pp. 96-97.

18. Report of the President's Commission on Migratory Labor, *Migratory Labor in American Agriculture* (Washington, D.C., 1951), p. 71.

19. Ibid. Their figures are for June of 1950.

20. "Mexican Agricultural Wage Rates, 1948 to 1953," Foreign Service Dispatch, from: American Embassy, Mexico, D.F. to: The Department of State (20 July 1953), in Record Group 166, Box 298, Foreign Agricultural Service, Mexican Labor Folder, 1953, National Archives, Washington, D.C. (hereafter cited as "Wages, 1948 to 1953," R.G. 166, Box 298, Mexican Labor Folder, 1953, N.A.).

21. Newton, *Mexican Illegal Immigration,* pp. 26 and 27; Robert D. Tomasek, "The Political and Economic Implications of Mexican Labor in the United States under the Non Quota System, Contract Labor Program, and Wetback Movement" (Ph.D. diss., University of Michigan, 1957), p. 199.

22. Ibid.

23. "Wages, 1948 to 1953," p. 4, R.G. 166, Box 298, Mexican Labor Folder, 1953, N.A.

24. Newton, *Mexican Illegal Immigration,* p. 12.

25. *Congressional Record,* 83d Cong., 2d sess., 1954, p. 8133.

26. Robert D. Tomasek, "The Political and Economic Implications of Mexican Labor in the United States Under the Non-Quota System, Contract Labor Program, and Wetback Movement" (Ph.D. diss., University of Michigan, 1957), p. 1. Opponents of the program in Mexico argued that it served only to foster an even greater economic dependence in the United States. Richard B. Craig, *The Bracero Program: Interest Groups and Foreign Policy* (Austin: University of Texas Press, 1971), p. 21.

27. Julian Samora, *Los Majados: The Wetback Story* (South Bend, Ind.: University of Notre Dame Press, 1971), p. 44.

28. Ibid.

29. Maroni, "Mexico's Economic and Financial Record," p. 3.

30. President's Commission, *Migratory Labor,* p. 72.

31. Harry Jerome, *Migration and Business Cycles* (New York: National Bureau of Economic Research, 1966), p. 208.

32. Craig, *The Bracero Program,* p. 60.

33. *Review of the Economic Situation of Mexico* 30, no. 334 (July 1954): 10.

34. Henry P. Anderson, *Fields of Bondage: The Mexican Contract Labor System in Industrialized Agriculture* (Martinez, Calif.: n.p., 1963), p. 23.

35. Comision de Planeccion Industria de la Camara Nactional de la Industria de Transformacion, *Proceso Ocupacional* (Mexico, 1956), p. 139.

36. Campbell, "Bracero Migration," pp. 116-17.

37. *Excelsior* (23 March 1956), p. 6A.

38. Pedro Alba, *Siete Articulos Sobre el Problema de los Braceros* (Mexico, 1954), p. 24.

39. Campbell, "Bracero Migration," p. 149.

40. John C. Elac, *Employment of Mexican Workers in U.S. Agriculture, 1900-1960* (San Francisco: R and E Research Associates, 1972), p. 101; and Arthur F. Corwin, "Causes of Mexican Emigration to the United States. A Summary Review," in *Perspectives in American History,* eds. Donald Fleming and Bernard Bailyn, vol. 7, *Dislocation and Emigration: The Social Background of American Immigration* (Boston: Harvard University, 1973), p. 561.

41. Roberto L. Ghisi, "Transportaron como Bestial des de Guadalajara, A 25,000 Braceros," *ABC* (7 September 1951), Reports in Record Group 166, Box 299, Foreign Agricultural Service, Mexican Labor Folder, 1951-1952, National Archives, Washington, D.C.

42. *Excelsior* (2 July 1953), p. 1.

43. Leo Grebler, *Mexican Immigration to the United States,* p. 9.

44. Ibid., pp. 10-11.

45. "Increase of Mexican Labor in Certain Industries in the United States," *Monthly Labor Review* 32 (January 1931): 65.

46. Anita Jones, *Conditions Surrounding Mexicans in Chicago* (San Francisco: R and E Research Associates, Inc., 1971), p. 55; Gilbert Cardenas, "United States Immigration Policy and Mexican Immigration" (Paper delivered at South Bend, Ind., Centro de Estudios Chicanos, September 1974), p. 7.

47. Speech delivered by Willard F. Kelly, Assistant Commissioner, INS, before the Annual Assembly of the Division of Home Missions of the National Council of Churches of Christ in the U.S.A., Buck Hill Falls, Penn. (15 December 1953), pp. 9-10, Record Group 166, Box 299, Foreign Agricultural Service, Narrative Reports, 1948-1954, Mexican Labor Folder, National Archives, Washington, D.C.

48. Ibid., pp. 11-12.

49. U.S. Department of Labor, Bureau of Labor Statistics, "Agricultural Labor Contractor System in California," *Monthly Labor Review* 52 (February 1941): 348.

50. Governor's Committee to Survey the Agricultural Labor Resources of the San Joaquin Valley, *Agricultural Labor in the San Joaquin Valley—Final Report and Recommendations* (Sacramento, Calif., 1951), pp. 21-28. For discussion of the conditions under which Mexicans were forced to travel, *see* Carey McWilliams, "Mexicans to Michigan," *Common Ground* 2, no. 1 (Autumn, 1941).

1
The Bracero Program

THE MOBILIZATION FOR World War II drew thousands of people from the migratory labor stream and created an increasing demand for unskilled labor in the Southwest. The advent of the war had not only stimulated industrial output but also increased the production of fruits, vegetables, and fibrous plants necessary to feed and clothe armies. Because such labor was not readily available in the United States, growers and processors began to appeal to the government for the importation of foreign laborers to fill their needs.

Apprehensive that not enough domestic labor would be available for the cotton harvest, the powerful Farm Bureau Federation of Arizona requested in July of 1941 that the United States Employment Service (USES) import 18,000 Mexican contract workers.[1] Although their request was denied by the USES, the agency did not prove insensitive to the needs of the growers. Instead it instituted a vigorous interstate recruitment program that sought to draw domestic migrant laborers to the area.

Similar requests for the importation of Mexican laborers from the states of Texas and New Mexico during the summer of 1941 also resulted in denials.[2] The requests were refused primarily because the Department of Agriculture and other governmental agencies such as the Farm Security Administration believed that the importation of Mexican contract laborers would hamper efforts to increase wages for domestic migrant farm workers.[3] In a similar vein, there were those who believed that labor shortages would not exist if the growers would pay better wages to farm workers.

Many of the large commercial growers were well aware not only that the competition for workers would increase because of the war effort, but also that wages would have to be increased if they were to keep people in farm work and away from the lure of the war industries. Yet, generally speaking, the large commercial growers were unwilling to pay higher wages because they might have to continue paying such wages once the war came to an end, undoing many years of effort to keep wages at a minimum and maintain a large but malleable labor pool.

Accomplishing this task had not been easy, for many still recalled the long and sometimes bloody encounters with union organizers during the Depression. Although unionization efforts throughout the Southwest had largely failed or had been squelched by strong-arm tactics on the part of growers and their law-enforcement allies, the struggle had nonetheless proved long and difficult. Yet the growers had survived it and in fact had emerged even stronger and better organized, especially in the state of California, which had witnessed a great number of strikes in its agricultural regions.[4]

California has four distinct geographic areas that contribute to crop differentiation. One of these areas is in Southern California, which includes the Imperial Valley.

The Imperial Valley has been described as one huge garden, an area reclaimed from desert by water imported from other states. Yet because of the intense heat most of its residents shun it most of the year. It is here that cotton and truck farms abound, while in the rest of southern California citrus and winter garden crops prevail. A second geographic area is the San Joaquin Valley where cotton, grapes, peaches, and tomatoes are planted. This area requires extensive irrigation, a good deal of which is supplied at public expense. The third area is the Sacramento Valley, known for its peaches, tomatoes, pears, and grain. The San Joaquin and Sacramento Valleys together comprise the great Central Valley, which makes up virtually two-thirds of the state's interior, from Chico in the north to Bakersfield in the south. Finally there are the coast counties, where the crops vary from one area to the other. For example, Monterey and Santa Barbara specialize in vegetables, Santa Clara in apricots and prunes, San Benito in wine grapes and apples, and Sanoma in hops.[5]

Almost all the land in these four geographic areas is owned by companies such as DiGiorgio and others. These "factories in the fields," as Carey McWilliams has called them, are vast and powerful complexes that wield considerable influence at the state and national level. They are cultivated by migratory laborers who miraculously turn up for the harvest and disappear once the crops are laid by. "This agricultural pattern was produced by a combination of land monopolization, the necessity for expensive irrigation, and the availability of a floating supply of cheap migratory labor."[6]

In his testimony before the LaFollette Committee, which was charged with investing violations of labor rights, the noted economist Paul Taylor stated that large-scale farms constituted about 2.1 percent of the farms in California. Nonetheless, this small percentage was responsible for about 28.5 percent of all agricultural production in that state and spent 35 percent of the total agricultural wage bill. They also employed the bulk of the 200,000 migratory workers.[7] In essence Dr. Taylor was saying that California agriculture was controlled by a small minority of growers who exercised power out of proportion to their numbers.

Much of this power had been consolidated during the 1930s, when California experienced a great wave of strikes by the state's 250,000 agricultural workers.

The strikes were triggered by further drops in wages, poor working and living conditions, and continued exploitation by some unscrupulous growers, who were quick to take advantage of the misery caused by the Depression and the large number of unemployed who were desperately seeking work.[8]

The unionization effort was doomed by two major factors. One was the Depression itself, which provided growers in California and throughout the Southwest with an abundant supply of labor via the arrival of the dust-bowl refugees collectively referred to as the "Okies." The second factor was the decision of California growers in 1936 to organize to fight labor organization. The California growers formed a voluntary association known as the Associated Farmers of California, Incorporated. This association soon developed into a formidable force that would dominate California agriculture and influence policies both locally and nationally for many years thereafter.

A few years later, when the LaFollette Committee launched its full-scale investigation of California's agricultural system, it subpoenaed and seized the files of the Associated Farmers. According to Carey McWilliams, a long-time sympathizer and supporter of agricultural workers, "These confidential records proved a bonanza: they betrayed a dismal story of labor-baiting, private strike-breaking armies and arsenals, collusion with local officials in exploiting labor, and violations of workers' civil liberties."[9]

Although such revelations stirred criticism against growers, they were not enough to weaken the growers' power. The arrival of the "Okies" had focused public attention on the problems and corruption in California agriculture. By displacing the Mexican and Asian labor force on California's commercial farms, the "Okies" exposed a caste system that had existed for three-quarters of a century but had been ignored because its victims were alien and nonwhite and therefore largely invisible. People such as the Mexicans, Asians, and blacks had always been viewed as racial inferiors in the social order, so much that race had combined with field work to produce a pattern of caste relationships between the "foreign minorities" and the "Californians."

Individuals such as John Steinbeck moved people to sympathy by their graphic portrayals of people like the Joads, who endured much at the hands of unscrupulous employers and their henchmen. With the end of the Depression many of the "Okies" left the fields and entered other lines of work, and the caste system that had been exposed by their presence was soon forgotten. In many instances the Mexican, Mexican American, and other minorities who had been displaced returned to the fields. They found that little had changed. The racial psychosis still existed, a psychosis based on revulsion against social intermingling with people of differing skin pigmentation.

The growers still maintained the belief that ethnic composition was a rationale for their continued exploitation of agricultural migrants. They continued to believe that they were entitled to a large supply of cheap labor, and that in fact they had an inherent right to it. This is important to remember, because these attitudes would persist throughout the existence of the bracero program and would affect the treatment of Mexican nationals throughout the series of international agreements under which it operated. These racial attitudes would play a key role in hindering the effective enforcement of the bracero agreement. They would also cause serious ramifications, one of which was to increase the number of "illegals" in the United States during the World War II period.

In time the growers overcame the reluctance of the United States to import foreign laborers, by stating that such a labor supply was necessary to overcome the manpower shortage created by the war and to help in harvesting crops vital to the war effort. Now all that remained was to get Mexico to acquiesce to such a program, something that would not prove easy to do.

Although the United States quickly warmed to the idea of importing Mexican labor, the Mexican government did not. Both countries formed a joint commission to study the possibility of an agreement concerning contract labor, but Mexico continued to display great hesitation about the matter for a number of reasons.

Mexico still harbored ill feelings over the mass deportation of many of its citizens from the United States during the 1930s. Although these deportations had been sponsored largely by local business and civic groups, the U.S. government had done little to intervene or speak out against such actions. Mexico not only had viewed this as an act of discrimination on the part of the United States but had also been upset that thousands of Mexicans had been unceremoniously dumped on its northern frontier, causing untold economic hardships on all those involved. Furthermore Mexico itself had been unprepared to absorb so many people into its already depressed economy.

Those who had longer memories also recalled the abysmal failure of an earlier contract program involving both nations. In 1917, because of a similar labor shortage brought about by the war, a contract labor program had been agreed to by both countries. Under its rules, employers in the United States had been obligated to go to the recruiting stations and contract the workers. There they would inform the immigration officers of the wages to be paid, the length of time for which Mexican nationals would be contracted (limited to no more than six months), and a description of the work to be done and accommodations to be provided for the Mexican workers. Growers also agreed to notify immigration officials should any of their charges break their contracts and to make some form of commitment to help locate the individual should this occur.[10] As it turned out few of the agreements were kept, the program was plagued by problems, and Mexico was more than happy to see it end on 31 December 1919.

This experience served to remind Mexico of the dangers inherent in undertaking another program without strict guarantees and enforcement. Furthermore, Mexico was bound to provide such guarantees by its Constitution of 1917. For example, Article 123, in addition to prohibiting unregulated mass emigration, stipulated that return transportation be guaranteed to emigrants.

Because growers in the United States ignored this stipulation during the first agreement, thereby forcing many Mexicans to make their own way home, more stringent legislation was enacted into Mexico's Labor Law in 1931. Under Article 29 employers of Mexican workers had to pay their transportation expenses, and bonds had to be placed in Mexican hands to insure the cost of their return. The same article also required that workers have fixed wages and written contracts, both of which had to be approved by Mexican authorities.[11]

The Mexican government had to contend with public opinion and the ever-present criticism of opposition groups, as well as opposition from some of its own officials. Unfortunately for the opposition groups, their reasons for opposing the bracero program rarely coincided, preventing them from presenting a united front. In any case, their chances for success were limited because most of them, particularly the industrialists and the landowners, were not members of the official party, the Institutional Revolutionary Party or PRI, and therefore lacked power.

For those who opposed the program, the greatest hope of blocking its passage lay within the ranks of the official party itself. Yet within the PRI only one group, the Mexican labor unions, was opposed to the contract labor program. Their opposition lay in the fact that they believed that the braceros would have a negative impact on domestic migrants in the United States, that Mexican nationals would encounter widespread discrimination, and that the mass exodus of Mexican workers would be harmful to the economy of Mexico by reducing its labor supply and by increasing the already high rate of inflation.

The labor unions were supported somewhat in their stance by top officials in the Ministry of Labor and Social Welfare and the Ministry of Agriculture. Officials from these ministries also believed that a contract labor program would hurt national production, contribute to inflation, impede unionization efforts in the United States among migrants once the war ended, and expose Mexican nationals to discrimination and mistreatment.[12]

Other Mexican government officials also had reservations about instituting another contract labor program. In fact in the late 1920s the Mexican government had not favored Mexican emigration because it believed that such an exodus was depriving it of its best people and because Mexicans were poorly treated in the United States.[13] These views were still quite apparent as late as 1942, when Miguel Aleman, Secretary of the Government, stated publicly that "the rightful place for Mexican labor is at home."[14] But Aleman and those who agreed with him in principle proved to be in the minority.

In Mexico the strength of the president's position as well as the dominance of one party were the important elements in determining the government's position on the question of a bracero program. Because they monopolized the decision-making process, it was they who would be the principle determiners of policy with regard to the labor contract program.[15]

When the United States approached Mexico about the resumption of a contract labor program, the Mexican government appointed a committee to study the request. This committee, consisting of members from the Ministries of Foreign Relations, Labor, and Interior, expressed doubts and reservations about the request. First of all they doubted the claim by the United States that there was not enough labor available. They expressed concern about workers who would return to Mexico once the war was over and the ability of Mexico's economy to absorb them. They feared that the United States government could do little to control, much less end, prejudice and discrimination against Mexicans that would then mar friendly relations between the two countries. They also expressed concern about the labor needs of Mexico's expanding wartime economy.[16]

In spite of these reservations, several factors forced Mexican officials to accept the offer. First of all, Mexico felt obligated to aid the United States by providing labor for its war effort. Second, the program would benefit the economy of Mexico via bracero remittances and increased purchasing power, as well as by providing work for the unemployed or underemployed sectors of Mexican society. Related to this was the possibility that braceros might learn new agricultural techniques that they could use in their respective villages upon their return. Third, the government viewed the program as a temporary program that would be terminated once the war came to an end. They were also aware that the United States was Mexico's best customer and thus did not want to antagonize it by refusing its request. Finally, and perhaps most importantly, government officials believed that they had learned much from the first contract labor program in the early 1900s. They now knew that they would not enter upon an unguaranteed contract program. They were aware of the potential pitfalls and were prepared to remedy them in the agreement to protect their people as much as possible from exploitation and discrimination. Mexico believed, and correctly so, that it would have a strong voice in establishing guarantees and controls over the operation and size of the program. They knew that they could withdraw from the discussions should the United States prove unwilling to meet their demands.

Other factors influenced Mexico to enter into an agreement with the United States. One was the assurance of Secretary of Agriculture Claude R. Wickard that guarantees in the program would be extensive and that they would be enforced. Another factor was Mexico's declaration of war against Germany, Italy, and Japan on 1 June 1942. Therefore on 23 July 1942, Mexico signed an agreement with the United States which became effective through an exchange of notes on 4 August 1942.[17] On 27 September 1942, the first Mexican agricultural laborers were admitted into the United States at El Paso, Texas.[18] Initially an emergency, wartime program, the bracero program would span a twenty-two year period, from 1942 to 1964. It would involve the importation of some 4.5 million Mexican workers, and it would present both Mexico and the United States with great benefits and even greater problems.

The agreement of 1942 was to serve as the foundation of the bracero program. (See Appendix 1) In line with its terms, the Farm Security Administration was designated as the administrative agency for the program. Its responsibility was to define the terms under which the Mexican workers would be employed.[19] The United States Employment Service was charged with certifying that local workers were unavailable in sufficient numbers to meet the demand for labor. When such a need was ascertained, the recruiting of nonlocal workers could get under way.

Under the terms of the agreement the governments of the United States and Mexico made provisions for the recruitment of temporary contract laborers in Mexico to work in specific occupations in this country. The way the agreement operated was fairly simple. The Farm Security Administration (and later the Agriculture and Labor Departments) signed a contract with individual Mexican workers. According to this contract, the worker agreed to provide his services for a certain specified period (usually one year) and to return to Mexico immediately upon the termination of his contract. The laborer also agreed to work only in certain specified occupations, usually agriculture. In return the government of the United States agreed to provide transportation expenses to and from Mexico. It guaranteed Mexican nationals the "prevailing wage" for the particular work they were engaged in, as well as adequate housing and medical services while in this country. The contract also guaranteed braceros employment for at least 75 percent of the working days covered by the contract. In the case of the 1942 Agreement, the United States would be the contractor to whom the employers' organizations in this country would apply for the hiring of braceros. Finally, the contract with the employers could be cancelled and the workers withdrawn if the employers did not comply with the standards set by the agreement.[20] (See Appendix 2)

The 1942 Agreement established four standards that were to serve as general guidelines throughout its twenty-two year history.

> First, Mexican contract workers would not engage in any United States military service. Second, Mexicans entering the United States under provisions of the agreement would not be subjected to discriminatory acts of any kind. Third, they would be guaranteed transportation, living expenses, and repatriation along the lines established under Article 29 of the Mexican federal labor laws. Fourth, Mexicans entering under the agreement would not be employed either to displace domestics or to reduce their wages.[21]

These guidelines were designed to allay some of Mexico's major fears and concerns over the bracero program. The section dealing with military service had been attached in an effort to avoid a repeat of the rumors and mass exodus that had occurred during the World War I program when reports filtered back into Mexico that Mexican nationals were being pressed into military service. Although the stories were unfounded, they did cause difficulties between the two governments.[22]

With regards to the guideline on discrimination, Mexico wished to avoid any embarrassing incidents that would draw criticism of the program from its own

people. Mexicans still recalled the deportation of their compatriots during the Depression; they were aware of the mistreatment suffered by United States citizens
of Mexican descent; and they knew of the long history of cultural conflict between
Mexicans and Americans, especially in the state of Texas.

The guidelines covering employment might well have represented a gesture by
the government to respond to the concerns of the labor group within the PRI. It
might also have been designed to aid unionization efforts in the United States
among domestic migrants, particularly as the targeted areas for bracero employment were located in areas heavily populated by Mexican American migrant workers, who were fighting for better wages and working conditions.

Overall, Mexico can be credited with having done a good job in planning its
part of the program; yet Mexico's plans also suffered from the fact that it did
not take into account the role that powerful interest groups would play in the
from the fact that they did not take into account the role that powerful interest
groups would play in the operation of the program. There was also the fact that
the program itself was not static and a myriad of factors continually impacted
upon it.

In looking at the objectives of both countries in negotiating the agreement,
one can immediately discern different philosophical and political reasons for
favoring such a program. The primary goal of the United States was to have
available, if necessary, an adequate supply of Mexican agricultural laborers for
special needs. However, its prime concern was to obtain the adoption of simple
and practical arrangements that would make the acquisition of such workers as
easy as possible. Mexico, on the other hand, wanted strict guarantees governing
wages, transportation, housing, and protection for its workers against discrimination and exploitation. In addition to this Mexico wanted frequent inspections
by the United States to make sure that the terms of the agreement were being
complied with. Finally, it wanted to administer the program in such a way as
to prevent a mass exodus of its work force. Mexico believed that by limiting the
number of contracts it could better manage the program and see to it that the
articles of the agreement were complied with as much as possible.[23] Throughout
the existence of the bracero program these priorities would increasingly harden,
especially as both governments were pressured by various groups not to give
way on them.

With regard to the pressure groups, there were very distinct differences between the United States and Mexico. In Mexico the political party and presidential action determined policy to a large extent, while in the United States
pressure groups played a more important role than political parties in determining policy. Groups such as agribusiness and, to a lesser extent, the railroads,
backed by various financial and industrial interests[24] "were able to alter the
course of an intended wartime emergency measure into a long-term profitable
program."[25]

The third factor that undermined Mexico's work was the very nature of the
bracero program itself. That is, the so-called bracero question was a problem

with many different sides and dimensions. It was a problem that was constantly changing because of the effects on it of war and peace, political change, and economic fluctuations. It was affected by the issues surrounding hemispheric solidarity and inter-American relations. During its lifetime unilateral actions on the part of the United States further complicated the bracero question. Finally, there were economic, political, and sociological influences in the United States and Mexico that affected it. What this all came down to was that as long as all of those concerned with the program, employers, labor, and the two governments, failed to understand each other's interests, motives, and goals, then there existed little or no chance of reaching a solution to the issues and questions that plagued the program throughout its existence.[26] This situation can be demonstrated by examining, in general, the goals, objectives, motives, and thinking of the commercial growers.

Although the commercial growers had wanted a contract labor program, they were not pleased with the one that emerged. From the outset they had wanted the program to be modelled along the lines of the 1917 program. At the time they had made the initial request for imported laborers, they had been well aware of the dangers inherent in such a request. They realized that importing laborers would require planning and that such planning would require the participation of the federal government. In this they had little choice, for private agencies were not geared to speedily deliver the necessary labor. To involve the federal government was a departure from the accepted norm among commercial growers, who were "committed wholeheartedly to self-helping free enterprise."[27] They had to be careful in their planning to make sure that they received the labor they needed without sacrificing their autonomy in the agricultural arena. They realized that once standards were set up to protect foreign laborers similar standards might easily be set up for domestic migrants as well.

When news of the contents of the 1942 Agreement reached the growers many of them voiced almost immediate opposition to the bracero program. In November of 1942, the American Farm Bureau, the National Grange, and the National Council of Farmers Cooperatives issued a joint statement requesting that the agreement be modified. In brief, they wanted the rules and regulations eased.[28] According to President O'Neal of the American Farm Bureau, the Administration "had messed it all up with a lot of rules and regulations." O'Neal wanted to know why all of this was necessary. Why not just let the growers go into Mexico and get the workers they needed as they had done in the past?[29]

This marked the opening salvo in the struggle by agribusiness and groups supportive of it to have the program regulations modified to meet the needs of the growers. That such groups as the American Farm Bureau and the National Grange took the lead in making such demands is not surprising, as they were among the largest of the three major farm organizations. Of the two, the American Farm Bureau was the largest and most powerful, with a membership of about 1,452,210.[30]

This group also had greater access to government agencies, especially the Department of Agriculture. Part of the reason for this lay in the fact that the Farm Bureau had originated from governmental stimulation in World War I through the efforts of agricultural extension agents. This close relationship with government agencies had continued and grown.[31]

Since its inception, the American Farm Bureau had maintained a consistently conservative stand in its support of nonquota immigration of Mexican labor. It had fought against social legislation designed to improve the plight of the domestic migrant in the 1930s, and it had helped form the Associated Farmers, helping them to disrupt unionization efforts during the turbulent 1930s.[32] Interestingly enough, over 50 percent of the American Farm Bureau's membership was in the Midwest, yet it had little trouble in getting groups there to support its efforts in the area of contract labor from Mexico. In return for such support, it aided the Midwestern groups in getting price supports.[33]

It should be made clear that while the commercial growers were, generally speaking, unhappy with the agreements, they did not necessarily oppose the importation of labor. Their main complaint was that although they supported the program in principal they were unhappy with all the rules and regulations that governed its operation. Thus the growers found themselves in the position of defending the importation of laborers while attacking the agreements that made the importation of those workers possible.

While groups such as the American Farm Bureau, the National Grange, the Vegetable Growers Association of America, the National Council of Farm Cooperatives, the National Farm Labor Users Committee, the Amalgamated Sugar Company, the National Beet Growers Federation, the National Cotton Council, state growers' associations, and the Council of California Growers all worked behind the scenes to alter the agreement, they all, either individually or collectively, publicly supported or countenanced the program.[34] They, along with other auxiliary groups, advanced various and sundry arguments designed to support the existence of the bracero program.

For example, growers stated that Mexican contract labor was necessary because domestic migrants refused to do stoop labor. They also claimed that, when domestic labor proved willing to do such work, they lacked skills, dependability, and character. Advocates of the program claimed that Mexican nationals were the answer to the problem because they possessed the physical ability and the needed skills to perform the backbreaking and difficult job of harvesting certain crops. What many of them meant by this was that Mexicans were physically built to be beasts of burden and that their physical stature made them more capable of withstanding heat and of maintaining stooped positions for longer periods of time without becoming weary.[35] The belief that Mexicans could handle hot, arid work because they were accustomed to it was fallacious, as the greater portion of braceros came from the cool central plateau.[36]

Supporters of the program depicted braceros as dependable, hard-working, and honest. They stated that because braceros were only temporary migrants, they would not adversely affect wages and working conditions and would not displace domestic farmworkers who were willing to work. Not only would braceros prove beneficial to the United States, but they themselves would gain as a result of the program. Through the contract labor program braceros would upgrade themselves financially, which would aid them in becoming upwardly mobile once they returned to Mexico. It was even possible to assume, some claimed, that while in the United States some braceros would be exposed to new farming methods they could use in their own villages.

Others argued that the program carried with it diplomatic benefits in that braceros would have their cultural horizons broadened while in the United States and that as a result they would carry back with them a positive image of the United States and its people. In a similar vein there were those who believed that it would help in continuing to improve relations with Mexico by helping to ease the increasing influx of undocumented workers. The controlled entry of Mexican nationals could go a long way in calming xenophobic Mexicans who were embarrassed by the alarming increase of emigrants seeking opportunity in the United States.

A strong argument among those who favored the importation of workers was based on pure and simple economics. They contended that the program would prove of economic benefit to both countries. Specifically, the United States would benefit because farmers could harvest their crops at lower costs and could thus pass the savings on to the consumer. Mexico would be aided because braceros would pump money directly into its economy, which in turn would help Mexico begin to reduce the deficit in its balance of payments.

While the war lasted growers had little need of these arguments, for they could justify the importation of foreign labor on the basis of a wartime emergency. However, as the war came to an end growers continued to claim that a labor shortage still existed and that a bracero program was still a necessity. As opposition to their requests mounted in other sectors of society, the growers became more vocal in expressing some of the views just discussed. Upon closer examination one can see that these arguments were not new and had been espoused by growers in one form or another for many years.[37]

Many of the same groups that had opposed the importation of foreign laborers during World War I and shortly thereafter also opposed the importation of braceros once World War II had ended. These groups included organized labor, social reform and human-rights organizations (some of which were Mexican American in make-up), and religious organizations. Among the more vigorous opponents of the bracero program were the National Council of Churches, the National Catholic Welfare Conference, the National Advisory Committee on Farm Labor, the National Share-croppers Fund, the National Consumers League, the American G.I. Forum, the National Association for the Advancement of Colored People, the American Friends Committee, the American Federation of Labor and the Congress of Industrial Organizations, the Bishop's Committee on the Spanish Speaking, the League of United Latin American Citizens, and numerous state-level subsidiaries of these groups and organizations.[38]

These groups, collectively and individually, contested the arguments set forth by the proponents of the bracero program. According to them, the argument that domestic farm workers were unavailable and refused to do the work was untrue. The fact was that growers made little effort to secure domestic workers and, if anything, made every effort to discourage native farm workers by paying low wages and providing poor working conditions. Opponents of the program argued that if wages and working conditions were improved there would be sufficient domestic labor to perform the work. With regard to the contention of growers that braceros had the physical ability and stamina lacked by the domestics, opponents attributed such arguments to racist thinking. Anyone capable of performing construction work or any of the numerous hard jobs available on the market could harvest crops. Antibraceroists claimed that the disparaging character references made against domestic workers by growers were a good example of lower-class character assassination and that such categorization was groundless. These groups also contended that imported labor did adversely affect wages, and they pointed specifically to a decrease in wages during different periods throughout the existence of the program. In addition, working conditions were also adversely affected by the importation of braceros. Opponents were upset that foreigners were guaranteed fringe benefits repeatedly denied to American citizens in the migrant labor stream. They also claimed that braceros took jobs away from domestic workers because growers preferred paying low wages to the braceros and refused to hire domestic workers.

Though antibraceroists found it difficult to refute the fact that braceros did earn good wages by Mexican standards, they nevertheless focused on the widespread exploitation of nationals by unscrupulous growers and their associations. They also argued that Mexican family life was disrupted, as only men were hired, which tended to remove husbands and fathers from their families for extended periods. Opponents deemed the program detrimental to United States-Mexican relations because it exacerbated the anti-Yanqui syndrome among Mexicans. They pointed to the fact that Mexicans at home were aware of the mistreatment and exploitation of their countrymen in the United States, whether there legally or not. Furthermore the fact that so many Mexicans were forced to become braceros to improve their economic status grated on the sensibilities and pride of those Mexicans who remained at home. Finally, while the earnings of braceros might personally benefit them, such earnings only served to drain money needed in the United States. A more definite impact could be made on the economy by hiring American citizens whose earnings would go directly into the economy.[39]

On the surface the bracero program appeared to have some strong positive points. It was seminal as well as unique in that "it marked the first time that Mexican workers had entered the United States under the auspices of an intergovernmental accord."[40] Braceros augmented incomes in northern Mexico and

were largely responsible for the 5 percent rate of growth per year in the Mexican
economy beginning with 1940. The program also eased Mexico's balance-of-
payment problems.[41] It also alleviated conditions of unemployment and underemployment, thus serving as a safety valve for the potentially dangerous unrest
brought about by Mexico's poor economic conditions. As a temporary war measure
the program also helped the United States in filling a manpower shortage.

As to the question of whether or not braceros learned skills in the United States
and, if so, whether these newly-learned skills were implemented, the answer is yes
and no. While braceros did learn new agricultural methods, studies have shown that
their new skills and their value to improving conditions in Mexico have been highly
overrated.[42] This was due to the fact that farming in Mexico was primarily non-
irrigated subsistence farming on small amounts of land, while braceros learned
agricultural methods suited to large corporate farms and orchards. Furthermore,
most of the braceros were landless jornaleros, and those braceros who returned
with skills to their villages often met resistance to the changes they suggested. After
their attempts to implement the new techniques met with failure because of local
resistance or because they were not applicable to their local situations, or both,
many braceros simply lost interest and returned to old ways.[43]

In the area of inter-American relations the results of the program were mixed.
Throughout its existence the abuses by growers, the lack of effective compliance
measures and grievance procedures, the "wetback" question, prevailing racial attitudes, the unilateral recruiting practices of the United States, and ever-changing
economic and political conditions in Mexico and the United States caused stress
between the two nations. To further complicate the matter, the bracero program
was closely watched by other Latin American countries, for it served as a baro-
meter of United States attitudes, policies, and intentions with regard to Latin
America. Mexico not only had to avoid incidents and issues that would increase
popular opposition at home to the program, but it also had to avoid appearing
subservient to the interests of the United States. Similarly, the United States
had to remain sensitive to the impact that things such as discrimination, exploitation, and the "wetback" influx had on Latin American opinion.[44]

In spite of numerous controversies that arose over the bracero program and
the question of the undocumented worker, Mexico largely maintained its pro
forma support of the program. For the most part Mexico's official position was
that relations between the two countries witnessed great improvement and that
part of the reason lay in their joint efforts in making the contract labor program function as smoothly as possible. Mexico repeatedly attempted to play down
any controversy or issue that endangered the program and would put both nations
in a bad light.

In the early 1940s Mexico's Secretary of Foreign Relations, Ezquiel Padilla,
credited the program with his country's economic growth and expansion. Like
Padilla, President Avila Camacho and other high-ranking government officials
expressed satisfaction with the program, especially because they viewed it as a

boon to improving relations between the two nations.[45] Yet it was during this time that Mexico had blacklisted the state of Texas because of widespread discriminatory practices against Mexican citizens and Mexican Americans.[46] 1943 also marked the outbreak of the so-called Zoot-Suit Riots in Los Angeles, which saw members of the Mexican American community attacked, beaten, and jailed. Mexican officials were aware of this situation but attempted to ignore it.[47] When word spread about the attacks against Mexican and Mexican Americans by marauding groups of sailors and the fact that the majority of those jailed were the victims of these attacks, Mexico City was shaken by protests on the part of university students. Some 400 students walked out of classes and gathered for a protest demonstration, during which they angrily denounced these actions and hurled insults at Ezquiel Padilla for his failure to protest these injustices.[48]

Because of the tense situation, Padilla and other officials released statements concerning the incidents in Los Angeles. However to the chagrin of many the statements criticized the Mexican American "pachucos" or zoot-suit gang members for the events that had led to the riots.[49] Lombardo Toledano, leader of the Mexican labor movement, who was at this time still supportive of the United States, accused the rioters of sabotaging the war effort. On 28 June, Padilla added his voice to the matter by accusing Nazi-Fascist agents of fomenting racial antagonism and helping to spur the problems in Los Angeles. This statement and the fact that it was issued a week after the riots occurred did little to enhance Padilla's popularity among students and other groups who were concerned with discriminatory actions against Mexicans.[50] Mexicans were upset that no formal complaint was made by Mexico to the United States concerning the incident and that neither country took any measures to prevent similar occurrences.

In 1944, because of increasing complaints by Mexican consuls and braceros concerning contract violations and inadequate grievance procedures, Pedro M. Asunsolo, a high-ranking official from the Ministry of Foreign Affairs, made unannounced visits to areas in the United States where Mexicans had been contracted. Although he did find that some of the grievances were well founded, he nonetheless announced that he was generally satisfied that braceros were well treated.[51] Because of the importance of Mexican labor to the war effort and because Mexico still exercised its blacklisting power, both growers and United States representatives proved receptive to his recommendations concerning the eradication of some of the problems. However, once the war had ended, such recommendations would be increasingly ignored.

Visits by Mexican officials were not unusual during the early years of the program. During the summer of 1944 the Mexican Secretary of Labor had visited the United States on an announced visit and reported that he had found conditions satisfactory.[52] Inspection tours continued intermittently throughout the life of the program, and the majority of the reports that were issued for public consumption generally reflected satisfaction with the operation of the program and the fact that bracero guarantees were being adhered to. Yet when one peruses the official correspondence between the two governments one finds a different picture. In confidential letters, memos, and telegrams Mexican officials often expressed concern about problems plaguing the program, including discriminatory acts against Mexican nationals, physical abuse, inadequate grievance procedures, and violations of civil rights and contract guarantees. When news of such incidents did become public, Mexican officials wrote with concern about how such news proved damaging to their efforts to keep the contract labor program in a positive light. They informed officials in the United States that, when news of abuses or of secret agreements leaked out, it placed Mexico in a difficult situation, forcing them to take harder stands in their demands than they ordinarily might. Thus it behooved the United States to be more selective in its news releases and more cautious in making sure that present agreements would be enforced and observed, thereby making both of their jobs easier.[53]

Foreign officials in the United States were also concerned about the damage that rumors and documented incidents could do to U.S.-Mexican relations as well as to the continuation of the program. Of particular concern to both countries was the continuation of racial discrimination against Mexicans in general, regardless of their status or position. Widespread complaints of racial discrimination against Mexicans and Mexican Americans led to the State Department's appointment of William Blocker, American Consul General at Cuidad Juarez, to undertake a secret investigation of these complaints and allegations.[54] Blocker's assignment, by the way, occurred as negotiations for the bracero program got under way.

In his report Blocker stated that although he found some of the charges substantiated he believed that discrimination was not as widespread as officials had been led to believe.[55] Blocker's conclusions, however, should be viewed with caution as interpretations were somewhat different as to what actions were deemed discriminatory and prejudicial at that time. Interpretations of such incidents vary according to the perceptions and values held during the time period in which they are being viewed and studied. In essence Blocker's report reflects several elements and statements that cast doubt over his conclusions. First of all, his interest was in investigating discrimination against white-collar or professional Mexicans and Latin Americans. Second, most of his conversations were held with state and local officials, although he did meet with Mexican consuls to ascertain the source of their complaints and to look at their files. What adds doubt to the validity of his view that discrimination was not widespread are the statements of Blocker himself, for they demonstrate that he was not free of bias.

For example, he made reference to the fact that in Mexico there had been an intense effort by the government to create a respect for the Mexican working classes. According to Blocker other organizations had sprung up in the United States with similar views. To Blocker these organizations had demonstrated a quicker tendency to take offense at any act which might be considered as radically discriminatory. The organizations he referred to in particular are the League of United Latin American Citizens (LULAC) and the League of Loyal Americans, whose membership mainly consisted of Mexican American citizens. It was his opinion that these groups were overreacting to the situation in an effort to take advantage of the groundwork laid by the Good Neighbor Policy of Franklin Roosevelt. In his estimate, both the Mexican consuls and the local Mexican organizations were "inclined to search out instances with a view of making mole hills into mountains."[56] He believed that these groups had gone too far in attempting to group discrimination against socially unacceptable Mexicans with discrimination against professional and socially acceptable Mexicans. Blocker admitted that the Anglo population had, in some cases, been lax in distinguishing between the white-collar "Mexican" and the peon, but that nonetheless he believed and feared that the Mexican consuls, the LULAC, and the League of Loyal Americans had been "overextending their concern to reach too far down into the lower strata of their countrymen for equal social recognition."[57]

Thus Blocker's concern during his investigation was primarily with offenses against the "better-class," culturally respected Mexican as opposed to the "sandal-footed peon" who lacked proper dress and was unschooled in proper practices of hygiene.[58] Given this approach and Blocker's own bias, one can question the conclusions presented.

Perhaps Blocker's report can best be summed up in his own words:

> Owing to the limited time at my disposal at various points visited and the discreet manner in which the subject matter had to be dealt with, I lay no claim to exhaustiveness or unfallibility in the study made. The scope, importance, and magnitude of the task doubtless make it deserving of examination by students and experts in sociological work better equipped in that science than the modest skill with which I am endowed. . . .[59]

Many such studies did little to change the prevailing stereotypes and negative attitudes concerning Mexicans. If anything, they served to reinforce prevailing attitudes detrimental to Mexicans and Mexican Americans and continued to blame the victims for their status in society.[60]

Even though Blocker's report was made in 1942, it had important implications. The fact that Blocker was ordered to undertake a secret study indicates that there was sufficient concern on the part of Secretary of State Cordell Hull, Assistant Secretary of State Sumner Welles, and other United States officials concerning actions by individuals or groups that might threaten relations between Mexico and the United States and raise criticism from Latin America.

Similarly, Blocker's report is important for it indicates that discrimination and prejudice against Mexicans did exist, and it implies that most of the discrimination was aimed at the Mexican peon because of his language, his dress, his low economic status, and the perception by many that he was an "unclean greaser." What is important to note here is that the majority of braceros would come from the so-called jornalero class, that is, braceros were primarily landless campesinos from the rural regions of Mexico. Although studies have shown that they were not necessarily from the poorest sector of society,[61] they nonetheless were people who, for the most part, lacked formal education, who knew or understood little English, who dressed differently, and who were not familiar with the customs and culture of the United States. Given these conditions, the chances that they would receive better treatment or that people would change their attitudes about the Mexican campesino or "peon" were not great. To make things worse, people were not readily able to differentiate among a Mexican from the professional ranks, a legally contracted bracero, an undocumented worker, and a Mexican American citizen. Finally there was a history in the United States whereby Mexicans and Mexican Americans regardless of their status or social position had been discriminated against by members of the so-called dominant society.[62]

Discrimination and prejudice did occur throughout the existence of the bracero program and struck at Mexicans whether here legally or illegally,[63] although the undocumented worker was exploited more since employers could threaten him with deportation by the INS if he complained too much. The widespread abuses and the discrimination were of grave concern to both countries, but more often than not they were powerless to do much about it because of the size of the program, the lack of inspection officers, the power of growers over local officials, the implied acquiescence of communities who sided with their own against outsiders, and the existence of parochial, nativistic attitudes that were ever-present under the surface of American society.[64] Nonetheless it was an issue that had to somehow be dealt with, given its far-reaching implications for American foreign policy. To no one was it more apparent than to Sumner Welles, Undersecretary of State, who was deeply concerned about the existence of this discrimination. In 1944 he stated: "No good relationships can long continue if these unfair, humiliating, and wounding discriminations are practiced, as they inevitably cut deep, create lasting resentments, and undermine the foundations of our policy."[65]

For Mexico this and other issues presented a dilemma. Could it countenance such actions against its people, clearly in violation of the agreements and its constitution, or would it take the necessary measures to insure that they ceased, even to the point of terminating the program? Certainly the blatant violations in the state of Texas could not go unanswered, especially as the United States had done little to end the abuses. Because of this Mexico decided to blacklist Texas, prohibiting the use of braceros in that state.

Mexico appears to have been hesitant about terminating the program. In spite of the problems, Mexican officials believed that the benefits far outweighed the drawbacks, especially economically. They also believed that world conditions strengthened their position at the bargaining table. They believed that the problems could be ironed out with more stringent requirements and guarantees and with closer supervision. In brief, they did not view the problems as insurmountable. Yet Mexico did not realize that conditions would not always favor them in the bargaining process. They overlooked the fact that the United States government was subject to the influence of pressure groups. Finally, they realized that simply terminating the program would not necessarily stop the flow of people unleashed by the outbreak of war and the news of opportunity in the United States.

Supporters of the bracero program had argued that it helped to improve relations between Mexico and the United States, but events and issues surrounding its operation often cast doubt on those claims. Instead the series of controversies and issues that surrounded the program created some tense moments between the two countries.

While Mexico did on several occasions win many of its demands for protecting its people, there existed a great gap between what the guarantees promised and what was delivered. At times the sense of cooperation by the United States coupled with Mexico's shrewd bargaining served to augment the latter's national pride, which helped to quiet critics at home and for a time contributed to a feeling of close and mutual cooperation between the United States and Mexico in the area of bracero politics. Yet time would dim the optimistic encomiums that accompanied the signing of the first agreement, for exploitation, misunderstanding, confusion, and conflicting interests would plague the bracero program and overshadow its predicted benefits.

Among the reasons that Mexico had decided to enter into a labor contract agreement with the United States was its realization that it could do little to stem the tide of workers entering the United States illegally in search of work. Faced with this fact Mexico decided that the flow should continue under government auspices to guarantee the rights of its people and protect them as much as possible from exploitation.[66] Mexico believed that with an international accord in effect it might be able to arrange for the protection of Mexicans in the United States who had already entered illegally. It sought to shroud "illegals" with the same guarantees provided for legally contracted braceros by legalizing them under terms of the accord. Because Mexico was not happy about the "wetback" problem it felt compelled to acquiese to a system of "legalization" as the lesser of two evils.

CONTRACT LABOR PROGRAM
AND ILLEGAL IMMIGRATION

The unregulated exodus of Mexican workers was not a new problem for Mexico. Mexican nationals had been entering the United States for decades, and the flow was increased with the completion of railroad lines to the northern frontier during the regime of Porfirio Diaz. The flow continued unabated during the 1920s, when the southwestern United States experienced an agricultural and railroad building boom that required large amounts of cheap labor. Because of immigration restrictions against Asians and East Europeans, employers increasingly turned to the readily available supply of Mexican laborers.[67]

In the late 1920s and early 1930s, Manuel Gamio, a noted Mexican sociologist who was deeply involved in the study of Mexican emigration, charged that the wholesale emigration of Mexicans to the United States was detrimental to Mexico, primarily because it drained the nation of its best working population. As an alternative he proposed the creation of a contract labor arrangement whereby Mexicans would go into selected agricultural regions in the United States for seasonal work. As part of the arrangement such workers would be covered by written guarantees and supervised by both governments.[68] Although not adopted at the time, his ideas would have a strong influence on the Mexican government when it developed its contract labor program during World War II.

Mexico's plan to use the bracero agreement as a means of controlling the "wetback" influx was to prove unsuccessful. Numerous reports and scholarly studies have established the fact that the bracero program played a major role in causing increased "illegal" immigration to the United States.[69] With the onset of World War II and the signing of the bracero agreement, "the bracero program was as important a catalyst as the Revolution of 1910 in the first exodus"[70] in increasing the influx of "illegal aliens" into the United States.

The bracero program catalyzed the second exodus of Mexican emigrants in several ways. The program acted like a magnet, drawing thousands upon thousands of hopeful applicants to the recruiting centers. Usually contract workers returned with exciting tales of the money that could be earned in the United States. With each new harvest season, those who had participated in the program wanted to return to earn more money. Naturally their friends also wished to participate and applied as braceros. The end result was that the number of those applying for admission into the United States far exceeded the labor needs certified by the Secretary of Labor. It was estimated by Miguel Calderon, who held the office of Director General of Migratory Workers Affairs in the Department of Foreign Relations from 1947 to 1960, that only one out of every ten applicants ever received a contract.[71]

Needless to say, those who had made the often long, arduous, and expensive trip to the recruiting centers were generally reluctant to return home empty-handed if they were refused a contract, and many of them entered illegally.[72] In this way the bracero program acted as a pump primer for a second wave of Mexican emigration, both legal and illegal.

Another cause for increased entry of undocumented workers was the widespread practice of bribery in the bracero program. Because so many people in Mexico were destitute, a bracero contract very often meant the difference between starvation and survival. That this made the contract a very valuable document, Mexican officials were not slow to recognize. Further, the very mechanisms set up to operate the program in Mexico provided a great deal of opportunity for graft. For one thing one had to go through a prolonged process even to be considered for application. Potential barceros had to receive clearance from their local authorities that no labor shortage existed in that particular area and that men were free to make application for a contract. Without some sort of bribe to local officials, the chances of receiving clearance were slim. Once clearance was obtained, an individual had to make his way to one of the recruiting stations, which often required a great deal of time and expense, as most of the recruiting stations were located along the United States-Mexican border. This worked a particular hardship on bracero applicants from the densely populated central plateau region of Mexico, which would provide the majority of braceros throughout the life of the program. For example, during the period from 1942 to 1954, the states of Durango, Zacatecas, Guanajuato, Jalisco, Michoacan, and Aguascalientes provided 74 percent of the braceros contracted by employers in the United States.[73]

By the time most Mexicans had reached a recruiting station they had paid a bribe of about fifty pesos to the Municipal President to be allowed to leave that particular municipality. Once at the contracting center the potential bracero had to pay some three hundred pesos to an official to gain admittance. Inside, Mexicans had to pass rigorous health inspections and run a gauntlet of quotas and security checks. Even before they had entered the United States, many Mexicans had already invested fifty dollars or more,[74] no mean sum when one stops to consider the extreme poverty of these people. For many, fifty dollars amounted to almost half a year's income.

Graft was widespread and, for those officials on the take, extremely lucrative. Various factors contributed to its prevalence, including the low salaries of officials, the refusal of many Mexicans to complain or file complaints, and the fact that more money in the economy made the opportunities greater than ever. Oftentimes, those who could afford to pay the bribes were braceros who had already been to the United States and had set aside money to acquire another contract. Graft was so widespread that in 1952 President Adolfo Ruiz Cortines started a cleanup campaign that led to the temporary dismissal of some one hundred Mexican immigration inspectors, largely because of complaints by foreigners concerning bribery attempts.[75] Of course the mordida trade (another name for bribery) was so lucrative that many inspectors and officials continued to risk the consequences. By 1957 it was estimated to involve more than 7.2 million dollars annually.[76]

Many Mexicans who would have preferred to enter the United States legally were discouraged by the way the bracero system operated. Moreover, not even paying the bribes guaranteed that a contract would be awarded. After all, almost everyone else at the contracting centers had also paid a bribe to get there.

Following admission to a center, an indeterminate period was spent waiting to be examined and checked. After that more waiting, this time to be contracted. For every job opening there were ten to fifteen applicants or more. These people were forced to mill around in large waiting areas, sleeping outside and eating whatever food they could afford.[77] This situation created headaches for local and federal officials in the Mexican government. It also aroused the ire of certain segments of the Mexican press, who criticized the government for its conflicting bracero politics and its inability to provide for the economic well-being of its citizens. [78]

In spite of the lack of shelter, food, and proper sanitation facilities, and temperatures that often exceeded 100° during the day, the great majority of Mexicans waiting to be contracted comported themselves so well that officials in border towns like Mexicali and Chihuahua sang their praises. For example, even though some 17,000 men were waiting for a contract in Chihuahua, Salvador Razura, manager of the Chamber of Commerce of Retailers of Chihuahua, commented that although many of the hapless braceros were hungry and lacked the money to buy food, they nonetheless behaved themselves, "so that I cannot do other than praise them." [79]

Officials recognized that when cities having recruiting stations became crowded with men hopeful for contracts a potentially explosive situation was created. Yet they also realized that these men were only seeking to better their lot and that if local officials could not house and feed them then the least they could do was to treat them with as much courtesy, kindness, and respect as possible.

Not only were aspirants for contracts subject to harsh climatic conditions or physical hardships, but they also often became the victims of unscrupulous "coyotes" who preyed upon their meager personal or financial holdings with the promise of a contract. Local officials did what they could to control this form of exploitation, but individuals were either afraid to testify or refused to identify culprits for fear of jeopardizing their chances for a contract—a contract that more often than not never materialized.

At times even the system served to discourage individuals, for even though the government tried to establish an orderly method of assigning contracts by issuing numbers to men as they arrived, the numerical ordering was usually not adhered to, through bureaucratic bungling or bribery or both. And so it continued until the contracting period ended, when the governor of the state would take the necessary measures to dislodge from the city those who had not been contracted. [80]

Because of such conditions, entering illegally proved to many an easier and far less expensive way to come to the United States. Through illegal entry many Mexicans avoided the numerous bribes, the waiting, anxiety, and bureaucratic red tape. Others entered illegally because they learned that if one had been in the United States before then the chances of getting a bracero contract were much better, a situation which will be discussed in more detail later. [81]

From the outset the Mexican government had been opposed to opening recruiting stations along the border. In 1942 it had opened a recruiting station in Mexico City, D.F., but found it was not prepared to deal with the mass of humanity that poured into the city in search of contracts. Within a very short period Mexico City's population had increased by about 50,000. Lacking the public facilities to house or feed the applicants, officials decided to move the centers away from Mexico City.[82] In 1944 centers were opened in Guadalajara and Irapuato, while in 1947 centers operated in the cities of Zacatecas, Chihuahua, Tampico, and Aguascalientes.[83]

Between 1942 and 1950 the majority of recruiting stations operated away from the border regions, which presented a point of controversy between Mexico and the United States because the latter, moved by grower pressure, consistently argued for centers located along the border. Both countries based their stance on well-defined economic interests. On the one hand, Mexico realized that border recruiting would hurt the large commercial growers along its own northern frontier by drawing potential laborers to the United States. Such a shortage of labor would force Mexican growers to pay higher wages if they were to be competitive with wages in the United States.[84] Mexico also wanted to limit the number of braceros who emigrated in an effort to operate the program more efficiently and to keep the demand high for braceros in the United States. Finally, from Mexico's perspective, if recruiting centers were located along the border then the probability of illegal entry by uncontracted applicants would be dramatically increased.

The United States, on the other hand, wanted recruiting centers along the border because contracting braceros would prove cheaper and more convenient for Americans. Under the agreement, first the government and later the employer was responsible for paying the cost of a bracero's transportation and meals from the recruiting center and back. The further the center was from the border the greater the expense. Congressional supporters of the program were quite sensitive to expenses as it cost hundreds of thousands of dollars to operate the program every year. The government and growers wanted to shift this expense to the applicants by making them pay their way to contracting stations along the border,[85] and supporters of the program hoped thus to alleviate some of the criticism about the high operating cost of the program from some individuals in Congress.

In August of 1950 Mexico reversed its position against border contracting stations when it opened centers at Hermosillo, Chihauhau, and Monterrey, which provided United States employers with all the braceros they needed. Mexico also acquiesced to the continued legalization of Mexicans who had emigrated illegally and dropped all demands for an entry cut-off date for those who were to be legalized. In essence this marked a triumph for proponents of the open border, reflecting the fact that for the moment Mexico's bargaining strength was at low ebb. Aware of the implications and ramifications that news of this might have in Mexico, the Mexican government requested that publicity concerning this concession "be restricted."[86]

Though one of the purposes of the bracero program had been to curb illegal entry, this purpose was never achieved.[87] In 1952, a spokesman for the National Agricultural Workers Union, which represented the small farmer, made the following statement:

Agreements with the Republic of Mexico for the legal entry of 45,000 to 200,000 contract workers each year since 1942 . . . acted as a magnet drawing hundreds of thousands to the border from deep in the interior of Mexico. When the worker arrives at the border and finds that he cannot be accepted as a legal contract worker . . . it is a relatively easy matter to cross the 1,600 miles of practically unguarded boundary. Once in the United States there are always employers who will hire them at wages so low that few native Americans will accept. Thus legal importation of Mexicans has created the vicious situation now prevailing.[88]

Subsequent figures have borne out such allegations. There were nearly 856,000 recorded expulsion cases in the last half of the 1940s as against a little over 57,000 in the first half of that decade. Deportation cases rose to 70,505 in the latter half of the 1940s as compared to 17,078 in the earlier period.[89]

In examining the statistics on the number of braceros, one can find further proof of the bracero program's impact in bringing about illegal immigration. As the number of braceros increased there occurred a concomitant rise in the number of illegal entries (see figure 1). Chihuahua, the largest state in Mexico, was the greatest supplier of braceros to the United States.[90] During the period from 1951 to 1964, however, the state of Guanajuato supplied the most braceros. During this period Guanajuato provided 12.91 percent or 567,514 braceros, Jalisco 10.59 percent, Michoacan 10.55 percent, Chihuahua 9.89 percent, Zacatecas 8.87 percent, and Durango 8.87 percent. (Table 5) For this eleven-year period these six states provided about 65 percent of all braceros.[91]

Approximately 94 percent of all braceros employed went to the states of Texas, California, Arizona, New Mexico, and Arkansas. Of these, California and Texas employed the greatest number of braceros. The remaining 6 percent were divided among twenty-four other states.[92]

The majority of undocumented workers came from the very Mexican states that provided the majority of the bracero population. It is also significant that the American states that contracted most of the braceros were the same states that contained the largest proportions of undocumented workers.

The state of Texas had a bad reputation among Mexican officials and Mexican citizens in general because of its preference for hiring "illegals," its early and blatant violation of bracero contracts, and its discriminatory practices against people of Mexican descent. These activities had led Mexico to blacklist Texas from 1943 to 1947, but even after Texas was removed from the list and was permitted again to contract braceros, word had gotten out about conditions there. Even as late as 1951, while thousands of braceros awaited contracts in towns along the border, their tendency was not to accept a contract in Texas. As some braceros put it, they preferred to work in the United States because most of them knew they would be paid fairly well. With regard to treatment, the truth

FIGURE 1

NUMBER OF MEXICAN UNDOCUMENTED PERSONS AND
CONTRACT LABORERS IN THE UNITED STATES,
1941-1956

Key: — — — — — — —   Contract Labor

————————   "Wetback" Apprehensions

Source: Records of U.S. Immigration and Naturalization Service

was "that with the exception of Texas," most of the places they went to treated them fairly well and only those who "misbehaved" were "punished."[93]

It appears that for the most part Texas employers were little fazed by the blacklisting and regarded the imposition of contracts for hiring Mexicans as burdensome, bureaucratic, and unjust. Many of them preferred to hire undocumented Mexican workers, the majority of whom came from the states of Guanajuato, Jalisco, Michoacan, Zacatecas, and San Luis Potosi.[94] Generally speaking, when Texas employers did hire legally contracted braceros, they often violated contract guarantees. When this happened, dissatisfied braceros either complained to officials or they "skipped" their contracts. If a bracero "skipped" his contract then he was classified as an "illegal alien" by immigration authorities.

"Skipping" one's contract meant that, once in the United States, a bracero left his assigned employer and struck out on his own to seek employment elsewhere.[95] The majority of those who "skipped" were forced into doing so by a

TABLE 5

Numbers of Braceros,
by State of Origin,
1951-1964

State	Total Number	Percentage of the Total
Mexico	4,395,622	——
Aguascalientes	80,970	1.84
Baja California	21,078	.48
Campeche	1,256	.03
Coahuila	191,074	4.34
Colima	12,190	.28
Chiapas	1,473	.03
Chihuahua	434,938	9.89
Distrito Federal	44,431	1.01
Durango	386,260	8.78
Guanajuato	567,514	12.91
Guerrero	133,821	3.04
Hidalgo	33,712	.77
Jalisco	465,396	10.59
Mexico	79,288	1.80
Michoacan	463,811	10.55
Morelos	38,376	.87
Nayarit	46,660	1.06
Nuevo Leon	185,311	4.22
Oaxaca	126,453	2.88
Puebla	63,381	1.44
Queretaro	50,853	1.16
Quintana Roo	75	——
San Luis Potosi	211,703	4.82
Sinaloa	42,546	.97
Sonora	44,527	1.01
Tabasco	16,032	.37
Tamaulipas	56,652	1.29
Tlaxcala	29,430	.67
Veracruz	10,802	.25
Yucatan	47,285	1.08
Zacatecas	390,061	8.87

Sources: 1951-1960 Oficina Central de Trabajadores Emigrantes cited in:
Gloria R. Vargas y Campos, "El problema del bracero mexicano"
(Ph.D. diss., Universidad Nacional Autonoma de Mexico, 1964),
table 7. 1961-1964 *Anuarios Estadisticos*, 1962/63-1964/65.

variety of reasons and circumstances, although the most frequent causes cited were abuse, exploitation, violation of contract guarantees, or a combination of these. Another factor involved in "skipping" was the character and background of the "typical" bracero.

Generally speaking most braceros were single and between the ages of 17 and 22 years of age, with the median age between 21.78 years.[96] Most of them came from communities with populations of 2,500 or less,[97] and largely belonged to the landless *jornalero* population. While not among the poorest of the poor, these people nonetheless felt compelled by economic circumstances to seek greater opportunity elsewhere.[98] Initially many of these rural *campesinos* migrated to urban areas in search of employment, thereby creating a surplus labor supply. Unfortunately many of them lacked the necessary skills to work in industrial occupations and thus became braceros employed primarily in the agricultural sector.

Those who sought contracts as braceros were generally the more aggressive and more determined to improve their economic condition. With their decision to emigrate they had developed certain economic expectations with regard to the wages to be earned while braceros. As they struggled to obtain a contract and as the cost of obtaining a contract increased, so did their expectation that the returns would make the effort and the expense worthwhile. To bolster their expectations there were the ever-present "success" stories of those who had already been there.

The initiative, determination, and assertiveness displayed by many would-be braceros in search of a contract did not bear out the incorrect stereotypes of their docility and laziness. For the most part these men were not prepared to accept anything less than what had been promised or perceived as promised. The awarding of a contract renewed their hopes for a better life for themselves and their families. It also reinforced in many the obligation to repay those who had provided the money to travel to recruiting centers. Most, if not all, of these factors were generally at work when a bracero accepted a contract, and although a large number of them swallowed the bitter pill of disappointment in terms of earnings, there were those who refused to accept their fate at the hands of unscrupulous employers. It was from this latter group that the majority of "skips" came.

According to the 1942 Agreement, which was to serve as the prototype for all subsequent bracero agreements, contractors had to fulfill certain obligations to the braceros once they were employed.

> The contract, legally supported by the United States government, afforded the bracero the following guarantees: (1) payment of at least the prevailing area wages received by natives for performing a given task, (2) employment for three-fourths of the contract period, (3) adequate and sanitary free housing, (4) decent meals at reasonable prices, (5) occupational insurance at the employer's expense, and (6) free transportation back to Mexico once the contract period was completed.[99]

Other provisions stated that deductions were to be made from paychecks only for those items that appeared in the contract, that adequate employment records be kept, and that each individual's earnings be itemized each pay period.

Unfortunately, the bracero program was to be plagued by widespread evasion of regulations, which victimized those the program was designed to protect, in part because some of the requirements were vague or contained loopholes that created a wide margin for interpretation and evasion of responsibilities on the part of employers. Perhaps the greatest weakness lay in the area of compliance, where enforcement was at best patchy and at times almost nonexistent.

A common problem that caused dissatisfaction among braceros and consternation among Mexican officials was the lack of clarity over the so-called prevailing wage rate. As stated in the agreements, all legally contracted braceros were to be paid the "prevailing wage" of the area in which they were hired or a minimum of fifty cents, whichever was higher. On paper this sounded fair enough, but in reality there were at least two significant drawbacks. The first was that the "prevailing wage" was determined before the season began by the growers themselves.[100] This was advantageous to the growers as it kept wage levels as low as possible. Although these wage levels were either equal to or slightly higher than those paid to domestic migrants, the fact remained that the pay was not significant. An amendment to Public Law 78 in 1955 changed this practice. According to this amendment both employees and employers would negotiate with respect to the wages to be paid.[101] Nonetheless, wages never reached the level expected by braceros or the Mexican government.

A second drawback was that the prevailing wage rate was extremely difficult to enforce, as it fluctuated from area to area. For the most part the size of the labor pool determined wage rates. In areas saturated with undocumented workers, wage rates were extremely low. For example, in 1950 the average wage for farm work in California was eighty-eight cents per hour. In Texas it was fifty-four cents per hour. In the lower Rio Grande Valley, an area highly saturated with "illegals," the wage was fifteen to twenty-five cents an hour.[102] Braceros assigned to low-paying areas were often dissatisfied, and many "skipped" in order to find better wage rates elsewhere.

In essence the minimum wage guarantee was a myth. According to Walter J. Mason, a member of the Legislative Committee for the American Federation of Labor, there appeared little hope that the issue would ever be resolved in favor of the worker. To support his views he cited the findings of Jerry Holleman who, as executive secretary of the Texas State Federation of Labor, had investigated conditions under which braceros worked. Holleman reported that:

> Most of the Mexican consular offices in the areas involved are reporting literally thousands of complaints in this minimum wage violation. There are more cases filed than the (Mexican) consuls can investigate. It may be

years before they can process the cases already filed with them. The same complaints cover housing, bedding, cooking utensils, and so forth.[103]

Critics of program abuses charged that things had become worse when the United States had ceased being the major contractor in 1947. From that year until 1951 individual growers or their representatives were allowed to directly negotiate with and contract braceros. Thus the individual contractor rather than the federal government was legally responsible for fulfilling the agreements in the contract. With the elimination of direct government supervision over working and living conditions, a plethora of abuses and violations arose.

While some braceros attempted to deal with employer-employee problems themselves, others turned to Mexican consuls for help and succour. Generally speaking, when consuls visited sites of alleged violations, they usually found evidence to substantiate bracero complaints.

For example, an inspection tour of camps in August of 1947 by the consul at Kansas City, Missouri, uncovered a series of contract violations. At one camp the consul found twenty-four nationals crowded into two wooden shacks measuring five meters by four meters. These shacks lacked proper ventilation and were in a state of complete neglect. The kitchen and dining area were "filthy," and the utensils used for cooking were "repellent for lack of cleanliness." To add to the distress of the men the camp lacked bathing and washing facilities.[104]

Inspection of other camps by this consul uncovered conditions worse than those he had encountered in the first camp. Workers in one camp complained of insults, abusive language, and brutal treatment on the part of the foreman, employees of the company, "and even at times by the representatives of the Department of Agriculture," some of whom were of Hispanic descent.[105] Workers complained to him that certain individuals had informed them that their contracts and guarantees meant nothing. Some stated that some of them had been threatened with expulsion from the camp or deportation if they got sick, were too exhausted to do the work, or protested against poor treatment, bad food, lack of work, or errors in their salaries.[106]

The consul heard similar complaints from workers at Montgomery, Minnesota, where some two hundred braceros were employed. Workers claimed that at times they had been forced to work from 15 to 19 hours a day and that the foreman frequently abused them. It was at this camp that the Regional Representatives of the Department of Agriculture had cancelled the contracts of five workers and had refused to pay for their return transportation after they had acted as co-spokesmen for the discontented workers. According to the consul, the Regional Representative had taken this action because he considered these men to be "agitators."[107]

Russek, who wrote a report based on his visits to some of the camps and on information provided by other consuls, placed much of the blame for the abuses on the Regional Representative, who, he said, had shown little sympathy for

Mexican workers in the past. In fact his attitude was one of "a great deal of cal-lousness" with regard to the plight of the braceros.[108]

Another common complaint voiced by braceros was that they had not received full payment of wages by the contracting companies. Numerous letters written either by the braceros themselves or by their legal representatives to consuls or directly to the companies asked that back wages be forwarded. In many instances such pay failed to materialize.[109]

In 1947 Karl L. Zander, a public health engineer, complained to his director about budget cuts that would make it difficult for him to do an effective job in the Southwest. He stated that upon hearing of the legislative directive to liquidate the federally operated farm labor supply centers he immediately contacted the State Health Department and the California Division of Housing in order to as-certain whether or not they could handle the responsibility of administering this program. Both state agencies indicated to him that they were unprepared to do so.[110]

Zander believed it was a mistake to lease federally owned camps to local growers, because past experience had proven that they did little to keep up the facilities. He stated that even when the camps had been federally funded, supervised, and in-spected they still suffered from substandard facilities and limited equipment.[111] He described many of the camps as battered by heavy use and in need of extensive repair. Furthermore, most of the housing available to California migrants was in the form of one-room cabins, shelters, or tents that contained an oil stove for cook-ing. Most of them lacked adequate food storage facilities, heating facilities, or run-ning water. He was very critical of the federal migratory program, which, he said, "wreaked [sic] with reports (and) citations of sordid conditions," largely because of the dominant legislative influence of farm groups, who were primarily concerned "with the economics of crops and a cheap and ready labor market."[112]

Although Zander was complaining about problems encountered by migrants in Arizona and California and was opposed to the control of housing by growers, his statements are relevant, as most of these facilities would be leased by growers in order to house braceros.

Complaints concerning contract violations also emanated from the Mexican government itself. In 1949 Mexican officials objected to the actions of an individual who had repeatedly violated portions of the bracero agreement. According to the complaint, the Foreign Office in Mexico had had problems with this person in the past and because of these "held him in low esteem." Officials were loath to permit him to contract braceros as he was "regarded as a slave driver who on every occasion would not fail to take advantage of Mexican workers."[113] Because of this the Mexi-can government informed U.S. officials that they would no longer furnish braceros to an organization that allowed the individual in question to contract braceros.

Another common complaint voiced by Mexican officials concerned the tendency of growers to violate regulations governing the employment and placement of bra-ceros. This was the subject of a complaint filed by Manuel Aguilar, a member of the

Ministry of Foreign Affairs. Aguilar informed the American Consul Harwood Blocker that a private contractor had transferred the braceros encharged to him to another employer in Mississippi without authorization to do so. To make matters worse the employer who had accepted the braceros was a person blacklisted by the Mexican government for repeated contract violations.[114] According to Aguilar about twenty of the fifty-one men who had been sent to work for this person had "skipped" their contracts as a result of inadequate housing and cooking facilities and being overcharged for food.[115] Others had "skipped" after some of their colleagues had been incarcerated by this person after they had verbally protested the poor conditions in which they were forced to live. Because the U.S. government had failed to take necessary measures to protect these braceros, wrote Aguilar, his government had ordered the Mexican consul in Memphis, Tennessee, to cancel the contracts of the remaining braceros and see to it that they were turned over to an employer who would abide by the terms of the agreement.[116]

In several incidents U.S. officials charged with enforcing the contract agreements were accused by Mexican officials of not fulfilling these responsibilities and failing to cooperate with them. One such incident involved a representative of the U.S. at the El Paso contracting station. This official had not demonstrated any desire to cooperate with Mexican officials and had repeatedly exhibited negative feelings toward them whenever any problems concerning braceros arose.[117] He had refused to intervene on behalf of 2,500 braceros who had filed complaints and claims for back wages against the Trans Pecos Cotton Association. The fact that he had not even bothered to investigate their claims had resulted, according to Liciencado Miguel C. Calderon, Chief of the Department of Bracero Affairs, in considerable financial losses to those involved.[118]

The tone of Calderon's report about the lack of cooperation by this person reflected his anger and frustration. What particularly irked him was the poor attitude toward Mexicans this person had displayed. The actions of Mr. B., wrote Calderon, mirrored his belief that the Mexicans had no rights in the operation of the program. In fact he had voiced this opinion to several Mexican officials when he had decided to furnish braceros to some California growers in spite of their protestations. According to one representative Mr. B. had told them that he would furnish braceros to whomever he pleased, "with or without the authorization of the Mexican representative."[119] When one of the Mexican representatives asked that he at least check with Washington, Mr. B. replied: "What for? What can they do to me?" Exasperated by these remarks Mexican representatives asked how U.S. officials could expect them to work with anyone who had expressed himself in this way.[120]

Both Blocker and the State Department were sympathetic to Calderon's complaints, and the transfer of Mr. B. was arranged. The United States apologized for his actions, although no personal apology came from the individual involved. American officials asked that Lic. Calderon do them the favor of not making incidents of this nature the subject of future official correspondence. Instead the

Embassy requested that matters such as these be taken up with them "unofficially," so that their handling could be accomplished more expeditiously. It is somewhat ironic that the U.S. Embassy asked the injured party to show his good faith by withdrawing his note of 2 February 1952, which asked for an official investigation and some satisfaction on the matter. Apparently Calderon was satisfied enough to acquiesce to the request.[121]

Much of the correspondence already alluded to points to the fact that lack of effective enforcement plagued the program. More often than not certain groups or companies were guilty of repeated violations, and the fact that sanctions were not imposed on them only encouraged continued violations on their part. Although Mexican officials repeatedly called for cancellation of contracts against groups, companies, or individuals, few if any were cancelled, even when such cancellation was clearly merited.[122]

Because of these widespread violations Mexico sought to regain closer control over the program by having both governments assume direct responsibility for the contracting of braceros again. To bolster its argument Mexico pointed to the increasing number of braceros who were "skipping" their contracts because of poor working and living conditions, violation of wage guarantees, and discriminatory practices in states such as Arkansas, Mississippi, and Texas.[123] Mexican officials, such as Manuel Tello from the Ministry of Foreign Relations, claimed that their offices were receiving more and more complaints from workers concerning contract violations. The lack of compliance made it imperative, in the eyes of Mexican officials, to revise the bracero agreement so that a new, more stringent contracting system could be implemented.[124]

Although it appears that both governments attempted to play down incidents, violations, and abuses because of political and diplomatic reasons, they could not keep information concerning these problems from leaking out. In Mexico the opposition seized upon this information and used it to attack the program and the government for its failure to provide adequate protection for braceros. The opposition also criticized the weak economic structure that forced people to leave their homeland in search of work.

The program and its accompanying abuses, particularly in Texas, also drew fire from critics in the United States. Pauline Kibbe, a member of the Texas Good Neighbor Commission, an organization established in the aftermath of Mexico's blacklisting of that state in the early 1940s, called the program "bankrupt" and a "shocking disgrace to the entire country." She charged the agencies responsible for enforcement with "open connivance with private interests" and said that the violations and the insults against Mexico on the part of these agencies could not be "overlooked or condoned."[125] According to Kibbe, Texas had been negligent in rectifying the unsavory conditions under which Mexicans had labored and had too long hidden behind the battle cry of states rights, which to her was merely a "smoke screen for bigotry, avarice, (and) failure."[126]

In 1952 the Most Reverend Leo F. Dworschak wrote that farmers in his area appeared to have no sense of responsibility towards braceros or any other workers they brought in. He remarked sadly that "in some instances they provide better care for their cattle than they do for 'their workers.' "[127]

Archbishop Robert E. Lucey of San Antonio was not surprised to receive such information as that found in Reverend Dworschak's letter. A strong advocate of rights for migrant workers, Lucey was a consistent critic of the bracero program. Although on several occasions he criticized the program because it provided contract guarantees to aliens instead of domestic migrants, he nonetheless realized that braceros were not that much better off. In a letter to Reverend Matthew Kelly, the Archbishop wrote that Reverend Kelly had been too "kind" in his remarks concerning the bracero agreement before a senate committee. Kelly had credited the agreement with providing braceros with proper housing, adequate pay, and humane treatment. The truth of the matter was, wrote Lucey, that "the housing is sometimes pretty atrocious and a wage of fifty cents an hour is pretty far below a decent income."[128]

Lucey complimented Kelly for his testimony concerning the abuses of migrant workers and told him that his appearance was an honor to the Church. "We cannot deny," concluded Lucey, "that in times past too many of our priests and practically all of our laymen were silent about the obvious crimes committed in our country in industry and agriculture."[129] Not all Catholic priests felt as Lucey did. Earlier Lucey had received a preliminary report from Reverend James A. Hickey, a member of the Diocese of Saginaw, Michigan, who said that seminarians were cautioned "to avoid entanglements with the farmers and (sugar) companies. . . . We feel it best to stress the religious character of the work rather than get into arguments over housing, etc."[130]

Yet members of the Catholic hierarchy in the United States believed that they should get more involved in the temporal problems and needs of their Mexican parishioners, for they were well aware of the fact that the Protestants had begun to make inroads into the Mexican community. That is one of the reasons that the Bishops Committee on the Spanish Speaking was formed in 1945.

Various Protestant denominations had been actively involved in proselytizing among Mexican migrants for years, although the number of converts had not increased dramatically. Nonetheless some ministers took a keen interest in the plight of the Mexicans, especially when growers or contractors abused them. One such complaint was voiced by Father John F. Godfrey, pastor of the Ascension Church in Chesterfield, Missouri, who wrote to Secretary of Agriculture Mitchell about the abuse of Mexican nationals by a local employer. In his letter Godfrey charged that "very few of the agreements in the work contract" were being observed by the contractor. He wrote that his church had made repeated efforts to get the braceros, whom he described as humble and hard-working, to attend church services on Saturday and Sunday. After some coaxing several of the braceros had come to the church dressed in ragged clothes. Most of them arrived barefooted, while others simply had tied old pieces of auto tires to their feet.

Godfrey, who was moved by their poverty, complained that the company did everything that it could to keep the braceros from church. Even though their contract did not require them to work on weekends, Godfrey explained, many of them were afraid to refuse work in order to attend services. Those who chose to attend often found themselves locked out when they returned to the compound. On other occasions the church vehicle was not allowed to pick up braceros so that they might participate in church activities. To Godfrey this situation was the "worst form of slave labor and denial to our Mexican neighbors of the fundamental rights of our country especially the right of religious freedom."[131] Informed of these conditions, Mexican authorities investigated the situation and shortly thereafter refused to contract any more braceros to this particular employer.

Another strong critic of the program and its abuses was Ernesto Galarza, a labor activist, who at this time was serving as Director of Research and Education for the National Agricultural Workers Union. Galarza had long been an advocate of social legislation for domestic migrants and, although he was sympathetic to the plight of braceros, he believed that the program served to undermine labor-organizing efforts among migrants and delay the passage of laws designed to help migratory workers. Galarza, a meticulous scholar, published a pamphlet in 1956 entitled *Strangers in Our Fields,* in which he exposed the widespread abuse suffered by braceros. In his pamphlet Galarza attacked those who exploited braceros, criticized government agencies for their lack of enforcement, and attempted to discredit the arguments of those who defended the program on a variety of levels. The contents of the pamphlet, based on interviews with braceros and examination of reports, statistics, and other relevant documents pertaining to the bracero program, elicited much attention. Most of it was critical in nature and emanated from the targets of Galarza's pen. Critics charged him with exaggeration, poor research, and character assassination. Several angry letters were fired off to different senators and congressmen and a few to the Secretaries of Agriculture and Labor demanding that they refute the charges or force Galarza to retract his statements.[132] Of course the latter proved an unrealistic and unworkable request, and Galarza's pamphlet was widely circulated.

Strangers in Our Fields addressed itself to issues that plagued the program and contributed to the "wetback" influx. Galarza charged that the wages paid braceros were insufficient to meet their normal living needs.[133] According to him, braceros were required to pay $12.50 per week for room and board. This amount was deducted from their wages whether they worked or not. Although $12.50 represented the maximum that could be deducted under contract guidelines, Galarza stated that in most cases the maximum became the minimum charged in the camps.

Other charges and costs further served to reduce bracero earnings. Braceros were required to pay between 69 cents and one dollar per week for premiums on nonoccupational insurance negotiated for them by the Mexican government. Yet in spite of insurance premiums, braceros complained that medical attention was costly and at times difficult to get. When injuries or disabilities did occur, braceros often found it difficult to collect on their health insurance.[134]

Depending upon the arrangements, braceros sometimes had to pay for their room and board separately. If this was the case, the most that could be charged for meals was $1.75 per day. As in the case of the maximum for room and board, $1.75 became the minimum charged.[135]

Again, braceros found the food not to their liking. In many cases the food was carelessly prepared, sometimes rancid, and not enough to satisfy their appetites.[136]

Another abuse concerned the wages paid. As growers often did not bother to post wages, braceros seldom knew exactly how much they were earning, and it was not surprising that many found themselves shortchanged when they were paid. This and other violations of contract guarantees were reported by the Reverend Joseph H. Crosthwait during a trip through the western states on behalf of the Bishop's Committee for the Spanish Speaking. According to Crosthwait, records of working hours were not properly kept in many instances. "I have seen certificates of men I knew were all working twelve hours a day and who were being credited and paid for six or seven hours of work."[137] Braceros he questioned were aware of this. When asked why they did not compalin to the employer, they responded that they did not want to be sent back until they had made a little money.[138] Crosthwait argued that the basic rights of freedom of speech had been denied to these braceros and that he had encountered these violations not only in California but also in other contracting states he had visited. In his opinion, these men were being treated worse than animals. "The very setup of the Program tends to herd them into a mass of nonentities."[139]

All of this worked to the detriment of the bracero and ate away at his earnings, which were meager to begin with. If, according to Galarza, a bracero had a contract for a period of 45 days,

> with a wage rate of 70 cents per hour and assuming steady work of 48 hours a week, a National will have $79.05 deducted from his total earnings, leaving an average of little over $20.00 a week. If he is paid 90 cents an hour he may expect to average, on a full work week, $29.70.[140]

From this amount a bracero set aside $10.00 per week to send to his family in Mexico. Subtracted from this was about $2.50 per week required for such needs as clothing and cigarettes. The tight budget on which braceros lived left no room for other deductions for work equipment such as gloves, blankets, or other needs. Many braceros also had to earmark about $5.00 from their weekly earnings to repay money they had borrowed to finance their trip.[141] Given this situation it is little wonder that many braceros decided to break their contracts and strike out on their own. Those who endured the contract period often did not return as braceros the following year. Instead they decided that the expense, the trouble, and the potential earnings were not really worth the effort and the investment and instead opted for entering illegally.[142]

In spite of the numerous complaints, growers and contractors generally believed that there was little to fear from government reprisals. The size of the program alone and the vast area involved tended to preclude strict enforcement. For example, in California the Division of Housing had some 4,818 camps of all types under its jurisdiction in 1953, some 1,200 camps short of the estimated number of camps in operation. That year the Division of Housing was able to inspect 2,375 camps, leaving 2,443 camps not inspected. If the actual number of camps operating in California is taken into account, the number of camps uninspected rises to 3,625.[143] Given the lack of inspections, there is little wonder that growers often failed to meet contract standards in working and living conditions.

The agency charged with enforcing the contract agreements was the Labor Department. Its compliance officers were charged with the responsibility of enforcing contract agreements and were empowered to deny contract labor to any employer who violated any of the guarantees or who abused or exploited braceros. They were also required to remove braceros from growers who used "wetback" labor, or during domestic migrant strikes. Unfortunately the job required a greater amount of manpower than the Department of Labor had or was prepared to furnish.

In the postwar period the Department of Labor had only ten to twenty compliance agents to enforce contract agreements and to investigate violations. Hampered by a lack of personnel, the department was not effective in fulfilling its role as a compliance agency, nor did it on occasion carry out its responsibilities with much zeal. For example, in several instances the Border Patrol offered some assistance by furnishing compliance agents with lists of employers who had been caught using "wetbacks," but the Department of Labor continued to allow these employers to use contract workers.[144] Critics of the program were not slow to point this out, charging the department with a conflict of interest as the Secretary of Labor had the responsibility of assuring that the use of Mexican workers would not adversely affect the wages and working conditions of domestic migrants while also certifying that a bona fide shortage of domestic workers existed before braceros could be contracted.

The problem was that grower associations set the prevailing wage, which was usually low. Most domestic migrants found that they could not earn a decent living on such wages and thus refused to work. In this way the growers themselves had created a labor shortage by offering low wages and the Department of Labor was, in a sense, forced to declare that a labor shortage existed and permit the importation of braceros.[145] Representatives of the Labor Department at times admitted that this was the case but added that the problem was not a simple one. According to Robert C. Goodwin, determining whether Mexican workers adversely affected the wages of domestic migrants was extremely difficult, because adverse effects occurred slowly and were not often discernable until the passage of more than one crop season. Even then, Goodwin concluded, it was difficult to prove that the foreign workers were the sole cause, as other intangible and unexpected factors such as climate, crop yields, earnings, competitive employment, and technological changes also influenced wage rates.[146] Goodwin nonetheless admitted that there had been a relative decline in domestic wage rates, particularly in those areas where braceros were employed.[147]

By 1951 the Department of Labor was responsible for covering thirty thousand growers and other employers who had contracted braceros, while the number of compliance men had grown only to fifty.[148] This apparent laxity in ensuring that contract guarantees were carried out and enforced frustrated groups and individuals concerned with the plight of braceros and their effect on domestic migrants.

In 1954 Jerry Holleman wrote that the Texas Federation of Labor had been unable to find any genuine sincerity of purpose in the administration of the bracero program. According to him, "The absence of a United States employment service compliance program and compliance staff has caused a complete breakdown in the International Migratory Labor Agreement. Practically all articles for the protection of the bracero are being flagrantly and openly violated."[149] To illustrate his point Holleman listed examples of failure to enforce the agreement. He noted the absence since April of 1953 of published blacklists providing the names of all contractors and growers who had been caught using "wetbacks." Failure to publish these lists, he said, was in clear violation of the terms of the agreement.[150]

Complaints of abuses were also forthcoming from the braceros themselves. They were among the first to point out that violation of contract guarantees was a major reason for the large number of "skips." An interview with Carlos Morales that appeared in the Washington *Daily News* in 1956 gave a clear indication of the plight of many Mexicans. Morales was a man who had seen both sides of the issue, as a bracero and as an "illegal," and the *Daily News* reporter referred to him as a "legal slave" who had worked on a Texas ranch. In the interview Morales indicated he would rather be a "wetback" than do it all over again the legal way. He was not alone in his feelings, he stated, for they were shared by thousands like him who believed they had been cheated by greedy American farmers and grafting Mexican officials and abused by tyrannical foremen.[151]

Morales spoke of his hopes of earning sixty dollars for three month's work, and of the forty-eight dollars he paid for a work contract, a contract that was supposedly free. He described his long wait in the courtyard with about fifteen thousand other hopeful workers.

> If your name is called, you may have a job. Sometimes it costs still more money to get your name called. If it is called you take a physical. After that someone pats your back, someone shakes your hand . . . it is all so friendly, you think the first time. Actually, they are finding out if your back is strong and your hands rough, as if they were buying a horse.[152]

Those interviewed by Galarza were simply expressing what men such as Morales and others had experienced as braceros. Although happy to have a contract, they found that its promises were far greater than its actual benefits. Experience proved to them that the contract had little value when it came right down to guaranteeing their rights. As one bracero told Galarza, the boss was not interested in what it said. In the words of one contractor, the contract was "a filth of a paper. If you want to see how useless (it is) try to tell somebody about it."[153] The same bracero told Galarza that he was the first person they had spoken to who was willing to listen. To him the sheep in the adjoining field were better off, for they had a shepherd to watch over them and a dog to protect them. "Here" the bracero concluded, "it is one bite after another. They bite your wages and they bite your self love."[154]

Different authors have questioned Galarza's study, claiming that the abuses were not as widespread as he asserted[155] or that although grievance procedures were inadequate, most of the guarantees were fairly well kept.[156] Others have pointed to the fact that most braceros who were interviewed held positive views about their experiences in the United States and made little or no reference to abuses and violations.[157] Yet their findings are subject to question for several reasons. One reason is the official records and statements of officials on both sides of the border and of braceros themselves that speak of the myriad violations that were never investigated because of indifference, political reasons, or lack of sufficient staff. There was the blacklisting of Texas by the Mexican government after World War II because of widespread violations and acts of open discrimination. So flagrant were the latter that popular weeklies and newspapers in Mexico carried numerous articles and editorials on the subject of American racism. One such weekly was the Mexican *Mañana*, which referred to the Texans as Nazis who, though "not political partners of the Fuhrer of Germany," were nevertheless "slaves to the same prejudices. . . ."[158] Even Hart Stillwell, a popular novelist, was moved to comment on the widespread discrimination extant in his home state when he wrote:

> We can bring ten thousand Tipica Orchestras to Texas and send five thousand Rotary Clubs and Kiwanis Clubs . . . into Mexico, yet so long as the Mexican knows that he may be killed with impunity by an American who chooses to kill him, then all our talk about being good neighbors is merely paying lip service to a friendship we both know is a joke.[159]

There is also the fact that for the most part the interviews were held with braceros who had served the full length of their contract terms. Braceros who had been returned or who had "skipped" appear not to have been interviewed.

Further supporting Galarza's work are the findings of the so-called *Secret Study* written during the administration of Harry S. Truman. This report, based on State Department files and correspondence, identified five critical problem areas affecting the bracero program up until that time, including numerous violations committed by Texas employers with regard to recruiting, wages, general living conditions, and the utilization of undocumented workers; the failure of the United States Employment Service to enforce certain wage requirements and its tendency to favor agribusiness; numerous violations of Article 9 of the 1949 Agreement, which guaranteed braceros work for three-fourths of their contract; employers returning braceros to Mexico without first notifying the appropriate authorities; and the unjust encarceration of Mexican braceros following an incident in the town of Tivoli, Texas.[160] Finally, adding further credence to Galarza's studies, there was the increasing number of braceros who "skipped" yearly because of widespread dissatisfaction with their treatment at the hands of unscrupulous growers. These "skips" often felt frustrated, for it was difficult to even begin to demand their rights. Those who were willing to complain often found their efforts thwarted by insensitive bureaucrats, by a complex grievance system, or by the very brevity of their contract term. Of the three obstacles, the latter two proved the most discouraging.

For example, if one filed a complaint and action was taken, the bracero was in danger of losing a lot of valuable time in processing the complaint and seeing it to its conclusion, which reduced his time in the fields and curtailed his earning capacity. Other braceros believed it did little good to complain. One described how fifty of them had stopped work in the fields one day in order to protest. The bracero said that one among them who could speak English spoke on behalf of the others. He told the foreman that they did not wish to strike, but that they wanted either eight hours of work or free board if conditions allowed them to work only one or two hours. The foreman assured them that he would look into the matter, and they returned to work. The following day the braceros noticed that the man who had spoken for them was not around. They were told that if they would not do the work for what they received, then there were plenty more to take their place.[161] The bracero stated that he had read his contract, but that it was not worth the trouble to insist that the terms be observed. "Here the contract has no value," said the bracero.[162] Another bracero who spoke with Galarza put the issue more succinctly. "Eight times I have been in the United States, four times as a wetback and four times as a bracero. . . . The new ones without any experience have the illusion of the contract, but not me. When you come as a bracero it passes the same as when you come as a wetback."[163]

Increasingly this became the attitude of many braceros, who either "skipped" or returned as "illegals." Rather than complain and protest, many braceros voted with their feet. Contract skipping became a frequent occurrence in many camps, and the growing numbers of "skips" attested to the poor conditions in the camps and to the belief by braceros that the grievance procedure of the Bracero Agreement was of little value. In skipping out many braceros expressed their basic agreement with the Department of Labor official who stated that "the National cannot change jobs freely, thus seeking better conditions or higher pay."[164] In the eyes of many braceros the undocumented worker had more freedom to do just that. Unfortunately the plight of the undocumented worker was little better, and more often much worse.

There exist no accurate figures as to the number of braceros who "skipped" their contracts, yet their numbers were sufficient enough to concern officials in the United States. A report to the Secretary of Labor written in 1953 stated that in addition to "wetbacks" there were "hundreds of abscondees from contracts."[165] According to Rocco C. Siciliano, Assistant Secretary of Labor, the percentage of "skips" during the period from July 1951 to July 1953 was about 4.4 percent, or about 8,000 out of some 180,000 braceros sampled.[166] In later testimony Siciliano stated that the number of "skips" was fairly substantial, ranging anywhere from 15 to 20 percent.[167] Nonetheless Siciliano inferred at this time that the fault lay not with the growers but rather with the Mexican braceros who set out on their own in an effort to make better wages. He made no mention of what may have been the root causes of the problem, which were employer abuse, exploitation, and contract violations.

Opponents of the program were not as hesitant to discuss the problem of bracero "skips" as were government officials. In testimony before a Senate Committee in 1952, reference was made to a study conducted in 1951 concerning the number of braceros who had not completed their contract terms. Of the 30,200 Mexicans involved in the study, 5,466 had left their employers because of dissatisfaction. Another 6,122 had returned of their own volition to Mexico before the end of their contract period. All told, 39 percent of the 30,200 braceros had broken their contracts.[168]

In 1954 Walter Reuther complained to Secretary of Labor Mitchell that as a result of gross abuses and violations "thousands" had "skipped" their contracts and had entered the "industrial areas, swelling the ranks of the several million illegal entrants estimated to come here each year."[169] In that same year the Executive Council of the American Federation of Labor stated that "wetbacks" and braceros were both part of the same problem, as evident from the fact that "thousands of contracted aliens have either 'skipped' their contract or have continued to live in the United States after the expiration of their contracts. In either case they have automatically become 'wetbacks' who work and live at the mercy of easy-money employers or unscrupulous labor contractors."[170]

While accurate figures do not exist as to the number of braceros who actually "skipped," the fact remains that those who did "skip" often did so because of real or perceived unfair treatment at the hands of their employers. Inadequate and cumbersome grievance procedures also tended to encourage "skipping," for in pursuing the grievance procedure the bracero was bound to lose, either through lost time and wages or by the loss of his job.

It was also not unusual to find employers who encouraged braceros to "skip" their contracts and return illegally to them. Growers were loathe to release braceros whom they had trained to perform skill-related work, as those braceros might not be available for the next contracting period. Through this arrangement braceros could avoid an uncertain fate at contracting centers, and growers were assured of the renewed services of individuals who were of value to them.[171] This arrangement also saved growers the cost of bracero contracts, which after 1949 ran as high as fifty dollars per contract.[172]

CONCLUSION

In discussing the ways in which the bracero program contributed to the illegal influx, this chapter raises a number of questions about the operation of the program. For example, if widespread abuse did exist, why did so many braceros crowd into contracting stations seeking a contract? Why did so many others return year after year as contracted braceros? Of the many questions raised about the program perhaps these are the most difficult to answer, and one must rely largely on speculation in attempting to answer them.

Existing records seem to leave little doubt that abuse, exploitation, and violations did occur. The sheer size of the program and the numbers involved precluded strict enforcement of the contract agreements. Those braceros who complained often found their grievances unanswered or thwarted. Others elected to "skip" and strike out on their own in hopes of finding better jobs and wages and greater opportunity, yet they soon found that they were subject to even greater exploitation as "illegals." Thus the majority of Mexicans, whether happy with their lot as braceros or not, decided to fulfill their contract obligations. While the wages and the living and working conditions were not what they had been led to expect, they were for the most part tolerable.

Those who stayed did so out of a sense of obligation to those they had left behind and to those they owed money to. Most had been unemployed or underemployed in Mexico, and as braceros they were at least working and eating. They also knew that acquiring a contract greatly improved their chances for renewal when the next contract period came about. Others stayed because they had little choice. They understood neither the language nor the alien culture in which they found themselves. While conditions might not have been that good where they were, the uncertainty of what lay ahead should they leave was great enough to dissuade them from striking out on their own. Still others decided to take advantage of their contract to learn some English and to pick up whatever knowledge they could so that one day they might return and seek employment on their own. Some felt that they had put too much money and effort into getting contracts and therefore were loathe not to complete their terms as braceros. They therefore completed their obligation and chalked it up to experience. Also, there was the concept of "honor," wherein braceros viewed their acceptance of a contract as a bargain they were obligated to fulfill even if the other party could violate it with impunity. Of course, there were those whose employers abided by the contract rules and treated braceros with kindness and respect, which made the contract period worthwhile both economically and personally. Braceros fulfilled their contracts for various and sundry reasons. Certainly the same question can be asked as to why undocumented workers risked so much and endured such hardships for the meager sums they were paid.

The question also arises as to why Mexico repeatedly acquiesced to renewals of the contract labor program, given the plethora of problems that plagued it. Here the answer appears somewhat more clear.

The bracero program proved of tremendous economic benefit to Mexico, although official Mexican sources tended to play down the program's economic impact. Nonetheless figures indicate that Mexico's economy experienced growth during the 1950s and 1960s, much of which was due to tourism, border transactions, and bracero remittances, all of which helped reduce Mexico's trade deficit with the United States.[173]

Conflicting figures exist as to the actual amount that Mexico received as a result of bracero remittances. It has been estimated that from 1942 to 1947 Mexico received $318 million from braceros. Of this, $118 million came as a result of the forced and voluntary savings sent to Mexico.[174] Another $31 million was brought back by returning braceros, while $106 million came from individuals who had entered without a contract.[175]

In 1952 it was estimated that bracero remittances totalled some $70 million.[176] Other sources stated that during the decade of the 1950s remittances ranged from $22 million to $120 million annually.[177] Mexico's statistics are at variance with these figures. Mexican sources listed remittances at slightly more than $200 million for the period 1954-1959.[178] In 1954 a nationwide survey of bracero earnings by the Mexican Bankers Association revealed that $67 million had been sent to Mexico through postal and bank money orders during the five-month peak of contracting. A report released by the Mexican Treasury Department in 1954 estimated that $67 million had been brought back by braceros, thus bringing the estimated total of bracero remittances for that year, which by the way represented the peak load for bracero contracting, to $134 million.[179]

Hancock estimated that between 1956 and 1957 braceros either sent back or took no less than $120 million dollars annually.[180] The U.S. Department of Labor estimated that braceros earned approximately $200 million in 1957, half of which went back to Mexico.[181]

Whatever the precise amount of the remittances, they were of crucial importance to Mexico's balance of payments.[182] Bracero remittances contributed between 1 and 2 percent annually to Mexico's national income (see table 6). The importance here is not so much the percentage but rather its "multiplier effect" on the national economy.[183] According to Henry P. Anderson, a strident critic of the bracero program, each bracero supported an average of six people, which placed the number of people dependent upon bracero earnings at two-and-one-half million people.[184] Thus, unlike other sources of foreign exchange, these remittances went directly to the most economically depressed groups (see table 7).

TABLE 6

Bracero Remittances as a Percentage of the Mexican National Income, 1954-1964

Year	National Income[a] (Billions of Pesos)	Bracero Remittances[b] (Billions of Pesos)	Percent
1954	64,432	938	1.46
1955	69,290	1,313	1.89
1956	75,470	1,613	2.14
1957	83,120	1,500	1.80
1958	88,560	1,463	1.65
1959	93,750	1,625	1.73
1960	101,150	1,400	1.38
1961	106,480	1,338	1.26
1962	113,570	900	0.79
1963	122,300	638	0.52
1964	137,200	588	0.43

[a]Real Terms, 1954 prices
[b]All figures rounded off.

Sources: Column 2, *Review of the Economic Situation of Mexico* 43, 498 (May 1967): 11.
Column 3, U.S., Department of Commerce.

Because of the economic importance of the program, Mexico allowed it to continue through 1964. Mexican officials well realized that their country's economy could not keep pace with the demand for jobs and land produced by the tremendous population growth that Mexico was experiencing. They also knew that the impoverished state of many *campesinos* made them a politically and socially explosive force. The bracero program, along with increasing illegal emigration, served as a safety valve that relieved Mexico of some of its hungry and discontented populace. This exodus probably spared Mexico a great deal of social unrest and upheaval.[185]

Even if Mexico had discontinued the program at the end of World War II, it is quite doubtful that large-scale emigration to the United States could have been prevented. Mexico well realized that it could do little to stop the exodus. Faced with this reality, Mexico opted for a contract program. At least an international agreement, reasoned Mexican officials, would allow for some protection of their citizens while in the United States. If mass emigration seemed inevitable, then let it occur under government auspices.

What Mexican officials failed to realize was that they were not dealing solely with the government of the United States. They were also dealing with strong interest groups who considered the bracero program as their own domain and had long resisted government interference or control in agriculture. These officials

TABLE 7

Average Remittance by Mexican Braceros,
1954-1964

Year	Dollar Amount	Peso Equivalent	Mexican Estimate
1964	264	3300	2026
1963	273	3413	2038
1962	369	4613	2038
1961	367	4588	1463
1960	355	4438	1425
1959	297	3713	1075
1958	270	3375	1025
1957	275	3438	957
1956	290	3625	1063
1955	263	3288	775
1954	243	3038	1125

Sources: Column 3, $1:12.50 pesos (all figures rounded off).
Column 4, González Navarro, "Historia Demográfica," p. 411.

also failed to recognize that their goals differed from those of the United States.

Generally speaking, Mexico can be credited with doing a good job in getting so many guarantees for its workers. Unfortunately they had little or no direct control over those who would contract workers. A contract could not change ingrained attitudes or historical relationships. For example, a pattern of caste relationships had developed in California between racial minorities such as Mexicans, Filipinos, and other Asian groups and the white population. To the white Californians who generally employed them, all field workers were social inferiors.[186]

Similar attitudes were perhaps even more evident in Texas, where Mexicans and white Texans had been in cultural conflict since the early part of the nineteenth century. The independence of Texas in 1836 and the end of the Mexican War in 1848 only served to intensify hatred between the two groups. Negative feelings and stereotypes hardened on the part of the "conquerors" and the "conquered." The Mexicans were viewed and depicted as either dirty, cowardly, bloodthirsty bandits or as ignorant, lazy, docile, childlike peasants who needed to be prodded along or cared for. These stereotypes tended to evoke feelings of hostility toward people of Mexican descent on the part of Anglo-Texans. Attitudes, stereotypes, and perceptions were slow to die; and the miserable conditions characterizing the lives of many Mexicans and Mexican Americans in the Southwest served only to reinforce negative views about them and their culture. Some perceived this situation as the natural order of things and resented anyone who attempted to change it. As one Texan expressed it: "As soon as you begin to Americanize a Mexican he's no longer any good. He just won't work anymore."[187]

In essence, a contract did not alter the fact that the braceros were Mexicans, a fact that determined in large part how the braceros were treated. Once braceros were contracted, employers generally reverted to the same practices of exploitation and abuse that have characterized much of the history of agribusiness in the Southwest. A contract without teeth and without enforcement mechanisms became just another piece of paper to most growers. It was, in most cases, a means to an end, with the end being a large supply of cheap labor.

While braceros theoretically had certain rights, in many ways they were no better off than the domestic migrants who suffered from many of the same abuses. Working and living conditions for both braceros and domestic migrants left much to be desired, although braceros did find themselves the objects of great concern on the part of their government while in the United States. The same was true of domestic migrants, whose cause was espoused by a vocal, although poorly organized and ineffective group of social-reform, labor, and religious advocates.

At the very bottom was the worker who had entered illegally. Living outside the law, he had no one to champion his cause. He had only those who sought to exploit him and those who sought to expel him. Of the three groups, bracero, domestic migrant, and undocumented worker, the last was the least understood and the most exploited.

NOTES

1. Wayne D. Rasmussen, *A History of the Emergency Farm Labor Program, 1943 to 1947* (Washington, D.C.: U. S. Department of Agriculture, Bureau of Agricultural Economics, 1951), pp. 200-201.

2. Ibid. In October of 1941 the Associated Farmers requested that the Immigration and Naturalization Service allow them to import 30,000 Mexican braceros for use in California. At the behest of the Governor of California the request was denied by the INS. Horace E. Newton, *Mexican Illegal Immigration into California, Principally Since 1945* (San Francisco: R and E Research Associates, 1973), p. 5.

3. Robert D. Tomasek, "The Political and Economic Implications of Mexican Labor in the United States under the Non Quota System, Contract Labor Program, and Wetback Movement" (Ph.D. diss., University of Michigan, 1957), p. 52.

4. Rudolfo Acuña, *Occupied America: The Chicano's Struggle Toward Liberation* (San Francisco: Canfield Press, 1972), chapter 7; Julian Samora and Patricia Vandel Simon, *A History of the Mexican American People* (South Bend, Ind.: University of Notre Dame Press, 1978), chapter 18.

5. Walter J. Stein, *California and the Dust Bowl Migration* (Westport, Conn.: Greenwood Press, 1973), p. 33; and Newton, *Mexican Illegal Immigration*, pp. 17-18.

6. Newton, *Mexican Illegal Immigration*, pp. 17-18.

7. Stein, *California and the Dust Bowl*, p. 21; and Jerome S. Auerbach, *Labor and Liberty: The LaFollette Committee and the New Deal* (New York: Bobbs-Merrill, 1966), chapter 8, *passim*.

8. Carey McWilliams, *Factories in the Fields: The Study of Migratory Farm Labor in California* (Boston: Little, Brown and Co., 1944), p. 230.

9. Carey McWilliams, *Ill Fares The Land* (New York: Barnes and Noble, 1967), pp. 16-19.

10. "Contract Labor Admitted for Farmers," *Survey* 38 (30 June 1917): 296.

11. Howard L. Campbell, "Bracero Migration and the Mexican Economy, 1951-1964" (Ph.D. diss., American University, 1972), pp. 39-40.

12. *El Universal* (10 February 1946), p. 1.

13. Mexico, Secretaria de Relaciones Exteriores, *La Migracion y Proteccion de Mexicanos en el Extranjero* (Mexico, D.F., 1928), p. 6.

14. *El Universal* (18 July 1942), p. 1.

15. Tomasek, "The Political and Economic Implications," pp. 155, 284.

16. Otey M. Scruggs, "Evolution of the Mexican Farm Labor Agreement of 1942," *Agricultural History* 34 (July 1960): 145-46.

17. Tomasek, "The Political and Economic Implications," p. 54.

18. Richard T. Jarnagin, "The Effect of Increased Illegal Mexican Migration upon the Organization and Operations of the United States Immigration Border Patrol, Southwest Region" (Master's thesis, University of Southern California, 1957), p. 151.

19. Nelson G. Copp, *Wetbacks and Braceros* (San Francisco: R and E Research Associates, 1971), p. 57.

20. United States, Statutes at Large, 56, pt. 2, 1942, p., 1757.

21. Richard B. Craig, *The Bracero Program: Interest Groups and Foreign Policy* (Austin: University of Texas Press, 1971), p. 43.

22. Mark Reisler, *By the Sweat of Their Brow: Mexican Immigrant Labor in the United States, 1900-1940* (Westport, Conn.: Greenwood Press, 1976), pp. 25-27.

23. Record Group 166, Foreign Agricultural Service, Narrative Reports, 1950-1954, Mexico-Labor, Box 299, Folder on Mexico-Labor, 1952-1951, National Archives, Washington, D.C. (hereafter cited as R.G. 166, FAS, Narrative Reports, Box 299, Mexican Labor Folder 1952-1951, N.A.).

24. Tomasek, "The Political and Economic Implications," p. 88. These interests include electric companies, canners and packers, sugar beet companies, and banks, all of which have vested interests in Mexican labor. However, they prefer that the commercial growers do the work before Congress while they remain discreetly in the background and support the movement for cheap labor with money instead of words.

25. Peter Neil Kirstein, "Anglo over Bracero: A History of the Mexican Worker in the United States from Roosevelt to Nixon" (Ph.D. diss., St. Louis University, 1973), p. 210.

26. R. G. 166, FAS, Narrative Reports, Box 299, Mexican Labor Folder 1952-1951, N.A.

27. Ernesto Galarza, *Merchants of Labor: The Mexican Bracero Story* (Charlotte, N.C.: McNally and Loftin, 1964), p. 43.

28. U.S., Congress, House, *Farm Labor Program*, 1943, Hearings before the subcommittee of the Committee on Appropriations, 78th Cong. 1st sess., 17 February 1943, p. 89.

29. U.S., Congress, House, *Farm Labor Program*, Hearings before the Committee on Agriculture, 78th Cong., 1st sess., 22 March 1943, pp. 70-71.

30. Grant McConnell, *The Decline of Agrarian Democracy* (Berkeley: University of California Press, 1953), p. 146. The national Grange had a membership of 850,000, while the National Farmers' Union had 500,000 members.

31. Ibid., p. 158.

32. Tomasek, "The Political and Economic Implications," p. 107.

33. McConnell, *The Decline*, p. 158.

34. Craig, *The Bracero Program*, p. 24.

35. Robert J. Lipschultz, *American Attitudes Toward Mexican Immigration* (San Francisco: R and E Research Associates, 1971), p. 3.

36. Tomasek, "The Political and Economic Implications," pp. 34-35.

37. Lipschultz, *American Attitudes*, chapter 1; Reisler, *By The Sweat*, chapter 2.

38. The list is gleaned from records, correspondence, and other materials found in R.G. 166, Secretary of Agriculture Records, National Archives, Washington, D.C. and from Craig, *The Bracero Program,* p. 29.

39. Craig, *The Bracero Program,* p. 29.

40. John C. Elac, *The Employment of Mexican Workers in United States Agriculture, 1900-1960: A Binational Economic Analysis* (Los Angeles: University of California, 1961), p. 36.

41. Richard T. Spradlin, "The Mexican Farm Labor Importation Program-Review and Reform (Part II)," *The George Washington Law Review* 30 (1961-1962): 319.

42. Richard H. Hancock, *The Role of the Bracero in the Economic and Cultural Dynamics of Mexico: A Case Study of Chihuahua* (Stanford: Hispanic American Society, 1959), pp. 97-106; Campbell, "Bracero Migration," p. 264.

43. Kirstein, "Anglo over Bracero," p. 210.

44. Elac, *The Employment,* p. 201.

45. *El Universal* (8 January 1943), p. 6; (21 April 1943), p. 9; and (30 April 1943), p. 4.

46. Craig, *The Bracero Program,* p. 51.

47. G. S. Messersmith to Secretary of State, Subject: "Disturbances in Los Angeles Involving Mexicans" (19 June 1943), Mexico, D.F.; in State Department Records, Document No. 811, 4016/570, National Archives, Washington, D.C.

48. David Thomasson to Secretary of State, Subject: "Student Demonstrations Regarding Alleged Racial Discrimination in the United States on June 25, 1943" (1 July 1943), Mexico, D.F., in State Department Records, Document No. 811, 4016/593, National Archives, Washington, D.C.

49. "Los Sucesos de California," editorial in *Novedades* (21 June 1943), p. 1.

50. *New York Times* (17 June 1943), p. 23; (27 June 1943), p. 28; (28 June 1943), p. 27; *El Universal* (26 June 1943), p. 1.

51. Mexico, Secretaria de Relaciones Exteriores, *Desde Mexico.* Boletin, Pedro Munro Asunsolo, "Como Viven y Trabajan Los Braceros Mexicanos en los Estados Unidos" (Mexico, D.F., 15 December and 30 December 1944), pp. 2-4 and pp. 2-4.

52. Mexico, Secretaria de Relaciones Exteriores, *Desde Mexico.* Boletin Quinceñal del Departamento de Informacion Para el Extranjero (Mexico, D.F.: 15 June 1944), p. 2.

53. R. G. 166, FAS, Narrative Reports, Box 299, Mexican Labor Folder, N.A.

54. Memo to William P. Blocker from Secretary of State (1942), in R. G. 59, State Department, Decimal File 811.4, National Archives, Washington, D.C.

55. William P. Blocker, "Results of a Confidential Survey of the Problem of Racial Discrimination Against Mexican and Latin American Citizens in New Mexico," American Consulate, Ciudad Juarez, Mexico (27 February 1942), Foreign Service of the United States of America, File Number 811.4016/377 PS/JMK in R.G. 59, State Department, Decimal File 811.4 to 811.4016/499, National Archives, Washington, D.C. (hereafter cited as *The Blocker Report,* 1942), N.A.

56. Ibid., p. 5.

57. Ibid., p. 21.

58. Ibid., pp. 21-22.

59. Ibid., p. 32.

60. For a discussion of such attitudes and their continued prepondernace *see*: Deluvinia Hernandez, *Mexican American Challenge to a Sacred Cow* (Los Angeles: Aztlan Publications, 1970); and Philip Wayne Powell, *Tree of Hate* (New York: Basic Books, 1971).

61. Campbell, "Bracero Migration," p. 180.

62. Robert F. Heizer and Alan J. Almquist, *The Other Californians: Prejudice and Discrimination under Spain, Mexico and the United States to 1920* (Los Angeles: University of California Press, 1971).

63. *See* R. G. 59, Mexican Labor Program Folders, N.A.

64. John Higham, *Strangers in the Land: Patterns of American Nativism, 1860-1925* (New York: Atheneum, 1972), pp. 3-11.

65. Sumner Welles, "Discriminating Against Our Neignbors," article cited in U.S., Congress, Senate, *Congressional Record,* 78th Cong., 2d sess., 23 February 1944, 90, pt. 8, Appendix, p. A899.

66. Craig, *The Bracero Program,* p. 59.

67. Juan R. Garcia, *A History of the Mexican American People of Chicago Heights, Illinois* (Chicago Heights: Prairie State College, 1976), chapter 1.

68. Manuel Gamio, *Mexican Immigration to the United States* (New York: Dover, Inc., 1971), pp. 177-82.

69. For example, *see:* Leo Grebler, *Mexican Immigration to the United States: The Record and Its Implications,* Mexican American Study Project, Advance Report 2 (Los Angeles: University of California, 1966); Eleanor Hadley, "A Critical Analysis of the Wetback Problem," *Law and Contemporary Problems* 21 (1956): 334-57; Julian Samora, *Los Mojados: The Wetback Story* (South Bend, Ind.: University of Notre Dame Press, 1971); Lyle Saunders and Olen E. Leonard, "The Wetback in the Lower Rio Grande Valley of Texas," in *Inter-American Education, Occasional Papers,* vol. 7 (Austin: University of Texas, July 1951).

70. Corwin, "Causes of Mexican Emigration," p. 567.

71. Personal interview with Manuel G. Calderon in November, 1969, Mexico City, cited in Campbell, "Bracero Migration," p. 93.

72. Hadley, "A Critical Analysis," p. 344.

73. Hancock, *The Role of the Bracero,* p. 21.

74. Tomasek, "The Political and Economic Implications," pp. 180-81 and 190-91; Otey M. Scruggs, "The United States, Mexico, and the Wetbacks, 1942-1947," *The Pacific Historical Review* 30, no. 2 (May, 1961): 163.

75. *New York Times* (2 April 1954), p. 2.

76. *Hispanic American Report,* no. 10 (November 1957), p. 520.

77. Record Group 166, Foreign Agricultural Service, Box 299, Folder on Mexican Labor, 1950-1948, National Archives, Washington, D.C. (hereafter cited as R.G. 166, Box 299, Mexican Labor Folder, 1950-1948, N.A.); the author was also provided with a special box of materials and documents dealing with Mexican labor from 1946 to 1949, no Record Group Number, National Archives (hereafter cited as Box on Mexican Labor, 1946-1949. N.A.).

78. Gustavo Duran de la Huerta, "17,000 Campesinos Sin Abrigo Ni Comida Luchan Por Emigrar," *Excelsior* (1 June 1951); Robert L. Ghisi, "Inhumana Explotacion Han Hecho Con Los Braceros Contratados," article in the Mexicali Daily *ABC* (6 September 1951); Robert L. Ghisi, "Transportan Como Bestias Desde Guadalajara, A 25,000 Braceros," *ABC* (7 September 1951).

79. de la Huerta, "17,000 Campesinos," *Excelsior* (1 June 1951).

80. Department of State, Washington, Foreign Service Dispatch (7 September 1951), Subject: "Arrival and Processing of Mexican Agricultural Workers at Calexico, California, under the Migrant Labor Agreement of 1951," located in R. G. 166, Box 299, Mexican Labor Folder, 1950-1948, N.A.

81. Scruggs, "The United States," p. 163.

82. Galarza, *Merchants,* p. 52.

83. Ibid.

84. Ibid., pp. 56-57 and 77.

85. Ibid., p. 57; and Craig, *The Bracero Program,* p. 82.

86. Kirstein, "Anglo over Bracero," pp. 170-71.

87. Hancock, *The Role of the Bracero*, p. 66.

88. U.S. Congress, House, Committee on the Judiciary, *Hearings before the President's Commission on Immigration and Naturalization,* 82d Cong., 2d sess., September and October, 1952, pp. 41-42. This union, a strong opponent of the illegal influx, consistently pointed to the bracero program as the chief cause of the great increase in the number of illegal entrants. National Agricultural Workers Union *Proceedings: Seventh National Convention of the National Farm Labor Union* (Memphis, 1951), Resolution 2.

89. Grebler, *Mexican Immigration*, p. 32.

90. Hancock, *The Role of the Bracero*, p. 3.

91. Gloria R. Vargas y Campos, *El Problema del Bracero Mexicano* (Mexico: Universidad Autonoma de Mexico, 1964), Table 7; and Mexico, Direccion General de Estadistica, *Anuarios estadisticos,* 1962/1963 and 1964/65 (distributed by Somerset House, Teaneck, New Jersey). The reader should note that percentages will vary among different authors.

92. Craig, *The Bracero Program*, pp. 130-31; and Hancock, *The Role of the Bracero*, p. 3.

93. de la Huerta, "17,000 Campesinos," *Excelsior* (1 June 1951).

94. Saunders and Leonard, "The Wetbacks," p. 30.

95. Samora, *Los Mojados*, p. 39.

96. Robert C. Jones, *Los Braceros Mexicanos en los estados unidos durante el periodo belico* (Washington, D.C.: Union Panamericana, 1946), pp. 29-42. According to the figures presented, 83 percent of the braceros contracted were under 24 years of age and 76 percent of those who were contracted were unmarried.

97. According to Nathan Whetten nearly 65 percent of the Mexican people in 1940 lived in rural communities of 2,500 or less. By 1960 the percentage had dropped to 49 percent. Nathan Whetten, "Population Growth in Mexico," *Report of the Select Commission on Western Hemisphere Immigration* (Washington, D.C.: G.P.O., 1968), p. 175.

98. Campbell, "Bracero Migration," p. 180.

99. Craig, *The Bracero Program*, p. 60.

100. Hadley, "A Critical Analysis," p. 354.

101. Ibid.

102. Sheldon L. Greene, "Immigration Law and Rural Poverty: The Problems of the Illegal Entrant," *Duke Law Journal* 1969, no. 3 (June 1969): p. 479. This practice was not new to Mexico or Mexicans since minimum wages were set biannually by wage boards made up of government representatives, workers, and employers in the municipios of Mexico. Because of this, Mexico also had wage rates that differed from state to state. Campbell, "Bracero Migration," p. 146.

103. Walter J. Mason to George Meany (18 October 1954), cited in U.S. Congress, House, Mexican Farm Labor Program, *Hearings Before the Subcommittee on Agriculture on H.R. 3822,* 84th Cong., 1st sess., March 1955, p. 160 (hereafter cited as *Hearings on H.R. 3822*).

104. Note #6770, from Mexican Embassy to Department of State, 10 September 1947, in Record Group 244, Office of Labor, General Correspondence, 1947, Health Services 6, Box 114, Folder 3, Laborers, National Archives, Washington, D.C. (hereafter cited as Note #6770, R.G. 244, Box 114, Folder 3, 1947, N.A.).

105. Ibid.

106. Ibid.

107. Ibid., p. 2.

108. Ibid.

109. Letters in Folder 3, Ibid.

110. Karl L. Zander to W. T. Harrison, Medical Director, District No. 5, 1947, p. 3, in Record Group 224, Office of Labor, General Correspondence, 1947, Box 114, Health Services, Sanitation, Folder 7, National Archives, Washington, D.C. (hereafter cited as Zander Memorandum, R.G. 244, Box 114, 1947, Folder 7, N.A.).

111. Ibid., p. 4.

112. Ibid., p. 5.

113. Airgram from Walter Thurston, American Embassy, Mexico, D.F., to Secretary of State, 26 August 1949, in Special Box, no Record Group, Folder, Mexico, 1949-1946, N.A.

114. Dispatch, to Department of State, from Mexico, D.F., 9 November 1950. Subject: "Braceros: Cancellation of Contracts," Record Group 166, Foreign Agricultural Service, Narrative Reports 1950-1954, Box 299, Mexican Labor Folder 1950-1948, National Archives, Washington, D.C. (hereafter cited as R.G. 166, Box 299, Mexican Labor Folder, 1950-1948, N.A.).

115. Ibid.

116. Ibid.

117. Foreign Service Dispatch from American Embassy, Mexico, D.F., to Department of State, Reference to Embassy's Dispatch No. 1806 of 25 January 1952, Subject: Braceros: Incident, 1 February 1952, in Record Group 166, Foreign Agricultural Service, Narrative Reports 1950-1954, Box 299, Mexican Labor Folder, 1952-1951, National Archives, Washington, D.C. (hereafter cited as R.G. 166, Box 299, Mexican Labor Folder 1952-1951, N.A.).

118. Ibid., pp. 1-2.

119. Ibid., p. 2.

120. Ibid.

121. Foreign Service Dispatch from American Embassy, Mexico, D.F., to Department of State, 26 February 1952, in R.G. 166, Box 299, Mexican Labor Folder, 1950-1948, N.A.

122. Foreign Service Dispatch to State Department from American Embassy, Mexico, D.F., Dispatch No. 1187, 8 November 1951, R.G. 166, Box 299, Mexican Labor Folder, 1952-1951, N.A.

123. Foreign Service Dispatch to State Department from W.K. Alshie, American Consul General, Mexico, D.F., Dispatch No. 1135, 31 October 1951, ibid.

124. Foreign Service Dispatch from Manuel Tello, Mexico, D.F., to Department of State, Dispatch No. 1, 2 July 1951, ibid.

125. Pauline R. Kibbe, "The Economic Plight of Mexicans," *Ethnic Relations in the United States,* ed. Edward C. McDonagh and Eugene S. Richardo (New York: Appleton-Century Crofts, Inc., 1953), p. 106.

126. Ibid., p. 197.

127. Most Reverend Leo F. Dworschak (Auxiliary Bishop of Fargo, North Dakota) to Most Reverend Robert E. Lucey, 27 October 1952, letter in Archbishop Robert E. Lucey Papers, Notre Dame Archives, University of Notre Dame, South Bend Ind. (hereafter cited as Lucey Papers, N.D. Archives).

128. Archbishop Robert E. Lucey to Reverend Mathew Kelly, July 1954, p. 1, Lucey Papers, N.D. Archives.

129. Ibid., pp. 1-2.

130. "A preliminary report on the work of Mexican 'Chaplains' for Migrants in the Michigan Area," p. 3, from Reverend James A. Hickey, Diocese of Saginaw, to Archbishop Robert E. Lucey, 8 July 1953, in Lucey Papers, N.D. Archives.

131. Father John F. Godfrey to James P. Mitchell, 23 November 1953, R. G. 174, Department of Labor, Box 54, Mexican Labor Program, Miscellaneous Folder, National Archives, Washington, D.C.

132. Correspondence in Record Group 174, Box 140, Department of Labor, Mexican Labor Program Folder, July-December 1956, National Archives, Washington, D.C.

133. Ernesto Galarza, *Strangers in Our Fields* (Washington, D.C.: Joint United States-Mexico Trade Union Committee, 1956), p. 35.

134. Rocco C. Siciliano, Assistant Secretary of Labor, to Estes Kefauver 6 July 1956, in R.G. 174, Box 140, Mexican Labor Program File, July-December 1956, N.A.

135. Galarza, *Strangers*, p. 30.

136. *Los Braceros,* pp. 97-99.

137. Excerpts from Report of Field Trip to the Western States by Reverend Joseph H. Crosthwait, Field Representative, Bishop's Committee for the Spanish-speaking, October 1957, BCSS File, Annual Report, Lucey Papers, N.D. Archives.

138. Ibid.

139. Ibid.

140. Galarza, *Strangers*, pp. 35-6.

141. Ibid.

142. There were braceros who felt that the contract was worth it. As the program continued, growers began recontracting many of the same braceros who had worked for them in previous seasons. There soon emerged a group of "professional" braceros who were repeatedly contracted, which served to reduce the number of new contracts available. Those unable to receive contracts because they were superseded by these "professionals" also entered illegally. Campbell, "Bracero Migration," pp. 103-4.

143. Galarza, *Strangers*, p. 26.

144. Tomasek, "The Political and Economic Implications," p. 132.

145. U.S., Congress, House, *Congressional Record,* 83d Cong., 2d sess., 1954, 100, pt. 2: 2432; President's Commission on Migratory Labor, *Migratory Labor in American Agriculture* (Washington, D.C.: G.P.O., 1951), p. 62; Ellis W. Hawley, "The Politics of the Mexican Labor Issue, 1950-1965," *Agricultural History* 40, no. 2 (July 1966): 169. Hawley states that contrary to outward appearances, the Department of Labor was not really a hostile agency with regard to the growers. Although the United States Employment Agency was charged with certifying labor shortages, it was only a coordinating agency for the state services and their farm placement divisions. The crucial day-to-day decisions were made on the local and state levels where employer influence was strong. It was usually certain that labor shortages would be certified so that growers and their associations would be eligible for braceros.

146. Robert C. Goodwin to Secretary of Labor James P. Mitchell, December 12, 1956, R.G. 174, Box 140, Mexican Labor Program File, 1956, N.A.

147. Ibid.

148. Tomasek, "The Political and Economic Implications," pp. 226-27.

149. *Hearings on H.R. 3822*, p. 159.

150. Ibid.

151. Don McLean and Walter Wings, "U.S. Farms Breed Wetbacks?" clipping from *Washington Daily News* (19 November 1956), p. 30, found in R. G. 174, Box 140, Mexican Labor Program File, 1956.

152. Ibid.

153. Galarza, *Strangers*, p. 79.

154. Ibid., p. 18.

155. Hancock, *The Role of the Bracero*, p. 126.

156. Tomasek, "The Political and Economic Implications," p. 75.

157. Norman D. Humphrey, "The Mexican Image of Americans," *Annals of the American Academy of Political and Social Science* 295 (September 1954): 116; William H. Form and Julius Rivera, "Work Contracts and International Evaluations," *Social Forces* 37 (May, 1959): 334-35; Campbell, "Bracero Migration," p. 276.

158. Carey McWilliams, *Factories in the Fields* (Boston: Little, Brown, 1939), pp. 270-71, citing *Mañana*, p. 21.

159. *The Texas Spectator* (11 October 1946), p. 21.

160. *Secret Study*, n.d., report housed in the David H. Stowe Papers, Truman Library, Independence, Mo. (hereafter cited as *Secret Study*).

161. Galarza, *Strangers*, p. 18.

162. Ibid.

163. Ibid.

164. Ibid.

165. Bureau of Labor Standards, "The Migratory Labor Story, 1953," report prepared for Secretary of Labor (July 1953), Folder 10, Box 78, A72-8, Dwight D. Eisenhower Library, Abilene, Kansas.

166. Ibid.

167. Ibid.

168. U.S., Congress, Senate, *Migratory Labor Hearings* before the subcommittee on Labor-Management Relations of the Committee on Labor and Public Welfare, 82d Cong., 2d sess., 1952, pt. 1: 888.

169. Walter P. Reuther to James P. Mitchell (11 January 1954), Record Group 174, Box 54, Mexican Labor Program-Miscellaneous (January-June), National Archives, Washington, D.C.

170. Harvey A. Levenstein, *Labor Organizations in the United States and Mexico: A History of Their Relations* (Westport, Ct.: Greenwood Press, 1971), p. 209.

171. Corwin, "Causes of Mexican Emigration," p. 568.

172. It appears that on occasion employers were given to extreme practices in protecting their investments. Fully aware that "skipping" was on the increase, some growers took the precaution of placing armed guards in the camps and fields to prevent runaways. Ted Le Berthon, "At the Prevailing Rate," *Commonweal* 67 (1 November 1957): 123. Similar precautions had been taken during the 1920s by labor contractors when they chained braceros together and delivered them under armed guard to the depots for transporting to their assigned areas. Victor S. Clark, "Mexican Labor in the United States," *Bulletin of the Bureau of Labor*, 17, no. 78 (Washington, D.C.: Bureau of Labor, 1908): 471-75.

173. Campbell, "Bracero Migration," p. 209.

174. Prior to 1951 all braceros were required to deposit ten percent of their earnings into banks specifically designated by the Mexican government. The monies were held there until the braceros returned at the end of their contract period, to insure that the braceros saved some of their earnings and to discourage them from remaining in the United States after their contracts expired. This practice was discontinued after 1951.

175. These figures are based on 52 percent savings figures. Pedro Merla, "El Bracero Mexicano en la Economia Nacional," *Revista del Trabajo* 3, no. 143 (December 1949): 9-10.

176. "Wetback Flood," *Newsweek* 41, no. 21 (25 May 1953): 56.

177. Craig, *The Bracero Program*, p. 17.

178. Secretaria de Industria y Commercio, *Direccion General de Estadistica*, M. 19:422, 421; 21:112; 22:108; 23:168.

179. A. C. McLellan, "Down in the Valley: A Supplementary Report on Developments in the Wetback and Bracero Situation of the Lower Rio Grande Valley of Texas Since Publication of 'What Price Wetbacks?' " (Austin: Texas State Federation of Labor, 1953), p. 3.

180. Hancock, *The Role of the Bracero*, p. 37.

181. U.S., Department of Labor, *Farm Labor Fact Book* (Washington, D.C.: G. P. O., 1958), p. 176.

182. U.S., Congress, Senate, Committee on Appropriations, *Department of Agriculture and Related Agencies' Appropriations. Hearings before Subcommittee on H.R. 10509*, 90th Cong., 1st sess., Fiscal Year 1968, pp. 55-57. A study completed three years after the bracero program ended showed that there was a substantial increase in the balance of payments in favor of the U.S. in those years following the end of the program.

183. Campbell, "Bracero Migration," pp. 212-13.

184. Henry P. Anderson, *The Bracero Program in California with Particular Reference to Health Status, Attitudes, and Practices* (Berkeley: School of Public Health, University of California, 1961), p. 17.

185. Craig, *The Bracero Program,* p. 60.

186. Stein, *California,* p. 60.

187. Hawley, "The Politics," p. 169.

2
Conflicting Immigration Policies in the United States and Mexico

BETWEEN 1947 AND 1951 the bracero program deteriorated as legislation governing its operation removed much of the previous governmental supervision and placed the contracting of Mexican workers into the hands of private employers, which gave rise to many problems and abuses. The Mexican government, hampered by inefficiency and by a weak bargaining position now that the war crisis had ended, repeatedly reminded the United States that the change in contracting procedures did not relieve either government of its responsibility for upholding program guarantees, but many of its protests went unheeded.

Under the new agreement employers were required to pay all transportation and recruitment costs. Unhappy with the red tape and high costs involved, many employers increasingly turned to the use of undocumented labor. The growing influx of undocumented workers and the growing concern of the Mexican government over the lack of protection and guarantees for its citizens led it to press for a renegotiation of the 1949 Bracero Agreement, which was scheduled to expire on 30 June 1951.[1]

Mexico entered into negotiation determined to wring as many concessions and guarantees as possible from the United States. Mexico wanted to continue the program because remittances from braceros were quickly becoming a prime source of income for Mexico's battered economy, but it also had to contend with growing criticism from its own people. The increasingly commonplace stories of inhuman treatment of braceros and undocumented workers by United States growers and processors evoked resentment from many Mexicans. What especially incensed Mexicans were reports that their countrymen were denied equal treatment in Texas because of their skin color and nationality. They also resented the apparent American belief that all Mexicans were illiterate peons.[2]

A 1951 report prepared in the United States pointed out that the contracting of braceros, the "chronic" violations of contract terms by corporation farmers, and the exploitation of "illegals" had all become major political issues in Mexico.[3] The report stated that working, social, and economic conditions endured by legals and "illegals" put President Miguel Aleman in a "delicate" position.[4] Of course

Aleman had not been the first, nor would he be the last, Mexican president to be placed in such a position by the bracero program.

Mexican officials had for the most part favored continuing the program even though it presented them with some difficult dilemmas. Although they would not openly admit it, the program did benefit the country socially, politically, and economically. For example, it acted as a safety valve for the large mass of unemployed workers in the agricultural sector. Observers believed that the government gained political benefits from it in that braceros showed their gratitude to the official party through their votes.[5] Yet the program also had its drawbacks, as it tended to deprive Mexico of valuable potential labor. The fact that many Mexicans had gone to the United States prior to the bracero agreements had been one of the reasons for Mexico's acquiescence to a regulated international agreement. However, even though the program supposedly had been negotiated to provide protection and to regulate the flow of emigrants, it had not proven very successful in accomplishing either goal.

Critics of the program in Mexico were not slow to point out these and other shortcomings. The weak opposition parties used the program to attack the official party; and their attacks, while politically motivated and recognized as such, nonetheless had to be reckoned with. Whether the attacks emanated from the ultra-conservative, highly nationalistic, religious Sinarquista Party, the moderately conservative Party of National Action, the agrarian, social-reform-oriented Popular Party, or the Communist Party, they all had the same effect of placing the official party of the PRI in the unenviable position of attempting to explain why such a program was necessary if Mexico's economy was as sound as the PRI claimed it was.[6] An even more damning critique was that based on arguments that appealed to Mexico's nationalism, for the opposition consistently hammered on the fact that Mexican citizens were performing demeaning tasks for paltry sums. The political left described the program as colonialistic and exploitative, while to the moderates it represented an affront to the dignity of Mexicans.[7]

American representatives in Mexico took exception to the attacks levelled against the "capitalistic gringos" by Mexico's opposition parties. One official was particularly disturbed by an article in the weekly magazine La Nacion, published by the Partido Accion Nacional (PAN). He stated that the article, entitled "Braceros Transported Like Slaves," proved that the opposition sought to seize every opportunity to promote anti-American propaganda. He believed that such propaganda almost always found fertile ground among the Mexican people. He stated that, although PAN was conservative, pro-Catholic, and anti-Communist, when it came to stirring up anti-American feelings it went hand-in-hand with the communists in efforts to berate and discredit the United States.[8]

Another strong opponent of the program was the Mexican unions, which comprised an important group within the official party. At the outset of the program the Mexican Confederation of Labor had sought to have the program ended, but by 1946 the leadership had changed its stance, realizing that the program would continue in spite of their vehement protests. After that they concentrated their efforts on obtaining stronger safeguards for legally contracted workers who went to the United States and for more stringent controls against those who entered illegally or those who aided individuals in entering illegally.[9]

The unions opposed the program and the emigration of undocumented workers because of the poor working conditions and living conditions under which many of them were forced to labor. They were also concerned about the impact the entry of foreign labor might have on migrant workers, many of whom were of Mexican descent, in the United States; and they feared that the continuing exodus of undocumented workers would prove harmful to the Mexican economy by draining the country of much-needed labor. Finally, the unions realized that each worker who left Mexico represented the loss of a potential unionist.[10]

Because they were members of the official party and because they tended to be better organized, the Mexican labor unions were somewhat successful in their efforts to make the program more effective in protecting Mexican braceros. For example, they played a key role in urging the Mexican government to locate contracting stations in the interior and to refuse contract labor to states where discrimination against Mexicans was blatant.

In 1954 the Mexican Condederation of Labor was responsible for getting the Inter-American Regional Organization of Workers to pass a resolution that urged the Mexican government to adopt penalties for farmers who abandoned their lands in order to enter the United States illegally. That same resolution also called upon the government to demand specific information as to where braceros would work, what kinds of work they would do, and how many hours they would be required to work while under contract.[11] Its strongest recommendations came on the "wetback" problem; the union demanded that legislation be enacted to curb the movement of undocumented workers at the point of origin. It also recommended that all vehicles used to transport undocumented workers to the border be confiscated. As added measures they called for better patrolling of the border region by both countries and for publicity by the government that would inform potential "wetbacks" about the dangers of crossing illegally and about the abuses they would be subject to if they entered without a contract.[12]

Mexican commercial farmers also called for an end to the contract labor program. After failing to bring it to an end, they concentrated on keeping contracting stations away from the border regions and on having stronger measures enacted to prevent the exodus of undocumented workers. For the most part they were not that influential, given the land reforms embodied in the ideals of the Revolution of 1910. Furthermore, they spoke out comparatively late against the exodus of farm workers from Mexico. In 1952 they came out against the program and illegal emigration, claiming that it disrupted the national economy by depriving them of the labor necessary to harvest their crops.[13] They also complained that the use of Mexican labor in the United States produced a surplus of American cotton that was often dumped on the world market, undermining the cotton industry of Mexico.[14]

Industrialists opposed emigration of Mexicans because a dearth of labor forced them to pay higher wages. But their complaints, like those of the agriculturalists, went pretty much unheeded, as they did not belong to the official party.

The Catholic Church in Mexico came out against the emigration of braceros and "illegals" because members of the hierarchy believed that it contributed to the disruption of family life. They were also concerned about the temptation of braceros to live immorally in the United States, as many of them were young and single and others would be separated from their wives and families for extended periods. Of course, they were fearful that the spiritual needs of braceros would not be attended to while in the United States, especially in light of the strong proselytizing efforts being undertaken by Protestant missions.

If the various groups both within and outside the official party had been able to unite and coordinate their efforts they might have effected change, but the various groups opposed the mass emigration for different reasons. Within the official party two of the five important sectors, the *ejido* (communal Indian property) organizations and the popular or bureaucratic groups, were largely noncommital about the whole situation. Thus, with only the labor unions of the official party dissenting, the president and high authorities were able to adopt the position they believed best served the interests of the country.

Although the opposition groups were not able to effect policy change, their criticisms of the bracero program, reinforced by outcries from the Mexican citizenry in general, did force the Mexican government to pressure the United States for more effective measures to enforce contract guarantees. At times this pressure worked, especially when the foreign policy situation placed Mexico in a strong bargaining position. One such instance occurred in 1950, when United States involvement in the Korean War created a need for Mexican labor.

The Mexican government believed that it held a strong bargaining position, and its assumption proved correct. Growers had convinced United States officials that braceros were vital to the war effort. Ironically enough, in doing so growers gave more control over agricultural matters to the very agency that they wished to limit—the federal government. Because of the need for Mexican labor, United States representatives acquiesced to many of Mexico's demands, including ones for stricter intergovernmental control over the operation of the program and stricter enforcement of guarantees.[15] Of course, not everyone was completely satisfied with the agreement, but it was for the time being, considered by Mexico, the United States, and the agricultural sector as a detailed, fairly workable agreement.

Public Act 78, as the 1951 agreement came to be known when President Harry S. Truman signed it into law on 12 July 1951, testified to the shrewd and tough bargaining abilities of Mexico. Yet Mexico was not completely satisfied with it, as issues such as penalties against employers of undocumented workers and a stronger voice in determining the prevailing wage remained unresolved. Because of this, Mexico decided to make the agreement effective for a period of six months in order to provide Congress with some time to demonstrate its good faith by enacting penalty legislation. Further, Mexico realized that P.L. 78 signalled the institutionalization of what had started out to be an emergency wartime program. Thus it appears that Mexico opted for a six-month agreement during which it could consider the implications of making the bracero program a long-term project, waiting to see if the United States would rectify some of the evils spawned during the tumultuous years between 1948 and 1951.[16]

That repeated violations of bracero contracts and acts of racism by the United States against Mexicans were the targets of recurring criticism on the part of braceros and Mexican citizens from all walks of life was embarrassing and galling enough to the Mexican government. As one Mexican editorial expressed the matter, it was a "satisfactory fact that they [braceros] constitute an important source of dollars for our country. Nevertheless, it is a sober truth that the Nation is enriching itself at the cost of the people."[17] Mexican officials could find some relief in arguing that they were doing their best to protect Mexican citizens in the United States via a binational agreement, and thus pass much of the blame along to Uncle Sam. The most glaring problem was the "illegal" workers, for their mass exodus was always a source of deep embarrassment to Mexican officials. No matter how much they proclaimed the principles of the Revolution and the progress of their country, that mass emigration brought those claims into question. Furthermore, the plight of the "illegal" in the United States played on the sensitivity of Mexicans.

From the outset Mexico held the view that control of the illegal influx was the responsibility of the United States. The United States believed Mexico had not taken sufficient measures to halt illegal emigration. Therefore neither Mexico nor the United States appeared willing to accept responsibility for curbing the flow of "illegals." In fact, the two powers could not even remotely agree on how to solve this problem. Owing to a genuine belief that curbing the "illegal" problem was in fact more of an American than a Mexican concern, a reluctance to assume the added cost of augmenting its border patrol, and a disinclination to place further controls on its citizens, the Mexican government refused to increase efforts to stop the flow.[18]   From its point of view, the Mexican Constitution guaranteed Mexican citizens freedom of movement, and to do anything to restrict this was in violation of their rights.[19] The remedy, according to many Mexican officials, lay in United States penalties against those who employed "wetbacks." The United States did not favor this idea, as the issue of such penalties was a sensitive one.[20]

The debate over which country was responsible for dealing with the "illegal" situation came to a head in 1948, when Mexico abrogated the labor treaty because of what it perceived were unfair actions on the part of the United States. These actions included the continued employment by Americans of undocumented workers instead of legally contracted braceros and continued violations of the contract agreements by employers of minimum wage agreements and standard working conditions.[21] Mexico was also dissatisfied with the prevailing wage rate of $2.50

per hundred pounds set by the growers in Texas and sought to increase the picking rate to $3.00 per hundred pounds picked.[22]

What finally triggered Mexico's decision to abrogate the agreement of 1948 was the "El Paso Incident," which occurred between October 13 and October 18, 1948. Texas growers, who had met earlier in the year and set the prevailing wage at $2.50, professed outrage at what they considered highhanded dealing by the Mexican government and refused to accede to Mexico's wage demands. In their view the right to set the prevailing wage had never been challenged by the U.S. government and they were not about to let the Mexicans dictate to them. Because of the increasingly tense situation and Mexico's refusal to provide braceros, the Department of Labor sent Donald Larin to El Paso to investigate and conciliate. Larin, who knew little about the situation, arrived in El Paso and quickly sided with the Texas growers. In Larin's opinion the fault lay exclusively with Mexico as it had violated the agreement that called for a picking rate of $2.50 per hundred pounds of cotton picked.

The United States Employment Agency (USES), which was responsible for determining the need for foreign labor, held similar sentiments. Representatives of the USES had expressed impatience with Mexico's failure to fulfill the agreement as early as September of 1948 and threatened to force Mexico to meet its commitment in full "under penalty of unrestricted border recruitment and immigration clearance of braceros thereafter."[23] The USES had the full support of the Department of Labor and the Immigration and Naturalization Service in its declared intent to use unilateral recruitment if necessary. The State Department, however, had grave reservations about unilateral recruitment because of the serious diplomatic problems it might create. Walter Thurston strongly opposed unilateral recruitment, as he believed that this "drastic" action would constitute a violation of the international agreement, provoke the resentment of the Mexican government, and "have the most regrettable and unnecessary . . . consequences."[24] An aide to President Truman stated that the president would not support either the violation or the termination of the agreement.[25]

However, officials on the scene chose to ignore the sentiments of those who opposed the whole idea of unilateral recruitment and opened up the border to the braceros, who were anxiously awaiting a contract. Many of these hungry men did not understand or even know about the issues being debated by Mexico and the United States. All they knew was that they had been milling around for a long time and that just a short distance away there were jobs that paid $2.50 per hundred pounds. When negotiations broke down, word quickly spread among the braceros that Mexico was planning to close the border and terminate the agreement. Some decided not to wait and began to wade across. It soon became apparent that immigration officials were not going to do anything to stop them, and in what has been described as a "massive break" thousands of braceros raced for the border.

As the braceros crossed the river into El Paso immigration officials seized them, placed them under technical arrest, and then quickly parolled them to members of the Texas Employment Commission.[26] According to Grover C. Wilmoth, the District Immigration Director in El Paso, the border was opened because the braceros needed the work and the farmers needed the braceros to harvest their crops.[27] Thus from October 13 to October 18, approximately 5,000 braceros were allowed to enter the United States "illegally."[28]

Mexican officials were outraged. They accused Washington of having tacitly agreed to permit the illegal entry of braceros into Texas. In a statement issued on 18 October 1948, Mexico expressed "profound disappointment" with officials of the Immigration and Naturalization Service for their complicity in the flagrant violation of the international agreement. It informed the United States that the "El Paso Incident" left Mexico with little recourse but to terminate the bracero agreement. Because the United States had not lived up to its obligations Mexico stated that it would hold the United States responsible for any damages that the actions of the INS would have on its economy and its braceros.[29]

The incident proved embarrassing to the United States, and some officials attempted to excuse their actions by stating that they had not opened the border. According to Deputy Immigration Commissioner John P. Boyd, there was little that officials could have done to prevent the braceros from crossing the border, as there were simply too many of them.[30] Yet American officials realized that the actions taken by the INS and USES were indeed in direct violation of the bracero agreement and the immigration laws of the United States and Mexico.[31] They were also quite aware of Mexico's outrage. Torres Bodet, the Mexican official who met with Thurston concerning the abrogation of the agreement, courteously but firmly expressed to him President Aleman's "surprise and consternation" at the action taken by American officials, especially those who had carried out their threats without approval from their superiors. What particularly angered Mexican officials was that this incident would serve to "aggravate Mexican public opinion," which had always disapproved of the program. Now the Mexican government would be forced to take measures to remedy the situation in order to quiet the people's anger. In brief, Mexican officials believed they had little choice but to terminate the agreement. If they did not, critics of the program would have further ammunition for their attacks. Mexico's Foreign Minister viewed the incident as an abuse of American power. Thurston cautioned the Secretary of State that Mexico's sense of outrage should not be underestimated. He believed that their feelings were accentuated by Mexican suspicions that the action of the border authorities had the tacit approval of their superiors in Washington.[32]

Because of the diplomatic implications involved, the desire to continue the program, and perhaps because some officials in the United States agreed with Thurston and wished to provide Mexico with an opportunity to extricate itself from serious repercussions at home, the United States issued a formal apology on 25 October 1948. In its statement to Mexico the State Department admitted that allowing the braceros to enter had constituted an illegal action. It would begin to deport those who had entered and had issued orders to immigration authorities to stop all further illegal immigration. Mexico found the apology satisfactory and accepted it.[33] However, no new agreement was signed until August of 1949.[34]

The "El Paso Incident" was not forgotten by the Mexican government. To Mexican officials and critics of the bracero program the incident clearly demonstrated open complicity between those charged with enforcing the immigration laws and the growers. Mexico realized that it was fairly powerless against the political strength that could be marshalled by the growers and the powerful interest groups who supported them, and it sought some form of leverage in order to offset some of that power. That leverage came with the need for labor created by the outbreak of the Korean War.

The penalty legislation requested by Mexico from the United States during the negotiations for the 1951 Agreement had received support from President Truman because, as he stated, if Congress did not enact such legislation the United States would lose Mexican labor.[35] After much debate in the House and Senate, S.1851, which had been originally authored by Representative Francis Walter of Pennsylvania, was signed into law by Truman on 20 March 1952. Under Public Act 283, as the measure was called once Truman signed it, it became a felony, instead of a misdemeanor, to willfully import, transport, or harbor "illegal aliens." It permitted Immigration Service officers to search private property for illegal entrants within a radius of twenty-five miles of the border without a warrant, although it did not permit these officials to enter private homes without a warrant. It was quite specific in stating that the employment of undocumented workers did not in itself constitute "harboring." Senator Paul Douglas of Illinois had proposed an amendment that would have made it a felony to employ any one who was suspected of having entered illegally, but that was overwhelmingly rejected.[36] Mexico, although not satisfied with the measure because it made no provision for penalizing employers of undocumented workers, nonetheless decided to begin negotiations in 1952 to extend the bracero program.

Mexico's dissatisfaction with both the 1951 Agreement and Public Act 283 is understandable, given the mood of its people and the press over the bracero program. Although Mexican officials had sought to carry on the negotiations in 1951 without publicity, their efforts had been unsuccessful. When negotiations began, editorial reaction in the conservative Mexican press was critical. Papers such as *Excelsior, Novedades,* and *Universal Grafico* called upon officials to drive a hard bargain. The press was even more critical of the United States for its seeming intransigence on the question of undocumented workers.[37]

When the recommendations were announced concerning the 1951 Agreement, press reaction was generally favorable. Mexican officials were praised for their diplomatic victory.[38] On the other side of the coin, the press continued to be hostile toward the United States. One paper blamed the illegal exodus of Mexican workers and their "pitiless exploitation" on American groups, while it praised its government's concern about the clandestine exodus of its laborers.[39] An editorial in another paper stated that only the adoption by the United States of punitive measures against growers employing "illegal entrants" would solve the problem of exploitation of undocumented workers.[40]

William R. Laidlaw wrote from Mexico City that although reaction to the agreement was favorable, there nonetheless continued to be opposition to the exodus of braceros. He stated that a group called the Comite Nacional de Defensa de los Derechos Agrarios (the National Committee for the Protection of Rights of Agricultural Workers) had petitioned the Mexican Senate to prohibit the exporting of braceros because their labor was needed in Mexico. The Sinarquistas had expressed their continuing disfavor with the program through a political cartoon that depicted Uncle Sam stuffing helpless Mexicans into a hopper from which they emerged as soldiers. The cover of the opposition publication *Mañana* depicted what Laidlaw described as "a repulsive but readily identifiable Texan enticing a Mexican across the border with a roll of greenbacks, while an even more repulsive figure representing the Texan's real nature awaited the hapless campesino with a poised axe."[41]

That Mexican officials continued to be sensitive to such criticism is attested to by their reaction to Senator Allen J. Ellender's statement that Mexico had promised to provide the United States with 85,000 braceros. This revelation proved embarrassing to Mexican officials since they had pledged to strictly limit the exportation of braceros until the growers and their government had shown that they would live up to program guarantees. In an effort to assuage Mexican public opinion after Ellender's story, the PRI printed a story in *La Prensa* that charged that rumors of a great demand for braceros in the United States were merely Texas trickery designed to encourage illegal entrants.

Ellender's statement also increased the Mexican government's anxiety that any more revelations would make the new agreement appear as less than a complete Mexican triumph. Therefore, Oficial Mayor Alfonso Guerra of the Foreign Office felt it necessary to issue repeated denials that any specific numbers of braceros had been agreed upon.[42] At the same time the Mexican government attempted to prepare the ground for issuing a large number of contracts by publishing stories that the destruction of crops in northern Mexico by recent freezing weather would increase the supply of braceros available to the United States.[43] Actually, as the decision to allow the contracting of large numbers of braceros by the United States had already been made, the Mexican government was attempting to defuse those sectors opposing the exodus of large numbers of braceros.

This was not the first time that Mexico had been less than honest with the public concerning predetermined agreements with the United States. In 1950 Mexican newspapers such as *Ultimas Noticias* had editorially attacked the Mexican government for permitting its braceros to suffer from deplorable conditions while at contracting centers such as Ciudad Juarez. The editorial was highly critical of border contracting not only because of the strain it placed on localities along the border but also because it encouraged illegal entry.[44] Mexican officials had consistently opposed border recruitment themselves because they wanted to discourage such entry.

However, Mexican officials were inconsistent in their efforts to discourage illegal entry and in fact agreed to measures that at times belied their sincerity, as when they signed an agreement with United States officials on 20 October 1950 that permitted the United States to contract up to 25,000 workers from those who had already entered illegally and been captured. Mexico indicated that it did not want news of the agreement leaking out,[45] but the news was given to newspapers in Laredo, Texas, by a constituent of Congressman Lloyd M. Benson. It seems that this person had written Benson for help in getting Mexican farmworkers, to which Benson had replied that he would have the workers once the agreement was consummated.[46] According to V. Harwood Blocker, the Mexican government was quite "perturbed" that this information had become public. The American Embassy apologized profusely, promising Mexican officials that it would take every step necessary to make sure that "no further publicity" would be given on the agreement.[47] Nonetheless, the damage had been done, according to Manuel Aguilar. Now the Mexican government "would be obliged to issue a statement to the press contradicting the dispatch."[48] Furthermore, the statement would attempt to make it quite clear that the government would not permit the further departure of Mexican agricultural workers from Mexico.

Aguilar informed Blocker that the Mexican government was under constant pressure from the Mexican Chambers of Commerce, farmers, politicians, and others who opposed the departure of workers from Mexico. According to Aguilar the public was so sensitive to this issue that every time the press made any reference to contracting of braceros, the appropriate Mexican government departments were "subjected to harsh criticism and unfavorable comment" from those opposed to the program.[49] Both countries would have to be careful about making public any agreements that would contradict Mexico's stated position concerning contract guarantees, border recruitment, and the contracting of undocumented workers.

Although Mexican public reaction to the 1951 Agreement was generally favorable, the traditional conservative opposition to a bracero program remained. Mexican officials and U.S. State Department observers were well aware that the opposition would become more outspoken if it appeared that Mexico had made any real concessions regarding braceros, if the United States did not live up to the agreements in P.A. 78, and if legislation aimed at penalizing those who employed illegal entrants were not enacted.

That opposition was not long in reemerging. Many Mexicans were dissatisfied with the "anti-wetback" legislation passed in 1952, as they believed that it did not strike at the cause of the "illegal problem"—the employer. Vicente Lombardo Toledano, a popular labor organizer in Mexico and founder of the Popular Party, was one of the men who spearheaded the attack. As the Popular Party's presidential candidate in 1952, Toledano made the bracero and "wetback" issues part of his campaign. In his speeches he described the bracero program as graft-ridden and harmful to Mexico's economy. He charged the United States with racial discrimination against Mexicans and claimed that "wetbacks" were mercilessly exploited by their employers without fear of recrimination or punishment.[50]

Others attacked the agreement because of the renewed hunger marches and the human misery that characterized life at recruitment centers. One newspaper wrote that braceros were transported like slaves and deplored the "infamous" treatment accorded to braceros. It described the braceros as mere chattel for the official government—chattel to be used in the international market.[51] The article accused the Mexican government of "spineless subservience" because it had extended the bracero program without major modifications to benefit Mexican workers, even though the government had claimed that it held the advantage in the negotiations because of labor needs in the United States.[52] Another newspaper exhorted the government to prohibit the departure of Mexican workers either as braceros or as "wetbacks" because the country needed all of its able-bodied men for employment on its own farms and ranches. According to a series of articles and editorials in *Mañana*, the government needed to develop new areas of production to help lower the cost of living in Mexico rather than to contribute to the betterment of a foreign economy. Of even more importance to the editors was that Mexican citizens not be oppressed and exploited by "foreigners" for their own selfish gain. Therefore it was necessary that the Mexican government protect its own people from such abuse by demanding that the United States enact penalty legislation for those who hired undocumented workers.[53]

These demands did not fall on deaf ears. The Mexican government was itself deeply concerned over the startling rise in the influx of illegal entrants into the United States. It believed that undocumented workers would undermine the bracero program and what little bargaining power remained to Mexico when it came to negotiating new and more favorable agreements. At the same time Mexico had begun to lose patience with the United States, who it viewed as dragging its feet on the question of "wetback" penalty legislation. Mexican officials believed that the "illegal entrant problem" was the responsibility of the United States because its growers were responsible for encouraging illegal entrants by employing them.

The 1951 Agreement was scheduled to expire on 31 December 1953. Mexico, because of the Korean War, the labor needs of the United States, and increasing pressure from bracero opponents at home, prepared itself to negotiate a more favorable agreement and thus quell some of the resistance to the program. As it developed, six main issues emerged that needed resolution if an agreement were to be reached by both countries. One issue involved Mexico's desire to participate in the determination of the prevailing wage, to which the United States and the powerful grower interest groups were strongly opposed. A second issue concerned Mexico's practice of bypassing compliance and grievance procedures. On several occasions Mexican consuls had, on their own initiative, blacklisted individuals and even counties which they believed were guilty of racial discrimination and violation of contract guarantees. The United States opposed these actions, charging that any unilateral act on the part of Mexico concerning the bracero agreement constituted a violation of that agreement. The third issue arose over the location of contracting stations, which Mexico wanted located in the interior again, while the United States wanted recruiting stations along the border. Other issues involved subsistence payments to braceros, nonoccupational insurance for braceros, and the increasing problem of bracero "skips." With regard to subsistence payments and nonoccupational insurance Mexico wanted higher payments for its braceros and mandatory insurance through companies that it approved. On the question of "skips" the United States demanded that braceros be made more responsible for fulfilling their contracts and that an enlarged system of wage holdings be instituted to discourage skipping.[54]

Although representatives of the United States had broached these issues with their Mexican counterparts when negotiations began, Mexico too had considered them of great importance and was not willing to sign a new agreement unless these issues were settled to its satisfaction. Further complicating matters was the question of the "wetback" and Mexican complaints charging that the United States had not enacted adequate penalty legislation. There were of course countercharges by the United States that Mexico had done little to stop the influx of undocumented workers.[55]

It appears that the United States had prepared itself for what it considered Mexico's usual intransigence. An indication of this was given on 8 November 1953, when Edward F. Hayes, Chief of the Farm Placement Service of the State Department of Employment in California, told members of the North Coast Chamber of Commerce that the United States Department of Justice was considering opening the border to Mexican braceros if negotiations over renewal of the program broke down.[56] Hayes was simply echoing what had already become apparent during the congressional hearings on extension of P.L. 78 held in March of 1953. Discussion at these hearings revealed a more militant stance concerning the agreement not only on the part of growers but also on the part of United States representatives. Under Secretary of Labor Lloyd Mashburn had called for a one-year extension of the bracero agreement. In his view an abbreviated extension would provide his department with a lever in its negotiations with Mexico. He did not want to buttress Mexico's bargaining position by giving it a long-term renewal that would lead the Mexicans to believe that they could get whatever they wanted because of America's need for their labor.[57] Some senators expressed similar sentiments. They wanted to make it clear to Mexico that if it continued to be inflexible in its demands then the United States would take matters into its own hands and resort to unilateral recruitment of Mexican workers.[58]

In spite of such threats Mexico remained adamant. Mexican officials believed that the United States would not adopt a unilateral recruitment policy at a time when United States-Latin American relations were deteriorating. The United States had taken a decidedly more aggressive stance against Communist influence in Latin America and had been pushing the Organization of American States to adopt a policy that would prevent such penetration. Of particular interest to the United States during its impasse with Mexico was the situation in Guatemala, where the Communists had influenced a popular movement to reform an archaic social system. While the United States had decided that it would do everything that it could to prevent Communism from gaining a foothold in the western hemisphere, it was nonetheless confronted with the fact that the popular movement in Guatemala had support from other Latin American nations. Although the United States succeeded in Caracas, Venezuela, in 1954, the resolution was adopted by many of the delegates without much enthusiasm. Many of those who voted in favor of the resolution aimed at preventing communist domination or control of any nation in the western hemisphere had done so under duress. Mexico, well aware of these developments, believed that the United States would attempt to avoid any embarrassing diplomatic incidents with its Latin American neighbors.

Another reason for Mexico's intransigence was pride. Its officials believed that they could no longer continue to compromise the welfare of its citizens, even if it meant a confrontation with the United States. This view was bolstered by Mexico's belief that it was bargaining from a position of strength, given the tense diplomatic situation in Latin American and the involvement of the United States in the Korean War. Mexican officials were confident that the United States would come around and see things their way.

Mexico's confidence might have been justified if its battle had been solely with the government of the United States, whose priorities were on a national and international level. However, Mexico either did not consider or underestimated the power of the special-interest groups in Washington that supported a Mexican contract labor program. Unfortunately for Mexico, these interest groups would play a key role in determining what actions the United States would take if the impasse in the negotiations continued.

Furthermore, American officials had entered the negotiations determined to bring about fundamental changes in the contract labor agreement to control what they perceived to be a Mexican propensity for unilateral actions. To bolster their arguments and demands officials had resorted to unofficial threats that the United States would resort to unilateral recruitment if Mexico refused to compromise.[59] Special-interest groups, determined to wring more concessions from Mexico, were very effective in using their political power to influence American negotiators not to back down. As it stood the Departments of Labor, Justice, and State needed little convincing to provide growers with the necessary labor with or without Mexico's approval.[60] By the time negotiations broke down in January of 1954, the United States had already committed itself to a course of action that would force Mexico to come around. In essence, it appears that officials in the United States were willing to risk the short-range consequences of an international incident in an effort to acquire an agreement that they could live with. Because neither side proved willing to bend, the 31 December expiration date arrived with no new agreement consummated. Both sides however were not willing as yet to end negotiations and terminate the agreement. Mexico therefore agreed to extend the old bracero agreement until 15 January 1954. The extension did not bring forth a new agreement, and for the moment the bracero program was considered terminated by both countries. On 16 January 1954, the United States carried out its threat by announcing the implementation of a unilateral recruitment program to begin on 22 January 1954.[61]

Mexico responded to this announcement with a sharply worded communique which stated that it would not "conform" to this action.[62] In another communique the Mexicans expressed disapproval of the illegal emigration of their citizens, stating that they had done everything possible to prevent it. They again reminded United States officials that such entry would be considerably reduced or even completely checked if the United States enacted "appropriate measures" against those who hired illegal entrants. With regard to the modifications to the agreement suggested by the U.S., Mexico stated that they "were not acceptable because they diminished the participation of the Mexican Government or its representatives in the execution of the Agreement and reduced the benefits granted braceros." As they could not reach a satisfactory agreement, they had decided to terminate the program.[63]

On the subject of unilateral recruitment the communique was quite succinct. It stated that the Mexican government would not agree to it and would not authorize the legal departure of braceros because "without guarantees such a situation would be in conflict with specific provisions contained in their Labor and Population Laws."[64]

The threat by the United States to resort to unilateral recruitment and its subsequent announcement that it would do so united the many diverse elements in Mexico behind their government's refusal to "conform" to the United States policy. Groups such as the unions, large landowners, ejido organizations, students, chambers of commerce, civil servants, and the opposition parties supported the position taken by the Mexican government.[65] Yet Mexican officials did not appear willing to totally abandon efforts to negotiate a new agreement. President Ruiz Cortines called for a calm approach to the issue and stated that failure to reach an agreement was "not a problem but only an incident that could be resolved within the norms of the Good Neighbor Policy."[66] The failure to negotiate a new agreement was not what disturbed the diverse Mexican elements, but rather they were angered over the audacity displayed by the United States. The latter's decision not only to by-pass the agreement but also to flaunt its power in the faces of the Mexicans was simply unacceptable to many. Unilateral recruitment was tantamount to a national insult, and feelings ran high.

While all of this was transpiring, thousands of Mexicans headed toward the contracting station at El Centro, California, where the United States had indicated that contracting would begin on 22 January 1954. The Mexican government attempted to deter its people from going there through threats and pleas but to no avail. About seven hundred Mexicans managed to cross the border into El Centro before the Mexican government was able to post armed guards there and at other points of entry. The presence of Mexican troops caused a tense situation along the border, exacerbated by United States officials, who resorted to a process of instant legalization of anyone who crossed the border. The legalization process was accomplished by having Mexicans who entered illegally run back to the official border crossing-point, put one foot on Mexican soil, and then dart back so that they could be legally processed.[67] At times this practice approached the absurd, as depicted in a photograph showing a hapless bracero being pulled south by a Mexican border official and north by a United States official.[68]

Between 23 January and 5 February 1954, a series of bloody clashes erupted between Mexican troops and desperate, hungry braceros at several cities along the border. Mexicans were repelled by hard-pressed troops using guns, clubs, fists, and water hoses. According to the *New York Times*, Mexican officials were dismayed and angered at the sight of thousands of their countrymen jammed like sardines and gasping for air in the crush to cross the boundary for a handful of harvest jobs. The *Times* quoted Tulio Lopez-Lira, who was in charge of emigration at the Mexican border port, as stating that this unpleasant situation was "the fault of the Americans." "My countrymen," said Lopez-Lira, "have been trapped here by American lies and propaganda that the border would be open to them."[69]

The Mexican government and people were furious and deeply embarrassed by the turn of events. The riots had involved Mexicans fighting Mexicans, which saddened people throughout the country. Furthermore the rush to the border and the rioting had served to further discredit Mexican claims of economic advancement.[70] Many Mexicans were shocked to learn that their countrymen were so desperate that they trekked hundreds of miles, suffered hunger, humiliation, beatings, and even danger of death just to contract for the most menial of tasks.

Generally speaking, Mexican officials were not only angered but shocked that the United States had instituted unilateral recruitment. This action appeared totally irrational to the Mexicans, particularly as it might have intensified the general crisis already extant between the United States and other Latin American republics. Even those who had taken these threats seriously were taken aback, realizing that such a policy would only unite Mexican public opinion against the United States and further endanger the chances for renewal of the bracero program. That the United States had adopted a go-it-alone policy led Mexicans to believe that a gross injustice had been committed against them. Many viewed this as the product of the new Republican administration headed by Dwight D. Eisenhower, signalling the demise of good neighborliness and a return to "big stick" diplomacy.[71]

Officials in the United States had not been blind to these considerations and were in fact well aware of the implications the unilateral recruitment policy carried with it. They realized that it entailed diplomatic risks, but many had come to the conclusion that Mexico had had its way too long in the bargaining and had in fact abused its generally strong position in negotiating agreements. Hard feelings had also been intensified by other incidents involving both countries. Mexico, for example, was still smarting from the fact that the United States had closed the border in 1953 because of charges that Mexican livestock were infected with hoof-and-mouth disease, an allegation which Mexico had vehemently denied. At about the same time Mexico had charged United States fishing boats with violating its territorial waters. Finally, the United States had increased tariffs on Mexican mining products.[72] All of these incidents had contributed to the declining relations between the two nations, which did little to create a suitable atmosphere for co-operation and compromise in the contract negotiations.

Objections to the unilateral recruitment policy were not confined solely to south of the border. The voices of opposition to unilateral recruitment of Mexican nationals had also made themselves heard north of the border. Editorials in the *New York Times* opposed the policy.[73] Congressman John F. Shelley of California lambasted the terms the United States had attempted to impose upon Mexico in renegotiating the bracero agreement. He accused growers of supporting the terms proposed by this country because they made it possible further to exploit the contract laborer, referring to the contract system with all its abuses as just another form of "peonage."[74] He also questioned the reasoning of the State Department, which had supported the legalization program on the basis that it would help wipe out the illegal crossings.

> Apparently their reasoning is that if we simply remove all restrictions on border crossing, as we have done since expiration of the agreement, all crossings will be legal and we will, therefore, wipe out the wetback program. This reasoning fits very nicely into the pattern of thought of the organized growers who have from year to year successfully propagandized against adequate border patrols to stop the traffic as it should be stopped. Their propaganda has been powerful indeed, as we who sit here each session and watch the appropriations for this purpose defeated know. The present administration apparently intends to make the propaganda no longer necessary.[75]

Shelley's views proved correct. The new approach did not halt the entry of undocumented workers. In fact it only served to further induce illegal crossings, as those who entered illegally were rewarded for their efforts by being processed and turned over to waiting employers. Even though legalization of "wetbacks" was not a new procedure, having in fact been carried out for some years, it had nonetheless been done previously with the consent of both governments. Furthermore, those who had been legalized in the past had been given contract guarantees. The unilateral program of 1954 differed sharply from the bracero program and the legalization process in that the 1954 action not only was unilateral but also placed responsibility for the braceros totally in the hands of United States officials. As it turned out, the declaration of an open border by the United States encouraged illegal entry, demonstrated the extent to which grower influence operated, represented a direct violation of Mexican and United States immigration laws, and undermined the efforts of those on both sides of the border who wished to discourage Mexicans from entering illegally. By literally taking the situation into its own hands the United States "ignored every consideration of human decency, international courtesy, and, in short, everything but the demands of the organized growers bent on an open door to cheap farm labor, regardless of consequences."[76]

One of the organizations adding their voices to those opposed to an open border was the American G. I. Forum. The G. I. Forum had been founded in 1948 by Doctor Hector P. García in Texas, when a local mortuary in Three Rivers, Texas, had refused to bury a Mexican American veteran killed in action. According to the director of the funeral home the young man could not be buried in the cemetery because he was not "white." This blatant act of discrimination served to mobilize other Mexican American veterans into organizing themselves to fight discrimination in public facilities and to work for fair employment practices. Unlike earlier Mexican American organizations, the G. I. Forum and others that emerged after World War II concentrated their efforts on politically organizing the Mexican American community, advocated direct involvement in the political system of the United States, and sought cooperation with supportive Anglo-American organizations and individuals in order to create some power base for implementing their goals and programs. The G. I. Forum aggressively demanded civil liberties as well as political and economic rights, while attempting to assimilate its people into the mainstream of American society. Because of its assimilationist tendencies and its efforts to create and project a positive image of its people, the G. I. Forum viewed the large influx of "illegal aliens" as a threat to its goals. Many of the leaders of the G. I. Forum on both the local and national level viewed the presence of "illegal aliens," most of whom were unlettered *campesinos,* as a retarding influence on their efforts to acquire equal rights for citizens of Mexican descent. Furthermore, as undocumented workers often deprived Mexican American citizens of much-needed work because of their willingness to work for substandard wages, the G. I. Forum advocated a closed border and strict control over the entry of undocumented workers.

When the border was opened in 1954 to Mexican workers, Edward Idar, Jr., Executive Secretary of the American G. I. Forum in Texas, sent a telegram to President Eisenhower asking for his personal intervention in stopping the unilateral recruitment of Mexican workers. Idar and his organization considered border recruitment "nothing short of legalized wetbackism, of benefit only to isolated agricultural interests bent on obtaining twenty-five cent an hour labor."[77] He stated that allowing the recruitment policy to continue would constitute "an incredible sell-out" and would reflect a "callous indifference to the needs of three million Spanish citizens in the Southwest."[78] In his opinion the action taken by the United States against Mexico constituted the worst diplomatic blunder this country had committed in the last two decades.

Elias Olivarez, Chairman of the District One G. I. Forum in McAllen, Texas, wrote to Attorney General Herbert Brownell to protest the unilateral recruitment policy. Olivarez voiced the Forum's concern that the illegal influx was being used as a screen by subversives and saboteurs to infiltrate the United States. Olivarez urged Brownell to stop this "wholesale invasion."[79]

Olivarez wrote a similar letter to Eisenhower. In it he took the president to task for permitting a handful of "self-serving Valley farmers" to influence his administration at the expense of the welfare of many citizens.[80] It is somewhat ironic that while both Idar and Olivarez were concerned about communist infiltration, the Rio Grande Valley Growers Union was charging the G. I. Forum and its leadership with communistic sympathies because of their reform efforts.

Another Mexican American organization, the League of United Latin American Citizens (LULAC), also expressed disapproval of the policy. They too were concerned with the economic, political, and social impact undocumented workers would have on their efforts to improve the quality of life for Mexican American citizens.

Founded in 1929 in Corpus Christi, Texas, LULAC members dedicated themselves to achieving economic, social, and political rights for all Mexican Americans. It sought to educate Mexican Americans in "good citizenship." Its main thrust was in the field of education, where the organization sought to increase the number of Mexican Americans in professional fields such as medicine, law, engineering, and business. To this end it sponsored scholarships and programs such as the "400 Clubs," whose purpose it was to teach Spanish-speaking children the English language. By necessity it avoided political assertiveness or militancy and any open demonstrations that demanded civil equality. This approach is understandable, given the prevailing attitudes of the 1920s and 1930s. LULAC, in order to survive, turned to adaptation and accommodation, for the decades preceding World War II were not conducive to movements that espoused social and civil rights. Rather the period witnessed the resurgence of fundamentalism, nativism, and the Ku Klux Klan. Related to this was widespread concern over foreign immigration, particularly from Eastern Europe. By the late 1920s the passage of the Quota Acts of 1921 and 1924 had curtailed immigration from Eastern Europe and concern emerged over the increasing number of Mexican immigrants in the United States. With the onset of the Depression in the 1930s Mexicans and Mexican Americans became unwelcome entities and were the victims of mass deportations. Through it all the small Mexican American middle class which comprised the larger portion of the LULAC membership was extremely vulnerable, yet they managed to survive the ordeal and expand their membership. While they continued to espouse pride in their culture, they nonetheless believed that accommodation was the only route to success. One of their main goals was "to develop within the members of our race the best, purest and most perfect type of a true and loyal citizen of the United States of America." To that end they opposed any "radical and violent demonstration" that would "create conflicts and disturb the tranquility of (the) country."[81]

The thrust of LULAC's objections concerned their opposition to any plan that would bring "alien" farm labor into the United States without guarantees. In the view of Frank Piñedo, Texas Regional Governor of LULAC, such a system would open the way for further exploitation of all Americans of Mexican descent. Piñedo said it was bad enough that the importation of foreign labor was not based on responsible determination by the Department of Labor on whether or not there was a lack of sufficient domestic labor before importing braceros. According to Piñedo the importation of such labor had a serious and detrimental effect on the economic welfare of American citizens, particularly those of Mexican extraction. He therefore urged the Secretary of Labor to end unilateral recruitment and to encourage the employment of domestic laborers at decent wages.[82]

In responding to Piñedo's telegram, Secretary of Labor James P. Mitchell assured him that the United States intended to continue providing the same protection given to braceros under the former bilateral agreement. Mitchell stated that the United States favored continuation of the bilateral agreement but that some changes would have to be made by Mexico in order to simplify it.[83] In essence Mitchell blamed the illegal influx on the complex rules and regulations of the agreement, which he believed discouraged employers from hiring braceros and led them to employ undocumented workers. Mitchell intimated that the fault for the influx of illegal entrants and the failure to reach a new agreement lay with Mexico.

The G. I. Forum and LULAC were supported in their views by the Executive Council of the American Federation of Labor, which described the policy of unilateral recruitment as "shocking." It warned the Labor Department that it was being used to create a surplus labor supply for the corporate farms and large ranches of the Southwest so that wage standards would become depressed. It charged that foreign workers were being imported at a time when unemployment was rapidly growing throughout the Southwest. The situation was particularly acute in California, according to the Executive Council, where unemployment had increased by 46,000 during the month of November, bringing the total of unemployed in the state to 197,000 as of 1 December 1954. Not only was it opposed to the bilateral importation of braceros, but it also vehemently disapproved of unilateral recruitment, since such a policy was "perilous and short-sighted" in its economic and diplomatic implications.[84]

There were of course other letters, telegrams, and statements sent to various government agencies and the president protesting the situation. But the protests of individuals, organizations, and even the Mexican government itself were of little avail. It appeared that the United States had decided upon its course of action with regard to the bracero agreement and was prepared to continue its policy until Mexico was forced to make the necessary concessions. Thus it might have continued, had it not been for the intercession of the Comptroller General of the United States.

At the time that the United States announced its intention to implement a unilateral recruitment program, Rocco C. Siciliano, Assistant Secretary of Labor,

had asked the Comptroller General Lindsey C. Warren if funds appropriated
for the bilateral bracero agreement could be used to continue the program on
an interim basis, pending the development of another agreement with Mexico
"satisfactory to the interests of the United States."[85] After some investigation
into the Department of Labor's querry, Warren reported to Siciliano that he was:

> Compelled to the conclusion that it [Congress] did not intend, by implication,
> to authorize or sanction the use of funds made available to your Department
> for carrying out such programs pursuant to 'arrangements' with Mexico when,
> admittedly, no such arrangements exist with that Government. Accordingly,
> it must be held that the funds here in question are not available to continue
> further the Mexican farm labor program on an interim basis as proposed in
> the letter of January 19, *supra*.[86]

Because of Warren's decision, the United States was forced to cease unilateral
recruitment for the time being.

On 11 February 1954, President Eisenhower announced that negotiations
would resume with Mexico. Yet the two-week recruiting of braceros on a unilateral
basis had received strong support from growers and other special interest groups,
who sought to continue it by working to make unilateral recruitment a legal policy.
Officials in the Departments of Labor, Agriculture, Justice, and State also favored
this action and added their voice of support to a bill introduced in late January
to authorize the use of unilateral recruitment in the future by amending Public
Law 78.[87]

The proposal was introduced by Congressman Clifford Hope, Chairman of the
Committee on Agriculture. The resolution, H. J. R. 355, amended Section 501 of
Public Law 78 by striking out the parenthetical clause "pursuant to arrangements
between the United States and the Republic of Mexico." This clause was replaced
by one which read: "pursuant to arrangements between the United States and the
Republic of Mexico or *after every practicable effort has been made by the United
States to negotiate and reach agreement on such arrangements.*"[88]

As amended, Public Law 78 made it clear to Mexico that its failure to accept
an agreement on terms offered by the United States would once again lead to
the implementation of a unilateral recruitment policy. In the words of one State
Department official, this amendment would hit Mexico in a sore spot, but its
passage was necessary because it was in the best interest of America's economy
and national security.[89]

A few days after Hope's proposal, Walter B. Smith sent a memorandum to
President Eisenhower on the occasion of the Mexican Ambassador's visit to
discuss the Migrant Labor Agreement. The memorandum referred to the unilateral
recruitment of Mexican workers following the expiration of the binational contract agreement on 15 January 1954. Smith told Eisenhower that the new recruitment process was working well, but that it would have to end because of Warren's

decision. He added that he was still hopeful that Mexico would be amenable
to the new terms and that its acceptance of full participation on mutually satisfactory terms "would eliminate the problem raised by the Comptroller General's
decision and save the United States considerable embarrassment."[90] Smith concluded by suggesting that if this did not prove feasible, then the United States
"might gain valuable time, during which legislation already introduced to eliminate
the Comptroller General problem may pass, by offering to assist Mexico to relieve
the problem created by thousands of workers assembling at border gates."[91]

While H. J. R. 355 enjoyed widespread support in both Houses of Congress,
there were a few who spoke out against it. In the House, Representative Harold
Cooley of North Carolina staged a vigorous fight against the bill because he believed that it would only do more harm to relations with Mexico.[92] Another outspoken critic of the bill was Congressman Ray Madden, Democrat from Indiana,
who also believed that unilateral recruitment would only serve to further antagonize Mexico as well as the rest of Latin America. He charged in addition that such
a bill would increase, not decrease, the influx of undocumented workers. To him
the idea that this bill was simply "a little weapon" that would make Mexico more
responsive in its negotiations was absurd. "My definition of a weapon with a little
weight," scowled Madden, "is . . . a blackjack."[93] Pennsylvania Congressman Francis
Walter nodded agreement to Madden's remarks. He too opposed the measure because it placed "a premium on the ability to cross the border surreptitiously."
In his view the enactment of the bill would throw all of our immigration laws "out
the window."[94]

New York Congressman Emanuel Cellar concurred with his colleagues. To him
the bill made little sense, and he resented the fact that Congress was "being used
as a catspaw for the ranching, cotton and fruit tycoons principally from Texas and
California." Cellar could not understand why the United States closed its borders
and ports in the north in order to prevent subversives from entering and left the
gates deliberately open along the Mexican border.[95] Representative Philip J. Phil-
bin of Massachusetts aimed his remarks at those who advocated the passage of
H. J. R. 355. Harkening back to his state's fight against the evils of slavery Phil-
bin said:

> We recall that in history the same arguments that are advanced today in be-
> half of this resolution were similarly employed to justify the slave traffic
> with its debasement of human and spiritual values—a traffic which denied
> the essential dignity of man and condemned him to be sold and bartered
> in the market places of exploitation as a common chattel.[96]

In addressing himself to the issue again, Representative Cooley told members of
Congress that he had called William White, American Ambassador to Mexico, in
order to ascertain his views on H. J. R. 355. White told Cooley that passage of this
bill would "definitely . . . have a bad effect on our relationship [with Mexico] ."[97]

Because of the antagonism that it would arouse in Mexico against the United States, Cooley urged his colleagues to defeat the measure. Cooley concluded his remarks by addressing the lawyers in the House, telling them that one could not have a unilateral agreement. "There is no such animal known to legal jurisprudence," said Cooley. "Whoever heard of a unilateral agreement? What our officials have done in Mexico is to slam the door on the recruiting offices and move north of the Rio Grande and carry on in an illegal fashion."[98]

Opposition in the Senate to H. J. R. 355 was led by Senators Hubert Humphrey, Herbert Lehman, and Allen Ellender. Humphrey of Minnesota was "shocked beyond words that the Congress, which investigates practically everyone from a baby sitter to a kindergarten teacher does not impose stringent controls in the case of immigration at the Mexican border."[99] Humphrey opposed the bill because its enactment would not only permit "aliens" to enter the United States illegally, but it would also put a premium on their ability to enter illegally.[100]

In his remarks to the Senate Humphrey said that neither Secretary of State John Foster Dulles nor Milton Eisenhower was aware that such legislation had been introduced in Congress.[101] He also stated that John Vorys, Chairman of the House Committee on Foreign Relations, was opposed to the resolution because it sought to recruit foreigners in the face of growing unemployment in the United States. In fact, Vorys did not want to see the bracero program become a fixed part of the economy of the United States. He believed that this country had "drifted into a situation where certain segments of our agriculture are developing vested rights in foreign labor."[102]

Humphrey stated that he was "proud" of the Mexican government. "At long last it is standing up for its people. We have become too accustomed to using Mexico for our own purposes. We have exploited her oil resources, and now we are attempting to exploit her people." Humphrey and others believed that the United States could not afford to take such an irresponsible approach in dealing with Mexico, particularly in view of the fact that the United States was demanding that other nations live up to their agreements and assume responsibility for their actions. He moved that H. J. R. 355 be referred to the Committee on Agriculture and Forestry for revision and reconsideration, but his motion was quickly voted down.[103]

There was little doubt that Mexico would react with great fury once news of the bill reached it. The predictions of White and others about the bill's negative impact on United States-Mexican relations were in part borne out by an article which appeared on 5 March 1954, in the *New York Times.* According to the article the passage of H. J. R. 355 "had stirred intense anger among unofficial groups" in Mexico City. One Mexican newspaper, *Novedades,* described the passage of the bill as a renewal of the "big stick" policy by the Republicans. The article in the *New York Times* quoted Novedades as stating:

> 'It is foolish, sheer ignorance of what our country is, to imagine that a North American law, even though conceived, proposed, and approved to exercise

undue pressure on decisions of our Government, can influence it to modify our position of legitimate defense of our citizens in favor of dealers in braceros, who seem to have forgotten they are compatriots of Lincoln.'[104]

Whereas opponents of H. J. R. 355 opposed it for various reasons, its proponents were pretty much one in their reason for supporting it. They were not so vociferous in their remarks, but only because they realized their opponents were on the defensive. As Congressman O. C. Fisher of Texas pointed out on 1 March 1954, the resolution had the strong support of the Departments of State, Justice, Labor, and Agriculture, as well as the endorsement of the American Farm Bureau, the National Council of Farm Co-Operatives, the National Grange, and scores of other farmer and grower organizations.[105] Fisher stated that the Department of Justice through the Attorney General's office had declared in its report to the Agriculture Committee that H. J. R. 355's passage was "of urgent importance to the efficient administration of the immigration laws of the United States, and to the needs of a substantial part of the agricultural economy of the western and southwestern United States."[106]

In the view of those who supported the bill, it was Mexico's intransigence, particularly its arbitrary and unilateral action in closing the border recruiting centers, that had brought about the problem. They pointed out that many Mexicans living along Mexico's northern border could not afford to travel hundreds of miles into the interior of Mexico to a recruiting center on the slim chance of being accepted. It appeared obvious to them that the farther into Mexico the recruiting centers were located the more inaccessible they were to Mexican workers in the border area. In this situation it was easy to understand why so many Mexicans were tempted to cross the border illegally.[107]

Congressman Fisher believed that unilateral recruitment of Mexican workers was an American concern and had nothing to do with Mexico. To him such recruitment was a domestic issue that concerned the processing of laborers already legally in the United States.[108] Congressman Harris Ellsworth concurred with Fisher's simplistic and unrealistic conclusion. According to Ellsworth the Bracero Agreement "gave to the Republic of Mexico the courtesy of joining us in an agreement regarding the admission of people who . . . perform labor in this country under certain conditions."[109] It was that pure and simple to him.

Members of Congress who supported the bill were simply echoing the sentiments expressed during the congressional hearings on H. J. R. 355 before the Committee on Agriculture. At those hearings Congressman W. R. Poage of Texas had stated that the only way by which the United States could hope to reach any deal with the Mexicans was to demonstrate to them that this country did not have to deal with them.[110] The best way to accomplish this was for the United States to approve a unilateral recruitment program.

Representative Cooley took issue with Poage's views. In a heated exchange between the two, Cooley told Poage that the United States should not attempt to negotiate an agreement with Mexico by putting a pistol to their backs. To which

Poage retorted: "They have been pretty successful in getting an agreement with a pistol in our backs."[111]

Opponents of H. J. R. 355, while vocal, constituted only a minority in both Houses. The bill gained ready approval in the Senate, where it was passed by a vote of 59 to 22 after Senator George Aiken's amendment was added. The amendment read:

> Resolved, etc., That section 501 of the Agricultural Act of 1949, as amended is further amended by striking out the parenthetical clause '(pursuant to arrangements between the United States and the Republic of Mexico)' and inserting in lieu thereof '(pursuant to arrangements between the United States and the Republic of Mexico or after every practicable effort has been made by the United States to negotiate and reach agreement on such agreements.)'[112]

It was then transmitted to the House of Representatives, where it again passed without difficulty.

After the bill was passed in Congress, its opponents concentrated their efforts on attempting to persuade President Eisenhower to veto it. They were not a very cohesive group, and they made little effort to pool their resources in order to convince the president. However, they generally agreed that H. J. R. 355 was nothing more than an instrument that would facilitate the exploitation of human misery and all the rationalization in the world could not conceal that ugly fact.

One of the earliest to appeal to Eisenhower was Archbishop Robert E. Lucey of San Antonio. Lucey wrote that even though many Americans sympathized with and were concerned about the unhappy plight of undocumented workers, the fact remained that they were still in this country illegally. He believed that their presence in this country was of benefit to no one except those who sought to exploit them. In his view the enactment of legislation that permitted unilateral recruitment would only serve to encourage further illegal entry. He urged the president to veto any legislation that would "legalize the lawlessness" of illegal entry.[113]

Representative Harlan Hagen of California also made an appeal to Eisenhower. The Fourteenth District Representative wrote that he was reluctant to make the request for a presidential veto of H. J. R. 355 but that he did so because he questioned the growers' estimate of the availability of domestic farm labor in this country. He noted that it was a very common practice for growers to claim that a shortage of domestic labor existed, even in the face of overwhelming evidence to the contrary. He further believed that the timing of enacting this legislation was poor, given that Mexico had already made overtures regarding the resumption of negotiations.[114]

Guy R. Brewer did not mince any words in asking Eisenhower to veto H. J. R. 355. Brewer, who was Chairman of the Legislation Committee of the Jamaica, New York branch of the NAACP, wrote that he hoped that Senator William

Knowland's statement that Eisenhower supported the bill was an error. He called upon Ike to veto this "unfortunate piece of legislation" because of its domestic and international implications.[115]

Brewer stated that he could understand the Dixiecrat mentality and what prompted many of their actions. However, when it came to comprehending the Republican mentality, he was at a complete loss. For example, wrote Brewer, he could not understand how the administration could take such action when the Secretary of State was in Caracas, Venezuela, pressing for greater inter-American solidarity and cooperation. What was really frustrating to him was that after committing such "asinine . . . boners" the United States would have to "squander hundreds of millions of dollars, extracted from our hard pressed taxpayers, in loans and gifts to Latin American nations in an attempt to repair the damage done by such stupid legislation as this."[116]

Brewer also questioned the validity of grower claims that there was a labor shortage. In his view such claims were pure "hokum," since the labor shortage was really caused by the extremely poor wages that employers offered to domestic workers. Therefore Eisenhower, even if he did not "give a damn" about inter-American relations, ought to veto the bill anyway as it would have a depressing effect on both white and nonwhite American laborers in the Southwest.[117]

Whether or not to veto the bill was for Eisenhower a difficult decision because the question was mired in a series of complex issues. Eisenhower knew that the bill had been easily passed in both Houses and that, should he veto it, the chances were good that Congress would override his veto. He realized that many in the government were determined to take a hard stand against what they perceived to be Mexican intransigence, and he was well aware that the powerful interest groups had marshalled their forces in order to get unilateral recruitment instituted as a permanent fixture in P. L. 78. Yet Eisenhower did not want to alienate Mexico. Those who argued that unilateral recruitment would increase illegal entry had struck a responsive chord in Eisenhower. Although he was not totally convinced of the validity of this argument against the bill, Eisenhower had nonetheless been greatly concerned about the growing influx of undocumented workers. He wanted measures to halt illegal entry, not to encourage it. Furthermore he had to take cognizance of Mexico's national honor, for if nothing else Eisenhower realized that to control the influx of undocumented workers would require the cooperation of both countries. Signing such legislation would certainly injure Mexican sensibilities and probably hurt chances for such cooperation. There was also the fact that both countries had come to an agreement over the bracero program. Would Mexico sign the new agreement if it appeared that it had done so under duress because of the enactment of the unilateral recruiting amendment?

Some individuals in Eisenhower's administration believed that the president should either veto the bill or at least delay signing it until the new bracero agreement had been consummated. For example, Thruston B. Morton, Assistant Secretary of State, believed that authority already existed for the admission of

Mexican workers in the absence of an agreement with Mexico and was thus inclined to support H. J. R. 355. However, in Morton's words, this bill had "caused serious concern to the Mexican government." That is, although Mexico was willing to sign a new agreement, it did not wish to appear to be doing so because of the passage of H. J. R. 355. Because of this the Mexican government had requested that United States officials do whatever they would to prevent the bill from becoming law.[118]

Since it was anticipated that Mexico would sign a new agreement by 10 March 1954 and because of Mexico's sensitivity to signing the agreement after H. J. R. 355 became effective and its official assurance that the problem would be less acute if the new agreement were signed before H. J. R. 355, the State Department recommended that presidential action on the unilateral recruitment bill be delayed until 15 March 1954. It also recommended that Eisenhower make a brief statement at the time of the signing about the benefits that would be forthcoming to Mexican workers under H. J. R. 355.[119]

The Department of State recommendations were supported by Walter B. Smith, a close friend and advisor of the president. Like Morton, Smith also wanted Eisenhower to issue a statement upon signing H. J. R. 355 to assuage Mexican feelings. To aid the president, Smith sent along a draft of such a statement for his consideration, which emphasized that the purpose of the legislation was to enable the United States to give Mexican labor the protection of its laws whenever it was necessary. It also emphasized the cooperative approach taken by both countries to achieve some sort of agreement and made specific reference to the agreement signed on 10 March with Mexico. Smith and others hoped to dispel the impression that the purpose of H. J. R. 355 was to provide a club to be held over Mexico's head during the operation of the current agreement and in the negotiation of any future agreements.[120] Of course, that is exactly what H. J. R. 355 did.

In his memo Smith told Eisenhower that important sectors of the press had begun to assume that legislation concerning unilateral recruitment was no longer necessary, as a new bracero agreement had been concluded. Similar sentiments were expressed by those who had opposed its passage from the outset. Yet Smith cautioned Eisenhower against such views. In his opinion, although such legislation did not have an immediate purpose, it nonetheless would have some utility should a similar impasse ever arise again over the bracero program. Smith recommended that the president sign the bill into law after the new agreement was consummated and that he issue a statement at the bill's signing assuring the Mexican government of continued respect and cooperation on the part of the United States.[121]

Eisenhower accepted the counsel of his advisors and signed H. J. R. 355 into law on 16 March 1954, six days after the United States and Mexico had signed a new bracero agreement. After signing, Eisenhower told the press that he believed such a law was necessary for the United States government to provide Mexican braceros with the protection of its laws.[122]

Mexican officials made few public statements concerning the passage of H. J. R.

355. They recognized it for what it was and realized that they could do little to prevent its passage. For the most part they had to be content that the United States had at least waited until the bracero agreement was signed before signing H. J. R. 355 into law. As far as Mexico was concerned it was best to play down unilateral recruitment as much as possible and not give critics of the program any more ammunition with which to further their attacks against the government.

To offset some of the criticism, Mexican officials played up the success in negotiating the new bracero agreement. Yet the agreement in actuality contained little to satisfy the Mexican demands that had prompted termination of the agreement a few months earlier, especially in the two areas of wage determination and legislation to penalize employers of undocumented workers. Whereas Mexico had initially demanded that it be allowed to fix minimum wages for braceros performing different work in different regions, the 1954 Agreement merely permitted Mexico to "protest and present evidence" when it considered a prevailing wage determination by the Labor Department too low.[123] With regard to penalty legislation Mexico had to settle for the creation of a Joint Migratory Labor Commission, which was to study issues pertaining to both the undocumented worker and the bracero program. The commission, which was to operate until October of 1954, was only empowered to make recommendations on these questions and had no administrative responsibilities or negotiating powers.[124] Nonetheless, when Mexico publicized the contents of the agreement in its press it presented the principal points in a manner that implied that they represented important new concessions on the part of the United States.[125] In actuality, the provisions concerning guarantees and government supervision were those that had, in practically every instance, been included in the previous agreements and did not represent any new concessions on the part of the United States. Thus, as one American official put it, the reports issued by the Mexican government to the press and the public merely represented a "face-saving device which the United States anticipated the Mexican authorities would resort to."[126]

CONCLUSION

Throughout this period Mexican immigration was essentially labor immigration, a fact that set the tone of overall United States immigration policy vis-à-vis Mexico. Through its policies the United States demonstrated that it was interested in bringing Mexicans in only as temporary laborers. To accomplish this the United States often undertook policies inconsistent with and contrary to its immigration laws and those of Mexico.

This "special United States policy toward Mexican immigration"[127] took many forms and only served to further compound the confusion surrounding both the bracero program and the so-called "wetback" problem. More often than not this special policy took the form of ad hoc exemptions and administrative adjustments to the immigration laws of this country.

One such adjustment was the initiation of the bracero program in 1941. While it was initially intended to be a temporary wartime program, the bracero program was extended repeatedly after the end of the war, although critics of the program charged that there was sufficient domestic labor in the United States to perform the work of harvesting crops. Interestingly enough, while the bracero program expanded the United States maintained stringent requirements for legal immigration from Mexico. Thus the message was quite clear. As far as the United States was concerned Mexicans were welcomed as laborers but not as permanent residents seeking citizenship status.

Another example of selective application and periodic relaxation of immigration laws on the part of the United States[128] can be found in the unilateral recruitment of Mexican braceros in 1948 and 1954. In each of these instances the United States adopted the attitude that Mexican intransigence had forced it to take such action. Whether this was true or not, the fact remained that unilateral recruitment clearly violated the international agreement with Mexico. It also represented a blatant disregard for the immigration laws of Mexico as well as those of the United States. In essence such acts made a mockery of the immigration laws and tended to break down the enforcement program that the Border Patrol was charged with carrying out.[129] It also fostered illegal immigration.

Ironically enough 1948 and 1954 also witnessed major efforts to control the influx of undocumented workers. As part of the 1948 Agreement the United States and Mexico pledged themselves to strict enforcement along the border in order to reduce illegal entry. In 1954 the Immigration and Naturalization Service undertook a massive deportation drive against undocumented workers. Thus the policy resembled a revolving door, and anyone caught up in it was at a loss to determine which policy was actually being observed.

Mexico appeared, at least on the surface, to be deeply concerned about illegal emigration into the United States, and for good reason. From the outset it had attempted to keep the bracero program at a moderate size, to better regulate the flow of workers into the United States and to maintain a strong bargaining position. Mexico realized that as long as the United States needed labor it would prove somewhat amenable to meeting Mexican demands for stricter contract guarantees. However, the growing influx of illegal entrants threatened to undermine this position, as disgruntled employers preferred to hire undocumented workers and bypass the legal program. Mexico was also concerned about the bad publicity that accompanied illegal emigration. The opposition used it to attack the Mexican government. Worse yet, the large numbers who left illegally brought in question all the government's claims of economic and social progress. If Mexico had made such great strides, people asked, then why were so many of its citizens fleeing their homeland to work at the most menial and demeaning jobs without protections or guarantees?

On the surface the solution seemed apparent. Tighten security along the border and impose stricter enforcement of the immigration laws. Yet there was another side to the story. While illegal emigration had its drawbacks it also provided Mexico with some positive features. For one thing, the little money sent back by "illegals" helped Mexico's economy. Perhaps more importantly, the emigration of Mexicans served as a safety valve for Mexico by drawing out potentially explosive elements who were unemployed and disgruntled. The dilemma, of course, was how to respond to the situation. Mexico adopted what it thought to be the best course. First, it concentrated on presenting public evidence of its effort to improve the lot of its workers in the United States, via the bracero contracts. It also called for penalties against those who employed undocumented workers as a price for renewing the contract on several occasions. Finally, it fought to have recruiting stations in the interior of Mexico instead of along the border. Beyond that it appears that Mexican officials were willing to do little. They preferred to take the offensive by focusing attention on the failure of the United States to penalize employers. As far as they were concerned the problem of illegal immigration belonged not to them but to the United States. If any decisive steps were going to be taken to control illegal entry, they would have to be taken by the United States and not by Mexico.

The United States was not willing to undertake the responsibility alone. American officials were particularly sensitive to the fact that any effort to enact penalty legislation against employers of undocumented workers would entail some serious political and economic ramifications. Representatives in the United States were cognizant of the powerful influence wielded by agricultural interests and their allies and knew that chances for the passage of such legislation were almost nonexistent. The United States found itself in difficult straits, as it was almost impossible to reconcile the efforts to strengthen inter-American ties while remaining responsive to the personal needs of domestic interest groups whose concerns lay outside the diplomatic arena. Nonetheless, the events of 1948 and 1954 proved to Mexican officials that the United States would support the needs of their growers first. Mexico also learned that the attitudes of United States officials had increasingly hardened against it because of perceived Mexican intransigence about renewing the bracero agreement.

In examining the course followed by the United States with regard to Mexican immigration, it becomes apparent that its policies generally favored the growers and processors. Policies such as unilateral recruitment, extension of the bracero program, permitting the direct recruitment of Mexican laborers by employers, and maintaining stringent requirements for legal immigration were all designed to encourage a large-scale influx of temporary Mexican laborers.[130] Such efforts proved successful, as reflected in the growing numbers of braceros as well as illegals who entered the United States between 1947 and 1954.[131] Yet it should be pointed out that the United States does not solely bear the blame for the increased influx. In many instances, with the exception of the unilateral recruitment policy, Mexico was also responsible for encouraging illegal entry by acquiescing to contradictory policies.

A prime example of this can be seen in Mexico's acquiescence in what was commonly referred to as the "legalization of wetbacks," which became quite prevalent after 1947. This policy had been conceived by officials in the United States as a means of reducing the embarrassment caused by its failure to restrict the number of people entering the country illegally. Furthermore, the process of "drying out" "illegals" was seen as a way of coaxing growers and processors to hire braceros instead of undocumented workers.[132] Officials on both sides of the border were concerned that the number of legally contracted braceros had remained relatively small. For example, in 1949 only 415 employers had contracted braceros.[133] In 1950 the United States Employment Service reported that it had received requests for only 1,500 braceros in the Rio Grande Valley of Texas. However, figures indicated a dramatic climb in the number of undocumented workers entering the country, which tended to dispel the myth that the legal contracting program was an effective deterrent to illegal entry.[134] Because of this, officials in the United States believed that a legalization program would serve to reduce the number of undocumented workers by regularizing their presence in this country. It would also serve to create a readily available pool of "legal" labor for use by employers. The plan was particularly appealing to officials because the process of legalization was both simple and inexpensive, as it did not require deportation or a formal reentry from Mexico.

Mexico was of course fully aware of the plans to initiate this program and supported the idea, even though it continued to decry the loss of manpower resulting from "wetbacks" and braceros who had skipped their contracts. By approving such a program Mexico found itself guilty of encouraging further illegal entry and of following contradictory policies with regard to its immigration laws. It encouraged its citizens to apply for contracts before entering the United States while strongly denouncing anyone who entered illegally. Mexico sought to further discourage entry by calling for penalties against those who employed undocumented workers. Yet by acquiescing in a legalization program it encouraged illegal entry. As both countries were rewarding those who had entered illegally by providing them with contracts and allowing them to bypass many of the procedures for acquiring a contract, little wonder that more people sought to enter the United States illegally.

In spite of the apparent drawbacks to this system Mexican officials continued to support it. In their view the system would help identify illegal entrants, give them the protection of a contract, and encourage their return to Mexico by eliminating the fear of fines or punishment.[135] The process allowed both the government and those who had left Mexico illegally to save face.

The legalization process made the bracero program a mere "supplementary program" to the widespread use of illegals.[136] In fact the legalization process was formalized through clauses in the bracero agreements of 1947, 1949, and 1950. From 1947 on, most of the braceros were in truth "legalized wetbacks."[137] By 1951 the program had so proved its merit in the eyes of its supporters that it was incorporated into Public Law 78 Section 501. Under this clause the Secretary of Labor was authorized "to recruit Mexican workers, including illegal entrants who had resided in the United States for the preceding five years, or who had entered originally under legal contract and remained after it expired."[138]

Yet its "success" did not hide the fact that it seriously undermined efforts at enforcement and the immigration laws passed to discourage illegal entry. One of the strongest condemnations of this policy came from the President's Commission on Migratory Labor, which had been appointed in June of 1950 to investigate the question of migratory labor in the United States.[139] In its final report the commission accused the federal government of having condoned the "wetback" traffic during the harvest season. According to its findings:

> wetbacks [who were apprehended] were given identification slips in the United States by the Immigration and Naturalization Service, which entitled them, within a few minutes, to step back across the border and become contract workers. There was no other way to obtain the indispensable slip of paper except to be found illegally in the United States. Thus violators of the law were rewarded by receiving legal contracts while the same opportunities were denied law-abiding citizens of Mexico. The United States, having engaged in a program giving preference in contracting to those who had broken the law, had encouraged violation of immigration laws. Our government thus had become a contributor to the growth of an illegal traffic which it has the responsibility to prevent.[140]

NOTES

1. Congressional Quarterly Service, *U. S. Agricultural Policy in the Postwar Years, 1945-1963* (Washington, D.C.: G. P. O., 1963), p. 83.

2. Marion Wilhelm, "Wetback Tide Overflowing Rio Grande Again," *The Washington Post* (Sunday, 7 June 1953), p. 3b, Records of Presidential Committee on Migratory Labor, 1941-1963, Secretary of Agriculture, Box No. 102, Folder M-1-2 Wetbacks, Dwight D. Eisenhower Library, Abilene, Kansas.

3. "The Wetback Strike: A Report on the Strike of Farm Workers in the Imperial Valley of California" (24 May, 25 June 1951, Published by the National Farm Labor Union, AF of L, Washington, D.C.), p. 21, in Records of President's Committee on Migratory Labor, 1941-1963, Secretary of Agriculture, Box Number 1, Folder-California, Dwight D. Eisenhower Library, Abilene, Kansas.

4. Ibid.

5. José Lazaro Salinas, *La Emigracion de Braceros* (Mexico, D.F.: Cuauhtemoc Press, 1955), p. 28.

6. Robert D. Tomasek, "The Political and Economic Implications of Mexican Labor in the United States under the Non Quota System, Contract Labor Program, and Wetback Movements" (Ph.D. diss., University of Michigan, 1957), p. 169.

7. Richard B. Craig, *The Bracero Program: Interest Groups and Foreign Policy* (Austin: University of Texas Press, 1971), p. 22.

8. American Embassy, Foreign Service Despatch From Mexico, D.F., to Department of State (7 August 1952), Subject: "The Bracero Question and Anti-American Propaganda," Record Group 166, Box 299, Foreign Agricultural Service, Mexican Labor, Narrative Reports, 1950-1954, Mexican Labor Folder, 1951-1952, National Archives, Washington, D.C.

9. Tomasek, "The Political and Economic Implications," p. 170. The Mexican Confederation of Labor is comprised of most of the important unions in Mexico.

10. Craig, *The Bracero Program*, pp. 19-20.

11. *El Nacional* (1 January 1954), p. 1.

12. Serafino Romualdi, "Hands Across the Border," *American Federationist* (June 1954), p. 20.

13. Tomasek, "The Political and Economic Implications," pp. 175-76.

14. Craig, *The Bracero Program*, p. 20.

15. *U. S. Agricultural Policy . . . 1945-1963*, p. 83. For a discussion of the specific contents of the 1951 Agreement and the interest group dynamics at play *see* Craig, *The Bracero Program*, chapter 3.

16. Craig, *The Bracero Program*, pp. 78-79.

17. Wilhelm, *Washington Post* (7 June 1953).

18. Otey M. Scruggs, "The United States, Mexico, and the Wetbacks, 1942-1947," *Pacific Historical Review* 30 (May 1961): 158.

19. *New York Times* (27 January 1953), p. 22.

20. Scruggs, "The United States," p. 158.

21. Sheldon L. Greene, "Immigration Law and Rural Poverty—The Problems of the Illegal Entrant," *Duke Law Journal* (June 1969), p. 479.

22. Ernesto Galarza, *Merchants of Labor: The Mexican Bracero Story* (Charlotte: McNally and Loftin Publishers, 1964), p. 49.

23. Walter J. Thurston, Mexico City, to Secretary of State (17 September 1948) in Special Folder-Mexico, 1946-1949, No Record Group, National Archives, Washington, D.C. (hereafter cited as Special Folder-Mexico, 1942-1949, N.A.).

24. Ibid.

25. David Stowe, *Secret Study*, p. 12; located in Harry S. Truman Library, Independence, Missouri.

26. *New York Times* (17 October 1948), p. 33.

27. *New York Times* (19 October 1948), p. 16.

28. *New York Times* (21 October 1948), p. 14.

29. *New York Times* (19 October 1948), p. 16.

30. *New York Times* (21 October 1948), p. 14.

31. Mexican statute law prohibited the unbridled illegal emigration of its citizens. When it was announced that the United States would resort to unilateral recruiting, Mexican officials warned that anyone crossing illegally would be prosecuted under Mexican law.

32. Walter Thurston, Mexico, D.F., to Secretary of State George C. Marshall (18 October 1948), pp. 1-3, Special Folder-Mexico, 1946-1949, N.A.

33. *New York Times* (26 October 1948), p. 35.

34. Craig, *The Bracero Program*, p. 69.

35. *El Universal* (4 January 1952).

36. S. 1851 had not been introduced as an agricultural or labor measure. Instead it was introduced as an amendment to the Immigration Act of 1917, *U.S. Agricultural Policy . . . , 1945-1963*, p. 2.283, U.S., 66 Statute, 26.

37. *See Excelsior* (1 February 1951); *Novedades* (2 February 1951), *Universal Grafico* (2 February 1951).

38. *See Novedades* (5 February 1951); *El Nacional* (7 February 1951).

39. *Novedades*, ibid.

40. *El Nacional* (7 February 1951).

41. William R. Laidlaw, Second Secretary of Embassy, Mexico, D.F., to Department of State (16 February 1951), Subject: "Mexican Reaction to Bracero Conversations," Record Group 166, Box 299, Mexican Folder, 1948-1950, in National Archives, Washington, D.C.

42. Ibid.

43. Ibid.

44. "Sorrowful Situation of Thousands of Braceros," *Ultimas Noticias* (23 October 1950), p. 1.

45. V. Harwood Blocker, American Consul, Mexico, D.F., to Department of State (25 October 1950), Record Group 166, Box 299, Foreign Agricultural Service, Narrative Reports, 1950-1954, Mexican Labor Folder, 1948-1950, National Archives, Washington, D.C.

46. Ibid.

47. Ibid.

48. Ibid.

49. Ibid.

50. *El Popular* (17 February 1952), p. 1.

51. *La Nacion* (4 August 1952), p. 1.

52. Ibid., p. 2.

53. William E. Price, American Consul, Reynosa, Mexico to Department of State (4 February 1952), Subject: "Local Press Comments Regarding Certain Aspects of Pending Bracero Agreement," Record Group 166, Box 299, Foreign Agricultural Service, Narrative Reports, Mexican Labor Folder, 1951-1952, National Archives, Washington, D.C.

54. Craig, *The Bracero Program*, pp. 105-6.

55. Tomasek, "The Political and Economic Implications," p. 258.

56. *Los Angeles Times* (8 November 1953), p. 8.

57. U. S., Congress, Senate, Committee on Agriculture and Forestry, *Extension of the Mexican Farm Labor Program: Hearings on S.1207*, 83d Cong., 1st sess., March 23 and 24, 1953 (Washington, D.C.: G. P. O., 1953), p. 23.

58. Ibid., pp. 24-26.

59. *New York Times* (8 October 1953), p. 21.

60. *New York Times* (12 January 1954), p. 33.

61. *New York Times* (16 January 1954), p. 15.

62. *El Nacional* (17 January 1954), p. 1.

63. William P. Snow, American Embassy, Mexico, D.F., to Department of State (19 January 1954), Subject: "Translation of Mexican Communique on Expiration of Bracero Agreement," pp. 1-2, Record Group 166, Box 298, Foreign Agricultural Service, Narrative Reports 1950-1954, Mexican Folder-Home, Economic and Welfare-Labor, 1953-1954, National Archives, Washington, D.C.

64. Ibid., p. 2.

65. *El Universal* (17 January 1954), p. 1; *El Nacional* (17 January 1954), pp. 1, 2, 6, and (20 January 1954), p. 1.

66. *El Nacional* (20 January 1954), p. 1.

67. Craig, *The Bracero Program*, p. 112.

68. *Hispanic American Report*, no. 7 (February 1954), p. 1.

69. *New York Times* (2 February 1954), p. 3.

70. Galarza, *Merchants*, p. 69.

71. American Embassy, Mexico, D.F., to Department of State (27 January 1954), Subject: "Provincial Reaction to Bracero Issue," pp. 1-2, R. G. 166, Box 298, Mexican Folder, 1953-1954, N.A.

72. *Hispanic American Report*, no. 6 (August 1953), p. 9.

73. *See New York Times* editorials for 22 November 1953; 12 January 1954; 13 January 1954; 17 January 1954; 20 January 1954; 24 January 1954.

74. *Congressional Record*, 83d Cong., 2d sess., 100, pt. 1, (4 February 1954), Extension of Remarks, p. 1387.

75. Ibid.

76. Ibid., p. 1388.

77. Telegram from Mr. Ed Idar, Jr., to President Dwight D. Eisenhower (18 January 1954), p. 2, Record Group 174, Box 54, Secretary of Labor, 1954 Mexican Labor Program, Misc. (January-June), National Archives, Washington, D.C. hereafter cited as R. G. 174, Box 54).

78. Ibid.

79. Elias Olivares to Herbert Brownell (22 January 1954), in File Number 8, Justice Department Records, Justice Department, Washington, D.C., District Number One of the G.I. Forum encompassed the length of the Rio Grande Valley from Rio Grande City to Brownsville, Texas.

80. Elias Olivarez to President Dwight D. Eisenhower (21 January 1954), ibid.

81. Douglas O. Weeks, "The League of United Latin American Citizens: A Texas Mexican Civic Organization," *Southwestern Political and Social Science Quarterly* (December 1929), p. 259.

82. Frank Piñedo to James P. Mitchell (19 January 1954), R. G. 174, Box 54, N.A.

83. James P. Mitchell to Frank Piñedo (27 January 1954), ibid.

84. Statement by the Executive Council of the American Federation of Labor, Miami Beach, Florida (4 February 1954), p. 2, File Number 8, Justice Department Records, Washington, D.C.

85. Rocco C. Siciliano to Lindsey C. Warren (17 January 1954), R. G. 174, Box 54, N.A. Interim basis was another term for unilateral recruitment.

86. Lindsey G. Warren to Rocco S. Siciliano (18 February 1954), ibid.

87. U. S. Congress, House, *Mexican Farm Labor,* Hearings Before the Committee on Agriculture on H. J. R. 355, 83d Cong., 2d sess. (Washington, D.C.: February, 1954), p. 2, Papers of James P. Mitchell, Secretary of Labor, 1953-1961, Box 46, Folder-1954 Mexican Farm Labor Hearings, A70-17, located in Dwight D. Eisenhower Library, Abilene, Kansas (hereafter cited as Mitchell Papers, Box 46, D.D.E.L.).

88. Ibid., p. 6.

89. Thruston B. Morton, Assistant Secretary of State, to Clifford R. Hope (5 February 1954), R. G. 166, Box 298, N.A.

90. Walter B. Smith, Memorandum for the President (3 February 1954), Subject: Mexican Ambassador's Visit to Discuss Migrant Labor Agreement in Central Files, Official File, OF 124-A-1, Box 634, Folder 124-C (1) Migratory Labor, Dwight D. Eisenhower Library, Abilene, Kansas (hereafter cited as Central Files, White House, Box 634, Migratory Labor Folder).

91. Ibid.

92. *Congressional Record,* 83d Cong., 2d sess., 100, pt. 2 (2 March 1954), pp. 2489-92.

93. Ibid., p. 2424.

94. Ibid., p. 2426.

95. Ibid.

96. Ibid., p. 2531.

97. *Congressional Record,* 100, pt. 2 (1954), p. 2491.

98. Ibid.

99. Ibid., p. 2558.

100. Ibid., p. 2560.

101. Ibid., p. 2566.

102. Ibid., p. 2569.

103. Ibid., p. 2570.

104. "Mexico Expecting a New Hiring Pact," *New York Times* (5 March 1954), p. 10.

105. *Congressional Record,* 100, pt. 2 (1954), p. 2427.

106. Ibid., p. 2428.

107. Ibid.

108. Ibid., p. 2429.

109. Ibid.

110. *Hearings on J. J. R. 355*, p. 9, Mitchell Papers, Box 46, D.D.E.L.

111. Ibid., p. 12.

112. *Congressional Record*, 100, pt. 2 (1954), pp. 2555 and 2571.

113. Most Reverend Robert E. Lucey, S. T. D., Archbishop of San Antonio, to Dwight D. Eisenhower (15 February 1954), Central Files, White House, Box 634, Migratory Labor File, Dwight D. Eisenhower Library, Abilene, Kansas (hereafter cited as Central Files, White House, Box 634, D.D.E.L.).

114. Harlan Hagen to Dwight D. Eisenhower (6 March 1954), pp. 1-2, ibid.

115. Guy R. Brewer to Dwight D. Eisenhower (6 March 1954), Mitchell Papers, Box 46, D.D.E.L. Brewer was probably referring to a story that had emanated from Washington that it was the intention of Vice President Richard M. Nixon, Senator William P. Knowland, and Speaker Joe Martin to persuade Eisenhower to delay signing a new bilateral agreement with Mexico until he had approved H.J.R. 355 "as a permanent big stick over Mexico." Gardner Jackson to Dwight D. Eisenhower (7 March 1954), pp. 2-3, ibid.

116. Ibid.

117. Ibid.

118. Thruston B. Morton to Joseph M. Dodge (4 March 1954), p. 1, Central Files, White House, General File 126-I-1, Box 968, D.D.E.L.

119. Ibid., pp. 1-2.

120. Memorandum for the President, Subject: "Mexican Migrant Labor Legislation," submitted by Walter B. Smith (12 March 1954), Mitchell Papers, Box 466, D.D.E.L.

121. Ibid.

122. Immediate Release, James C. Hagerty, Press Secretary to the President, The White House, Statement by the President on signing H.J. Res. 355 (16 March 1954), Central Files, White House, Box 634, Migratory Labor File, D.D.E.L.

123. *U.S. Agricultural Policy . . . 1945-1964*, pp. 7-8.

124. U.S. Department of State *Bulletin*, "U.S.-Migratory Labor Commission Membership," (12 April 1954), p. 565.

125. *El Universal* (12 March 1954), p. 3; *El Nacional* (12 March 1954), p. 3; *Excelsior* (11 March 1954), p. 1.

126. Foreign Service Despatch from William P. Hudson, Mexico City, to Secretary of State (15 March 1954), R.G. 166, Box 298, Folder-Mexico, Labor, 1953-1954, N.A.

127. Corwin, "Causes," p. 617.

128. Julian Samora, *Los Mojados: The Wetback Story* (South Bend, Ind.: University of Notre Dame Press, 1970), p. 33.

129. *Task Force Report on Migratory Labor in Agriculture*, p. 24, Migratory Labor File, Stone Papers, Truman Library, Independence, Missouri.

130. Gilbert Cardenas, "United States Immigration Policy and Mexican Immigration" (South Bend, Ind.: Centro de Estudios Chicanos, 1974), p. 30.

131. Between 1 July 1949 and 30 June 1950, more than 220,000 undocumented workers were deported to Mexico from the McAllen section of Texas. Saunders and Leonard, "The Wetback," p. 56.

132. Corwin, "Causes," p. 627; Samora, *Los Mojados*, pp. 46-48; Galarza, *Merchants*, pp. 63-64. The legalization program encouraged many growers to join farm labor associations between 1951 and 1954, because under this program growers could legally contract "wetback specials" (that is, undocumented workers who had received special training by their employers and who returned annually to that employer because of a guaranteed job). It is interesting to note that these employers were the same ones who claimed that they had dif-

ficulty in identifying undocumented workers. Yet despite this disclaimer they were usually able, when the legalization process went into effect, to identify their "specials," who had entered illegally. Galarza, ibid., p. 64.

133. Most of its employers were packers and canners.

134. Corwin, "Causes," p. 627; Samora, *Los Mojados*, pp. 46-48; Galarza, *Merchants*, pp. 63.

135. Under Mexican law it was a crime to leave the country illegally.

136. *Migratory Labor Hearings, 1952*, p. 2571.

137. Horace E. Newton, *Mexican Illegal Immigration into California* (San Francisco: R and E Research Associates, 1973), p. 27. There was heated debate over Senator Ellender's proposal, yet Ellender attempted to quiet the opposition by stating that the five-year standard would be strictly adhered to. The question nonetheless remained as to how one would prove that a legalized "wetback" met the five-year requirement.

138. Galarza, *Merchants*, p. 63; Craig, *The Bracero Program*, p. 72.

139. Craig, Ibid., p. 66. The commission was composed of Noble Clark, William Liesenson, Robert E. Lucey, Peter Odegard, and Maurice Von Hecke.

140. *Migratory Labor in American Agriculture*, pp. 74-75. Also *see* Samora, *Los Mojados*, p. 47.

3
The Border Patrol

THE UNITED STATES did not follow a clear, consistent, or coherent policy
on Mexican immigration throughout most of the period preceding "Operation
Wetback." Instead, on several occasions, it chose to selectively relax its immigration policies along its southwestern border to acquire the Mexican labor it
deemed necessary to its economic security. Even though such practices often
violated existing immigration statutes, the Immigration and Naturalization Service,
which was charged with enforcement of those laws, usually did little to publicly
protest or block such actions. On several occasions the Immigration and Naturalization Service became a willing partner in violating the laws it was supposed to enforce, which led to charges of open complicity with vested interests and undermined its already limited effectiveness in controlling the border against an increasing influx of undocumented workers.

On the other hand, when Mexican labor was no longer needed in large quantities, the United States would apply its immigration policies. When such a decision
was made the responsibility for carrying it out fell on the shoulders of the Immigration and Naturalization Service. The result was again a barrage of criticism, this
time from other sectors who opposed strict enforcement. Ironically enough, by
enforcing such policies when ordered to do so, the INS fell prey to the charge that
it was a mere creature of powerful vested interest groups who were only concerned
with keeping the gates opened until their labor demands were met and getting
rid of their miserable charges when that need no longer existed. Yet it was these
same interest groups, whose interests the INS was supposedly serving, who repeatedly undermined the effectiveness of the INS by cutting its appropriations. Thus it
is very difficult to paint the INS in simple terms, for a myriad of factors affected
its ability to operate.

A great many things hampered its operation, some imposed by forces outside
its control, and others self-inflicted and self-imposed.

Migration from Mexico into what is today the southwestern part of the United
States has been going on since the Spanish conquest of New Spain. For more than
half a century before World War II Mexicans had been crossing the border illegally.

Prior to 1882 there existed no international restrictions on immigration, and Mexicans moved freely across the border to work in the mines, the railroads, and the ranches of the Southwest. *De facto* free movement continues relatively unabated to the present.

In June of 1924, the United States government founded the Border Patrol in an effort to check and control illegal entry from Mexico. Interestingly enough the targets of this action were not the Mexicans, but the Europeans and the Asians who were entering the United States via Mexico.[1] Their illegal entry had been prompted by quota and immigration laws that limited the number of European entrants and all but excluded Asians. People of the western hemisphere had had no quota placed upon them, and the need for a large labor pool in the Southwest made the Mexican national a welcome sight to many growers and railroad men.

Throughout the 1920s the Border Patrol was situated in the Department of Labor. Because there existed little precedent for their activities, early Border Patrol officials concentrated their efforts on controlling smuggling activities along the border. Most of the men in the Border Patrol had little or no knowledge about immigration or international law and found little need for such training. They allowed Mexicans looking for work to enter pretty much unmolested. Many of the men assigned to the Border Patrol viewed themselves more as police officers than as immigration officers, given the nature of their duties.[2]

The Border Patrol continued to function as an anticontraband force throughout the 1920s and until the Volstead Act was repealed in 1933. When Francis Perkins became Secretary of Labor a review of the Border Patrol was undertaken. As smuggling activities had decreased for the moment, people in Washington began to question the need for a Border Patrol. For a time Secretary of Labor Perkins seriously considered transferring the Border Patrol back to the Treasury Department, where it appeared to belong. However, Perkins decided to keep the Border Patrol within the Labor Department after she was convinced that immigration was linked to economics and labor needs. By 1934 the Border Patrol had begun to concentrate more on the job it had been created for—controlling illegal immigration.[3] Although the force was reduced in 1933 because of a bureaucratic shake-up, the Border Patrol was again increased in 1935. In that year members of the Border Patrol had their pay increased and began to receive training as immigration officers.

In spite of these changes, the Border Patrol remained relatively small and obscure. The economic depression that swept the United States during the 1930s did little to enhance the reputation, much less the need for a Border Patrol. Throughout much of this period Mexican immigration was reversed because of adverse economic conditions in the United States. Uncounted numbers of Mexicans returned to Mexico voluntarily, while an unknown number were forcefully deported. Unfortunately for the Border Patrol, many of the deportation activities conducted in the 1930s were carried out by local agencies or organizations in cooperation with local law enforcement agencies. The Border Patrol was thus relegated to a very minor role during this period, giving rise to renewed questions concerning the need for a Border Patrol or at least the need for large appropriations to support it. Throughout the 1930s the Border Patrol remained poorly staffed, poorly equipped, poorly administered, and largely disorganized.

In 1940 the Immigration and Naturalization Service was transferred from the Labor Department to the Justice Department. The move was prompted by growing concern on the part of Franklin D. Roosevelt's administration that Germany and Italy would have their agents infiltrate the United States through its unpatrolled borders. Although the United States had not declared war against the Axis Powers, the indications were quite clear that American sympathies lay with England and its allies. Because of this it was not unlikely that foreign agents would undertake activities detrimental to the security of the country. This concern brought about a change in how the service's role was viewed. Whereas in previous years immigration had been looked at in terms of labor, now immigration began to be viewed in terms of national security. The INS and its Border Patrol were placed under a branch which, in the eyes of immigration officials, was more in line with what they believed were the purposes and functions of the INS, the Justice Department.

Nonetheless strict enforcement of immigration laws along the southwestern border did not materialize with the transfer of the INS into the Justice Department. The entry of the United States into World War II and the concomitant shortage of labor in industry and agriculture brought amnesty to the undocumented worker. Effective control of the Mexican border was also affected by the Border Patrol's increased attention to national security problems and by the fact that the war depleted its ranks, as many officers entered military service.

The laws and policies under which the Border Patrol functioned also served to further weaken its enforcement capabilities. These laws and policies pretty much reflected a laissez-faire attitude toward illegal immigration from Mexico. They also reflected the desire of powerful interest groups to keep the enforcement of laws to a minimum and the interest of supporters in providing the Border Patrol with flexibility so that it could provide a modicum of enforcement.

Prior to 1929 apprehended aliens who had entered without documents were not subject to any charges or penalties. This policy was modified in 1929 when Congress enacted a law that made it a misdemeanor for any alien to enter illegally. Those who were apprehended and who were offenders for the first time were subject to a fine and up to a year's imprisonment, although such penalties were seldom imposed. Subsequent convictions could lead to imprisonment for a maximum of two years and a fine of one thousand dollars. Although specific efforts were made to try offenders, such efforts usually proved futile. The large numbers of apprehensions made it almost impossible to handle the case loads, while detention facilities quickly became overcrowded. It was not uncommon to place first offenders on probation or to parole apprehended aliens to local employers until the Border Patrol could make arrangements to return them across the border.[4] Such practices were common throughout the 1930s, 1940s, and 1950s and helped to undermine the Border Patrol's effectiveness. It also meant that undocumented workers did not take the enforcement efforts of the Border Patrol seriously.

Beginning in 1939 economic reasons forced the Border Patrol increasingly to rely on the voluntary departure method for aliens who had entered the country illegally and who had been apprehended.[5] Although this method did prove more economical than going through time-consuming and expensive deportation proceeding, it did little to discourage the influx of undocumented workers. Instead this procedure encouraged illegal entry, as undocumented aliens were often released on their own recognizance and permitted to make their own way back to Mexico without any kind of penalty. In the 1940s a new wrinkle was added when the United States and Mexico agreed to "drying out" wetbacks. Through this process "illegal aliens" who were apprehended were permitted to temporarily cross back into Mexico and then return to be processed as braceros. Instead of punishing offenders, this process rewarded them with contracts. Again the end result was an increased influx of "illegals."

On other occasions the Border Patrol openly acquiesced to the violation of the laws it was charged with enforcing. The most blatant examples involved the unilateral recruitment of Mexican workers in 1948 and again in 1954, after Mexico had terminated the bracero agreements following impasses during negotiations. Whether Border Patrol officials were ordered to permit the entry of braceros by superiors or whether they acted on their own initiative did not change the fact that they had disregarded the law. The Border Patrol served as a regulator or "balance wheel." According to the President's Commission on Migratory Labor the Border Patrol permitted enough "wetbacks" to enter to do the necessary work but also sent back enough of them "to prevent serious overcrowding."

The Border Patrol's record in regulating the influx of "illegals" along the Mexican border was not impressive. This lack of performance, when coupled with the efforts of southwestern congressmen to keep the Border Patrol from being effective, lead to repeated reductions in its budgets and to a mounting tide of criticism from all sectors. Every year the Border Patrol was forced to fight an uphill battle to obtain sufficient funding to operate, and every year it became more apparent that it was fighting a losing battle. Appropriations were usually cut to the bone, causing reductions in equipment and a decline in personnel. From 1946 to 1954, the number of Border Patrol personnel decreased.[6] During roughly the same period the total increase in annual appropriations amounted to $1,613,603, an increase of less than 23 percent, while during the period from 1948 to 1954 apprehensions increased 400 percent.[7]

In Congress the fight to repeatedly cut Border Patrol appropriations was primarily led by congressmen and senators from the southwestern states. Though their motives were obvious to many observers, these men usually attempted to disguise them in terms of the need to economize and cut down on federal expenditures.[8] Those who were not from commercial farming areas usually supported their colleagues in cutting appropriations because they knew little about the "illegal" situation along the border and because they often needed to secure support from southwestern congressmen for their own legislation. Other congressmen supported proposed cuts because they confused illegal crossings with the bracero program, whose cost they considered excessive. In fact, those who were of this persuasion began as early as 1947 to demand the termination of the program. As far as they were concerned, the bracero program had been proposed and passed only as an emergency wartime measure. They questioned the need to expend $3,000,000 per year to run a program that was no longer necessary now that the war had ended. Unable to bring the program to an end, its opponents concentrated on reducing costs related to it as much as possible. As the issue and the program involved Mexican immigration, there was a tendency to view Border Patrol costs as part of the overall bracero program budget. Of course this was a mistaken notion, but the Border Patrol continued to suffer as a result of it.

In retrospect, it appears that the Border Patrol was caught up in a vicious circle. Its critics, both in and out of Congress, accused the Border Patrol of gross inefficiency and pointed to the growing number of "illegal" entrants to support their arguments. Yet part of the reason for its failure to stem the influx lay with its outdated equipment and its lack of personnel. However, until it could prove that it could do the job, Congress was not prepared to increase its appropriations enough to purchase the equipment and hire the extra personnel necessary to control the border.[9]

The Border Patrol also had to share part of the blame for its difficulties. Its inefficiency provided effective ammunition for its critics and undermined the efforts of its supporters. Plagued by internal problems and often lax in performing its duties, the Border Patrol made itself an easy target. From its inception it had suffered from a lack of organization and autonomy. For example, its three divisions were each responsible to separate immigration heads who had little or no direct contact with one another, which led to duplication and overlapping in patrolling assignments. It also led to jurisdictional disputes between the divisions and to little or no cooperation among department heads. When the INS was moved from the Labor Department to the Justice Department in 1940, no steps were taken to reorganize it.[10]

In 1950 there was some improvement in the operation of the Border Patrol after Argyle Mackey was named its commissioner. It was he who suggested transporting apprehended "illegals" into the interior of Mexico by naval transport. The outbreak of the Korean War caused the plan to be scrapped. Not to be deterred, Mackey in 1951 recommended the airlifting of "illegals" by using Flying Tiger planes.[11] Though it appears from various reports that the plan was effective, it had to be dropped because of the high cost. Nonetheless, despite Mackey's initiative, dynamic leadership and organization were still lacking.

Prior to 1954 the Border Patrol was divided into thirteen sectors along the Mexican border.[12] Lacking coordination, inspectors went where they chose. As they had no assigned territory, it was not uncommon to find two or three cars covering the same area within minutes of each others' patrol, leaving other areas unvisited for relatively long periods. Inspectors also traveled in pairs in small cars. As this made it impossible to transport large numbers of apprehended "illegals," inspectors and patrol officers seldom raided larger farms.[13]

When Joseph Swing became Commissioner of Immigration he noted that the Border Patrol lacked "any real fervor to get anything done."[14] This was in part because of the low morale prevalent among many officers and because of pressure exerted on Border Patrol Inspectors by some of their superiors in the INS, who indicated that they were not eager for their officers to be zealous in performing their duties.

From time to time Border Patrol officials and line officers testified publicly that they had been ordered to hold back until after the harvest season was over. In testimony before the President's Commission on Migratory Labor, three officials from the INS in Arizona testified that a powerful group of agribusiness interests had compelled the suspension of law-enforcement activities against undocumented workers. Carson Morrow, Arizona Chief Border Patrol Inspector at Tucson, stated that he had received orders from the District Director at El Paso, Texas, to stop the deportation of undocumented workers. According to Morrow these orders had been issued during each harvest season. O. W. Manney, Phoenix Chief of the Immigration Service, told the commission that the legal and illegal contracting of Mexican workers because of domestic labor shortages had been abused to the extent that there always seemed to be "a year around emergency."[15]

According to the commission, incidents involving nonenforcement of immigration laws were more frequent than generally imagined and there had been a good number of "deals" aimed at securing nonenforcement until the harvest season had come to an end.[16]

In 1951 the District Director of the Immigration and Naturalization Service in El Paso, Texas, told the commission that farmers had in the past complained to the Secretary of Labor about labor shortages. The purpose of such complaints was to exert pressure on the Immigration Service to "go easy" on their apprehensions until the cotton chopping or picking season was over. It appears that such coercion or "cooperation" often occurred. For example, in the late 1940s the Immigration Commissioner had assured Representative Clinton McKinnon that "the Border Patrol would not go on the farms in search of 'wetbacks,' but would confine their activities to the highways and places of social gatherings."[17] An excerpt from a 1949 report to the Idaho State Employment Office included the following statement: "The United States Immigration and Naturalization Service recognizes the need for farm workers in Idaho, and, through cooperation with the state employment service, withholds its search until such times as there is not a shortage of farm workers."[18]

In June of 1950, William F. Kelley, Assistant Commissioner of Immigration, admitted that the Border Patrol continued the practice of "cooperating" with local growers. Kelley and others in the service recognized that cooperation of this kind was at times necessary. This was especially true during manpower shortages and the critical need to increase production. At times such as these "Service Officers were instructed to defer the apprehension of Mexicans employed on Texas farms where to remove them could likely result in loss of the crops."[19] Four years later, during the impasse in renegotiating the bracero agreement, Kelley made a stronger statement concerning this issue. As far as he was concerned, the Immigration Service had the authority to allow "aliens" to remain the United States, "whether they are here legally nor not!"[20]

Critics of the Border Patrol latched onto statements such as these as proof positive that it was a tool used by growers and other employers to obtain cheap labor. One report called the exploitation of "wetback labor" a "degrading and depressing spectacle" and stated that "the most dismaying aspect of this unsavory picture is the fact that governmental agencies, notably the Immigration Service . . . [is] participating in the introduction . . . of these thousands upon thousands of wetbacks."[21] Others charged that the INS and the Border Patrol not only permitted undocumented workers to enter illegally but also miraculously appeared at the close of the harvest season to remove them once their services were no longer required. In support of these charges critics pointed to the increased number of apprehensions once the harvest season had ended. One report pointed out that apprehensions in Texas were the highest during the month of August, the month that marked the end of the seasonal need for stoop labor in the southern portions of that state.[22] The President's Commission on Migratory Labor also noted that apprehensions and deportations tended to rise very rapidly once the seasonal harvest period had ended. In its opinion, wrote the commission, this could "be interpreted not alone to mean that the immigration officer suddenly goes about his work with renewed zeal and vigor, but rather that at this time of the year 'cooperation' in law enforcement by farm employers and townspeople rapidly undergoes considerable improvement."[23]

Mexico was of course aware of these charges against the Border Patrol, and it occasionally asked the United States not to condone such activities. For example, in 1952 Mexico became aware that the Border Patrol was being removed from the immediate border near the Rio Grande Valley to positions some eighty kilometers from the border in order to stop incursions farther north. Concerned about this, Mexico requested that the United States not go through with its plans to remove the Border Patrol. Mexico also informed the United States that it was aware that roundups of undocumented workers often occurred after the cotton crop had been harvested and implored this country to remove them before the harvest and not after.[24] The Mayor of Matamoros, Lic. Cardenas Montemayor, charged that farmers in the Rio Grande Valley of Texas worked "wetbacks" for a time and then called in the Border Patrol just before payday. He considered this a highly unethical practice and was particularly angered that his city had to assume the costs for feeding and transporting the penniless Mexicans the Border Patrol had apprehended following such actions.[25]

While criticisms of this nature against the Border Patrol were at times justified, they did not take cognizance of the pressures under which the Border Patrol operated. Just as it antagonized individuals and groups opposed to the illegal influx by not enforcing the laws at times, it also antagonized proponents of cheap labor when it did take measures to slow down the influx. The Border Patrol was in no position to antagonize the powerful interest groups in Congress by being overly effective. For the time being it had more to lose by alienating these groups than by alienating the weak and loosely organized groups that favored a closed border. Furthermore, other factors affected the performance of the Border Patrol prior to 1954.

Pressure on Border Patrol and other immigration officials was not limited to the political and economic sphere. Officers along the southwestern border, particularly those stationed in Texas, also found themselves and their families subject to social pressure. Officers were often insulted by growers and farmers while attempting to perform their duty. They were also, on occasion, denied hotel accommodations, housing, and service in restaurants. Their wives were socially ostracized and their children harassed at school. Incidents between Border Patrolmen and undocumented workers who resisted arrest were played up in local newspapers and blown all out of proportion, although at times Border Patrolmen did abuse their charges, thereby adding credence to stories of brutality. Incidents of personality clashes between immigration officials and local employers were also given wide publicity and were usually detrimental to the former's image,[26] especially in the Rio Grande Valley of Texas, where the Valley press sided with local growers. Articles about the Border Patrol usually referred to officers as "villains" or "goon squads," while the Border Patrol itself was called the "gestapo."[27]

Hampered by contradictory laws, low appropriations, poor organizational structure, ineffective leadership, and direct and indirect pressures, the morale of Border Patrol personnel continually declined. The low morale made itself apparent in many ways. For one thing Border Patrolmen took little pride in their appearance. Their dress was usually casual and based largely on the personal taste of the individual.[28] At times the men themselves expressed a lack of self-esteem and reflected the belief that they were not effectively enforcing the laws. Most of them readily admitted that they were not holding their own against the increasing traffic of undocumented workers.[29] They generally conceded that they were carrying on a holding operation. One Border Patrol officer in California expressed his exasperation by stating that attempting to stop the influx of "illegals" was just "like trying to bail out the ocean with a bucket."[30] Unofficial sources made repeated references to the fact that the "chotas" (Spanish slang for Border Patrolmen) often found the task of patrolling the border a hope-

"Wetbacks" rounded up by the Border Patrol. *Courtesy of the Texas AFL-CIO Collection, The University of Texas at Arlington Library.*

Some of the one thousand "wetbacks" processed daily at the McAllen detention center. *Courtesy the Texas AFL-CIO Collection, The University of Texas at Arlington Library.*

less one. It was not unusual for them to allow undocumented workers to roam the Valley and concentrate their efforts on keeping them away from the industrial jobs further north.[31]

Another indicator of the low morale was in the high turnover rate which plagued the Border Patrol. Although the Border Patrol had been plagued by high turnover before the beginning of the "wetback decade" in 1940 because of long and irregular hours, night duty, and extended periods out in the field, the turnover rate in the late 1940s and early 1950s was largely attributed to disillusion- ment and the lack of prestige associated with the Service.[32] The Border Patrol could ill afford additional losses to its already understaffed force. By 1950 the Border Patrol counted 700 officers on the Mexican border. With annual leave, holidays and the five-day week, this number was reduced by 39 percent, leaving it with 427 officers to patrol the border on a daily basis. When this number was divided by three in order to have twenty-four-hour coverage, the number dwindled to 142 men to patrol some 1,600 miles of border. To further reduce their effective- ness, Border Patrolmen could not enter commercial farms unless they were ab- solutely sure that there were undocumented workers there. Officers could not enter private dwellings to search for "illegals," and even if they managed to cap- ture some undocumented workers there were no penalties for the employers who had hired them. The most that officers could do was to place the employer's name on a list and forward it to Labor Department compliance officers. As this so-called blacklisting seldom resulted in an employer's being refused contract labor, many Border Patrolmen did not bother to submit lists.[33]

While the number of critics on both sides of the "illegal" question grew and continued their assault on the shortcomings of the Border Patrol, a few staunch advocates and supporters fought for increased appropriations and for more strin- gent laws aimed at ending the influx of "illegals."

Throughout the late 1940s and early 1950s Senators Hubert Humphrey, Paul Douglas, and Herbert Lehman repeatedly argued for increased appropriations for the Border Patrol.[34] Generally, these men typified those in Congress who supported such appropriations: they were from the Midwest and Northeast, they usually sided with or were sympathetic to labor, and they felt some concern about the plight of domestic migrants. Because of such interests and the impact that the undocu- mented worker had on these concerns, they advocated an expanded, well-equipped, well-staffed Border Patrol.

While they were generally successful in cajoling or convincing the Appropriations Committee to increase funds for the Border Patrol, their proposals usually failed to pass once they reached the floor of Congress.[35] The simple fact was that they were going up against a powerful and well-organized group of representatives from the Southwest who could muster more than enough support to have any proposals concerning the Border Patrol voted down. This group was in the driver's seat, and they were helped along by the fact that the Border Patrol was caught up in a vicious circle. On the one hand, detractors pointed to its ineffectiveness and ques-

TABLE 8

Number of Border Patrol Line Officers, 1942-1956

1942..........1,592	1947..........1,319	1952..........1,259
1943..........1,637	1948..........1,160	1953..........1,079
1944..........1,360	1949..........1,125	1954..........1,079
1945..........1,251	1950..........1,110	1955..........1,479
1946..........1,352	1951..........1,098	1956..........1,526

Source: Eleanor Hadley, "A Critical Analysis," p. 348.

tioned whether increased appropriations was the answer. Immigration officials were told repeatedly that they had to convince legislators that they could do the job, and then perhaps they would receive increased funds. On the other hand, when the Border Patrol did undertake intensive measures to stop the influx, the same detractors accused it of being wasteful and inefficient. A case in point occurred in 1951 and 1952, when Border Patrol officials airlifted undocumented workers into the interior of Mexico to discourage their immediate return. This was a departure from the usual method of simply depositing apprehended individuals across the border in Mexico. From all indications the airlift plan appears to have had some effect in reducing the number of repeaters. During this period, the overall number of "illegals" apprehended showed a small downward trend. Nonetheless, the program quickly became the object of congressional criticism that further swelled the ranks of congressmen who opposed increased appropriations for the Border Patrol. What particularly irked most congressmen was the high cost attached to the venture. It cost the government $43.00 for every "illegal" airlifted back to Mexico, which led one critic of the program to describe it as "one of the most extravagant ideas any bureaucracy ever thought up."[36] Given the high cost of the project, funds quickly ran out and the project had to be scuttled. This and the reductions in personnel in 1953 clearly indicated to Border Patrol officials what they could expect if they antagonized grower interests and their spokesmen in Congress.[37] Nonetheless, they continued to argue for more money.

A short time before the intense drive in 1954, Senator Harley Kilgore added his voice to those who sought to strengthen the Border Patrol. Once a severe critic of the Border Patrol, Kilgore, like other representatives, had become concerned by the "illegal question." In 1953 the media began to pay more attention to the influx of undocumented workers from Mexico, which sparked an interest as well as an increased concern in many who had either been unaware of the growing stream of "illegals" or had simply been unconcerned about it. Kilgore now supported the Border Patrol and in fact believed that more needed to be done to help it close the border.

Kilgore asked his colleagues to go beyond simply increased appropriations for more personnel. He was not convinced that increasing the manpower of the Border Patrol would suffice. Other services were required to assist the Border Patrol in their enforcement efforts, and he decried the fact that such services had been allowed to atrophy. He called for a proper handling of cases in the courts to punish those who violated the immigration laws, and he called for a more active role on the part of the Justice Department in helping its fellow officers. It was of course no secret to the Border Patrol that one of its worst enemies had been the Justice Department, which at times had appeared more responsive to vested interests than to the Border Patrol.[38] Then too there was the fact that the Border Patrol had just joined the Justice Department in 1940 and was still a relative newcomer with the unsavory task of tracking down hungry and unarmed people. Certainly there was little glamor in this, and it provided very little to which Justice Department officials could point proudly. Finally, there was the Border Patrol's tendency to become entangled in appropriations battles, which did little to ingratiate it with some high-level officials in the Justice Department who wished to avoid a lot of publicity and congressional attention.

In Kilgore's estimation all the hard work in the world would not bring about noticeable results unless Congress funded associated agencies and services to help the Border Patrol in the performance of its duties. Failure to fund such services, noted Kilgore, would be equivalent to "putting a policeman on the beat, and not providing him with a jail or stationhouse into which to place the criminals he captures."[39]

Officials of the INS were not loathe to express their views either, and in fact they actively campaigned for increased funds. Generally their arguments were the same. They needed more money and more personnel in order to operate effectively.

In 1952, Argyle R. Mackey, Commissioner of the Immigration and Naturalization Service, testified at a hearing on migratory labor before a Senate subcommittee that even though greater demands had been placed on the Border Patrol because of the increased influx of undocumented workers, it was repeatedly denied supplemental funds necessary to its operations, in spite of the fact that the United States and Mexico had pledged themselves to end the illegal influx. He stated that funds were refused for continuing the airlift operations even though figures showed that of the thousands of "wetbacks" flown into the interior of Mexico only about 1.7 percent returned.[40] Mackey went on to say that Public Law 78 further depleted the manpower resources of the Border Patrol in that it required more than 170 men out of a total of 750 in 1951 to process and examine legal "aliens" being brought in under contract.[41]

Senator Hubert Humphrey of Minnesota told Mackey and Willard Kelley of the INS in the course of their testimony that until Congress gave them some more money he would "never be convinced that a majority around here are sincere about wanting to do anything about the wetback problem."[42] Kelly concurred, adding that the INS was becoming a "little cynical" about the whole matter.

In fact, Kelley added, "It would almost seem that the reason for the failure of the United States to properly protect its border is to make way for the illegal entry of cheap alien labor into certain privileged areas."[43]

Reductions in budget and personnel in 1953 and 1954 appeared to underscore Kelly's remarks, as 1953 witnessed a further decrease in the number of Border Patrol personnel. While a 1954 bill before Congress gave the INS an additional thirty-nine million dollars, only two-and-one-half million dollars of it was earmarked for the Border Patrol. Of this amount, only one-sixth was allocated for the prevention of illegal entry from Mexico and Canada, with the remaining sum earmarked for activities connected with immigration from Europe and Asia.[44] It should be noted that two-thirds of the personnel of the Border Patrol was situated along the southwestern border and that this area was receiving only one-sixth of the allocation, some of which was allocated to carry on operations along the Canadian border.[45]

In addition to a strong congressional bloc that could mobilize its resources when necessary, the INS and its Border Patrol had also to contend with local interest groups determined to undermine any effort at closing the border. Immigration officials were well aware that local cooperation was essential if they were to carry out their responsibilities in an effective manner. However, they also realized that such cooperation from local grower groups would not be forthcoming. To make matters worse officials could expect little community cooperation and support, as many communities relied on local growers to support their economy by providing jobs for residents, markets for local businesses, and investments. Given this reliance and the fact that these men were often influential citizens, it is little wonder that many communities shared, in large part, the prevailing negative attitudes of growers toward Mexicans and the Border Patrol. Certainly acquiring increased funding was not the sole solution to the enforcement problem. As long as the community countenanced the employment and exploitation of undocumented workers, there was little that enforcement agencies could do to halt the illegal entry of workers.

No where was this more clearly demonstrated than in the Rio Grande Valley of Texas, an area where large concentrations of undocumented workers lived and worked. Because of the blacklisting of Texas by the Mexican government for widespread bracero contract violations during the 1940s, many Texans had turned to using undocumented workers instead of braceros. The practice was so common that many employers in that state had come to view the hiring of undocumented workers as an inherent right. From their perspective they were entitled to get the labor necessary to harvest their crops, and they were not about to allow anyone, especially the INS, to upset an economy of many years' standing. Thus it was that in 1951 a proposal was set forth by members of the South Texas (Growers) Association that the Valley Chamber of Commerce join them in bringing an end to the red tape associated with contracting braceros and in working to limit the effectiveness of the Border Patrol.[46] According to General

Manager R. C. (Tommy) Tomkins, the South Texas Association had set a goal of $50,000 in order to finance lobbying activities in Washington and Mexico City. Although discussions at the initial planning meeting were supposed to be kept in strictest confidence, information leaks disclosed that the organization was going to fight to block further appropriations aimed at augmenting the Border Patrol's personnel. It also sought to cut off funding for support of the airlift initiated by the Border Patrol.[47] Just how much influence this group actually had and how successful they were in raising the necessary funds is not known. However, they were not alone in their sentiments; and the repeated cuts in the budget of the INS and the repeated failure to increase appropriations to support Border Patrol activities is testimony to the overall effectiveness of local interest groups and their representatives in Congress in achieving some of their goals.

The influence of interest groups can be seen in the series of proposals from 1951 to 1952 designed to provide funding to deal with the so-called Mexican border problem. For example, on 25 July 1951, President Harry Truman, who had expressed deep concern over the increasing number of illegal entrants from Mexico, requested a $6,500,000 supplement for fiscal year 1952. Some three weeks later, on 17 August 1951, the House committee reduced the figure to $4,000,000. Three days later, on 20 August 1951, by floor action the House voted to eliminate the entire item.[48]

In October of 1951 a Senate committee recommended that $3,000,000 be restored in order to effect border operations. The Senate acquiesced and passed the bill. On 19 October 1951, a Joint Committee of Conference reduced it to $1,000,000, an amount subsequently approved on 7 November by the Supplemental Appropriation Act of 1952.[49]

On 14 February 1952, President Truman requested a supplemental estimate of $2,000,000 for the INS for fiscal year 1952. The House Committee recommended a sum of $1,390,000. The entire amount was eliminated by floor action in the House on 13 March 1952.[50] However, the Senate later restored the proposed $1,390,000 on 22 April, following action by a Senate committee on 10 April 1952. On 3 June, a Joint Committee of Conference recommended that this amount be approved. On 5 June the supplemental estimate was granted under the Third Supplemental Appropriations Act (Public Law 375).[51]

The INS budget for fiscal 1953 requested an additional $4,001,000 in order to continue the border program covered by Public Law 375. A House committee recommended on 28 March that the amount be reduced by $1,000,000. The House felt otherwise and voted to eliminate the entire item from the INS budget. An appeal by Commissioner of Immigration Argyle Mackey to a Senate committee was of little avail, and the additional funds requested were not granted to the INS.[52]

In summary, it seems apparent that Congress never intended to adequately finance the INS to control illegal immigration. Senators and representatives from the border states successfully led the fight for reduced appropriations. They and their constituents fully understood that "with the purse half shut the gate could remain half open."[53]

The INS and its supporters fared little better in their efforts to have penalty legislation enacted against those who employed or harbored undocumented workers. However, the battle for penalty legislation was not so one-sided as the battle for increased appropriations, for the INS received support from a variety of interest groups and social-reform organizations. The movement for penalty legislation was also pushed along by the Mexican government, which had long advocated such measures.

At times the international situation provided Mexico with needed leverage in pressing for its demands. Such an opportunity arose with the outbreak of the Korean War, which once again increased the demand for Mexican labor in the United States. Taking as much advantage of the opportunity as it possibly could Mexico demanded stricter contract guarantees for its braceros and penalties for those who employed undocumented workers.[54] While some officials recognized the validity of Mexico's demands with regard to bracero contracts and penalty legislation, they still balked at the idea of proposing such legislation because of the storm of controversy it would arouse in the United States. Officials were well aware of the great power that could be marshalled by the farm bloc in order to defeat such proposals, and few were willing to stake their careers in supporting something which would inevitably go down to defeat in Congress.

In spite of Mexico's strong bargaining position, it failed in its efforts to have penalty legislation enacted. Instead it had to settle for a weak provision in Public Law 78, which denied employers of "illegals" the right to contract braceros.[55] While some proponents of Public Law 78 hailed it as an effective measure for curtailing illegal entry, others recognized that it contained too many loopholes to be effective. Among those who held this view was Truman, who had signed the bill reluctantly because of its lack of provisions for penalizing employers for hiring "illegals." Commenting on the law, Truman stated that it did little to address the issue of undocumented workers; he urged the Congress to pass supplemental legislation that would impose criminal penalties on those who concealed, harbored, or smuggled in "wetbacks."[56] It should be noted that Truman did not include a request for penalties against employers, probably because of his belief that such legislation would have little chance of passing in Congress and that the courts would never uphold such a provision. At any rate Truman failed even in getting penalties against those engaged in smuggling or harboring "illegals."

Understandably, Mexico was not totally satisfied with the new bracero agreement. Even though it had gone into the bargaining with pretty good leverage, much of that had dissipated as negotiations progressed because of the powerful influence wielded by the farm bloc and their legislative representatives. Nonetheless, Mexico chose to view its setback over the "wetback" issue as only temporary, realizing that the bracero agreement would have to be renegotiated. Furthermore, Mexican officials could not afford to drop the issue, as its press had given wide publicity to the "wetback" question. After the 1950 Agreement the Mexican press demanded that its government not renew the bracero agreement with the United States in 1951 unless that country enacted strong "anti-wetback" measures.[57] Between 1950 and 1953 Mexico's position on the subject became more rigid because of public pressure, the increasing numbers of illegal emigrants, and stories concerning the abuse and exploitation of "illegals" by employers and by enforcement agencies in the United States.[58] Mexico's increasingly rigid stance over penalty legislation made it apparent to United States negotiators that there existed a direct correlation between the number of "wetbacks" and the manner in which negotiations progressed on the contract labor program.[59] Meanwhile, there was growing support for penalty legislation on the part of many groups who were moved to action for a variety of reasons.

One such group was organized labor, which opposed the entry of "illegals" because it believed that they depressed wages and disrupted unionization efforts by acting as strikebreakers. In the eyes of many labor leaders a tacit agreement existed between Immigration Service officials and powerful growers whereby the INS ignored the presence of undocumented workers during the harvest season.[60] George Weber, the AFL organizer in the Southwest, called the undocumented worker "the number one enemy of organized labor at the border."[61] In 1950 labor attributed an economic downswing and increased unemployment in the Southwest to the large number of "illegals" and braceros in the region. While little was said about the presence of braceros, given that the AFL-CIO had never really opposed the bracero program as such, labor leaders made a great deal of commotion over the rising influx of "illegals" from Mexico. Although the economic downswing receded and employment opportunities increased because of the outbreak of the Korean War, labor was quick to point out that so long as no control was placed on illegal immigration from Mexico and no penalties were imposed on those who employed them, there would continue to exist the danger of a similar occurrence in the future. Other labor leaders warned that "wetbacks" not only depressed wages but also served as a shield for communist infiltration.[62] While this was somewhat doubtful, there were those who were not prepared to take a chance when it came to communism. In 1954 Senator Pat McCarran also made a similar charge, claiming that communist agents were among the "wetbacks" who crossed the Rio Grande. This led the Senate Internal Security Subcommittee, chaired by William E. Jenner of Indiana, to appoint McCarran and Senator Herman Welker from Idaho, to conduct an investigation of this matter.[63] However, labor's efforts to control the influx and to have penalty legislation enacted by Congress met with failure because of the power of the farm bloc, labor's relative weakness in the political sphere, and the lack of a coordinated effort with other groups and organizations with similar goals.[64]

Social reformers and religious groups also intensified their efforts to have Congre enact penalty legislation. Such efforts in the past had usually failed because of the lack of coordination among the various groups, public apathy concerning the issue of "illegals," the power of the farm bloc, and a general lack of attention paid to the implications of the influx by the popular media. This began to change in the early 1950s when the "wetback phenomenon" began to receive an increasing amount of exposure in the popular media. Journals, magazines, newspapers, reports, and radio programs ran countless articles and programs on the accompanying evils of this so-called invasion. The majority of the information dealt with the negative aspects of such immigration and attributed increased problems in health, disease, crime, narcotics, soaring welfare costs, and infiltration by subversives to the mass influx of "illegals."[65]

In 1952 a crime survey of Arizona, New Mexico, Texas, and southern California attributed 11.5 percent of the crimes committed in those states to "wetbacks."[66] Austin W. Mathis, M.D., health officer from Imperial County, California, called the Valley a "powder keg . . . as far as communicable diseases go," because of the large concentration of "illegals" there.[67] The President's Commission on Migratory Labor report characterized the infant mortality rate along the Texas-Mexican border as high. According to the report, infant mortality represented one of the most sensitive indicators of the state of public health. Defined as the number of deaths under one year of age per 1,000 live births, in 1948 the mortality rate for the United States was 32 for every 1,000 live births. In Texas, the statewide average was 46.2. However, this rate climbed to 79.5 deaths for every 1,000 live births in the 28 countries of Texas on or immediately adjacent to the border. In the three counties of the lower Rio Grande Valley, the infant mortality rates were startlingly high. Cameron County's rate was 82.5, Hidalgo County's average 107.2, and Willacy County's ran as high as 127.6.[68] Other counties in Texas, Arizona, New Mexico, and California that also had high concentrations of "illegals" tended to have correspondingly high rates of infant mortality, according to the report.[69]

In 1954 Willard F. Kelley of the INS wrote about the high number of illegitimate births in counties containing large numbers of "illegals." For example, Riverside County in California reported that as many as 900 illegitimate births occurred each year, most of which were attributed to "illegals." The report also claimed that a high percentage of the "illegals" in the area were dependent on county care. According to Kelley, these facts were reflected in soaring welfare costs for such counties, not only for hospitalization and health care but also for removal of "aliens" to Mexicali, which cost the county 75 dollars per case.[70] Kelley concluded that officials did not pretend that they could accurately compute the costs of the "wetback" to the taxpayer. However, wrote Kelley, "one county supervisor said he could clearly trace to him in one way or another twenty-seven cents out of every tax dollar."[71]

Opponents of the "wetback" influx compiled an imposing arsenal of facts, figures, and studies to bolster their arguments for more stringent enforcement along the border and for penalty legislation against smugglers and employers of "illegal aliens." The problem was that a clear distinction was seldom made as to whether "illegals" actually contributed to, for example, the crime problem or whether they were more victims than victimizers. What people mainly referred to was that crime increased in areas that contained high concentrations of "illegals" without really stopping to study just what this meant. A similar view could be set forth concerning health statistics, whose accuracy could be questioned. Would people so afraid of being apprehended risk being exposed, even to take advantage of health-care services? Furthermore, most "illegals" could speak or comprehend little English, which often deterred them from seeking aid. Finally, there was the whole psychological aspect of someone entering the bowels of any institution with all of its formalized rituals, forms, and bureaucracy. Would many "illegals" choose to expose themselves to this kind of cultural shock in a strange country? These of course are difficult questions to answer, for the answer largely depends on the individual and his or her needs and background. Nonetheless, many of the facts and figures so often quoted were in reality "guesstimates" and difficult to substantiate. At times the issue became confused by all the information and misinformation floating around. Was the concern expressed by opponents of the "illegals" based on the exploitation of these people? Was it based on a desire to identify and hopefully solve some of the social ills plaguing the country? Was it the desire of anti-wetback groups to attach an onus to anyone who employed or smuggled "illegals" by emphasizing and perhaps exaggerating the ills created by the illegal influx? Or was it a combination of these things? The answer is difficult to ascertain. One thing becomes apparent from all this. Whether it was done intentionally or not, the tendency was to vilify the "wetback" and to depict him or her in largely negative terms. Thus many tended to perceive the "wetback" as a problem rather than as a human being or as the symptom of much larger social and economic problems in both Mexico and the United States.

In confronting the issue of illegal immigration Mexican Americans often found themselves in dire straits. Should they oppose illegal immigration and espouse penalty legislation? What about the idea of turning "illegals" in to the authorities or preventing their exploitation by Anglo and Mexican American alike? This was a real dilemma, given that most "illegals" were of Mexican descent. Further complicating the issue was that illegal immigration from Mexico directly affected Mexican Americans through job displacement, lowered wage scales, or the belief that "illegals" further retarded assimilation efforts. Largely as a result of the impact that "illegals" had upon Mexican Americans, they and their organizations generally supported stricter control of the border and penalty legislation against employers.

In 1952 Senator Hubert Humphrey of Minnesota held hearings on the question of migratory labor in the United States. Exponents of penalty legislation and of a closed border found Humphrey strongly sympathetic to their goals. Among those testifying at the subcommittee hearings were a number of Mexican Americans, much of whose testimony reflected a concern about the negative effects illegal immigration had on the Mexican American community in the Southwest.

According to Jacinto Cota, a migrant worker from the Imperial Valley in California, the "wetbacks" were "poison" to people such as himself, for they were willing to work for the most meager of wages.[72] Gus García, General Counsel for the American G.I. Forum of Texas, testified that something had to be done to bring the situation under control and asked that the Immigration and Naturalization Service be given the authority to do the job they really wanted to do. He was supportive of the idea of airlifting apprehended "aliens" into the interior of Mexico, something which had proven effective in 1951, he said, until outcries from grower interests had brought an end to it. While the motives of the growers in Texas had been clear, García indicated, they had attempted to veil them by charging that the airlift was cruel to Mexicans.[73]

García told Humphrey's subcommittee that he believed that illegal immigration had also served to increase racial discrimination against Mexican Americans because it had accentuated tensions between Anglo and Mexican Americans. In García's opinion, this had led to "an aggravation of practices of discrimination and segregation springing up where none had existed before." According to García, signs began to appear in public places reading "No Mexicans allowed" where none had been seen before. "We have had an increased number of violations of civil rights where none had occurred before," said García.[74]

In many ways García's testimony was misleading and incorrect. Discrimination and segregation against Mexicans, whether citizens, braceros, or "illegals," had been part and parcel of the mores of many communities and had roots dating back to the 1820s, when Anglo-Americans had begun settling in lands belonging to Mexico. The image of the lazy, shiftless peon or of the cruel, bloodthirsty bandido were commonly accepted stereotypes and were often used in rationalizing the poor treatment people of Mexican descent received at the hands of Anglos. Although the presence of "wetbacks" might have served to reinforce negative feelings and beliefs, they by no means were responsible for creating the conditions García described in his testimony.[75]

Not only were "illegals" accused of lowering wages scales, disrupting unionization efforts, and increasing welfare costs, disease, and crime rates, but they were also viewed as responsible for low educational achievement in certain areas of the country. This was one of the findings in *The Uneducated*, a study initiated by Dwight D. Eisenhower while he was president of Columbia University, which revealed a striking correlation between areas having large numbers of "illegals" and high rates of illiteracy.[76] The high rate of illiteracy was revealed by rejection rates for military service in World War II. According to the study, high rejection rates were found south of a line drawn from El Paso to Houston, an area which included two-thirds or more of the Spanish-speaking population of Texas. While the statewide rejection average for Texas was 63 per 1,000, the rate in the counties along the Rio Grande Valley was just under 400 per 1,000.[77] The study indicated that Mexicans and Mexican Americans generally had low achievement scores, poor attendance records, and large numbers of dropouts. According to the findings, much of this was due to the heavy seasonal migration these people undertook because of job displacement by undocumented workers.[78] Thus the study placed much of the blame for the educational problems of Mexican Americans on the shoulders of the "illegals" and made little mention of the institutional barriers that contributed to the problem.

"Illegals" did have a few defenders, like Pauline Kibbe of the Texas Good Neighbor Commission, who considered them a humble and needy people who were encouraged to violate the immigration laws of the United States by what she termed "a fifth column in Texas."[79] A great majority of the people, however, simply viewed them as invaders and a problem, a view perhaps best summarized by an immigration official who described the large influx of "illegals" as "the greatest peacetime invasion ever complacently suffered by any country under open, flagrant, contemptuous violations of its laws."[80]

Of course, most undocumented workers did not view themselves as dangerous, malicious, or subversive. Instead, they thought largely in terms of their needs and their survival. This view was best exemplified in the following exchange between an undocumented Mexican worker who was brought before a judge for having repeatedly entered illegally. The judge asked the man: "Don't you respect the laws of this country?" To which he replied, "Our necessities know no law."[81]

Reports such as those issued by the President's Commission on Migratory Labor and the publication of studies such as "What Price Wetbacks," written, according to its authors, in an effort to "produce a document which no politicians or newspaper men could dismiss as an unfounded smear,"[82] along with a concomitant growth of media coverage and increased pressure by various groups and organizations, all served to revitalize the efforts of those legislators who had in the past expressed concern about illegal entry and the lack of measures taken to prevent it. The result was renewed activity in Congress for the next few years to rectify this situation and a growing hope among some INS officials that they would finally be given more power with which to carry out their duties.

Most of the congressmen and senators who advocated stronger "anti-wetback" measures came from the Northeast and Midwest. Their support of these measures was due to a variety of reasons. Some favored penalty measures for employers and increased appropriations for the INS because of their ties with labor groups who had consistently fought for stronger regulation of the border. Others supported these measures because of a growing number of complaints from agricultural constituents who argued that they could not compete in the agricultural market with those who used cheap "wetback" labor.[83] Still others were concerned about the ill effects in the social and economic spheres which were increasingly being attributed to the illegal influx, while a few expressed concern that "illegals" would soon penetrate further northward in search of industrial work if nothing were done to discourage their entry. Finally, there were those who either resented or were quite baffled by the conflicting policies concerning Mexican labor and who wanted to impose some rational consistency in the area of immigration regulation. As one senator wryly remarked: "We shall be using more than a million dollars in the next 2½ months to get Mexican laborers into our country legally, and at the same time the Department [of Immigration] is asking for $4,000,000 for the next 2½ months to keep illegal entrants out."[84] Because of such reasons, certain members of Congress believed that a practical solution lay in taking stronger measures against those who either smuggled, harbored, or employed "illegal aliens" from Mexico.[85]

In 1952 Representative Francis Walter of Pennsylvania authored S.1851, a bill that would make it a felony, instead of a misdemeanor, to aid anyone in entering the country illegally or to harbor or conceal an illegal entrant. The bill also aimed at correcting a hiatus in the penalty provision brought out in the 1948 Supreme Court decision in the *Evans* case. "In its decision the court ruled unenforceable various punitive provisions of the 1917 Immigration Act, holding that Congress had never supplemented the act by enacting appropriate penalty measures."[86] Much of the debate on the Walter bill centered around the question of its constitutionality and around an amendment proposed in conference by Senator Paul Douglas that would have made it a felony to employ an "alien" suspected of having entered the country illegally.

In the Senate the bill encountered opposition from different senators in the wake of the 5 February Douglas amendment.[87] Senator William Langer of North Dakota argued that if a farmer hired ten workers and one of those ten was an "illegal alien" then the farmer might fall victim to blackmail on the part of that person. To Langer it would take "less proof to send a farmer to the penitentiary for trying to harvest a crop than it would to convict a professional crook for receiving stolen property."[88] Langer termed this an unfair law, for it would also place on farmers the responsibility of guarding the borders, a job that was supposedly the responsibility of the federal government.[89] Senator John McClellan of Arkansas also opposed the amendment because it made the farmer the victim of the government's failure and inefficiency in policing the border.[90] Senator Welker of Oregon, himself a farmer in the eastern part of the state, had earlier termed Douglas' amendment "vicious" in that it singled out the farmer for punishment.[91] Senator Dennis Chavez of New Mexico held sentiments similar to those of Welker and McClellan. Yet careful reading of the amendment shows that no special reference was made to the farmer, but rather to "any person" who knowingly hired an "illegal alien."[92]

Other senators opposed the bill because they resented Mexico's refusal to renegotiate the bracero agreement until penalty legislation was approved. Among those especially perturbed by this situation were Senators Allen Ellender (Louisiana), Tom Connally (Texas), and William Knowland (California). Ellender believed that Mexico was unloading the entire "wetback" issue on the United States while itself doing nothing about the problem. Mexico, he stated, had a law on its statute

books that made it a crime punishable by fine and imprisonment if a person returned to Mexico was shown to have crossed illegally.[93] In addition, other critics
of Mexico pointed out that the Mexican government had done little to inform its
people who were planning to enter illegally about problems faced by "wetbacks"
in the United States.[94] Furthermore, Mexico had been lax in enforcing its laws
against smugglers involved in the trafficking of "illegals." Under the 1936 General
Population Law of Mexico a smuggler was subject to imprisonment for up to two
years if convicted. In 1951 this law was revised and the penalty was increased to
nine years in prison. Yet the fact remained that Mexican officials seldom apprehended, much less convicted, smugglers.

Those who believed that Mexico should assume greater responsibility for controlling illegal emigration pointed out that Article 80 of the General Population
Law of 1936 also gave it the authority to stop "wetback" crossings at the border
in that this article prohibited emigration when the public interest required it.
Articles 87 and 88 of the same law stated that Mexicans could emigrate only if
they had sufficient salaries awaiting them,[95] and that should anyone leave the
country illegally such a person could be fined up to $1,600 upon returning to
Mexico.[96]

Senator Ernest McFarland (Arizona) objected to Douglas's amendment because
its insertion would prove detrimental to the passage of S.1851 and thus serve to
impede a quick agreement with Mexico over the braceros. Furthermore McFarland saw S.1851 as merely a stopgap measure only designed to enable the farmers
of the United States to obtain the needed labor from Mexico for another six
months.[97] Douglas disagreed with McFarland's reasoning. To him acceptance of
the amendment was "the real test and the real milk in the coconut [for it would]
actually determine whether we are to have a really effective law or whether we
are to have no law at all."[98] Douglas said that his amendment was merely re-
proposing what the Senate had proposed a year earlier and had been eliminated
in conference. The argument that it was not the proper time to discuss such legislation had been used before, Douglas continued, but he believed that now was the
proper time.[99]

Both Humphrey and George Aiken of Vermont voiced support for Douglas's
amendment. Humphrey believed that some action on the whole "wetback" issue
was long overdue. Aiken was more cautious in his support of Douglas. He wanted
Douglas to modify his amendment and asked him if he would be willing to delete
the word "Mexican" from the provision. Aiken wished to have the provision on
hiring "illegals" apply to hiring "anyone" who had entered illegally. He questioned whether a law could discriminate constitutionally against "aliens" from a
particular nation. Douglas recognized the validity of his point and agreed to the
change.[100]

Douglas's amendment to S.1851 was defeated by a vote of 69 to 12, with 15
abstentions.[101] After the vote Douglas proposed a second amendment in many
ways identical to the one just voted down by a healthy margin. This time, in an

effort to gain more support for his amendment, he deleted the words "or has reasonable grounds to believe" that an "alien" had entered illegally. Douglas explained to his colleagues that he was not prepared to admit defeat. He was determined to fight for penalty legislation because of his desire "to eliminate the magnet by which large numbers of Mexicans are drawn illegally across the border. That magnet which pulls them across the border is the employment which is now open to wetbacks."[102]

In spite of his arguments, Douglas's second amendment also went down to defeat by a one-sided margin. As no further amendments were offered, S.1851 was put to a vote and passed. As approved by the Senate, S.1851 provided penalties only against those who harboured or concealed "illegal aliens."[103]

S.1851 was sent to the House for action on 6 February 1952. The bill was not well received and encountered vigorous opposition from southwestern representatives, who opposed the bill for various reasons. First, they questioned the bill's constitutionality. Second, they argued that the measure was designed to penalize one particular sector and thus lacked universality. Those who would suffer the most from S.1851 would be southwestern growers, while other employers in other parts of the country would hardly be affected at all. Third, opponents of the bill in the House resented the atmosphere of foreign coercion surrounding its consideration and debate. Opponents of the bill contended that passage of the bill would be construed as giving in to Mexican demands,[104] an idea they found distasteful. That is why they had, in the past, advocated the implementation of a simple crossing-card system so that the whole cumbersome issue of renegotiating agreements with Mexico could be dispensed with.

Some opponents of S.1851 expressed resentment over the recurring attacks and innuendos against their constituents over the "wetback" issue. They believed that the stir over the whole "wetback" issue was exaggerated and overblown. John Fiske of Texas termed the charges of widespread exploitation and abuse of "illegals" "fantastic" and "distorted." He said that those who lived along the border had come to regard such stories as "monstrous jokes."[105] A few weeks later Congressman Phillip Regan of Texas made the statement that "illegals" received wages equal to those paid to American workers employed in the same area. If "illegals" were treated so badly, querried Regan, then why did they continue to come? The fact was, he said, that they came because wages in the United States were good. Congressman Wier of New York took issue with Regan, stating that he had grown weary of hearing this during the debate over the "wetback" crisis. Such arguments, said Wier, always emanated from those areas in which the problem was most prevalent. He then accused the proponents of "wetback servitude" of always adding crippling amendments to legislative efforts in order to keep the back door of the Rio Grande open.[106]

Some of those who opposed the passage of S.1851 did so because they questioned the constitutionality of Subsection C. According to this provision, "When the Attorney General or any district director or any assistant district director of the Immigration and Naturalization Service has information indicating a reasonable probability that in any designated lands or other property aliens are illegally within the United States, he may issue a search warrant."[107] In their view this provision infringed upon the protection of the Fourth Amendment to the Constitution guaranteeing protection to citizens of the United States against unreasonable search and seizure.[108] One of the most vehement in attacking this section was Congressman Fisher of Texas, who told his colleagues that "The Constitution does not authorize search warrants for fishing expeditions."[109] He could not understand how anyone could propose, much less support, a law that would authorize "a search for the purpose of obtaining information upon which a search warrant might be legally issued in the first place." To him Subsection C was nothing more than a "blank check" that would allow the Border Patrol to harass and abuse farmers and growers.[110]

Congressman John Shelley of California disagreed with Fisher and took issue with his arguments. Shelley said that the bill permitted only the issuing of administrative warrants to six officials in the three Immigration Service districts between the Gulf of Mexico and the Pacific Coast. Furthermore, the authority to search a place would be bestowed only on one immigration official named in the warrant and that official might have to cover hundreds of thousands of acres. Finally, provisions in S.1851 limited the use of the warrant to a certain specified time of the day or night and placed a thirty-day time limit on its use. Thus Subsection C did not really threaten anyone's constitutional rights, according to Shelley. In fact the law, if enacted, would impose so many restrictions on the issue and exercise of a warrant that it would practically be a useless piece of paper.[111] Subsection C, in Shelley's opinion, was a farce. What was really needed, he told his colleagues, was to give border officials more authority and more personnel. "No law," he said, "is any better than its enforcement provisions. S.1851, without more drastic powers for uncovering evidence of violators, would be hardly better than no law at all."[112]

Shelley had not finished. Looking over to some of the more outspoken congressmen from the Southwest he levelled a final blast at the ones he deemed responsible for such an emasculated version. The debate over the bill and its contents had once again pointed up to Shelley and others the power that large grower interests exercised in Congress. Shelley continued. If his fellow legislators allowed the bill to pass with all of its loopholes intact and if they accepted the provision that "employment (including the usual and normal practices incident to employment) shall not be deemed to constitute harboring," then such an act would be tantamount to a "mandate from Congress that farming corporations are a privileged class, and that they may not be interfered with in their pernicious practices." Furthermore, said Shelley, "it would constitute a barefaced admission that our only reason for passing the bill is to throw a sop to the Government and people of Mexico who demand that we do something to clean house before they will permit any more of their contract nationals to cross the border."[113]

In spite of his impassioned arguments, Shelley's efforts to muster support for a stronger bill failed. Since little further was said on the matter, the members of the House passed S.1851 in an amended form. The bill was then returned to the Senate on 26 February 1952. Because neither chamber accepted the other's version of the bill, a conference was called between them.[114] As finally passed, S.1851 did not contain the provision that would have given the Attorney General, the district director, or the assistant district director the authority to issue a search warrant. Instead the measure stated that search warrants were to be issued by a federal court.[115] Final action on the bill was completed by Congress on 13 March, and President Truman signed it into law on 20 March 1952. S.1851, which became Public Law 283, stood as the sum total of federal legislation to control "wetbacks" for the next eight years.[116]

Public Law 283 granted the Immigration Service about the same general authority as that held by a game warden.[117] It permitted immigration officials to search property without a warrant within twenty-five miles of the border. It made it a felony to aid anyone in entering the country illegally or to harbor or conceal anyone who had entered illegally. However, according to Public Law 283, employing illegal entrants did not constitute harboring.

In a 1952 editorial, the *New York Times* criticized Congress for its failure to enact penalty legislation against those who employed "illegals."

> It is remarkable how some of the same Senators and Representatives who are all for enacting the most rigid barriers against immigration from Southern Europe suffer from a sudden blindness when it comes to protecting the southern border of the United States. This peculiar weakness is most noticeable among members from Texas and the Southwest, where the wetbacks happen to be primarily employed.[118]

CONCLUSION

The debates and discussions surrounding increased appropriations for the Immigration and Naturalization Service and the enactment of penalty legislation prior to "Operation Wetback" demonstrated the importance of pressure politics and interest groups. While the so-called farm bloc was a force to be reckoned with, other factors contributed to its ability to consistently defeat increased appropriations for the INS as well as efforts to pass effective penalty legislation against those who employed undocumented workers. At times the farm bloc was helped along by its opponents. Certainly the events surrounding the appropriations battles and the debates over S.1851 bring this out.

The Border Patrol, like any other government agency whose work is of direct interest to various groups, is sensitive to the political configuration of a given time. For the most part it appears that the Border Patrol had little difficulty with grower interests as long as it confined its efforts to curtailing smuggling activities and making token raids against undocumented workers once the harvest season had ended. If anything, the evidence indicates that the Border Patrol was in fact subservient to the growers. From outward appearance it seems that those in positions of authority within the INS were fairly content with this state of affairs. In return for a lack of zeal on the part of the Border Patrol, grower interests and their representatives were content to provide the Border Patrol enough funds to operate at minimal levels.

However, the complacency of these groups changed as the INS was increasingly called upon to enforce the immigration laws along the southwestern border and to curtail the illegal influx from Mexico. This change placed the INS squarely between two warring factions, each of which accused the Border Patrol of being a tool used by the other to achieve its goals. The Border Patrol's lackluster record became ready ammunition in the hands of detractors, and certainly the most effective in using such ammunition were the grower interests. Soon the Border Patrol was enmeshed in a vicious circle. Enforcing the laws and effective performance of duty further antagonized representatives and growers dependent on illegal labor. Generally speaking, such antagonism adversely affected the Border Patrol's chances for increased appropriations. On the other hand, failure to carry out its responsibilities would expose it to charges of inefficiency and subservience to the interest of growers bent on exploiting "wetback" labor.

Interestingly enough, the farm bloc also used the Border Patrol's inefficiency to have appropriations reduced or blocked. They had little trouble in convincing other members of Congress that no increased funds should be forthcoming until the INS had shown that the borders were being effectively patrolled with what had already been given it. Border Patrol officials responded that this would not be possible until they had sufficient funding to purchase needed equipment and to hire added personnel. Thus the vicious circle. Effective control antagonized powerful elements. Lax enforcement led to demands on the INS to make better use of what they had before asking for more. Either way the INS was placed in a poor and extremely vulnerable position.

Further complicating matters and adding to the agony of its situation, the INS found itself plagued by poor organization, poor leadership, low morale, lack of support from the communities in which it worked, outdated equipment, contradictory national policies with regard to labor immigration, insufficient personnel, and very little in the way of laws to aid its officials in controlling the influx of undocumented workers.

Legislative efforts to impose penalties against those who smuggled, concealed, harbored, or employed undocumented workers also experienced rough sailing.

From the outset S.1851 had a great number of things working against its passage, at least in a form that would make it an effective piece of legislation to help control the influx of "illegals."

The brevity of debates in both the Senate and the House on the bill pointed out that the bill had few supporters. Once again the forces of opposition were led by those supportive of grower interests, and once again many factors favored their stance. First and perhaps foremost was the knowledge that they had the necessary votes either to defeat the bill or to so weaken it by crippling amendments that it would pose little threat to the interests of their constituents. Although the farm bloc was not a monolithic organization that agreed on all issues pertaining to agriculture, it nonetheless possessed the ability to draw together when it needed to. By and large they had little to fear from "the other side," which was plagued by a lack of organization. Furthermore, representatives sympathetic to labor, small farmers, and migrant workers constituted a small minority in both houses that often opposed the farm bloc for different reasons. More often than not they were frustrated in their efforts to enact legislation such as S.1851 primiarily because it was so diluted that they themselves either were forced to vote against it or abstained from voting altogether.

Another factor that favored the farm bloc and worked against the antiwetback, antibracero forces was their inability to swing uncommitted legislators to their cause. Richard Craig has described the struggle over bracero legislation as "a classic example of pork barreling among legislators." Generally speaking, representatives from the midwestern and northwestern states supported southwestern interests simply because they could not be convinced that the importation of braceros was detrimental to their interests. It was not uncommon for legislators to confuse or to equate "illegals" with braceros or vice versa. They often became impatient with the so-called bleeding-heart urban liberals from the Northeast. They could not understand what all the hullaballoo was about. Their attitude was that the Mexicans, whether legal or illegal, were confined to the Southwest and were therefore the concern of the Southwest. They were not prepared to lose southwestern votes for their pet legislation over a bunch of Mexicans or overzealous liberals.

Things were not much better for antiwetback groups such as labor. Labor too was plagued by a series of handicaps that needed to be overcome before they could launch an effective campaign against the vise-like grip growers exercised in Congress.

There had been a ray of hope when Truman had added his voice to the call for penalty legislation. However, it had not been the characteristic call of the feisty President. It had been more of a garbled whisper, for he had called for penalties against only those who harbored, smuggled, or concealed "illegals." His remarks to Congress and the public had made no mention of penalties against employers and thus had compromised the issue before it was actually brought up for debate in Congress. Nonetheless, had circumstances permitted, Truman might have come out more strongly and openly in favor of penalty legislation against employers. However, he believed that the courts would never uphold legislation designed to penalize employers. Second, he might have viewed such legislation as discriminatory against the agricultural sector, and he was still mindful of the important role that group had played in his stunning election victory in 1948.

Furthermore, the farm problem was a thorny issue, and perhaps he wanted to avoid widening the rift that had developed between him and farm groups. Fourth, he knew that he did not have the necessary support in Congress to enact such legislation. Fifth, he probably believed that any legislation designed to deal with the "wetback problem" represented a positive step that might help convince Mexico of his country's sincere desire to do something about the border situation. He might have been happy to take whatever he could get rather than to risk having nothing enacted.

Because of the limitations imposed on Truman and sympathetic legislators, labor needed to take more positive steps to achieve its goals; but labor too was plagued by a lack of organization and the absence of a solid plan of action. Labor had already taken a beating with the passage of the Taft-Hartley Act, and most of its energies were directed at overturning it and to closing ranks by merging the AFL and CIO. When United States labor did turn its attention to the issue of Mexican labor it found itself confronted by a major roadblock, the stance of the Mexican unions.

Generally speaking, the AFL and the CIO had not objected to the bracero program. In fact they had often joined forces with their Mexican counterparts in order to obtain fair treatment for braceros and more effective grievance procedures. When the 1951 economic downswing brought about increased unemployment, the union leadership decided to take more aggressive steps to deal with the question of Mexican labor. However, they chose to focus their attack not on the bracero, but on the undocumented worker. They chose this focus because they knew that their chances for having the bracero program terminated by Congress were almost nil. In a similar vein, labor leaders realized that an attack on the bracero program might well serve to alienate the powerful CTM labor union in Mexico, whose position on the bracero program fell in line with the official Mexican view of desiring the existence of the program. Like their government the Mexican labor unions favored a continuation of the program so long as braceros were well treated and did not suffer undue or excessive discrimination in the United States.

Given this situation the AFL, the primary power in this effort, decided to deal with the "illegal" situation, as leaders of this organization recognized that Mexico and its unions had long advocated stronger measures on the part of the United States to control illegal immigration. As expected, the support for penalty legislation was forthcoming, but it did little to shift the balance of power, in part because of the failure of the AFL and CIO to implement fully a coordinated effort. Unionism in agriculture was still in its embryonic stages and thus lacked the influence or support even within its own ranks to mount a strong and effective legislative campaign.

Yet in spite of the failures in 1951 and 1952 to gain increased appropriations and strict penalty legislation against employers, there were a few bright spots in the fabric for antiwetback and antibracero groups. The legislative support was in many ways perhaps the most aggressive launched to date. It had helped identify potential new allies as well as problems and issues that had to be resolved within their ranks before they could hope to take on effectively the entrenched power of agribusiness.

NOTES

1. John M. Myers, *The Border Wardens* (Englewood Cliffs, N.J.: Prentice-Hall Inc., 1971), pp. 15-16 and 24-25.

2. Ibid., pp. 33-34.

3. Ibid., p. 57. An executive order issued on 10 June 1933 combined the previously separate bureaus of Immigration and Naturalization into the Immigration and Naturalization Service.

4. Arthur F. Corwin, "Causes of Mexican Emigration to the United States: A Summary Review," p. 625, in *Dislocation and Emigration: The Social Background of American Immigration,* vol. 7 of *Perspectives in American History,* ed. Donald Fleming and Bernard Bailyn (Cambridge: Harvard University, Charles Warren Center for Studies in American History, 1974).

5. Richard T. Jarnagin, "The Effect of Increased Illegal Mexican Migration upon the Organization and Operations of the United States Immigration Border Patrol, Southwest Region" (Master's thesis, University of Southern California, January, 1957), p. 174.

6. The only year that no decline in personnel was registered was 1952. Ibid., p. 91.

7. Ibid., p. 95.

8. *See*, for example, U.S. Congress, House, *Congressional Record,* 82d Cong., 2d sess., 1952, 98, pt. 2: 2200-03.

9. Robert D. Tomasek, "The Political and Economic Implications of Mexican Labor in the United States under the Non-Quota System, Contract Labor Program, and Wetback Movement" (Ph.D. diss., University of Michigan, 1957), p. 149.

10. Report of the President's Commission on Immigration and Naturalization, *Whom We Shall Welcome* (Washington, D.C.: G.P.O., 1953), p. 128.

11. U.S., Senate, *Migratory Labor,* Hearings Before the Subcommittee on Labor and Labor-Management Relations of the Committee on Labor and Public Welfare, Part 1, 82d Cong., 2d sess., February and March 1952 (Washington, D.C.: G.P.O., 1952), pp. 323-40, *passim* (hereafter cited as *Migratory Labor,* hearings, 1952).

12. U.S., Congress, House, *Reorganization of the Immigration and Naturalization Service,* Hearings before the Subcommittee on Legal and Monetary Affairs of the Committee on Governmental Operations, 84th Cong., 1st sess., 9, 17 March 1955, p. 33 (hereafter cited as *Reorganization Hearings, 1955*).

13. Lyle Saunders and Olen E. Leonard, "The Wetback in the Lower Rio Grande Valley of Texas," in *Inter-American Education,* Occasional Papers 7 (Austin: University of Texas, 1951), pp. 77-78.

14. *Reorganization Hearings, 1955,* p. 13.

15. President's Commission on Migratory Labor, *Stenographic Report of the Phoenix, Arizona, Hearings on Migrant Labor, August 7 and 8* (Washington, D.C.: Ward and Paul Official Reporters, 1950), p. 166.

16. President's Commission on Migratory Labor, *Migratory Labor in American Agriculture* (Washington, D.C.: G.P.O., 1951), p. 78.

17. U.S., Congress, House, *Congressional Record,* 81st Cong., 1st sess., 1949, 95, pt. 13, Appendix, p. A2283.

18. *Migratory Labor in American Agriculture,* p. 76.

19. Ibid., p. 152.

20. Quoted in Stan Steiner, *La Raza: The Mexican Americans* (New York: Harper and Row, 1969), p. 128.

21. "The Wetback Problem of the Southwest," p. 2, in Secretary of Agriculture, Member, Records of the President's Committee on Migratory Labor, 1941-1963, Box 94, A72-8, Folder-Migratory Labor-Mexican Agricultural Laborers in the United States, Dwight D. Eisenhower Library, Abilene, Kansas (hereafter cited as "The Wetback Problem").

22. Ibid., p. 3.

23. *Migratory Labor in American Agriculture*, p. 78.

24. Foreign Service Dispatch from American Embassy, Mexico, D.F., to Department of State (17 July 1952), in R.G. 166, Foreign Agricultural Service, Narrative Reports, 1950-1954, Box 299, Folder-Mexico, Labor, 1952-1951, National Archives, Washington, D.C.

25. "The Wetbacks Are Back," *Texas Observer* (19 September 1956), clipping found in Box 4, Folder Texas, in Records of the President's Commission on Migratory Labor, 1941-1963, D.D.E.L.

26. Tomasek, "The Political and Economic Implications," p. 140.

27. "Down in the Valley: A Supplementary Report on Developments in the Wetback and Bracero Situation of the Lower Rio Grande Valley of Texas Since Publication of 'What Price Wetbacks?' " (Texas State Federation of Labor, Jerry R. Holleman, Executive Secretary, A.S. McLellan, Consultant: Austin, Tex. 1953), p. 2.

28. Ibid.

29. Ibid.

30. Don Wiggins, "Influx of 'Wetbacks' Snags Border Patrol; 30,000 Enter Yearly," Los Angeles *Daily News* (21 December 1953).

31. John McBride, *Vanishing Bracero: Valley Revolution* (San Antonio, Tex.: The Naylor Company, 1963), p. 2.

32. Ibid.

33. Ibid., p. 139; U.S., Congress, House, *Congressional Record,* 82nd Cong., 1st sess., 1951, 97, pt. 5: 954.

34. Tomasek, "The Political and Economic Implications," p. 150.

35. Ibid.

36. U.S., Congress, House, *Congressional Record,* 82d Cong., 2d sess., 1952, 98, pt. 2: 22.

37. In 1953, the Border Patrol had requested an additional 355 men. However, the Republican revision of what had been a Democratic budget not only removed this item but further cut the force by 200 men. "Wetbacks in the Middle of the Border War," *Business Week* (24 October 1953), p. 66.

38. Myers, *Border Wardens,* p. 122.

39. U.S., Congress, House, *Congressional Record,* 83d Cong., 2d sess., 1954, 100, pt. 6: 8139.

40. U.S., Congress, Senate, *Migratory Labor.* Hearings before the subcommittee on Labor and Labor-Management Relations of the Committee on Labor and Public Welfare, 82d Cong., 206 sess., pt. I, 5, 6, 7, 11, 14, 15, 17, 28, 29 February, 27 and 28 March 1952 (Washington, D.C.: G.P.O., 1952), p. 738-45, *passim* (hereafter cited as *Migratory Labor Hearings,* 1952).

41. Ibid., p. 743.

42. Ibid.

43. Ibid.

44. U.S., Congress, House, *Congressional Record,* 83d Cong., 2d sess., 1954, 98, pt. 1: 8127.

45. Jarnagin, "The Effect of Increased Illegal Mexican Immigration," p. 92.

46. "Valley C.C. Ponders Joining Labor Fight," *San Antonio Express* (5 October 1951).

47. Ibid.; Hoyt Hager, "Antilabor Squeeze Group Discussed by Citrus Agency," Corpus Christi (Texas) *Caller-Times* (4 October 1951).

48. U.S., Congress, House, *Congressional Record,* 82d Cong., 2d sess., 1952, 98, pt. 2: 8120.

49. Ibid.

50. Ibid.

51. Ibid.

52. Ibid.

53. Ernesto Galarza, *Merchants of Labor: The Mexican Bracero Story* (Charlotte: Mc-Nally and Loftin, 1964), p. 61.

54. Ellis W. Hawley, "The Politics of the Mexican Labor Issue, 1950-1965," *Agricultural History* 40, no. 3 (July, 1966): 159.

55. Richard Craig, *The Bracero Program: Interest Groups and Foreign Policy* (Austin: University of Texas Press, 1971), p. 74.

56. Harvey A. Levenstein, *Labor Organizations in the United States and Mexico* (Westport, Conn.: Greenwood Press, 1971), p. 206.

57. Craig, *The Bracero Program,* p. 94.

58. "Newspaper Publicity Relating to Matters Concerning Mexican Agricultural Workers," Report from the American Embassy, Mexico, D.F., to the Department of State (24 March 1950), in Record Group 166, Box 299, Mexican Folder, 1948-1950, National Archives, Washington, D.C.

59. Tomasek, "The Political and Economic Implications," p. 187.

60. George I. Sanchez and Lyle Saunders, "Wetback: A Preliminary Report to the Advisory Committees Study of the Spanish-speaking People" (University of Texas, 1949), p. 11.

61. Ibid., p. 24. Weber made this statement in 1948.

62. Henry C. Todd, "Labor's Viewpoint on Mexican Nationals and 'Wetbacks,' " *The Commonwealth* 29, no. 16 (20 April 1953): 164.

63. "Brownell Scouts Spy Ring Reports," *New York Times* (3 May 1954), p. 14.

64. Levenstein, *Labor Organizations,* pp. 205-06.

65. Craig, *The Bracero Program,* p. 126.

66. U.S., Congress, House, *Congressional Record,* 82d Cong., 2d sess., 1952, 98, pt. 2: 2201.

67. U.S., Congress, House, *Congressional Record,* 83d Cong., 2d sess., 1954, 100, pt. 6: 8132.

68. President's Commission, *Migratory Labor,* p. 78.

69. Ibid.

70. Willard F. Kelley, "The Wetback Issue," *The I and N Reporter* 2, no. 3 (January 1954): 38.

71. Ibid.

72. U.S., Congress, Senate, Subcommittee on Labor and Labor-Management Relations of the Committee on Labor and Public Welfare, *Hearings, Migratory Labor,* 82d Cong., 2d sess. (Washington, D.C.: 1952), p. 231 (hereafter cited as *Migratory Labor Hearings,* 1952).

73. Ibid., pp. 144-45.

74. *Migratory Labor Hearings,* 1952, p. 132.

75. Edward C. McDonagh, "Status Levels of Mexicans," *Sociology and Social Research* 30, no. 6 (July 1949): 452; Robert J. Lipschultz, *American Attitudes Toward Mexican Immigration, 1924 to 1952* (San Francisco: R and E Research Associates, 1971); Cecil B. Robinson, *With the Ears of Strangers* (Tucson: University of Arizona Press, 1971).

76. Eli Ginzberg and Douglas W. Bray, *The Uneducated* (New York, 1952), p. 51.

77. Ibid., pp. 46-47 and 174.

78. Ibid., p. 175.

79. Pauline R. Kibbe, "The Economic Plight of Mexicans," in *Ethnic Relations in the United States,* ed. Edward C. McDonagh and Eugene S. Richards (New York: Appleton-Century-Crofts, 1953), p. 196.

80. Kelley, "The Wetback Issue," p. 39.

81. William Korick, "The Wetback Story," *The Commonwealth*, 54 (13 June 1951), p. 327.

82. Myers, *Border Wardens*, p. 77. "What Price Wetbacks?" was a pamphlet published in 1953 under the auspices of the American G.I. Forum in Texas.

83. U.S., Congress, House, *Congressional Record*, 82d Cong., 2d sess., 1952, 98, pt. 1: 798.

84. U.S., Congress, Senate, *Congressional Record*, 82d Cong., 2d sess., 1952, 98, pt. 3: 4069.

85. Ibid., p. 3552.

86. Craig, *The Bracero Program*, p. 98.

87. U.S., Congress, Senate, *Congressional Record*, 82d Cong., 2d sess., 1952, 98, pt. 1: 798. His proposed amendment to Section 8 of the Immigration Act of 1917.

88. Nelson G. Copp, *Wetbacks and Braceros* (San Francisco: R and E Research Associates, 1971), p. 37.

89. Ibid., p. 38.

90. U.S., Congress, Senate, *Congressional Record*, 82d Cong., 2d sess., 1952, 98, pt. 1: 808.

91. Ibid., p. 806.

92. Ibid., p. 809.

93. Ibid., p. 795.

94. *New York Times* (13 August 1952), p. 22.

95. *El Nacional* (17 January 1954), p. 1:4.

96. *New York Times* (21 May 1951), p. 47.

97. U.S., Congress, Senate, *Congressional Record*, 82d Cong., 2d sess., 1952, 98, pt. 1: 798.

98. Ibid.

99. Ibid.

100. Ibid., p. 799.

101. Ibid., p. 811. The twelve liberal senators who voted for Douglas's amendment were Gordon, Flanders, Humphrey, Johnson (South Carolina), Lehman, Monroney, Moody, Morse, Murray, Neeley, Pastore, and Douglas.

102. Ibid., p. 812.

103. Ibid., p. 813. Senator Kilgore said that S.1851 would be beneficial to the Spanish-speaking person who had come to the United States legally or was already a citizen, for under the protective provision defining harboring, etc., employers would not be as hesitant to hire Spanish-speaking people who might be here illegally and thus to expose themselves to prosecution. Senator Chavez of New Mexico concurred with Kilgore's view of the bill. Ibid., pp. 794-95.

104. Craig, *The Bracero Program*, pp. 95-97.

105. U.S., Congress, House, *Congressional Record*, 82d Cong., 2d sess., 1952, 98, pt. 2: 2201.

106. Ibid., pp. 2201-02.

107. U.S., Congress, House, *Congressional Record*, 82d Cong., 2d sess., 1952, 98, pt. 1: 1354.

108. Ibid., p. 1352.

109. Ibid., p. 1353.

110. Ibid., pp. 1353-54.

111. Ibid., p. 1414.

112. Ibid.

113. Ibid. The Truman administration favored the provision which stated that employing "illegals" did not constitute harboring. This was important, for according to Richard Craig, "It constituted a clear indication that the administration had already compromised on the issue prior to introduction." Craig, *The Bracero Program*, p. 95.

114. U.S., Congress, House, *Congressional Record*, 82d Cong., 2d sess., 1952, 98, pt. 2: 2283.

115. Copp, *Wetbacks and Braceros*, p. 39.

116. Ibid.

117. Ibid.

118. *New York Times* (28 November 1952).

4
Undocumented Persons

AFTER THE REINSTATEMENT of the bracero program in 1954 the "wetback" or *mojado* had again become a focal point of controversy, not only between the United States and Mexico but also between the various interest groups embroiled in the struggle over the whole issue of Mexican labor in the United States. Much of the controversy centered on the ill effects the "wetback" created. For Mexico, undocumented workers were an embarrassing reminder that all of the promises of the Revolution had not been fulfilled. In many ways they seemed to epitomize Mexico's social and economic problems and the other critical issues that still confronted Mexico's leadership. Furthermore, undocumented workers threatened to undermine the bracero program itself by entering in such large numbers that many employers chose to hire them instead of braceros. "Illegals" had no rights or contract guarantees and were thus more subject to exploitation. Because Mexico appeared powerless to prevent their entry, it was determined to have them come under the protection of an international agreement and in such regulated numbers that Mexico could keep a handle on its people. Such was not possible if undocumented workers continued their emigration in ever-increasing numbers. Finally, an increasing number of stories about their exploitation were given wide play in Mexico's national press, which engendered increased ill-feelings toward the United States, the bracero program, and the Mexican government itself for failing to protect its citizens regardless of their status in the United States.[1]

On the national level officials in the United States were also concerned about the "wetbacks" and their negative effects on what they considered generally good relations with Mexico. Antiwetback groups in the United States were particularly vehement in pointing out the negative effects that illegal immigration from Mexico had on the social, political, and economic well-being of the United States. The views of labor concerning the "wetback" have already been discussed, and labor was joined by other groups who were becoming more vocal in their demands that the government do something about the invasion that they felt this country was complacently ignoring just to satisfy the insatiable need for cheap labor of a small group of selfish individuals.

Among those who added their voices to labor's was the Bishops' Committee for the Spanish Speaking. The committee of sixteen bishops from the West and Southwest was chaired by Archbishop Robert E. Lucey, long a critic of the bracero program and of the ills created by it and the "wetback" influx.[2]

The committee had originated in 1945 in partial response to the perceived inroads being made by various Protestant missions into the Mexican American Catholic population. Portestant denominations such as the Baptists, Methodists, and Presbyterians had proselytized among Mexican and Mexican American migrant workers since the early 1920s. For the most part the Catholic hierarchy had chosen to overlook such efforts because they had more crucial issues to deal with, particularly in the area of anti-Catholic feelings that had plagued the Church and its hierarchy in this country. It was assumed by many Catholic clergy that Mexicans were strongly loyal to the Catholic church, and they felt that they had little to fear from the Protestants. There were also the problems of insufficient funds, a dearth of trained clergy, and the belief of many churchmen that the main goal of the Church was to meet the pastoral needs of the people and avoid involvement in social action programs.[3]

This attitude had changed by the end of World War II because of the zeal displayed by Protestants, an increasing number of converts, and signs of growing discontent among Mexican Americans who believed their loyalty to the Catholic Church had been taken for granted and had therefore done little to alleviate their problems. Added pressure had been exerted on the Catholic Church in the United States by its Mexican counterpart, which had asked the former to oversee the spiritual and physical well-being of Mexicans coming to the United States to work. It seems that the Catholic Church in Mexico had opposed the bracero program because of its negative effect on the morals and family life of braceros. According to the Mexican hierarchy, the bracero program contributed to the disruption of family life. It was also concerned about the allegedly immoral lives led by many braceros while in the United States.[4] For these reasons and because Mexicans were predominantly still employed as migrant workers, the Catholic Church undertook to improve the working and living conditions of domestic migrants by demanding the termination of the bracero program.[5]

Unable to achieve the termination of the bracero program, church leaders began to demand that domestic migrants be given the same contract guarantees provided braceros. Lucey and others questioned how the government could deny rights and guarantees to its own citizens that it so readily granted to foreigners.

Those who advocated grater protection for the domestic migrant recognized that a major step in dealing with the illegal question could be taken if they could enact legislation to provide minimum wages and working guarantees to domestic migratory laborers in the United States. They had to discredit the argument that employers hired "wetbacks" because of continuing labor shortages. Supporters of the migrant worker charged that labor shortages were created by the low wages paid workers. As long as the migratory workers lacked minimum wage guarantees or recourse to such bodies as the National Labor Relations Board, growers and employers would continue to exploit their workers. Yet employers realized that there was a limit to how far domestic migrants could be pushed when it came to wages and living conditions before they began to fight back. Many growers and organizations were well aware that migrant workers had proven themselves militant and determined adversaries when it came to fighting for their rights against unscrupulous employers. Migrant workers, although difficult to organize, could and would, if necessary, close ranks and take on their employers as they had done in the turbulent 1930s. Braceros and undocumented workers posed no such threat to employers and thus presented a more appealing alternative for employers in filling their labor needs at the lowest cost possible.

The National Association for the Advancement of Colored People also expressed concern about the bracero program and the use of illegal labor. They charged that braceros and "illegals" had made their way into states such as Arkansas where they had displaced black migrant workers. The NAACP stated that conditions for migrant laborers of all colors were bad enough in the South. The importation of foreign labor would only make things worse. Black leaders were also upset that the president had not appointed a black representative to serve on the President's Commission on Migratory Labor.[6]

The cause of the migrant was also championed by other groups, including a number of ethnic groups. In addition to Mexican Americans and blacks, there were Jewish and Native American groups. In 1951, for example, a representative for the National Congress of American Indians presented testimony before a congressional subcommittee about the ill effects that braceros and "illegals" were having on the 33,000 Indian migrant workers in the United States.[7] Promigrant civic and educational organizations which also spoke out against the bracero program included the National Consumer's League, which for years had published pamphlets and documents on the poverty and misery of migrants. It had also actively worked for federal legislation to aid migrants. A similar course of action was followed by the American Association of Social Workers and the National Education Association.[8] The groups listed by no means exhaust the list of those who opposed the bracero program or the influx of undocumented workers. Other groups and organizations added their voices to the ranks of the opposition, but it was to little avail. For the most part, antibracero and antiwetback proponents were poorly organized and did not have access to the important governmental decision-making bodies and those who served on them.

Although it must be said that their efforts were largely diffuse and ineffective, they nonetheless at times appeared to be making progress in their struggle against the vested interests of agriculture. One such instance occurred when the President's Commission on Migratory Labor issued its final report. This Commission was appointed in June of 1950 ostensibly to investigate the question of migratory labor in American agriculture. However, it was viewed by some within the administration, and particularly within the Labor Department, as a means of absorbing some

of the "political heat" stirred up by the bracero program and the "wetback" phenomenon, which were receiving an increased amount of exposure in the popular
press. It was also hoped that such a commission would provide a factual foundation
for future policy decisions in the area of domestic and international farm labor in
the United States.[9]

The final report of the President's Commission on Migratory Labor pretty
much verified what antibraceroists and antiwetback proponents had contended
for some time. The commission found that the bracero program only contributed
to the influx of undocumented workers, that undocumented workers lowered
wages and increased unemployment, that they increased social ills and were subject
to widespread abuse and exploitation, and that the needs of domestic migrants
were being neglected by meeting the needs of powerful interest groups in agriculture. It also denounced the practice of legalizing "wetbacks" and criticized various
government agencies for their failure to take action on these issues and problems.
It set forth several recommendations on how to curtail the influx of undocumented
workers, including penalty legislation against employers who hired "illegals" and
more support for the INS.[10]

Reaction to the report was mixed and tended to reflect views and stances generally taken by interest groups on both sides of the question concerning migratory labor.
For the most part the report was discounted and attacked by rural spokesmen. They
called the report "ridiculous" and quite "devoid of justifiable evidence." They
described it as illustrative of the "erroneous" thinking that had once permeated
the Farm Security Administration. To them, the report represented the work of
social reformers, urban do-gooders, and union people.[11]

As already indicated, labor, along with many of the social-reform groups, hailed
the findings of the commission not only because it supported many of their charges
but also because it served as a bright spot in what had often been a difficult and
losing cause. They believed that the report would encourage others to rally to their
side and force legislators to consider their demands a little more seriously.

At the administrative level the Departments of Justice, Labor, and State pretty
much agreed with the commission's findings and recommendations. For example,
the Justice Department agreed that some legal measures needed to be enacted in
order to deal with the "wetback" traffic. However, it favored measures which were
less harsh than those espoused in the report. Justice Department officials did not
wish to employ injunctions, restraining orders, and bans on interstate commerce of
products produced or harvested by undocumented workers. Further tempering the
Justice Department's view was a skepticism concerning its ability to enforce immigration laws. It also had serious doubts about any punitive legislation Congress
could enact. According to Attorney General J. Howard McGrath, the enforcement
of immigration laws would not keep out undocumented workers. He believed that
it was a mistake to place the blame on employers for encouraging illegal immigration. In McGrath's opinion the "wetback" influx was due more to the "push"
factors of Mexico's declining economy, which wreaked hardship on the already

impoverished masses. What was really needed was a virtual overhaul of the Mexican economy. Without this "the invasion would continue regardless of whether the Commission report (on Migratory Labor) became administrative policy or not."[12]

The Labor and State Departments agreed with the report that the legislation on "wetbacks" was counterproductive. The State Department was particularly concerned about the "wetback problem" because of the negative effect that it had on relations with Mexico. However, it continued to favor a bracero program even though the report had pointed to it as a poor deterrent to the entry of "illegals." Although certain officials in the State Department concurred with this view, they nonetheless saw little value in discontinuing the bracero program. They reasoned that without it the United States might have to use force in order to check the influx of "illegals."[13] That the "wetback" was of extreme concern to State Department officials was best reflected in a remark made by Roy R. Rubottom, deputy director of the Office of Middle American Affairs, in 1952. According to Rubottom, "The ramifications of the wetback problem are perhaps one of the more difficult problems in foreign affairs and domestic affairs that the agencies of this government have ever been up against."[14]

Government agencies and officials appeared to be aware of the serious dimensions surrounding the "wetback" influx, but when it came to undertaking concrete measures designed to stop it there was a lot of balking, discussion, and confusion.

What antiwetback groups needed was broad popular support for their efforts in order to force public officials to take some action, yet such support had not been forthcoming, for in spite of the importance of the issue the public at large was not well informed about it. The tendency on the part of the general public was to view the "wetback" influx as a local problem confined to the border regions. For the most part, many people seemed oblivious to the fact that "wetbacks" even existed. Until 1951 popular pictorial magazines, weekly news magazines, and newspapers paid little heed to the miserable plight of undocumented workers.[15] This began to change during the latter part of 1951, when the mass media began to exhibit an increased interest in the influx of undocumented workers and their impact on the American way of life. Then, seemingly overnight, the public was flooded with a mass of articles and feature stories concerning undocumented workers. The majority of stories and articles portrayed the adverse effects that this unchecked tide was having on the economy and the public welfare. They bemoaned the many ills of illegal entry, charging that "wetbackism" was responsible for increased disease rates, crime rates, narcotics traffic, soaring welfare costs, and infiltration by subversive elements. By and large stories about undocumented workers painted a negative picture of the "wetback." That they were more often the victims of filth, disease, crime, and exploitation was often overlooked. What became imbedded in the public mind was a distorted picture of poor, hungry, wretched, and sinister "aliens" who were invading the United States. The media generally used terms such as "horde," "tide," "invasion," and "il-

legals" to describe the "wetback," thus causing many people to view them in
unfavorable terms. Instead of individuals, the "wetbacks" came to be viewed
as a faceless mass. Undocumented workers were often represented in the media
as faceless, shadowy, sinister-looking beings who skulked across the border in
the dead of night in order to deprive American citizens of their jobs and liveli-
hood.

There was, however, another side to the story, a side that occasionally found
its way into print. It told of the exploitation, the danger, the anguish and suffering, and the dreams that drove so many to risk so much for so little. A small
number of scholars and a few reporters were able to look at this side of the question and examine it both in terms of its international ramifications and in terms
of its human cost. What they found was that Mexican "illegal aliens" came to
the United States not so much because living conditions were better in this country,
but rather because there was not enough work in Mexico. A limited sample taken
from interviews of one hundred and sixty "wetbacks" at the McAllen Center in
July of 1950 provides an insight into their motivation.

When asked why they had come to the United States 64 or 43.5 percent replied that there was little work in Mexico. Only 50 or 34.0 percent said that they
came because better wages were offered in the United States. In all, 116 or 81.7
percent told the interviewers that they had learned of work opportunities here
through word of mouth.[16] Not one of them made any mention of the American
dream of streets paved with gold and unlimited opportunity. Not many of them
indicated that they wished to remain. All they wanted to do was to earn a little
money and return to Mexico, for many of them knew of the harsh realities that
awaited them if they remained in the United States.

According to Gladwyn Hill, who wrote a series of articles on the "wetback" in
the *New York Times* in 1954, it took "more than ordinary initiative to marshal
a grubstake, get to the border and run the Border Patrol's gauntlet, all for the
purpose of working harder at lower wages than most United States citizens will accept."[17] Crossing the border was by no means as easy as many people believed. Those
intending to cross the border illegally had to walk across scorching deserts. Those
lucky enough to ride often stowed away in boxcars of freight trains or rode the
rods. Others hid in empty tank cars, "from which, on occasion they [were] , extracted, dead, in northern yards."[18]

Those who could manage it often paid 150 dollars or more to professional
smugglers to travel north in cars, sometimes even in San Diego taxis.[19] It was a
long and often dangerous journey that took its toll on unknown numbers. Death
could come in many ways. Thirst, rattlesnake bites, starvation, exposure, gunshot
wounds, and drowning were just some of the ways in which "illegals" lost their
lives trying to cross the border. In 1953, some four hundred "wetbacks" drowned
attempting to cross rivers swollen by the big flood of that year.[20] In August of 1954,
the *New York Times* reported that some thirty bodies had been washed ashore near
Edinburg, Texas.[21] The bodies lacked any identification papers and thus were buried

in unmarked graves. The article stated that the number of "illegals" who drowned yearly attempting to cross was unknown.[22]

Those who survived the journey and reached the border had to contend with other obstacles. In addition to the Border Patrol, there were sometimes barbed wire fences to cross. Occasionally, more enterprising Mexicans made holes in the fence with a blowtorch and then charged their compatriots a dollar to enter through it. If no holes were there, one could pay a dollar for the use of a mattress to slide over the fence. If one lacked money but was athletic and agile, he might vault the fence. Those who succeeded became respected *alambristas* (fence climbers) and were the subject of as much respect as a bullfighter receives. Others merely crossed the fence less heroically by piling up a few cardboard boxes or orange crates.[23]

The Immigration Service of course attempted to control this flow by stationing officers at strategic points on important highway and rail routes leading from the border to the interior of the country. In addition to traffic-checking, the INS constructed sand or dirt track roads. Dirt track roads were inspected at regular intervals for footprints that would betray a crossing. However, they were largely ineffective as many "illegals," aware of such roads, either avoided them or covered their tracks. In certain areas, like Eagle Pass and the McAllen sector, the earth is so hard that it is not possible to use dirt track roads. For these reasons the Border Patrol relied mainly on sign cutting, leapfrogging, and air-search methods.[24]

In 1953 interviews of an "illegal alien" by Ruth Newhall appeared in the *San Francisco Chronicle*. In the series of interviews Refugio Sandoval, an "illegal" from Aposol in Zacatecas, told of his life as an undocumented worker. Sandoval had entered this country illegally five times. He told Newhall that the thing most forgotten about "illegals" was that "illegal aliens are people."[25] Sandoval described the economic hardships in Mexico that brought him to this country, the ways that he used to cross over, the hard journeys, and his search for a job. Once he had gotten past the border guards, he told Newhall, there was little to fear from their patrols.[26]

In 1954 Carlos Moreno posed as an illegal entrant and described for CBS Radio the steps and routes followed by "wetbacks." According to Moreno the first three legs of the trip (Calexico to Heber, Heber to El Centro, and El Centro to Brawley) were fairly easy. The most dangerous stage was the fourth one, from Brawley to Indio. Once out of Indio, said Moreno, the "illegal" was out of the danger zone. If one could afford it, most of the distance in the four stages could be covered by taxi.[27]

Moreno informed listeners that the route to Indio was about 75 miles long, across hard-packed desert. "There are two routes to Indio that go around the Salton Sea. The northern route and the southern route. The information I have says that there is less patrolling on the northern route."[28] After Indio there were no checkpoints, and at this point "illegals" often ended their taxi ride and proceeded by bus to Los Angeles.[29]

Many of those who managed to make the crossing and avoid injury or capture often found that things only became harder. They usually worked long hours at backbreaking labor. In return they received meager wages. On the average a worker could pick from 200 to 250 pounds of cotton per day. At this rate a person might earn about $26.25 per week if the going rate were $1.25 to $1.50 per hundred pounds picked. Earnings such as these were more often than not the exception, as the rates cited were considered high. In areas saturated with "illegals" the going rate was closer to fifty cents per hundred pounds of cotton picked.[30]

Most of their money was spent on purchasing the bare necessities such as food and clothing. Price gouging was a common practice because dealers knew that many of their customers were afraid to go into town to make their purchases. Like others who lived outside the law, undocumented workers had little choice but to pay whatever the seller asked.

Those lucky enough to save some money often sent it home to family and relations, yet it seldom amounted to much. Furthermore, in many cases, the money sent to family and relatives seldom went directly into their pockets. More often than not aspiring braceros who had turned "illegals" had had to borrow money in order to reach the border, and the small amount that had trickled home usually went to repay such loans. Those who returned to their homes, whether voluntarily or involuntarily, usually returned with a few dollars in their pockets, some new clothes, a new hat, and a few store-bought items.

In addition to poor wages, undocumented workers had to contend with poor living conditions. In some instances covered holes with tentlike structures above them, camouflaged by straw and dirt, served as homes for these people. Others lived in cavelike structures, in irrigation ditches, or in groves of trees. Most of the makeshift structures lacked running water and sanitation facilities, literally making them disease-breeding holes.[31] Perhaps the most tragic aspect of the undocumented workers' dilemma was that their children were also victims, for they often suffered from malnutrition, dysentery, diarrhea, and other infantile diseases.[32]

Not only were Mexican "illegals" exploited by growers, processors, and professional smugglers, but they were also victimized by members of their own ethnic group. There were instances where local Spanish-speaking people in the United States charged "aliens" excessive rent to live in mere shacks. At times they were charged high prices for food and transportation or were given short weights on harvested goods by the Spanish-speaking overseers. There was one recorded incident wherein a "wetback" who was picked up by the Border Patrol in McAllen proudly displayed a receipt for eighty dollars that a Spanish-speaking lawyer had charged him for filling out a form for a suspension of deportation request. These forms were actually quite simple to complete. Usually they were completed for "wetbacks" by an Immigration Service employee or Patrol Inspector without charge.[33]

There was in fact very little that Mexican undocumented workers could do to protect themselves against their exploiters or against the adverse conditions under

Covered holes that served as homes for some undocumented persons. Photograph taken on a farm adjacent to the Rio Grande River, Texas

Courtesy the Texas AFL-CIO Collection, The University of Texas at Arlington Library.

which they lived in the United States. "Illegal aliens" lived outside the law and on the fringes of society.[34] Their major fear lay in being apprehended, which left them at the mercy of those who chose to exploit them.[35] In addition, "illegal aliens" were seldom integrated into or able to participate in the society, whose culture was strange to them.[36] According to the President's Commission on Migratory Labor, "illegal aliens" lived as fugitives and those who employed and exploited undocumented workers had little to fear, while the "illegals" who suffered so much under this system always came out the losers.[37] Apprehension meant deportation or repatriation, while evasion meant continued exploitation, abuse, and fear.

Even when "wetbacks" had performed their work and had eluded apprehension, their troubles were not over. In 1953 it was reported in the State of California monthly report that the Division of Labor Law Enforcement had begun to take action on wage claims by "wetbacks." Though there was widespread opposition to this by grower interests, the report stated that such action was necessary if something were to be done about the "vicious practice of labor contractors and other people of working illegals and then refusing to pay them."[38] This practice left the "illegal" without legal remedies, the report stated, "thus creating an added incentive for unscrupulous persons to bring such workers into the state."[39] Though ameliorative efforts were made on the part of some authorities, they proved for the most part ineffective. The practice continued to be widespread.

If not cheated out of their pay by unscrupulous employers, "illegal aliens" were often robbed, beaten, or murdered by others for their meager earnings. In 1946 *Collier's* magazine ran a story about an organized murder ring operating along the border that had been uncovered by the Mexican government. According to the article, this ring specialized in preying upon "wetbacks" who were returning to Mexico with their year's earnings.[40]

The repeated exploitation of undocumented workers over the years grew and spread until it eroded the values and mores of the people and the communities where the use of "wetback" labor existed. In time, growers and processors came to believe that they had a vested right to use "wetbacks."[41] The manager of the Agricultural Producers Labor Committee reflected this attitude when he testified before the President's Commission on Migratory Labor in Los Angeles. He told the commission that if they could not contract the needed help during the peak of the harvest seasons, then the growers would use "wetbacks."[42] He had no qualms about admitting that they were already employing "wetbacks" and that one of the association's representatives was at El Centro and Calexico contracting legalized "wetbacks."[43]

From the outset, the use of "wetback" labor had its moral, ethical, and economic justifications. The economic reasons were obvious. Such laborers were cheap. There was no need for contracts, minimum wages, health benefits, housing, or transportation.[44] Not only were they good stoop laborers, but many became adept at different farming operations, serving as handymen, irrigators, pruners, tractor drivers, sorters, and pickers. Many employers, because of the training that they provided "illegals" for performing specialized tasks, perenially rehired them and exerted extra efforts to keep them from the grasp of the Border Patrol. These "specials," as they were called, and countless others who were able to perform jobs that put them a degree or two above the fieldworkers, "cast doubt on the common assertion of farm employers that they hired wetbacks only 'because they will do the hard, disagreeable tasks that white men simply won't take.' "[45]

Various authors have described the moral and psychological climate that prevailed in regard to the use of "wetback" labor. Critics of the system depicted it as the survival of peonage[46] or a form of slavery far worse than that which existed in nineteenth-century America.[47] Certain areas, such as the Rio Grande Valley were described as colonial empires. According to a federal employee, "the major or key configuration of the Valley is certainly the economic welfare of the producer. Other factors are secondary and minor."[48]

Anglos in communities and areas that employed undocumented workers had come to believe that they knew and understood the characteristics of Mexicans. This belief underlay and supported many of the attitudes and practices that affected Mexicans and Mexican Americans in those areas. According to a report issued in 1951, this belief permitted "the rationalization of the raw, sometimes vicious, sometimes paternal exploitation of wetback labor with the statement that 'they never had it so good in Mexico. . . .' "[49] In essence these attitudes and beliefs made the Spanish-speaking population in many areas, whether they were citizens, braceros, or "illegals," a mere commodity—something to be used when needed and discarded when no longer necessary. Their problems were ignored as not being those of human beings.[50] What follows are just a few examples of the beliefs that permeated the thinking of people who lived in the Rio Grande Valley of Texas.

A Valley politician who was a member of the Texas legislature in 1951 told interviewers that "relations in the Valley between English-speaking and Spanish-speaking people [were] good." He said that there was no discrimination in the Valley, but that there was of necessity segregation. The reason for this was hygienic and not racial. After all, he said, "we just can't have all those dirty, possibly diseased people swimming with our wives and children."[51]

Another Valley resident interviewed was an employee of the Texas Employment Commission. According to the report this individual had been awarded a Master's degree and had written a thesis on education in Mexico. In talking about "the lower class Mexicans" he said: "They have behind them five hundred years of burden bearing and animal-like living and just can't adjust to civilization in the way a white man does." In his opinion a "good Mexican" was hard-working, docile, and very loyal. Unfortunately, he continued, few Mexicans possessed these traits. For the most part Mexicans were lazy and undisciplined, characteristics already quite apparent when they were young, according to this self-proclaimed expert.

He was disturbed by the fact that all Mexican children were undisciplined and that they all carried knives by the time they had reached the age of twelve. To top things off, he believed all Mexicans to be cowardly, a characteristic that appeared transferable even to their pets, for according to this individual a Mexican dog would never attack a white man.[52]

Such derogatory and negative stereotypes more often than not were representatives of the attitudes held by many people in areas that had large numbers of undocumented workers or large populations of people of Mexican descent. Generally speaking, the only positive traits attributed to Mexicans were that they were good workers (if properly supervised) and that they labored for low wages. In line with these views people believed that Mexicans were satisfied with this arrangement as long as outside agitators were not permitted to come in and stir things up. As far as a large number of employers were concerned, efforts to Americanize Mexicans only served to make them lazy and ungrateful. Some even believed that the government had gone too far when it instituted the bracero program. Contract guarantees only served to spoil them and to shortchange those who employed them. According to a prominent employer, braceros were men whom Mexico wanted to get rid of. He described them as "drunks, bums and halfwits." He wrote that he was inclined to agree with the head man of his orange-picking crew who told him that if he had the power, "he would machine-gun all his contract laborers and get 'wetbacks.' " In his view the "wetback" had automatically screened himself by walking several hundred miles to find "honest work."[53] Therefore he urged that the United States continue to allow the entry of undocumented workers.

In discussing Mexicans, individuals seldom made distinctions between citizens, braceros, and "illegals." The tendency was to lump braceros, undocumented workers, and citizens of Mexican descent all under the rubric of "Mexican" and to pronounce the word in such a disparaging and distasteful manner that it left little doubt to those hearing it in what way the host society viewed Mexicans and Mexican Americans in general.

CONCLUSION

The debate concerning Mexican undocumented workers largely emanated from two groups. Those opposed to illegal entry usually represented labor and social welfare groups and organizations, Mexican American organizations, religious groups, and small farmers. Their opposition stemmed from the belief that "illegals" were a menace to the working community in the United States, that they posed a danger to the social, political, and economic stability of the country, and that they were in open and flagrant violation of this nation's immigration laws. Those who favored or encouraged illegal entry did so because they saw the undocumented worker as indispensable to the needs of agriculture.

In arguing their case before the public and before legislators, proponents of penalty legislation and increased Border Patrol appropriations presented an arsenal of facts and figures that attributed most social ills to the "illegal." Their case was strengthened when the President's Commission on Migratory Labor issued its report. However, it was not enough. In large part, both the findings and the recommendations of the commission were ignored, and they failed to generate concrete reforms.[54] Nonetheless the appointment of the commission represented the first major success by labor and its supporters on the issue of migrant workers and their plight in this country.[55] It also added further credence to their arguments concerning the ill effects that "illegals" had on this country.

On the other side of the fence were the large vested interests. By and large they seldom felt the need to defend their hiring practices. They realized that their opponents had a long row to plow before they could even begin to make headway in the area of legislation and increased appropriations. Furthermore, the opposition was hampered by poor organization, an unsympathetic public, and poor access to powerful committees and members in Congress. Even if something were enacted, there appeared to be little to worry about in the minds of most growers and processors. Enacting legislation was one thing, while enforcing it was something else. Local employers had been hiring undocumented workers in open defiance of the law, and if need be they would continue to do so.

While grower interests and their supporters were able to downplay the importance of the findings of the President's Commission on Migratory Labor and in fact largely ignore its report, they could not accomplish the same thing with public opinion.

A second major step by opponents of illegal immigration in gaining support for their cause was taken in the early 1950s when the popular press began to focus attention on the question of "illegals" and their impact on this country. Because of what amounted to a lot of sensationalistic reporting, the American public became aroused over the "invasion of illegal hordes" streaming in from Mexico. Antiwetback groups were delighted by this surge of interest on the part of the media, for now they could disseminate their information to a wider audience. Unfortunately for the "illegal," much of the information was designed to play up the ill effects of illegal immigration. Soon there emerged a negative and distorted picture of the undocumented worker as a sinister and dangerous person who was responsible for increased crime rates, disease rates, and welfare costs.

Very seldom was the "illegal" presented as an individual with needs, desires, and dreams. The press and proponents of penalty legislation seldom discussed the positive contributions of these people or lauded their drive, spirit, and motivation in seeking to improve their lot. What compliments or plaudits they did receive came largely from those who sought to exploit them or profit from their presence. Statistics used in stories were often "guesstimates," which were inflated with every retelling. Then, as now, no one really knew how many "illegals" were in the country and what their impact really was. Although there were criminal elements among those who entered, the great majority appear to have been law-abiding people genuinely interested in finding work and in remaining as unobtrusive as possible in order to avoid detection. In truth undocumented workers were not so pernicious or so sinister as they were depicted. More often than not undocumented workers were the victims of crime rather than the criminals. The mere fact that the great majority of apprehended "illegals" were given the opportunity to depart voluntarily attests in part to the fact that they were largely people in search of a job and a better way of life rather than a menace to American society.

One thing that does emerge for certain from all of the facts, figures, testimony, and viewpoints about undocumented workers is that they had many detractors on both sides of the issue, and almost no one to champion their cause. The struggle between organized labor and social welfare groups on one side and the grower interests on the other did not take into consideration the human factor. Nor did either side attempt to deal with the needs and problems that "illegals" faced and that led to their sojourns from Mexico. Instead the debates over legislation and appropriations served as a battleground where each group sought to discredit and to dominate the other. This did not augur well for "illegals," as this strategy made them a bone of contention between two quarreling factions. No matter which side would emerge victorious, the "wetbacks" would still be the real losers. If the growers and processors won, they could and would continue to exploit them. If labor and social-welfare organizations triumphed, it meant repatriation, deportation, and reduced opportunities for "illegals" to earn a living.

What about the undocumented workers themselves? In view of the miserable conditions under which many of them were forced to live and work, it is a wonder that they took so many risks to come to the United States. The fact that they were often abused and exploited raises questions as to why they stayed around at all, for according to one reporter "the black slave of pre-emancipation years was far better off" than the illegal migrant.[56] Another stated that undocumented workers in the Imperial Valley of California represented "one of the most highly concentrated survivals of peonage that exist anywhere in the southwest."[57] A third source wrote that the exploitation of "wetback" labor was a "form of slavery far worse than that which existed in the United States . . . one hundred years ago."[58]

To some, such statements may seem extreme. However, the squalor, the abuse and the exploitation of "illegals" has been documented as fact. What at times made the situation of the "illegal" appear worse was that unlike most slaveholders most "wetback" employers felt no responsibility for their workers. Because slaves were considered property, most slaveholders exercised some control over how much they abused or exploited their slaves. "Wetbacks," in contrast, were not property that employers had purchased, and thus unscrupulous individuals felt no sense of responsibility. Like the black slaves, "wetbacks" had been dehumanized because of pernicious stereotypes depicting them as subhuman and inferior. According to Edward C. McDonagh, a sociologist at the University of Southern California, Mexicans were assigned a low social status by Anglo-American society because they were viewed as persons who spent much of their time sleeping against a shady wall. Such a stereotype was detrimental to the Mexican, particularly in a "go-getting" culture.

The stereotype, however, did not fit the reality. Certainly people who trekked across dangerous terrain, risked their lives, left their families, and worked long hours for meager wages could not be classified as lazy, shiftless, and good-for-nothing. It is ironic that in many ways these people exhibited the same character-istics that Americans had displayed in settling this country. Undocumented persons had shown determination, courage, and strength; and they had set out for "unknown lands" in search of a better life. Yet these people were treated as inter-lopers and trespassers.

The reasons they came are as numerous as the people involved. A good number were driven here by hunger and unemployment, by stories of economic opportunity and the desire to improve their way of life by earning enough money to buy a parcel of land or needed equipment to grow more crops. A far smaller number were drawn here by the promise of adventure. Whatever the reason, few of them planned to make the United States their permanent home.

As to why they continued to come or why they stayed even in the face of discrimination, prejudice, and exploitation, the answer is a little more difficult to discern. According to some critics in Mexico, people continued to come to the United States because their government had failed adequately to inform them of the dangers and problems awaiting them if they entered illegally.[59] Government officials responded that this had nothing to do with it and that even those who knew about the dangers of "going wetback" were nonetheless willing to risk it. Undocumented persons who were interviewed explained that the wages paid in Mexico were not enough to keep up with the high cost of living there and this forced them to come to the United States. Furthermore, employers in Mexico usually paid lower wages than they had promised. According to one "illegal," Mexican employers usually kicked their workers in the pants when they no longer needed them.[60] It appears that those who entered illegally were willing to tolerate poor conditions for a short time in hopes of improving their lot.

Once in the United States it was sometimes too late for "illegal" workers to do much about their situation. They often arrived penniless and hungry and took whatever work they could find. Some employers did not pay their work-ers until the work had been completed and thus "illegals" had little choice but to stick it out. Other employers promised to hide them from the immigration officials. Oftentimes this offer of security was enough to keep "illegals" in a person's employ. Some workers were forced to stay with employers who threat-ened to turn them in. Still others stayed on because they had no basis upon which to compare their earnings or their housing. To the desperately poor some income and some shelter represented a definite improvement over what they had had in Mexico. Some stayed on in spite of the mistreatment and consoled themselves with the thought that this was just a temporary situation.

Of course not all "illegals" were abused and exploited by their employers, and of course not all "illegals" quietly endured their mistreatment. Unknown numbers left unscrupulous employers in search of better treatment and better opportunities. Just how many there were will never be known. What is known is that the poor treatment accorded to undocumented workers was indeed a blot on the history of this country. "It engendered an atmosphere of amorality and warped thinking which extended from the grower to the local and state officials to the highest levels of the Federal Government."[61] Yet growing public concern over this situation would soon bring increased pressure on government officials to deal with this critical and complex issue. Government officials, employers of undocumented workers, and their elected representatives could no longer openly sanction or encourage illegal immigration without arousing the public and the media. Steps had to be taken to quiet concern and criticism and yet not deprive the growers of a large pool of cheap and readily available labor. This was certainly a challenge to those who advocated the use of legal and illegal Mexican labor and, as it turned out, they were able to meet this challenge.

NOTES

1. Louis F. Blanchard, American Consul, Mexico, D.E., to Department of State (24 March 1950), Subject: "Newspaper Publicity Relating to Matters Concerning Mexican Agricultural Workers," in Foreign Agricultural Service, Record Group 166, Box 299, Mexican Labor Folder, 1950 to 1948, National Archives, Washington, D.C.

2. Leo Grebler, Joan W. Moore, and Ralph C. Guzman, *The Mexican-American People: The Nation's Second Largest Minority* (New York: The Free Press, 1970), p. 462.

3. Ibid., pp. 450-56.

4. Richard B. Craig, *The Bracero Program: Interest Groups and Foreign Policy* (Austin: University of Texas Press, 1971), pp. 19-20.

5. There was also an underlying philosophy within the Catholic Church as a whole that supported the idea of labor unionism. This and the desire for an equitable wage level had been promulgated by Leo XIII in 1891 in his papal encyclical *Rerum Novarum*. Grebler et al., *The Mexican-American People*, p. 455.

6. President's Commission on Migratory Labor, *Steneographic Report of the Washington, D.C., Hearings on Migratory Labor*, 13 and 14 July 1950 (Washington, D.C.), pp. 65-75.

7. For more on the views of these groups *see*: U.S., Congress, House, *Farm Labor, Hearings Before the Committee on Agriculture*, 82d Cong., 2d sess. (February and March 1952), pp. 652-55.

8. Robert D. Tomasek, "The Political and Economic Implications of Mexican Labor in the United States under the Non-Quota System, Contract Labor Program, and the Wetback Movement" (Ph.D. diss., University of Michigan, 1957), pp. 123-24.

9. Ellis W. Hawley, "The Politics of the Mexican Labor Issue, 1950-1965," *Agricultural History* 40, no. 3 (July 1966): 159. The commission was made up of five members and an executive secretary. Appointed to serve on this commission were: Maurice T. Van Hecke, a lawyer and professor of law at the University of North Carolina (Van Hecke was also the chairman of the commission); Archbishop Robert E. Lucey from San Antonio, Texas; William E. Leiserson, a labor mediator; Peter H. Odegard, a political scientist from the University of California; Noble Clark, who had replaced Paul Miller, following Miller's resignation. Serving as executive secretary was Warden Fuller from the University of California. Truman did not appoint any Blacks, females, or labor representatives to the Commission.

10. President's Commission on Migratory Labor, *Migratory Labor in American Agriculture* (Washington, D.C.: U. S. G.P.O., 1951), p. 180 and throughout.

11. Hawley, "The Politics of the Mexican Labor Issue," pp. 160-61.

12. Peter Neil Kirstein, "Anglo over Bracero: A History of the Mexican Worker in the United States from Roosevelt to Nixon." (Ph.D. diss., St. Louis University, 1973), pp. 207-08, citing J. Howard McGrath to President Truman (5 June 1951), Attorney General Desk Correspondence Folder, J. Howard McGrath Papers, Truman Library, Missouri.

13. Craig, *The Bracero Program,* p. 63.

14. U.S., Congress, Senate, Committee on Labor and Labor-Management Relations, *Migratory Labor,* Part 1: Hearings before Subcommittee, 82d Cong., 2d sess. (February-March 1952), pp. 129-30.

15. Tomasek, "The Political and Economic Implications," p. 221.

16. Lyle Saunders and Olen E. Leonard, "The Wetback in the Lower Rio Grande Valley of Texas," *Inter-American Education,* Occasional Papers VII (Austin: University of Texas, July 1951), p. 33.

17. Gladwyn Hill, "Two Every Minute across the Border," *New York Times Magazine* 31 January 1954), p. 13.

18. Ibid.

19. Ibid.

20. *Excelsior* (2 July 1953), p. 2.

21. "Rio Grande Drowns Many 'Wetbacks,' " *New York Times* (12 August 1954), p. 9.

22. Ibid.

23. Richard P. Eckels, "Hungry Workers, Ripe Crops, and the Non-Existent Mexican Border," *The Reporter* (13 April 1954), p. 28.

24. Interview with A. V. Nelson, Immigration Inspector, Sub-District Office of the Immigration and Naturalization Service, Hammond, Indiana (10 February 1975).

25. Rufugio G. Sandoval as told to Ruth Newhall, "Mexican Tells of Border Crossing," *San Francisco Chronicle* (5 October 1953), p. 1.

26. Ibid.; also (6 October 1953), p. 2.

27. Excerpts from the CBS Radio presentation of "The Wetback" (4 April 1954), cited in U.S. Congress, House, *Congressional Record,* 83d Cong., 2d sess., 1954, 100, pt. 6: 8135.

28. Ibid.

29. Ibid.

30. Saunders and Leonard, "The Wetback in the Lower Rio Grande," p. 55.

31. "The Wetback Menace," *International Teamster* 51, no. 3 (March 1954): 5.

32. Ibid., p. 6.

33. Saunders and Leonard, "The Wetback in the Lower Rio Grande," p. 62.

34. Julian Samora, *Los Mojados: The Wetback Story* (South Bend: University of Notre Dame Press, 1971), p. 4.

35. Ibid.

36. Ibid., p. 97.

37. President's Commission on Migratory Labor, *Migratory Labor in American Agriculture,* p. 78.

38. Excerpt from the State of California *Monthly Report* (September 1953), Records of the President's Committee on Migratory Labor, 1941-1963, Secretary of Agriculture, Member, A72-8, Box 102, Dwight D. Eisenhower Library (hereafter cited as *Records,* Box 102).

39. Ibid.

40. *Collier's* 118 (17 August 1946): 24-26.

41. *New York Times* (17 August 1946), p. 31; Nelson Copp, *Wetbacks and Braceros* (San Francisco: R and E Research Associates, 1971), p. 35.

42. President's Commission on Migratory Labor, *Migratory Labor in American Agriculture,* p. 73.

43. Ibid.

44. Samora, *Los Mojados*, p. 9.

45. Ernesto Galarza, *Merchants of Labor: The Mexican Bracero Story* (Charlotte: McNally and Lofton, 1964), p. 60.

46. "The Wetback Strike: A Report on the Strike of Farm Workers in the Imperial Valley of California" by the National Farm Labor Union (Washington: AFL, 24 May, 25 June 1951), p. 9, pamphlet in Records, Box 1, California Folder, D.D.E. Library.

47. Ibid., p. 1.

48. Saunders and Leonard, "The Wetback in the Lower Rio Grande Valley," p. 72.

49. Ibid., p. 66.

50. Ibid., pp. 70-71.

51. Ibid., pp. 66-67.

52. Ibid., pp. 67-68.

53. Letter to J. Lee Rankin from a retired Army Major in Escondido, California (24 August 1954), File Number 11, located in the Justice Department Records, Department of Justice, Washington, D.C.

54. Kirstein, "Anglo over Bracero," p. 209.

55. Tomasek, "The Political and Economic Implications," p. 237.

56. George T. Sanchez and Lyle Saunders, " 'Wetbacks:' A Preliminary Report to the Advisory Committee Study of the Spanish-speaking People" (University of Texas, 1949), p. 19.

57. "The Wetback Strike. A Report on the Strike of Farm Workers in the Imperial Valley of California" by the National Farm Labor Union (Washington, AFL, 24 May, 25 June 1951), p. 9, pamphlet in Records, Box 1, California Folder, D.D.E. Library.

58. Ibid., p. 1.

59. "The Bracero Situation in the Rio Grande Valley," p. 1. Report from Culver E. Gidden, American Consul, to Department of State (16 April 1951), Record Group 166, Foreign Agricultural Service, Box 299, Mexican Labor Folder, 1951-1952, National Archives, Washington, D.C.

60. "Arrival and Processing of Mexican Agricultural Workers at Calerico, California, under the Migrant Labor Agreement of 1951," p. 2, Report from Antonio Cortosime, American Consul, ibid.

61. Tomasek, "The Political and Economic Implications," p. 185.

5
Legislative Proposals for Curtailing Illegal Immigration: S.3600 and S. 3661

ALTHOUGH ADVOCATES OF penalty legislation had had their hopes buoyed up during the latter part of Truman's administration, early indications from Eisenhower's camp tended to cast a shadow over their optimism. Early statements from the newly appointed Attorney General Herbert Brownell suggested that he planned to do little about the situation and that for the moment the "wetback" issue was not a priority to him. However, events would soon change the Attorney General's thinking and force him to take action.

According to various reports and sources one of the areas most affected in social and economic terms by the illegal influx was the Imperial Valley in California. One article stated that "illegals" were costing the Valley at least $250,000 a year.[1] County officials began to request that the governor do something about it. "Was there not some way the state or federal government could reimburse Imperial County for its disproportionately high police, hospital, and welfare costs?" Governor Earl Warren felt that the magnitude of the situation called for federal intervention, particularly in view of the fact that the issue of illegal immigration from Mexico carried with it international implications. He therefore appealed to Eisenhower for help.[2]

No immediate action was taken on Warren's request. In fact, shortly thereafter Brownell told the House Appropriations Committee that he was opposed to granting the Border Patrol increased funding as in his opinion they simply did not need it.[3]

Brownell and Eisenhower could not ignore the problem for long. An aroused press and an angry public continued to voice concern over the "wetback" problem and its impact on the country. Advisors close to the president recommended that he at least study the issue and make a report to respond to the public concern. Eisenhower, who knew little about the subject but who understood the importance of keeping up good relations with Mexico as well as with the American public, asked Brownell to look into the situation along the border and come up with some recommendations. Brownell decided that it would prove helpful to him if he familiarized himself with the Mexican border area. Thus, with a little encouragement from immigration officials, Brownell undertook an inspection tour of southern California in August of 1953.[4]

During his tour Brownell spoke with over one hundred people who were affected in one way or another by the influx of "illegals" from Mexico. He met with mayors, judges, district attorneys, county supervisors, chiefs of police, and sheriffs, most of whom complained about how "illegals" drained their limited resources. Brownell also spoke with county welfare directors, county and federal health officers, small farmers, state employment authorities, and representatives of labor and the clergy. They too largely complained about the ill effects of uncontrolled immigration from Mexico. It appears that only those who represented large farm organizations had anything positive to tell the Attorney General about the "wetbacks." In their view "wetback" labor was necessary for harvesting their crops. When Brownell asked about braceros, many grower representatives complained that the procedures for contracting them were too complicated and expensive. While in California Brownell also conferred with Border Patrol officials, who argued that they needed more money, more equipment, and more personnel. In order to show him what they were up against they took Brownell along on patrol, where he witnessed the arrest of a large number of undocumented workers. Following this he was escorted to an area where he actually saw another large group of undocumented workers crossing the border on foot.[5]

For the uninitiated Brownell, the trip to California changed his views concerning the problems along the border. During one point in his tour he described what he had heard and seen as "shocking" and unsettling.[6]

Upon his return to Washington, Brownell reversed his earlier statements concerning increased funding for the Border Patrol. Whereas he had once opposed any increases, he now termed any reductions in money and personnel as "penny-wise and pound-foolish."[7]

To Brownell increased appropriations represented only one approach to dealing with the influx of "illegals." He unveiled three other approaches at a meeting in Denver, Colorado, in August of 1953. Brownell proposed that the United States work closely with Mexico in order to seek a mutual solution to the problem of illegal immigration. He also suggested that the Department of Justice investigate ways to make federal laws tougher to curb illegal entry from Mexico. Third, the Attorney General recommended that state district attorneys study the possibility of making similar changes in their laws. His ideas met with strong support from President Eisenhower.[8]

Circumstances appeared to favor the proponents of penalty legislation now that the Eisenhower administration had recognized that illegal immigration from Mexico was a major issue affecting this country's well-being. Furthermore, the economic arguments set forth by antiwetback groups in support of penalty legislation were given added credence by the economic slump the United States was experiencing during 1953. While the rise in unemployment and the economic downswing were caused by a number of factors, many people attributed much of the fault to the presence of large numbers of undocumented workers. Reports that the United States was simply undergoing an adjustment closer to the normal rate of production were largely ignored.[9]

According to the *Congressional Record* only about half of those unemployed were men 25 years of age and older.[10] Of these, some were unemployed because they lacked skills or experience. Others refused to work because to do so meant being downgraded from their previous jobs or accepting lower-paying jobs. It seems that during the Korean War many workers were upgraded to jobs for which they were not really qualified. With the end of the boom many marginal workers were laid off, while others were hesitant to return to their former tasks. In addition, there were union men who were reluctant to take jobs outside of their industry lest they risk their seniority and their pension rights; many opted for a temporary idleness instead of risking their benefits. Unemployment insurance acted as a spur to this trend.[11] However, these circumstances received little publicity, and their effect on the unemployment situation were largely ignored by the general populace.

On the other hand the bracero and the "wetback" were constantly in the public eye, and to many they were the real cause of many of the nation's ills. While little could be done about braceros, there was something that could be done about the "wetbacks." After all, had not the media, labor leaders, and now the Justice Department said that the "illegals" had created "a grave social problem involving murder, prostitution, robbery, and a gigantic narcotics infiltration [as well as] a malignant threat to the growth of our society?"[12]

Generally speaking, the public had either been largely indifferent to the presence of "wetbacks" or had been unaware that a problem existed at all. These attitudes began to dissipate as the media took a greater interest and as many began to "feel" the negative economic effects attributed to their presence. As this interest and concern grew, there arose a greater call for the government to do something about it. Such demands could no longer be ignored or shunted aside.

On 29 March 1954, Brownell called a conference in his office in which he and Deputy Attorney General William P. Rogers met a labor delegation representing all of the major national labor organizations. Also present were representatives of the three major national religious organizations.[13] Brownell told the delegation, which was headed by Lewis G. Hines, special representative of the AFL, and Victor G. Reuther, assistant to the president of the CIO,[14] that he would take immediate administrative and legislative action in order to deal with the "wetback" situation. The administrative measure would involve a substantial increase in the number of Border Patrolmen along the Mexican border.[15] In promising this Brownell evidently overlooked the fact that in the past increased appropriations for the Immigration Service for equipment and increased personnel had not been forthcoming. Nonetheless, it represented quite a change from his earlier statements wherein he had said that he hoped the volume of illegal traffic could be relieved by negotiating a new farm-labor contract with Mexico "before we go ahead and indiscriminately increase the number of the border patrol."[16] Legislatively the program would involve enacting measures that would discourage the hiring of "illegal aliens" and provide for the seizure and confiscation of any vehicle or vessel used to bring or transport "illegals."[17]

Although Brownell made these pledges in March, no formal action on his promises occurred until 9 June 1954. It was at this time that Brownell unveiled plans for a massive roundup of undocumented workers and some legislative proposals that would be sent to Congress for action. With regard to the latter, Brownell stated that the proposed legislation would "provide the Department of Justice with much needed weapons to assist in bringing to a halt the increasing illegal crossings . . ."[18]

According to Brownell the proposals would authorize a court injunction to restrain an employer from continuing to hire "aliens" who were in the country illegally if the employer had knowledge that the "alien" was an illegal entrant. They would also authorize seizure and forfeiture of any vehicle or vessel used to transport "aliens" in violation of the immigration laws.[19] With regard to the first proposal Brownell told the press:

> The bill would not, per se, impose criminal liability upon a person who knowingly employs such aliens. The principal objective sought is the immediate suppression of employment practices which directly encourage and induce border violations. It is the opinion of the Department of Justice that this can be effectively done by employing the injunctive processes. As a regulatory device, it has proven to be both swift and effective. Moreover, persons who engage in the proscribed activities will be fully on notice before criminal sanctions can be applied, for only in cases of knowing violation of a court order can criminal contempt proceedings be instituted.[20]

The proposed legislation, which would be embodied in S.3660, differed in one major way from that discussed in 1951 by Truman in that it now contained language that would penalize those who employed undocumented workers. In this sense the legislation proposed during 1954 incorporated ideas espoused by Senator Paul Douglas during debates over S.1851 in 1951.

Yet S.3660 did not, in reality, represent a radical departure in the federal government's attitude concerning penalty legislation against those who employed undocumented workers. For one thing Douglas's amendment in 1951 would have made it a felony to hire "illegals." The 1954 bill did not make it a felony, and for that matter it imposed no criminal liability of any kind on employers of "wetbacks." It also included a provision in Section C that penalties could be imposed only on those employers who "knowingly" employed illegal entrants, something exceedingly difficult to prove. Another "safeguard" for employers was that the goal of the Justice Department was to discourage employment and not to punish offenders. Thus implicit in the legislation was the idea that employers would be given sufficient opportunity to change their waywardness before any criminal sanctions would be applied against them. In short, the law contained several loopholes that would provide employers of "illegals" with enough opportunities to avoid prosecution. It sought to apply the injunctive process as a way of reeducating those who were chronic employers of "illegals" and to encourage more growers to take advantage of the bracero program. In this way Justice Department officials and members of the Eisenhower administration attempted to make penalty legislation more palatable to the powerful grower groups and their representatives and supporters in Congress, while attempting to assuage an aroused press and public.

An interesting aspect of S.3660 was that, if enacted, it would further increase the opportunities for exploiting hapless "illegals," for it made the payment of money "or anything of value" for services rendered by "illegal aliens" unlawful.[21] Under this law employers could claim that they were unaware that the individual or individuals they had hired were in the country illegally and that to pay them would put them in jeopardy of criminal prosecution. Therefore employers could legally refuse to pay their workers for services rendered, and the workers (if here illegally) would have little or no legal recourse for demanding payment of their wages.

On 24 June 1954, S.3660 and S.3661 were introduced in both houses by Senator Arthur Watkins of Utah and Representative Louis E. Graham of Pennsylvania.[22] By that time Brownell had already instituted the other phase of his program to deal with the "wetback issue." On 9 June the mass roundup and deportation of undocumented workers had begun in California.

In introducing the bills to the Senate, Watkins, who was chairman of the Senate Judiciary Subcommittee on Immigration and Naturalization, made reference to "Operation Wetback" in his opening remarks. He called upon his colleagues to pass the bills before them and not to allow themselves to be lulled into inaction by the current operations in California and New Mexico. Watkins described the mass roundup as "salutory" and warned the Senate that it would not solve the problem of illegal immigration from Mexico.[23] What was needed was decisive action on these measures by the Senate. However, no immediate action was taken on the bills; instead, the bills were referred to the Senate Judiciary Committee for hearings.

The hearings, held in mid-July, produced the first public hearings focused specifically on curtailing illegal immigration from Mexico.[24] Wishing to press the advantage offered by these hearings and by the progress of the mass roundup, which had now moved to Texas and Arizona, proponents of penalty legislation appeared before the committee in force to present their arguments.

In appearing before the committee, antiwetback forces were assured a fairly sympathetic hearing because most of the senators serving on the committee came from the urban and industrial areas of the country. Proponents also knew that any bill that involved penalty laws against those who employed undocumented workers would require the revision of the 1917 Immigration Law. Such revision would require action by the Judiciary Committees, who had jurisdiction over such matters. Generally speaking, these committees had been favorable to the efforts of those who supported penalty legislation.

Commercial farm groups and their supporters were well aware of this and girded themselves for action. They realized that efforts at enacting penalty legislation would have to be blocked once they reached the floor. However, a better strategy appeared to be to have the bills reported out so late in the session that there would not be enough time left for action on them until Congress reconvened.[25]

Among the first to testify on behalf of the bills was Joseph Swing, the newly-appointed Commissioner of Immigration and Naturalization. Swing strongly supported the bills because he viewed them as a necessary complement to the mass deportation of undocumented workers still going on in the Southwest. According to Swing, something had to be done to convince employers of "illegals" that they would not be allowed to go unmolested any longer. Something had to be done to dissipate the belief by employers that they held a vested right in the use of illegal labor.[26] To Swing, S.3660 would prove a useful tool in persuading individuals to use legal contract labor. The law would make use of the injunction in order to stop employment of "illegals." If a person violated that injunction then he or she would be found in contempt of court.[27] Swing had no desire to have laws enacted that would be viewed as unduly harsh by the growers. Instead, he wanted laws to help in his program to reeducate people into using braceros instead of "illegals."

Watkins, who had introduced the bills in the Senate, favored them for other reasons. According to him the problem of the "illegals" could no longer be viewed as simply an agricultural or regional problem. Increasingly a large percentage of "illegals" apprehended in border districts and elsewhere had indicated that they considered employment in agriculture only as a temporary necessity. Their main goal, said Watkins, appeared to be a desire to filter into the industrial centers to find employment in defense plants and other industries.[28]

Rocco Siciliano, Assistant Secretary of Labor for Employment and Manpower, reinforced the views of Watkins by testifying that "wetbacks" were no longer limiting themselves to seeking employment in agriculture. Siciliano told members of the committee that the Immigration and Naturalization Service had apprehended 40,860 "illegals" in industries and trades throughout the county during the first eleven months of 1954. He stated that apprehensions had been made in cities such as San Francisco, Chicago, Detroit, Kansas City, and Seattle.[29] Moreover, overall apprehensions of "illegals" had risen dramatically from 8,000 in 1941 to 510,000 in 1952.[30]

Adding his voice in support of the measures on behalf of organized labor was Nicholas Dragon, a CIO Regional Representative from Phoenix, Arizona. Dragon told the committee that the CIO fully supported the "wetback" bills, but that his organization wanted to see amendments added to eliminate some of the loopholes contained in the bills.[31]

Reverend Matthew H. Kelly, Executive Secretary of the Regional Offices of the Bishop's Committee for the Spanish-Speaking in Houston, also appeared before the committee to urge passage of S.3660 and S.3661.[32] Kelly argued that failure to enact the legislation would only continue to encourage the exploitation of "illegals" by unscrupulous employers. He believed that something had to be done in order to remove one of the major reasons for crossing illegally, the promise of employment. Kelly not only criticized those who employed "illegals" but also levelled a few volleys at those who supported them and who publicly criticized law-enforcement officials for trying to do their job. According to Kelly such acts had bred a contempt and hatred of Border Patrolmen. In many instances, said Kelly, they became the "victims of ludicrous charges, dishonest innuendo, and open hostility." He questioned the real motives of editors in the Rio Grande Valley of Texas who carried on this campaign of defamation while claiming "to be motivated by a Christian sense of compassion for the multitude of wetbacks."[33] In his opinion the Border Patrol was to be commended for performing its duties in the face of such strong criticism and opposition.

Farmers and growers who ran small operations also expressed their support of the two bills. In their view the use of illegal labor by large grower corporations placed them at a distinct disadvantage in that the latter could harvest and process their crops more cheaply than the independent grower. A few commercial farm associations such as the El Paso Cotton Growers Associations, the Imperial Valley Farmers Association, and a few small associations in Arizona echoed the sentiments of the small farmers. However, favorable statements concerning penalty legislation from grower associations were the exception and were often made without much support from their membership.[34] For the most part growers and processors described the imposition of penalties against employers as "a very harsh type of police state measure."[35]

In spite of the sympathetic hearings that the two "wetback" bills received in committee, they still faced a strong uphill fight for passage. The commercial growers and farmers had a strong coalition of farm groups, and the farm organizations could pull together when they had to in order to block or push through legislation beneficial to them.

The power of this coalition had been amply demonstrated through the continued renewal of the bracero program. This was especially noteworthy when one considers that only about 2 percent of the nation's farms employed most of the domestic migrant and bracero labor available.[36] Thus only 125,000 large scale farms were reaping the benefits of the contract labor program in effect with Mexico.[37]

In addition to the voting strength of their representatives in Congress, grower interests have also dominated some of the key committees in the legislative branch, especially the Appropriations and Agriculture committees, in effect giving the large grower interests jurisdiction over the bracero program. Their influence in the area of appropriations, when coupled with the congressional desire to economize, made it possible to control the size and power of the Immigration Service and to keep the pool of contract labor compliance officers at a minimum.[38]

Why such power when only a relatively small percentage of people benefitted from such a massive and expensive program? Much of the success of these organizations came from their ability to garner the support of farm groups outside the Southwest. Of crucial importance was the support from midwestern farm organizations, who usually backed southwestern interests in return for support from them on price supports for midwestern farmers. Furthermore, some grower organizations, such as the American Farm Bureau Federation, had over 50 percent of their membership in the Midwest, and another 30 percent in the South. Because the American Farm Bureau Federation was the largest of the three major farm organizations and had a large national membership, legislators at all levels had to remain sensitive and responsive to its wishes.[39] Antiwetback and antibracero proponents were well aware of this, for they had often experienced frustrating defeats at the hands of this group. Thus, though they were hopeful of some success because of the climate of great public interest and concern, they were nonetheless not totally surprised by the slow progress that S.3660 and S.3661 made after the Judiciary Committee favorably reported them out in early August.

What angered those who favored their passage was the sudden lack of initiative displayed by Brownell in fighting for the bills before Congress. By late August the attorney general was under fire from labor, the elected friends of labor, and religious groups for permitting his much-heralded legislative program to flounder in Congress. Brownell responded that he was doing everything possible to have the "wetback" bills enacted.

In the Senate, Wayne Morse of Oregon questioned Brownell's commitment to the legislation. Was the attorney general in fact "doing everything possible" or making only a token effort?[40] Certainly, said Morse, the program had not gotten off to a good start, particularly since the Senate Judiciary Committee had not received drafts of the bills until three months after Brownell's promise to take action against the illegal influx. Morse told the Senate that he was sympathetic to the members of the Senate Judiciary Committee who had worked hard to complete the hearings on the bills and get them on the floor "with little or no further help from the Attorney General or the White House." Was it any wonder then that many had come to question Brownell's concern and sincerity?[41]

In the course of his remarks Morse also levelled some broadsides at the Republicans in general and the president in particular. He dismissed Republican charges that the bills had been delayed in coming to the floor because of Democratic actions as mere "excuses." This was just a feeble attempt to cover up the failure of the Republicans to take decisive action. To him the attempt to blame the Democrats represented "as abject a passing of the buck . . . as any I've seen in my political life." As far as he was concerned the responsibility for not passing the legislation rested squarely upon the shoulders of Eisenhower and his administration.[42]

Morse was of course being partisan in his remarks, particularly with regard to Eisenhower. From the outset Eisenhower had been opposed to the "wetback" influx because of the serious implications it carried in social, economic, and international terms. It is true that his administartion had acquiesced to the use of unilateral recruitment and to the "legalization" of "wetbacks," which had only served to further encourage illegal immigration. Yet Eisenhower himself had grown stronger in his own personal resolve to do something about the problem, as was reflected in his support of his friend Joseph Swing and in some of his statements concerning the problem of illegal immigration. For example, in 1951 Eisenhower wrote to Senator Fulbright commending him on a speech the senator had made on the need for more morality in American affairs. Ike agreed with his views and took occasion to tie the senator's remarks in with the question of illegal immigration. "The rise," wrote Eisenhower, "in illegal border crossings by Mexican wetbacks to a current rate of more than 1,000,000 cases a year has been accompanied by a curious relaxation in ethical standards extending all the way from the farmer-exploiters of this contraband labor to the highest levels of the Federal Government." He said he was troubled by the fact that southwestern cotton, citrus, and vegetable growers saw nothing wrong with employing, harboring, or even actively recruiting workers who were fugitives from justice. With reference to the fact that some had characterized Fulbright as naive for his views, Ike stated that he too had had that adjective applied to him, but that whereas his critics had meant it as an insult, he had "come to look upon it as a very distinct compliment . . . At the very least," he concluded, "it would seem to imply the opposite of deliberate racketeering."[43]

Yet when it came to political matters Eisenhower realized that personal feelings had to be set aside. This was the case with regard to S.3660 and S.3661. Although Eisenhower might have personally favored their passage he realized that his administration would have to pay a high political price for it. At this time Eisenhower was not willing to risk it, particularly in light of the support that the growers had demonstrated for the mass roundup in California. Of course, there was "Operation Wetback" itself. By the end of August the operation was winding down, and the INS and the media were heralding it as an unqualified success. Whether it was or not did not really matter to Eisenhower at this point. What did matter was that people viewed it as a positive step in dealing with a serious problem. The operation had served to relieve some of the pressure emanating from the antiwetback sector, and it had been carried off without creating too much antagonism among the powerful grower interests. To push for penalty legislation would only stir up the whole nest again. Therefore Eisenhower was content not to interfere in the legislative debate over the bills since they were doomed to defeat anyway.

CONCLUSION

Brownell's legislative proposals were never acted upon by Congress. Although they were favorably reported by the Senate Judiciary Committee, powerful interests in Congress saw to it that they were reported out so late in the session that no action was taken on them. Even if they had appeared on the floor early enough for debate and action, it is very doubtful that S.3660 and S.3661 would have passed, given the overwhelming influence that commercial farm interests exercised in Congress.

Although two bills were proposed, their fate from the outset was linked to S.3660, which contained provisions for imposing injunctions against those who "knowingly" employed "illegals." In scrutinizing the contents of this bill one is struck by its relative leniency, as it does not contain any criminal penalties against employers. In this sense the bill reflected the attitude of Justice Department officials that had so often frustrated enforcement officers in the Border Patrol, one of not wanting to impose criminal penalties against employers. Instead, the Justice Department had advocated the use of the injunction and of moral suasion to deter employers from hiring "illegals." In part this thinking had been shaped by a desire not to antagonize the powerful growers or their representatives and by the knowledge that more stringent penalty legislation would have no chance of being enacted.

Yet the Justice Department, which was responsible for overseeing the enforcement of immigration laws, could not afford to ignore the issue completely. In an attempt to do something about it, and at the same time not appear to be overly antagonistic to growers, it proposed relatively lenient legislation in hopes that it would prove palatable to most groups. Commercial growers were determined not to give ground on this issue. Any type of legislation designed to curb their power or their ability to hire the necessary labor was anathema to them. On the other side of the coin were those who sought to curtail the power of commercial growers and curb the illegal influx from Mexico. Although these individuals and groups recognized that S.3660 contained a number of loopholes favorable to employers, they nonetheless saw it as a step in the right direction. They were loathe to give up any gain or any promise of change that might signal that the battle was beginning to swing toward their side. Therefore they were insistent that Brownell follow through on his pledges.

Men such as H.L. Mitchell, President of the National Agricultural Union, and O.A. Knight of the CIO were quick to remind Brownell of his pledges. Mitchell questioned his lack of action in working to get the bills through Congress, while Knight expressed skepticism concerning the attorney general's sincerity.[44]

Throughout the hearings and discussions surrounding S.3660, very little mention was made of its companion, S.3661, which would have provided for the seizure and forfeiture of any vehicle or vessel used to knowingly transport "illegal aliens" into their country. In some ways S.3661 was designed to bolster the laws that made it unlawful to harbor, conceal, or smuggle in persons who had entered or were planning to enter "illegally."

Although S.3661 did not represent a great threat to a majority of the growers, its proposal in tandem with the more objectionable S.3660 also insured its defeat. Yet even if no such handicap had been imposed on it and it had been enacted, chances are that it would have had little effect in curtailing smuggling activities. This view is based on the ineffectiveness of the 1952 law, which imposed heavy penalties and prison sentences against anyone convicted of smuggling "aliens" into the country. The first conviction under this law occurred in March of 1953, when three building contractors were indicted for transporting "illegals" from Monterrey, Mexico, to Fresno, California. Their conviction was based on the fact that they had "knowingly" smuggled and transported aliens, as they were caught in the act by authorities, but they did not receive very stiff sentences.[45]

The first conviction of growers occurred in October of 1953. Of the three, one was convicted because he had used a shortwave radio to warn "illegals" that the Border Patrol was entering their area. The other two were convicted because they were caught while smuggling in eight "wetbacks," making them subject to a possible four years in prison and a fine of $8,000.00. Instead, both men were given only thirty days in jail.[46]

Few were ever captured, much less convicted, under the 1952 law. In fact, most juries refused to find defendants in trials involving smuggling, concealing, or harboring "illegals" guilty of any wrongdoing.[47] It is quite likely that the same lax enforcement would have been applied to the laws embodied in S.3660 and S.3661 if they had been enacted. As it was, interest in enacting such legislation quickly dropped off. The implementation of "Operation Wetback" and its much-publicized "success" lulled many proponents of such legislation into believing that the influx of "illegals" was under control and that perhaps penalty legislation, which would always face a tough uphill fight, was not the solution after all.

NOTES

1. Richard P. Eckels, "Hungry Workers, Ripe Crops, and the Non-Existent Mexican Border," *The Reporter* (13 April 1954), p. 28.

2. Ibid.

3. *San Francisco Examiner* (17 August 1957).

4. Willard F. Kelley, "The Wetback Issue," *The I and N Reporter* 2, no. 3 (January 1954): 37.

5. Ibid.

6. *New York Times* (18 August 1953), p. 16.

7. San Francisco *Examiner* (17 August 1953), Robert D. Tomasek, "The Political and Economic Implications of Mexican Labor in the United States under the Non-Quota System, Contract Labor Program, and Wetback Movement" (Ph.D. diss., University of Michigan, 1957), pp. 150-51.

8. Anthony Levieros, "Eisenhower Backs Wetback Drive," *New York Times* (18 August 1953), p. 16.

9. U.S., Congress, House, *Congressional Record,* 83d Cong., 2d sess., 1954, 100, pt. 2: 2393.

10. Ibid.

11. Ibid.

12. *Burner's Weekly Magazine* no. 126 (24 October 1953), p. 63.

13. U.S., Congress, House, *Congressional Record,* 83d Cong., 2d sess., 1954, 100, pt. 12: 15174.

14. " 'Wetback' Bill Pledged," *New York Times* (30 March 1954), p. 19.

15. U.S., Congress, House, *Congressional Record,* 1954, 100, pt. 12: 15174.

16. U.S., Congress, House, *Congressional Record,* 83d Cong., 2d sess., 1954, 100, pt. 2: 2526.

17. U.S., Congress, House, *Congressional Record,* 1954, 100, pt. 12: 15174.

18. Department of Justice News Release, 9 June 1954, p. 1, found in U.S. Department of Justice, Border Patrol Branch, Subject-General File: Special Border Patrol Force, "Wetback, Operation" Task Force General (May-June 1954), Volume 1, located in Office of Immigration, Washington, D.C. (hereafter cited as Records, *S.B.P.F.,* 1954, Volume 1).

19. Ibid.

20. Ibid.

21. Ibid.

22. U.S., Congress, House, *Congressional Record*, 1954, 100, pt. 12: 15174.

23. *Congressional Record*, 83d Cong., 2d sess., 1954, 100 pt. 7: 8792.

24. Gilbert Cardenas, "United States Immigration Policy Toward Mexico: An Historical Perspective" (South Bend, Ind.: Notre Dame, Centros de Estudios Chicanos y Investigaciones 1974), p. 55.

25. Robert D. Tomasek, "The Political and Economic Implications of Mexican Labor in the United States under the Non-Quota System, Contract Labor Program, and Wetback Movement" (Ph.D. diss., University of Michigan, 1957), pp. 150-51.

26. U.S. Congress, Senate, Committee on the Judiciary, Subcommittee on Immigration and Naturalization, *Hearings, to Control Illegal Immigration*, S.3660 and S.3661, 83d Cong., 2d sess., 1954, p. 5.

27. Ibid., p. 9.

28. Ibid., p. 16.

29. Ibid., p. 35.

30. Ibid., p. 37.

31. Ibid., pp. 43-45.

32. Ibid., p. 54.

33. Ibid., p. 56.

34. Tomasek, "The Political and Economic Implications," p. 202.

35. *Hearings, To Control Illegal Immigration*, p. 22.

36. President's Commission on Migratory Labor, *Migratory Labor in American Agriculture* (Washington, D.C.: G.P.O., 1951), p. 7.

37. Ibid.

38. Tomasek, "The Political and Economic Implications," p. 145.

39. Grant McConnell, *The Decline of Agrarian Democracy* (Berkeley: University of California Press, 1953), pp. 108-09.

40. U.S., Congress, House, *Congressional Record*, 1954, 100, pt. 12: 15174.

41. Ibid.

42. Ibid.

43. Dwight D. Eisenhower to Senator William Fulbright (19 June 1951), Central Files, White House Correspondence, located in Dwight D. Eisenhower Library, Abilene, Kansas.

44. H.L. Mitchell to Herbert Brownell (17 August 1954), cited in U.S., Congress, House, *Congressional Record*, 1954, 100, pt. 12: 15174; and O.A. Knight to Herbert Brownell (17 August 1954), cited in ibid., p. 15175.

45. *New York Times* (17 April 1953), p. 24.

46. *New York Times* (18 October 1953), p. 27.

47. Tomasek, "The Political and Economic Implications," p. 255.

6
Planning
"Operation Wetback"

WHILE ATTORNEY GENERAL Herbert Brownell's legislative proposals floun-
dered in Congress, the second phase of his plan to stem the illegal influx from
Mexico was put into action. Calling for the mass roundup and repatriation of
"illegal aliens" in the United States, this plan was given the name "Operation
Wetback."

During the initial planning of the operation Brownell had approached Secretary
of Defense Charles Wilson about the possibility of using the army to conduct the
mass roundup. According to Pentagon officials, Brownell had suggested that army
troops, assisted by light planes, patrol the 250-mile stretch along the California-
Arizona sector of the border, thus permitting the Border Patrol to concentrate its
strength in the border areas of Texas and New Mexico.[1]

Army officials reacted coldly to Brownell's proposal. They believed that such
a task would "seriously disrupt training programs at a time when the administration's economy slashes were forcing the service to drastically cut its strength."[2]
Army generals also opposed the idea because a division would be needed just to
begin to control the influx, while sealing off the border would require even more
troops.[3]

Brownell's plan to use the army had not met with favorable response from other
quarters. Robert C. Goodwin sent a memorandum to Secretary of Labor James
Mitchell stating that "if the Army proposal were to be followed, we (the United
States) would get a similar reaction from a rather large group in this country."[4]
The "reaction" that Goodwin referred to was embodied in a confidential foreign
service dispatch from the Embassy in Mexico to the State Department on 25 August
1953. The dispatch called attention to a 22 August cartoon on the editorial page
of *Excelsior,* Mexico's leading newspaper. The cartoon portrayed a terror-stricken
Mexican with his back to the wall and a huge bayonet marked "U.S. Troops"
pointed at his chest, with the legend "Between the Sword and the Wall." Franklin
C. Gowan, counselor of the American Embassy, said that the cartoon had caused
numerous anti-American comments because many assumed that we really intended
to use federal troops to stop illegal entry from Mexico. Gowan wrote:

> The slant of these comments, which are being overheard in typical local cafes, restaurants, and other like places patronized by Mexicans, is that we are an imperialistic, war-mongering and ruthless people and that the poor and wretched wetbacks who want to return to the lands which the United States forcibly took from Mexico, will be met by a hail of American bullets.[5]

Gowan concluded that these public comments were a clear indication to the ambassador of the disastrous effect that the use of federal troops to close the border would have not only in our relations with Mexico but with all of Latin America. It was also feared that such an act would be "fruit for the communist mill in other parts of the world."[6]

The concern of certain Washington officials was understandable, as Mexican sensitivities had already been stirred when newspapers in that country had charged immigration officials with inhuman treatment of captured "illegals." The charges stemmed from a newspaper account in the *Laredo Times* on 6 June 1953. According to the article, immigration officials had forced captured "wetbacks" to return to Mexico on foot through "45 miles of rattlesnake-infested desert" as "punishment." While immigration authorities and Justice Department officials either denied the charges or refused comment, the *Laredo Times* sent some of its correspondents to confirm the stories. According to Jack Yecman, one of the correspondents dispatched to confirm the charges, "wetbacks" were indeed forced to walk through an extremely hostile terrain once they had been dropped off by border patrolmen near Zapata, Texas.[7]

At first glance it might have appeared that the report by the *Laredo Times* was fabricated in order to discredit the Border Patrol. It was already a well-known fact that many of the newspapers in Texas supported the growers and their use of "wetbacks" and seldom missed an opportunity to place the Border Patrol in a bad light. Be that as it may, this was not the case this time. While immigration officials publicly denied such charges, privately they worked to change their handling of deportees now that it had been brought to light by what they termed "adverse publicity."[8]

This was not the first time that immigration officials had been charged with mistreating apprehended "illegals." In 1949 Waldo E. Bailey, the American consul in Tijuana, wrote a memorandum to the secretary of state deploring the fact that certain officials were completely shaving the heads of "illegals" just before deporting them. While the consul acknowledged that there might be some hygienic reasons for doing this, he also believed that completely depriving them of their hair was unnecessary and served only to anger and humiliate them.[9] A year later Mexican newspapers carried banner headlines charging immigration officials with conducting police-state raids against undocumented workers. An editorial in *El Popular* charged that Border Patrol officers were instructed "to fire without qualms" at those who attempted to enter illegally. Though these and other stories concerning abuses were jointly denied by Mexican and United States officials, such disclaimers did little to quell Mexican public resentment against the roundups.[10]

In 1952 another wave of stories concerning the mistreatment of Mexican "illegals" appeared in many of Mexico's northern newspapers. Again the stories charged immigration officials with "discrimination" and "harshness" and with treating Mexicans much as the "victims of Nazi concentration camps" were treated. While officials in the United States admitted privately that there had been a few abuses, they publicly decried the exaggerated stories in Mexican newspapers. One official suggested that the United States counteract these stories by publishing information reflecting the concern exercised by this country in the care of braceros. What this person appeared to overlook was that the stories dealt with the mistreatment of undocumented workers and not braceros.[11]

Because the Mexican press remained vigilant against mistreatment and abuses of Mexicans in the United States, whatever their status, and because the Mexican populace could be aroused to exert pressure on their government as a result of press coverage, officials in the United States had to exercise caution in their treatment of "illegals." It is therefore of little surprise that knowledgeable officials frowned upon the use of federal troops to patrol the border or the indiscriminate abuse of "illegals."

In 1956, General Joseph Swing testified that Brownell had asked him in 1953 to prepare a plan to send American troops to the Mexican border to stop the "illegal invasion of . . . 'wetbacks.' " Swing told the investigating committee that he had drawn up the plan, which was called "Operation Cloudburst," while he was commander of the Sixth Army in California. The plan, according to Swing, would have entailed stationing four thousand men along the border from east of the Yuma-San Luis area to the Pacific Ocean. Swing said that the plan was dropped after he had told Brownell that it was "a perfectly horrible" way to handle the situation because any such move would "destroy" relations with Mexico. After Swing retired from the army on 24 February 1954, Brownell invited him to "come on down and show us how to do it without closing the border." Swing took him up on the offer and was appointed Commissioner of Immigration.[12]

Brownell had been mulling over how to deal with the "wetback" situation after his inspection tour, for he viewed it as one of the most important problems awaiting resolution.[13] In addition to calling out the army, he had proposed that the Department of Defense make available certain resources and appropriations to meet the situation caused by illegal entrants, including ten million dollars to construct a 150-mile fence along the border. The Bureau of the Budget refused to grant the request because the construction of a six-mile fence a few years earlier had not proven an effective deterrent, and maintenance costs had been about $10,000 to $20,000 annually. A request for transfer of funds to resume airlifting of "illegal aliens" into the interior of Mexico was also denied, primarily because it was a violation of rules prohibiting such transfers.[14]

Brownell was accused of having considered even more radical methods to stop "illegals" than calling out troops and building a Mexican wall. In May of 1954, William P. Allen, publisher of the *Laredo Times,* wrote to Eisenhower about a charge made by leaders of the International Labor meeting. According to Allen labor leaders from Washington had told him at dinner on 11 May that they had discussed the "wetback problem" with Brownell, who had suggested that "one method of discouraging wetbacks would be to allow the border patrol to shoot some of them."[15] Allen said that shooting "illegals" and beating them up was nothing new and that it constituted a "vulgar page that is already smeared with blood." What irked Allen was that Brownell had asked labor leaders to support him in this matter when the shootings came to public attention. Allen demanded that Eisenhower look into this.[16] His telegram was referred to James Hagerty for the necessary action, but the records do not indicate what, if anything, was done about it.[17]

Although Brownell was unable to get the Army, he did manage to have a military man appointed to the post of Commissioner of Immigration. In 1954 Joseph M. Swing had retired with the rank of lieutenant-general from the United States Army.[18] A classmate of Dwight Eisenhower at West Point in 1911,[19] he had accompanied General John Pershing in 1916 on the "Punitive Expedition" against Pancho Villa.[20] Swing was reputed to be a "professional, long-time Mexican hater,"[21] which, if true, did not augur well for Mexicans in the United States.

In many ways Swing was a perfectionist. A stern task master, he was easily angered when anyone failed to carry out responsibilities. Yet, according to a close associate of his, underneath this harsh exterior there lay a person concerned about the welfare of others. As commissioner, Swing did not tolerate misconduct. If somebody allowed the "heat to get to him" and resorted to force and brutality, Swing would immediately have that person transferred to a post along the Canadian border. Harlon Carter, a key figure in "Operation Wetback" described him as "a tough boss" for whom he had a great deal of respect. According to Carter, Swing, who was in his late fifties when he became Commissioner of Immigration, was in constant pain from injuries he had suffered while making paratrooper jumps, yet he never complained about his discomfort.[22]

Swing's military experience was to prove a valuable asset to the Immigration Service, but of even greater importance was his close friendship with Eisenhower. On several occasions Swing met with the president without needing an appointment. Sources close to Swing believe that these informal gatherings with Ike proved beneficial to the service in getting needed support from the White House.

After taking office in May of 1954, Swing began to formulate plans for an all-out offensive against the "illegals." To help him in his planning he hired Generals Frank Partridge and Edwin Howard as consultants to the Immigration Service. Later Swing was to say that he attributed "the success of the stemming of the wetback program" to General Partridge's great experience in the handling of large organizations and his administrative ability.[23] Prior to Partridge's arrival, according to Swing, the Border Patrol branch pretty much ran around in circles.[24]

What developed into "Operation Wetback" had from the outset all the ear-marks of a military offensive. Not only did Swing bring in military consultants, but the terms and strategies used were also along military lines. Swing and his co-horts established an intelligence service and began to function with the "precision, timing, and efficiency of a trained military or semi-military body."[25]

The initial phase of the operation involved a personal tour of the border area by Swing.[26] After that, he and Partridge began the reorganization of the Border Patrol around two primary requisites: flexibility of organization to insure maximum efficiency and mobility of force to provide multiplied strength in regions where it was needed.[27]

When Swing toured the border area he found no coordination or cooperation among the thirteen Border Patrol sectors. No one on either side knew what the other was doing. This situation hindered operations as a tangle of confusion was created by a duplicating of areas patrolled and an overlapping of duties.[28] Surveys also showed that there was a serious lack of supervision and that top administrators in Washington were bogged down with routine operational activities that left them little time for policy-determining functions. To correct this, regional headquarters for supervision and management of districts were established.[29] This meant that the Border Patrol in these areas or regions was now directly under the control of a regional chief, thus eliminating district control and making for more unified plan-ning and action throughout the border area.[30] Supervision of the entire southern border was vested in one command instead of three. "Thus, where the movement of personnel and material were [sic] formerly restricted to the three district bound-aries in an area where there existed a single problem demanding a uniform response, now personnel and material [were] moved where and when needed to meet the demands of any situation along the entire border."[31] In addition, it was shown that the country naturally could be divided into four district areas with respect to service work, with the Southwest region being one of the four. District boundaries were realigned to make them coextensive with state boundaries whenever possible, another way of improving the old system.[32]

In addition to making the Border Patrol a more unified and autonomous branch, Swing created new positions to help it function more effectively. One such post was that of Senior Patrol Inspector. The Senior Patrol Inspector assigned to each sector had the responsibility of developing informants for the purpose of correlating, evaluating, and disseminating any information of value in dealing with smuggling operations as well as illegal entry.[33] The Senior Patrol Inspector was also authorized to enlist the aid of any patrol officer in a position to assist him, and he had the authority to bypass regular channels and deal directly with officers in different sectors, districts, or regions when events required immediate attention.[34]

The capstone of Swing's reorganization of the Border Patrol was the Mobile Task Force. The idea of using highly mobile task forces in roundup operations did not emerge from Swing or his consultants. The concept had been proposed prior to Swing's arrival by Harlon B. Carter, a veteran of the service, but the idea had not caught on primarily because of the overlapping in jurisdiction and because of the potentially high cost.

When Swing became commissioner and began to formulate plans for the mass roundup, he turned to some of the younger and more experienced Border Patrol officers for advise. Harlon Carter was one of the men chosen by Swing to oversee the planning and organization of the operation, and at this time Carter again set forth the idea of using mobile task forces. Swing liked the idea and told Carter to prepare detailed plans of how they would operate.

On 10 June 1954, all border chiefs met in California to discuss their assignments for the roundup. Among them were Charles Kirk, G.J. McNee, and John P. Swanson. It was to these three veterans that Carter gave the assignment of providing him with a design for the Mobile Task Force. Already familiar with the concept, the three of them worked feverishly for a few days to come up with a design. After a few days they gave their plan to Carter, who approved it and forwarded it to Swing.[35]

The design, which pleased Swing, was well suited to the needs at hand. For the moment Swing showed little concern over the fact that it was costly. According to the design each "task force" consisted of a twelve-man unit, highly mobile and self-sufficient. Each squad had radio-equipped automobiles, jeeps, trucks, and even buses and planes and thus had the necessary equipment available to more effectively patrol the border in their sector.[36] The reorganization of the Border Patrol into these squads made it possible to assemble "Special Mobile Forces" of four hundred men aided by seventy auxiliary personnel within four to forty-eight hours notice. This "Special Mobile Force" was assigned the areas within the Brownsville and McAllen sectors of the San Antonio District and the El Centro and Chula Vista sectors of the San Francisco District.[37] The purpose of the "Special Mobile Force" was to concentrate manpower in designated areas containing high concentrations of "illegal aliens." It would then conduct a mass roundup in that area and begin to work in widening circles. This method served to push the "aliens" across the border to avoid capture while the patrolmen conducted mop-up operations as they went along. In addition to the concentration of personnel, the Border Patrol enlisted the help of local and state law enforcement agencies to help in the operation. As already stated, the only drawback to this strategy was its costliness, for it involved the payment of per diem and other travel expenses for employees away from their official stations.

Swing and his staff also reinstated operating techniques that had proven fairly effective in the past and made them a part of standard operating procedure for the mobile task force. These techniques included the airlift, the buslift, the trainlift, the boatlift, and a new air-to-ground and car-to-car radio communication system. In conjunction with these steps, the reorganization brought to bear the resources of other divisions of the Immigration Service. Where no divisions existed to fill the needs, new ones were created. This included the Border Patrol Air Transport Arm[38] and an intelligence unit that provided the Border Patrol with strategies, tactical input, and counterintelligence information. Swing also increased the use of dogs on line operations.

The actual course of action for "Operation Wetback" was planned in May of 1954 at a meeting held in the office of William Belton of the Mexican Affairs Desk in the State Department.[39] Representatives of the Immigration, Labor, and State Departments had gathered to discuss the Immigration Service's proposal to control the entry of undocumented workers.[40] The proposal met with warm approval from all of those present. However, the Labor Department requested that the roundup not be limited solely to "illegals" employed in agriculture. Its representatives believed that efforts should be made to apprehend "illegals" working in the industrial sector in order to gain greater support for the INS in states where governors had already expressed concern over the growing number of "illegals" in industry.[41]

Labor officials also told those present that they would cooperate to the fullest extent in giving the program considerable advanced publicity so that employers of "wet labor" would have ample opportunity to recruit legal labor. This advance warning proved more beneficial to California growers than to Texas growers, as the former had better organized associations with which to recruit laborers.[42]

The method of removing captured "illegals" to Mexico was also discussed at this conference. Immigration officials clearly favored the use of a buslift. Their plan was to transport those who were apprehended from California to Nogales, Arizona. Once in Nogales, they would be taken to Mexico, where they would be transported to the interior of that country by Mexican officials. It was hoped that this approach would reduce the number of repeaters.[43]

In contrast to earlier episodes involving the deportation of "illegals," State Department officials decided to seek the full cooperation of the Mexican government in providing proper and adequate facilities for the removal of deported "illegals" into the interior of Mexico. In the past the United States had been satisfied to transport "illegals" to Mexican border cities, where their presence had added to health, economic, and social problems. W. Belton expressed the hope that the Immigration Service would in turn provide proper facilities for detaining "illegals" at Nogales until the trains that would take them to Mexico arrived. Belton also told those present at the conference that he would see to it that the United States Information Service was thoroughly briefed at the appropriate time concerning the operation to disseminate information to offset any adverse propaganda in the Mexican papers.[44]

The Mexican government fully approved of the planned roundup. It had advocated and demanded that the United States do something to control the border. While it would have preferred that the action be in the form of penalty legislation against employers, it nonetheless viewed the operation as a positive step in the right direction. Unable and unwilling to put an end to the outward flow of undocumented workers from its borders because of inadequate enforcement resources, legal technicalities guaranteeing free movement of its citizens, the need to have a safety valve for its large, unemployed population, and a fear of adverse reaction to any kind of enforcement effort on their part, Mexican officials were more than happy to let the United States assume the initiative, responsibility, expense, and onus of controlling the border.

Interestingly enough, there was little coverage of the mass roundup in the Mexican press. Most of what did appear in the newspapers involved a straightforward account of the operation. Seldom did the stories in Mexico's major newspapers make any editorial comment regarding the mass deportation of "illegals" from the United States. When such comments did appear they usually reflected governmental support and praise for the effort, indicating that illegal emigration was detrimental to Mexican citizens, the bracero program, and relations between Mexico and the United States and should therefore be stopped or controlled.[45]

The lack of intense coverage in Mexico's official press was probably due to Mexico's desire not to stir up adverse public reaction to what Mexicans might have deemed as just one more instance of strong-arm tactics against them by the Colossus of the North. Furthermore, Mexico saw some benefits deriving from the operation. For one thing, it provided Mexican officials with a temporary solution to its dilemma over the plight of undocumented workers in the United States. Because it was largely unable to protect them from abuse, exploitation, and discrimination, the Mexican government had been subject to much criticism from different segments, including newspapers, labor unions, and opposition political parties. The mass deportations provided Mexico with an opportunity to have many of its citizens returned to the fold. Mexico also mistakenly saw in the operation a short-term bonus in that it believed that the money brought in by deported "illegals" would be beneficial to its economy. In truth, there was little hard fact to support this view. Like so many others, Mexican officials had been misled into believing erroneous and exaggerated estimates concerning the earnings of "illegals." While it was estimated that undocumented workers earned anywhere from $7.00 to $24.00 per week, most of that money never left the country. A large portion of their earnings was spent on food and other necessities, for which unscrupulous profiteers charged exorbitant prices. Unable or afraid to go into town, many "illegals" had little choice but to deal with these people. From the little money which was left to them they usually paid off loans from friends or relatives. After these expenses, if any money remained, most of them would send it to their relatives or family. Estimates that "illegals" sent out as much as $150 million per year appear exaggerated.[46]

Finally, Mexico knew that many of the "illegals" who were apprehended would be reprocessed and contracted as legal braceros, which meant that for the time being they would not be a burden to the country.

Whereas the drive against the "wetbacks" received relatively little press coverage in Mexico, it did receive widespread attention in the popular media in the United States. Such coverage was particularly intense in the Southwest, where it had the greatest impact. Although some of this coverage was negative and was the result of local support for grower interests and local opposition to the Border Patrol, a large portion of it was supportive of the drive. Much of the positive coverage and "propaganda" was the result of specific efforts and informational input from the Immigration Service, which saw such coverage as vital to its plans and even its future.

Immigration officials realized that they lacked the manpower to conduct such a widespread operation. What they palnned to do was to deluge the southwestern region with advance publicity about the upcoming campaign against "illegals." As part of these announcements, undocumented workers were urged to avoid apprehension and deportation by leaving before the campaign actually began.[47] Longstanding media coverage concerning the ills created by the "illegal invasion" was also viewed as a positive thing by INS because it aided in creating an increasingly hostile environment against "illegals" and their employers. It was hoped that the threat of mass deportation and their increasingly unwelcomed status as "invaders" would serve to pressure many of them into leaving the country voluntarily.

The emphasis in widely publicizing the upcoming drive was also part of a planned effort on the part of the INS to drum up public and legislative support for itself. The increasing influx of "illegals" had been used by opponents of the INS to discredit it in the eyes of those who voted on its operational funds. The proposal to utilize the army had not only injured the pride of the INS but also served to further confirm growing suspicions that the continued existence of the Border Patrol might be in jeopardy. Thus meticulous attention was given not only to publicizing the drive but also to making sure that sympathetic correspondents accompanied some of the task forces. As H.L. Landon reported to Swing, "the desired coverage" had been arranged "so that very favorable publicity" would be attained, "not only on the local but national level."[48]

"Operation Wetback" was an important project for the Border Patrol, providing it with the opportunity to prove its public, private, and congressional detractors wrong and to begin to change its image as an inept, slovenly, and ineffective branch of the government. High officials in the service now saw a chance to reaffirm the need for its continued existence and operation while concomitantly pressing for increased operating appropriations from the congress. As Herbert Brownell pointed out to Senator Thomas Kuchel of California, "I am hopeful that the results of the experimental force of the Immigration and Naturalization Service . . . will justify asking the Congress for funds to organize and continue such a force on a permanent basis."[49]

The carefully planned media blitz accomplished its purposes. First of all, by sensationalizing the activities and deployment of the Border Patrol it created the impression that a veritable army was being assembled. In order to maintain that impression, "maximum security prevailed throughout the operation . . . [I]nformation concerning exact officer strength and the organization of the units was kept strictly within the ranks of the officers assigned to the operation. Cleverly worded press releases plus an ostentatious display of men created an impression of greater strength than actually existed." The press was misled into overestimating the size of the actual force. Even those papers hostile to the drive inadvertently helped contribute "to the illusion by constantly referring to the Task Force as an invading army and by using such superlatives as 'hordes' and 'battalions' when writing about small groups of officers. Without a doubt this 'show of strength' contributed greatly to the exodus of aliens that fled across the border."[50]

In California the exodus was so great, according to immigration officers, that it was impossible to count them. In Texas more than 63,000 "illegal aliens" returned to Mexico of their own accord, unassisted and at no cost to the United States.[51] The publicity was also credited with the sudden increase in the contracting of braceros by employers who did not wish to take a chance in having "illegals" who might be frightened into leaving or be captured during the raids.

The actual campaign had been scheduled to begin on 1 June 1954, deemed a good date with regard to seasonal factors. This date had also been selected because officials of the INS wanted to utilize funds appropriated for fiscal year 1954.[52] However, the drive did not begin until 10 June because the Mexican government was unable to meet the 1 June deadline for completing railway arrangements necessary to transport deportees into the interior. Another reason for the delay was that Mexico wanted to ascertain if illegal entrants could be recruited under the Bracero Agreement. W. Belton of the Mexican Affairs Desk stated that the recruitment of "illegals" would be carried out if there was a shortage of workers at the Mexicali staging area.[53]

Although Carter, who was at the time chief of the border patrol branch, and some patrol chiefs had been assigned the duty of designing the plan in detail, Swing had not yet selected the person who would oversee the operation in the field. When Swing met with Carter early in May, he asked the young officer whom he would recommend for the post. Carter responded that he favored Marcus Neelly, the district director at El Paso. Swing's response to Carter's suggestion was: "It seems to me that if you knew that the question as to whether there is going to be any Border Patrol in the future depends upon the success of this [operation], it seems to me that you'd want to be in charge of it." Carter responded that if this were indeed the case, then he most definitely wanted to be in charge of it.[54]

As it turned out, Swing's appointment of Carter as director of field operations was a good one. Although he was still a relatively young man, Carter was an experienced veteran. The first problem that he tackled was how to augment the meager force along the border without decreasing backup strength along travel routes and places of employment. To overcome this he proposed that extra personnel be brought in from the Canadian border and from the districts of El Paso, Texas, and Florida, which would maintain the vital backup strength while increasing the number of officers along the border.[55] His proposal was accepted although it was accurately pointed out to him that following this procedure would involve leaving other areas understaffed and subject to large-scale illegal entry and smuggling activities. Carter acknowledged this as a strong possibility but thought it worth the risk.

As the plan developed, it was decided to bring in an additional five hundred officers from the other sectors. The operation was to center in the McAllen Sector of the San Antonio District and the Los Angeles District, where the concentration of "illegals" was considered the greatest and where the favorable effects of a successful operation would be more pronounced.[56] Those apprehended would be returned by various methods, including buslift and airlift. "Illegal aliens" who were captured would pay the cost of travel if they could afford it. The operation was to be under the direction of the District directors of the area in which the drive was conducted, and the major effort was to be directed against "illegal aliens" entering, traveling, or employed in farm or ranch work.[57]

Designed to concentrate the efforts of the Immigration and Naturalization Service in the most "troublesome" areas for an indefinite period, the project was not to be a hit-and-run affair. To remove every element of surprise and in order not to operate in a drastic fashion that might work hardship on any employer or employee, the project was given wide publicity. Growers were reassured that an adequate supply of legal labor would continue to be available for those who applied for it. The Department of Labor assigned a special liaison officer to assist the Immigration Service in this matter.[58] The desire not to cause undue hardship on employers was in keeping with the Justice Department goal of not alienating the powerful grower interest groups and their allies. Swing agreed with this view, as it was not his goal to punish those who hired undocumented workers. Rather, he hoped to reeducate employers so that they would contract braceros. Swing's patient but firm reminders that the INS would no longer tolerate entry convinced growers, particularly in California, of the wisdom of using braceros.

NOTES

1. John A. Giles, "Wilson and Brownell Disagree over Plan for 'Wetback' Patrol," *Washington Star*, (30 August 1953), article found in Records of the President's Committee on Migratory Labor, 1941, 1963, Secretary of Agriculture, Member, Box 102, A72-A, Folder M1-2, Wetbacks, located in Dwight D. Eisenhower Library, Abilene, Kansas.

2. Ibid.

3. Ibid.

4. Robert C. Goodwin, Memorandum to James P. Mitchell, Subject: State Department Dispatch No. 395, "Unfavorable Public Reaction to Possible Use of Force to Repel Illegal Entries into the United States," found in Record Group 174, Department of Labor, Office of the Secretary, 1953, Departmental Subject Files, Mental-Solicitor's Office, File 1953, Mexican Labor Program—Misc. (July-December), Box 6, located in the National Archives, Washington, D.C.

5. Foreign Service Dispatch, Disp. No. 395, 25 August 1953 (Confidential) from American Embassy, Mexico, D.F., to the Department of State, Washington, found in ibid.

6. Ibid. In a letter dated 18 August 1953, Walter Williams wrote President Eisenhower that General Walter B. Smith had phoned him to request "that no action be taken with respect to calling out United States troops to control the 'wetback' situation on the Mexican border until the State Department had the opportunity to express itself on the matter." Walter Williams to Dwight D. Eisenhower (18 August 1953), Central Files, Official File, OF 124-A-1, Box 634, Folder 124-C (1), Migratory Labor in the Dwight D. Eisenhower Library, Abilene, Kansas (hereafter cited as Central Files, Box 634, Folder 124-C (1)).

7. "Paper Charges U.S. Deports Wetbacks into Desert Peril," *Washington Post* (7 June 1953), p. 3.

8. James C. Powell, Jr., American Consul, to State Department, Foreign Service Despatch (17 June 1953), Subject: "Movement of Mexican Farm Laborers Being Returned to Mexico Through Parts of Zapata and Laredo, Texas," pp. 1-2 R. G. 166, Foreign Agricultural Service Narrative Reports, 1950-1954, Box 298, Folder, Mexico-Labor, National Archives, Washington, D.C.

9. Waldo E. Bailey, American Consul, Tijuana, Mexico, to Secretary of State (22 July 1949), Subject: "Apparent Violations in the United States of Civil Rights of Mexican 'Wetbacks'," pp. 1-3, Special Box, Folder, Mexico-Labor, 1946-1949, National Archives, Washington, D.C.

10. Louis F. Blanchard, American Consul, Mexico, D.F., to Department of State (24 March 1950), Subject: "Newspaper Publicity Relating to Matters Concerning Mexican Agricultural Workers," pp. 1-14, R.G. 166, Box 299, Folder, 1948 to 1950, National Archives, Washington, D.C.

11. Gerald A. Mokma, American Consul General, Monterrey, to Department of State (23 September 1952), Subject: "Steps Needed to Counteract Bad Publicity on Migratory Labor Questions," pp. 1-2, R.G. 166, Box 299, Folder, Mexico-Labor, 1951-1952, National Archives, Washington, D.C.

12. U.S., Congress, House, *Improper Use of Governmental Equipment and Government Personnel* (Immigration and Naturalization Service), Twenty-sixth Intermediate Report of Session, House Report 2948, 1956, p. 12 (hereafter cited as Report, *Improper Use of Government Equipment and Government Personnel.*)

13. Oral History Interview with Herbert Brownell, O H-157, by Ed Edwin on 5 May 1967, Columbia University Oral History Project, Volume 3, pp. 147-56, *passim*, Dwight D. Eisenhower Library, Abilene, Kansas.

14. Joseph M. Dodge, Director, Bureau of the Budget, to Attorney General Herbert Brownell (16 October 1953), Central Files, Box 634, Folder 124-C(1), pp. 1-2.

15. Telegram WA 029 PD, Laredo, Texas, William P. Allen to President Eisenhower (12 May 1954), p. 1, Central Files, General File, GF 126-I-1, Box 968, Folder 126-J, Migratory Labor (1), Dwight D. Eisenhower Library, Abilene, Kansas.

16. Ibid., p. 2.

17. Ibid.

18. Allen Drury "U.S. Aide Scored on Hunting Trips," *New York Times* (7 July 1956), p. 14.

19. Lyle Saunders and Olen E. Leonard, "The Wetback in the Lower Rio Grande Valley of Texas," *Inter-American Education,* Occasional Papers VIII, (Austin: University of Texas, July, 1951), p. 73.

20. Rodolfo Acuña, *Occupied American: The Chicano's Struggle to Liberation* (San Francisco: Canfield Press, 1974), p. 212.

21. Ibid.

22. Interview with Harlon B. Carter, Washington, D.C., 18 January 1979.

23. U.S., Congress, House, Hearings before the Subcommittee on Legal and Monetary Affairs of the Committee on Government Operations, *Reorganization of the Immigration*

and Naturalization Service, 84th Cong., 1st sess., 1955, p. 13 (hereafter cited as *Hearings, Reorganization*, 1955). For his consulting services Partridge received fifty dollars per day for a year.

24. Ibid., p. 69.

25. "Down in the Valley. A Supplementary Report on Developments in the Wetback and Bracero Situation of the Lower Rio Grande Valley of Texas Since Publication of 'What Price Wetbacks?' " (Austin: Texas State Federation of Labor, 1953), p. 2.

26. *Hearings, Reorganization*, 1955, p. 76.

27. Richard T. Jarnagin, "The Effect of Increased Illegal Mexican Migration upon the Organization and Operations of the United States Immigration Border Patrol, Southwest Region" (M.A. thesis, University of Southern California, January 1957).

28. *Hearings, Reorganization*, 1955, p. 33.

29. Jarnagin, "The Effect of Increased Illegal Immigration," p. 181.

30. Ibid., pp. 1-2.

31. U.S., Department of Justice, *Annual Report of the Immigration and Naturalization Service* (Washington, D.C., 1955), p. 10.

32. Jarnagin, "The Effect of Increased Illegal Immigration," p. 181.

33. Ibid., p. 105.

34. Ibid., p. 106.

35. Interview with Harlon B. Carter, Washington, D.C., 18 January 1979.

36. Department of Justice, *Annual Report*, 1955, p. 10.

37. Ibid., pp. 10-12; U.S., Department of Justice, Immigration and Naturalization Service, *Border Patrol Management* (Washington, D.C.: G.P.O., 1955), p. 32.

38. The inaugural flight of this branch was made on 18 September 1954, when fifty Mexican "aliens" were transported from Chicago, Illinois, to Brownsville, Texas. In 1954 a total of 11,459 aliens were transported by this branch. Department of Justice, *Annual Report*, 1955, p. 20. For operational purposes the air arm of the Border Patrol was divided into two branches, the small observation aircraft and the large transport ships, which consisted of eighteen and five aircraft respectively.

39. Memorandum from A.C. Devaney, Assistant Commissioner, Inspection and Examinations Division (20 May 1954), Subject: Special Border Patrol Force, "Wetback, Operation," Task Force, 1954, Volume 1, located in the Immigration and Naturalization Service Branch, Washington, D.C. (hereafter cited as Records, *S.B.P.F.*, 1954, Volume 1).

40. Ibid. The representatives were Generals Partridge, Howard and A.C. Devancy from Immigration; D. Larin, E. Keegan, and A. Schoenthal from Labor; W. Belton and J. Neal from State.

41. Ibid.

42. Ibid., p. 2.

43. Ibid.

44. Ibid., pp. 2-3.

45. *See* in particular *Excelsior* (10 June 1954), p. 1; (11 June 1954), p. 9A; (28 June 1954), p. 1; (16 July 1954), pp. 1 and 12A; (23 July 1954), p. 8A.

46. This estimate is drawn from Robert D. Tomasek, "The Political and Economic Implications of Mexican Labor in the United States under the Non-Quota System, Contract Labor Program, and Wetback Movement" (Ph.D. diss., University of Michigan, 1957), p. 271.

47. Nelson G. Copp, *Wetbacks and Braceros* (San Francisco: R and E Research Associates, 1971), p. 40. The man in charge of publicity during the drive in California was H.R. Landon, District Director in Los Angeles. Publicity of the Justice Department was handled by Fred Muller.

48. Memorandum, H.R. Landon to J.M. Swing (11 June 1954), p. 2, Records, *S.B.P.F.*, 1954, Volume 1.

49. Herbert Brownell to Thomas Kuchel (7 June 1954), p. 3, ibid.

50. Department of Justice, *Border Patrol Management,* 1955, p. 53.

51. *Annual Report of the Immigration and Naturalization Service,* 1955, p. 14.

52. Outline for discussion, Subject: Special Patrol Force (19 May 1954), p. 2. Special Border Patrol Task Force, Part 1, Volume 7, "Wetback, Operation: General, California Section," Volume 7 (hereafter cited as Records, *S.B.P.F.,* 1954, Part 1, Volume 7).

53. Memorandum from A.C. Devaney (24 May 1954), Records, *S.B.P.F.,* 1954, Volume 1.

54. Interview with Harlon B. Carter, Washington, D.C., 18 January 1979.

55. Memorandum from Harlon B. Carter (12 May 1954), Records, *S.B.P.F.,* 1954, Volume 1.

56. Outline for discussion, Subject: Special Patrol Force (19 May 1954), p. 1, Records, *S.B.P.F.,* 1954, Part 1, Volume 7.

57. Robert H. Robinson to D.L. McClaran, Director of the Border Patrol Training School, El Paso, Texas (18 May 1954), ibid.

58. "Back up Information" to Muller from W.F.G. (25 May 1954), ibid.

7
The Buslift
and the California-
Arizona Operation

ON 9 JUNE 1954, Herbert Brownell announced that a special program to apprehend and deport "aliens" illegally in this country from areas along the southern border would begin on 17 June. Its initial movement would begin in California and Arizona.[1]

Brownell's announcement signalled the beginning of the initial phase of "Operation Wetback." The day after his announcement the Border Patrol set up road blocks along the border area in order to prevent "illegal aliens" who were already in the United States from fleeing further northward. In addition, the Border Patrol intensified train inspections, increased its line patrols, and made a concerted effort to establish control of the border in order to deter Mexicans from entering illegally.[2]

On 10 June 1954, the governors of the states of California and Arizona received letters from the Immigration and Naturalization Service informing them of the impending drive. The letters requested their cooperation in encouraging local law enforcement agencies to aid in the mass roundup. The chiefs of the state highway patrols in California and Arizona received similar letters. After explaining the purpose of the mass roundup, the letters asked for their cooperation in alerting all of their stations throughout their respective states to the drive and requested that they authorize their officers to work with immigration officials.

The Peace Officers Association in California, which met on 10 June, was also approached, and its officers willingly offered their assistance. In fact H. R. Landon found the positive response from all of the law-enforcement officials who were contacted most gratifying. He informed Swing that in the County of Los Angeles the sheriff and the chief of police each assigned sixteen officers on a full-time basis to assist in the drive. They also issued alerts to all of their stations informing officers to apprehend and hold all "illegal aliens" on charges of vagrancy until they were picked up by the INS.[3] Through the mobilization of other law enforcement agencies and the assistance of a growing number of employers, the drive against undocumented workers assumed the earmarks of a "campaign." Such support was never extended to the INS during routine operations.[4]

As part and parcel of the first phase, the Immigration Service also instituted a buslift on 10 June. The purpose of this was twofold. First, it would act as a prod in getting "illegal aliens" in the area to begin fleeing southward prior to the 17 June roundup.[5] Second, it would initiate deportation of all "wetbacks" apprehended in the California-Arizona district to Nogales, Sonora, Mexico, whence they would be taken by train into the interior of Mexico. Most of those buslifted before 17 June had been apprehended at road blocks or had been in detention centers at Chula Vista and El Centro, California. When the operation shifted to Texas, the buslift was also employed. Apprehended "aliens" were bussed to Presidio, Texas and loaded onto waiting trains. (see map)

As they boarded the buses and as they rode along, apprehended "illegals" saw bilingual billboards and signs bearing the following inscription: "NOTICE: The United States Needs Legal Farm Workers! The Mayor of Your Town Can Arrange for Your Contracting. WARNING: The Era of the Wetback and the Wire Cutter Has Ended! From This Day Forward Any Person Found in the United States Illegally Will be Punished by Imprisonment."[6]

The publicity and the buslift created unrest among "illegal Mexicans." It also provided the Mexican government with some anxious moments because it lacked the funds and railway cars needed for the daily transportation of large numbers into the interior. *Gobernacion,* or Mexico's Interior Department, asked the State Department for help in convincing the United States to recruit as many of the "illegals" as possible for the bracero program.[7] Interestingly, several sources indicated that "drying out" "wetbacks" and recruiting them as braceros would not be necessary, as enough local labor was available.[8] Another revealing entry in the Border Patrol records concerning the buslift was that 30 to 40 percent of those buslifted were unemployed at the time of their apprehension.[9] Such a high rate of unemployment among "illegals" does not lend credence to the contention that undocumented workers deprived U.S. citizens of jobs.

At 11:00 P.M. on 10 June, the first of twenty-eight Greyhound buses left El Centro, California, for Nogales. In all, the buses transported 1,008 "illegal aliens," 216 were from detention centers from the San Francisco district, while the remainder were people apprehended in line operations, freight train inspections, and roadblocks. It was estimated that when the final reports for the day came in the number of apprehensions would reach 2,000. According to the telegram no incidents were reported, but two problems did arise. One involved the limit placed on expulsions, which Mexico had set at 1,000 per day. The second problem involved the repatriation of women and children who had entered illegally to join their husbands or fathers in the United States.[10] Because the INS had not made plans for handling family groups, officials were instructed to encourage them to return voluntarily to Mexico. Therefore throughout the deportation drive only males were expelled through the staging areas, while children and families were permitted to depart on a voluntary basis through Mexicali and Tijuana.

On 11 June Carter reported to Swing that California Farm Association representatives had notified the senior patrol officer at Indio that there were "illegal aliens" working among their contracted nationals. They requested that the Border Patrol move in and apprehend them. To Carter this was a significant indication of the effect of the publicity.[11] It is also significant because growers were now able to identify "wetbacks" they had not been able to identify in the past.

During the first phase of the operation, road and railroad blocks netted 10,917 apprehensions, not including those apprehended in raids and those who returned voluntarily before they could be captured.[12] As the drive gathered momentum, the Immigration Service received increasing support in California from various grower organizations. Especially supportive were organizations of small farmers. Representatives of the Fresno County Farm Bureau, for example, telephoned Joseph Swing and told them they hoped the intensified campaigns in California would continue unabated "until all illegal aliens regardless of nationality" were apprehended and returned to their native country.[13] In a similar telegram E. G. Blayney, President of the Associated Farmers of Fresno County, expressed support for the drive. However, his group, like the County Farm Bureau, requested that the service "spare no efforts to prove illegal status of all deportees, thus protecting the civil rights of legal residents."[14]

The support of the growers for the campaign surprised many observers who had become accustomed to hearing them argue that "wetback" labor was indispensable. Yet, in retrospect, the sudden cooperation exhibited by the growers appears to have been a shrewdly calculated move. The decision to support the drive did not emanate from one person or organization. Rather, it appears to have come about by consensus and a desire by grower organizations not to alienate the public because of their continued use of undocumented workers. They did not want to endanger the image of the honest dirt farmers that they had so carefully cultivated in the public mind. Related to this, particularly among California growers, was the desire not to endanger the bracero program. In arguing for the renewal of the program in the past, grower interests and their supporters had argued that the bracero program discouraged illegal entry. They had also claimed that its continued operation helped to carefully regulate the entry of foreign workers so that they would not displace domestic workers. They also credited the bracero program with contributing to improved relations between Mexico and the United States by the existence of a mutually beneficial agreement.

Though the validity of these arguments can be questioned in retrospect, they nonetheless were convincing enough to have the bracero program repeatedly renewed. However, even though grower organizations and their supporters held the votes necessary to guarantee renewal of the program on a long-term basis, they nonetheless had to maintain a constant vigil not to undermine their own arguments by following practices that would be detrimental to those arguments or to their public image. In 1954 the continued use of "wetback" labor in the face of adverse publicity and the impending roundup presented the growers with an instance that might be detrimental to their goals as well as their image. They therefore opted,

FIGURE 2

ROUNDUP OPERATIONS IN THE SOUTHWEST

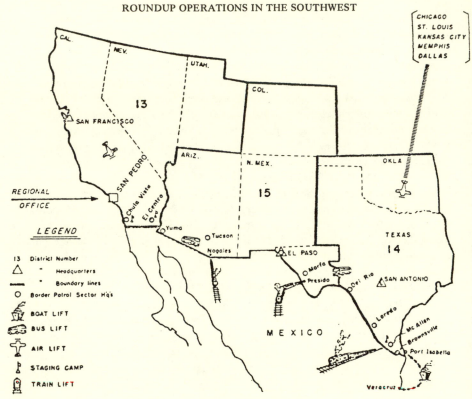

Source: *Mexican Farm Labor Program, 1955,* p. 91.

in large part, to publicly support the forces of law and order in their fight against what was described as the "wetback menace." Such support would not only enhance their public image but also cost them little, as the government had already assured them of an ample supply of labor via legally contracted braceros. Certainly when they looked at the advantages to be gained by declaring themselves in favor of what was already a fait accompli with regard to the mass roundup of "illegals," many grower organizations believed that this was the logical stance to adopt. Furthermore this action would be in keeping with the image of the farmers as "the nation's chosen people, the guardians of its most cherished virtues, and the defenders of individual freedom, republican simplicities, and old-fashioned morality."[15]

There were other practical considerations prompting the "sudden change" in attitude among most growers in the Southwest. For one thing there were rumblings of increasing discontent emanating from growers and farmers in other agricultural areas. Complaints were increasing about unfair competition, in that users of braceros and "illegals" paid far less in terms of wages than those who used domestic migrants. Although pressure groups outside of the Southwest were willing to continue backing the contract labor program, they were not willing to stand by and see their cohorts in that region continue to have the best of both worlds by continuing to employ "wetbacks" as well. Besides, if southwestern growers were utilizing "wetback" labor, why was the continuation of a bracero program so important? Southwestern growers, who relied on midwestern votes in Congress, had no satisfactory answer to this question. Therefore a logical step appeared to be to support the "wetback" drive and hopefully avoid alienating their perennial allies.

Another consideration was that growers had been informed by the INS and the Labor Department that they would be allowed to keep their "specials" once they had been legalized.[16] "Specials" were undocumented workers who had received special training by their employers in skilled and semiskilled jobs. This training made them valuable employees and helped guarantee their employment year after year by the same employer. This announcement made grower acceptance of the drive a little easier.

Finally, most employers realized that the mass roundup was only a stopgap measure and that Brownell's legislative efforts to enact penalty legislation would be thwarted. The best strategy was to forget about the "wetbacks" for the time being, concentrate on defending the bracero program, and work for the permanent enactment of Public Law 78.[17] In the final analysis, events supported the soundness of the reasoning of those who followed this route. The roundup of undocumented workers cleared the air and relieved much of the public pressure and criticism against those who employed "illegals." As for the bracero program, it was continually renewed for another ten years.

Not all employers accepted this viewpoint. In Texas, growers in the lower Rio Grande Valley bitterly opposed the drive and openly espoused the use of undocumented workers over braceros. Their drive to block the drive ended in dismal failure. As the drive shifted to Texas and as it gathered momentum, many growers were forced to contract braceros. Defiant to the end, many Valley growers were forced into a headlong rush to obtain legal contract labor in order to have their crops harvested.

The second phase of "Operation Wetback" began on 17 June 1954, when the Border Patrol, assisted by local law enforcement officials, began their sweep of the agricultural regions of California and Arizona. The Special Task Force assembled for this operation consisted of 750 men. After assembling at El Centro and Chula Vista, California, these men were divided into two task forces, which were given the designations of Task Force "A" and Task Force "B." These forces were then further subdivided into command units of twelve men. Each unit was under the command of a Senior Patrol Inspector and was equipped with trucks, jeeps, and automobiles. All of the vehicles were radio-equipped, which made it possible for officers to form a line of communication between themselves, the patrol aircraft, and task forces headquarters.[18] The patrol aircraft served as the "eyes" of these command units by locating "illegal aliens" from the air and then directing ground units to them. Once apprised of the location, the units quickly moved in with jeeps, cordonned off the area, apprehended the "illegals," loaded them onto waiting trucks, and transported them to detention camps and staging areas.[19]

The concentration of personnel in southern California began spreading in ever-widening circles almost immediately, and it was soon apparent to the planners that the mobile task force technique would prove more effective than initially believed. By 19 June 1954, the Border Patrol task forces had begun surpassing General Joseph Swing's goal of one thousand apprehensions per day,[20] and officials of the INS began to claim that they had brought the influx of "illegal aliens" into California under control.[21]

The operation, which centered in California and western Arizona, covered an area of about two hundred miles and represented only a small portion of the two-thousand-mile boundary. Yet immigration officials had decided to concentrate their efforts here because, according to them, this two-hundred-mile area had attracted more than 60 percent of the illegal influx.[22] Once the border was sealed off the two task forces began moving northward. Between the border and San Francisco, apprehensions reached about two thousand per day at the beginning of the drive.[23]

After 20 June the Immigration Service began the second phase of the operation as it moved four hundred men of the task force of seven hundred men into northern California.[24] These men were assigned to two mobile task forces, consisting of sixteen teams of twelve men each. The same procedure used in the initial phase of the roundup was used again. One of the forces was stationed at Fresno, the second at Sacramento.[25]

From the outset it was apparent that the task forces were going to move

against all undocumented workers, whether they worked in industry or agriculture. This helped ease some of the tension created by the drive among the farm
interests, who had indicated that they viewed the planned roundup as something
designed to strike only at agriculture. Thus the move by the INS against "illegals"
in industry helped to create further support among farm groups for the drive.

Between 17 June and 26 July, 1954, the special detail operating out of Los
Angeles apprehended 4,403 undocumented workers. Of these, 2,827 were employed in industrial jobs when they were apprehended. Of the remaining number,
1,069 were employed in agricultural work, while 507 were captured in transit or
in search of employment.[26]

The main body of "illegals" in industry was apprehended during 17 June through
30 June 1954, when the Border Patrol netted 2,157 "aliens." Between 1 July and
26 July the number of apprehensions decreased to 670.[27] During the 17 June
through 1 July period the main thrust of the roundup took place in Los Angeles.
At this time the Immigration Service was aided in its efforts by officers of the Los
Angeles Police Department and the Los Angeles County Sheriff's Office. After
July 1, two-thirds of the force that had engaged in the Los Angeles operation was
divided into groups of four and assigned to certain suburban cities to work with
local police organizations in those areas. This assignment was carried on for two
weeks. During this period 45 percent of the "aliens" apprehended were employed
in industry, 35 percent in agriculture, and 20 percent in other areas. Following
their two-week assignment, these groups were reassigned to the Los Angeles metropolitan area and left it only when they received specific information, complaints,
or requests from suburban city police departments.[28]

C. R. Porter, who supervised the Los Angeles roundup, told his superiors that
the police agencies within that area had been very cooperative and had "rendered
assistance far in excess of what could be expected." At times more assistance was
offered than necessary as when the Azusa Police Department advised the service
that a local theater in that town showed Mexican films on Wednesday nights.
The police told immigration officials that the place was packed on these nights
and that many of the patrons were known to be Mexicans who had entered the
United States illegally. The Azusa police said that they had made arrangements
with the management to stop the movie, turn on the lights, and have immigration
officers check for identification. The Azusa police also offered to furnish enough
officers to guard the exits while this took place. According to Porter the offer was
declined, "inasmuch as it is believed that such an operation would, without doubt,
be seized by certain factions to create a very undesirable type of publicity for this
service."[29]

Porter also reported on the progress of rounding up undocumented workers
employed in nonagricultural pursuits. He pointed out that the INS in California
had long been aware of employers who generally employed large numbers of "illegal aliens." However, few raids had been conducted against them since such raids
only netted a handful of "illegals." Officials attributed the low number of appre-

hensions to the high absentee rate prevalent among undocumented workers, thus making it difficult for them to determine when a large number of "illegals" would actually be at work. Second, traffic conditions were such that it required a considerable amount of time to travel to those places which allegedly employed "illegals." When a raid resulted in any apprehensions, INS officials were obligated to take their charges to their place of residence to pick up their belongings. INS officers found this type of duty frustrating and tedious, as they felt that very little of their time was being spent in "productive apprehensive ability."[30]

Porter pointed out that the industries that usually employed "illegals" were foundries, railroads, ceramic companies, brick industries, garbage and rubbish disposal companies, fertilizer plants, processing plants, meat-packing industries, auto-painting and body firms, and garages. By far the biggest single employers of "illegal aliens" were hotels and restaurants. Unlike the situation for other industires, absenteeism caused by fear of raids appeared to be no problem in the hotel and restaurant business, probably because the majority of "aliens" employed by restaurants and hotels served as bus boys, kitchen help, and waiters, who were "young, well-dressed, of better than average appearance, and educated, and by nature . . . more adventurous." Furthermore checks had to be made in the evening and night time, which meant that apprehensions, processing, getting clothes, and wages would make it an all-night operation. Because of this hotels and restaurants were checked less and thus created the illusion among "illegals" that they were immune from discovery and apprehension.[31]

The drive soon shattered that illusion, and "aliens" in increasing numbers failed to report to work. According to the report, many hid in their hotel rooms or other places of residence until the raids stopped. The drive worked a hardship on many "aliens" in terms of fear and mental anguish. It also worked a hardship on many "aliens" who were literally starved out by the Immigration Service because they were afraid to show themselves and face deportation.[32]

Porter reported that there were an estimated two or three thousand women employed in the downtown area working in garment and other kindred industries. Although no concentrated effort was made to close in on women who had entered illegally, there were instances when recently arrived single women were apprehended. Porter said that these women had invariably expressed surprise and indignation at being apprehended, stating that it was their understanding that the Immigration Service was not apprehending women.[33]

During the California roundup INS officials estimated that a large percentage of the Mexicans whom they apprehended had effected entry into the United States by using their Non-resident Alien Border Crossing Cards. Once here they found jobs and remained as long as possible, which violated the conditions under which the card had been issued. In order to avoid having this valuable card confiscated, individuals would mail it back to their homes in Mexico. Some INS officials believed that this practice could be controlled if apprehended "illegals" were fingerprinted and new cards were issued containing the fingerprints of the holder. This system

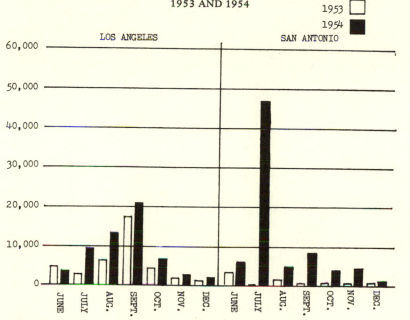

FIGURE 3
COMPARISON OF CONTRACTING BETWEEN LOS ANGELES AND SAN ANTONIO, 1953 AND 1954

1953 ☐
1954 ■

LOS ANGELES   SAN ANTONIO

Source: *Mexican Farm Labor Program,* 1955, p. 95

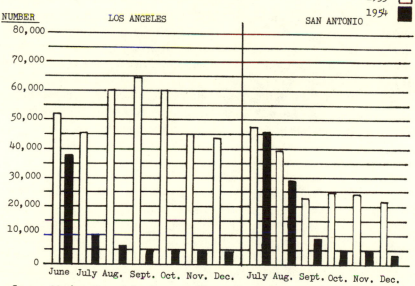
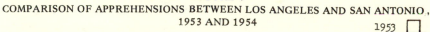

FIGURE 4
COMPARISON OF APPREHENSIONS BETWEEN LOS ANGELES AND SAN ANTONIO, 1953 AND 1954

1953 ☐
1954 ■

NUMBER   LOS ANGELES   SAN ANTONIO

Source: *Mexican Farm Labor Program,* 1955, p. 93

would permit them to more easily identify illegal entrants who had used the card to effect entry and to reclaim the card so that it could no longer be used in this manner by its holder. Of course this method would require an increase in personnel, but INS officials in the field believed that it would be well worth the added costs, as the illegal use of these cards presented "one of the largest potential methods" of illegal entry into the United States.[34]

While the INS raids on nonagricultural targets helped to further assuage the fears of the farm bloc, the results in terms of actual apprehensions were not that significant. The raids carried out against industry did not, according to H.R. Landon, bear out the contention among growers that there were over 70,000 "illegal aliens" employed in industrial jobs in California. Furthermore, continued Landon, the allegations by growers that the INS had been negligent in conducting raids against industry were unjustified and unfounded. The INS had made concerted efforts throughout much of the drive in California to apprehend undocumented workers wherever they were.

Landon's report stated that raids on manufacturing concerns and commercial services resulted only in "normal" apprehensions even after the INS had visited some places as many as four times. For example, out of 43,342 apprehensions in the California District during the month of June, only 3,740 had been employed in industry. Of the 620,207 apprehensions between 1 July 1953, and 30 June 1954, only 18,245 were employed in industry. During the mass roundup in California, which lasted from 11 June to 26 July 1954, agents netted 51,865 "illegals." Of these, 10 percent were working in industry when they were apprehended. Thus, concluded Landon in his report to Swing, the sweep in California, particularly in the Los Angeles area, "established definitely that 'wetbacks' are not being employed in industry to the same extent as they are in agriculture."[35]

While INS officials were inclined to agree with Landon's findings, they were not unconcerned about the growing number of undocumented workers who had found work in the industrial sector. In fact certain top officials in the INS held the view that an increasing number of "illegals" were opting for agricultural employment as a temporary expedient until they could find jobs in industry or commerce. To men such as Swing, the roundup of "illegals" in industry in the Los Angeles metropolitan area only represented the tip of the iceberg. They recognized that something had to be done to control this trend soon, or apprehending "illegals" would become increasingly difficult and more expensive.

While the sweep proceeded throughout California and Arizona, Joseph Swing held what was described as a "series of cordial meetings" with growers throughout California and Texas.[36] Swing told the farmers that the government was determined to eliminate the illegal entry problem. However, he assured them that every effort would be made to provide growers with legal contract labor through the United States Employment Service. This assurance, along with his pledge that the roundup would be pressed with vigor all along the southern boundary of the United States, helped assuage many farmers who had long protested the unfairness of the Border Patrol's haphazard raids.[37]

In California many of the growers took heed of the Immigration Service's warnings concerning the roundup. Growers from the Imperial Valley, an area with high concentrations of undocumented workers, began contracting braceros in larger numbers, thus encouraging others to follow suit. According to Walter B. Francis, manager of the U.S. Labor Department's Labor placement center, some 663 braceros had been contracted during one day. Francis reported that as of 15 July the total number of braceros contracted since 1 January 1954 was 37,969. Because of the success of the drive Francis predicted that some 7,000 braceros would be contracted in July alone, as opposed to only 2,778 for the previous July.[38]

According to a report issued on 29 July 1954, apprehensions had reached their peak during the first week of the operation when a daily average of 1,727 "illegal aliens" were apprehended.[39] By 27 July, a total of 52,374 Mexican "aliens" had been apprehended and expelled.[40] Of this number 38,414 were transported to Nogales for their return to the interior of Mexico by the Mexican government.[41] After 25 July, the daily number of apprehensions in California had declined to about four hundred.[42]

As the task forces continued what immigration officials termed "mopping-up" operations, those "aliens" already apprehended were taken to Nogales to be sent into the interior of Mexico. Those apprehended in the roundup usually had to pay their own bus fare to Nogales. If unable to do so, their fares were paid by the Immigration Service.[43]

Immigration officers were ordered not to collect fares from "aliens." According to a note from Harlon B. Carter, the bus companies were responsible for collecting the fares. Carter said that experience had shown that immigration officials had in the past collected from 10 to 20 percent more money from undocumented laborers, and thus officials of the service could communicate with those apprehended and explain to them that they had to pay their own way. However, actual cash payment by the "aliens" was to be made to the bus driver or the bus company representative.[44]

Although on the surface the operation appeared to be going smoothly, problems did arise, stemming from reported incidents between Border Patrol officials and "illegal aliens." From the outset, media coverage had been an important factor in the overall plan of the operation.[45] Not only had the media played an instrumental role in encouraging large numbers of "illegals" to flee the country before the drive began, but it also served the purpose of giving wide exposure to a reorganized, revitalized Immigration Service.

Yet the wide publicity given to the operation was a double-edged sword in that any slipup by the service or any incident involving violation of human or civil rights would come to the surface. The service had to be careful not to injure or harm any of the apprehended "aliens," for such an incident would surely cause serious political and international repercussions. Swing was aware of this from the outset and attempted to see that every precaution was taken by Immigration Service officials to minimize the hardships and distress of apprehended "aliens." Yet he did not delude himself, for he realized that "in such a large-scale operation individual instances of an unfortunate nature will occur."[46]

And occur they did, although they were not given much press coverage in California. In fact, most of the information concerning "instances of an unfortunate nature" in the California sweep were gleaned mainly from the records of the INS and not from newspaper accounts. That numerous incidents occurred is beyond question. Yet unlike the Texas media, which was largely hostile to the Border Patrol and its operations, the California media was very favorable toward the Immigration Service in reporting its activities. This situation was probably due to the climate of cooperation on the part of many growers in California.[47] As much of the media was either controlled or strongly influenced by grower interests and large numbers of people favored the roundup, the media saw little reason to take a critical view of the operation and some of the incidents surrounding its implementation.

Most of the complaints against the INS concerned violation of rights of both "illegals" and of citizens of the United States. For example, members of an American Legion post in Placer County, California, sent telegrams to Senators Knowland and Kuchel and to Congressman Engle protesting the misconduct of some immigration officers during the roundup. They charged that American citizens of Mexican descent and, in one case, an American of Japanese descent had been unreasonably detained and subjected to treatment "that no American citizen should have to stand for."[48] After Kuchel contacted Swing about this matter, the Commissioner of Immigration took immediate action by ordering Bruce G. Barber, district director in San Francisco, to carry out an investigation of this incident. Barber then dispatched Robert H. Lowry to investigate the various charges levelled against certain officers and to report his findings to him.

Lowry contacted Victor Mar and Lawrence A. Wood, the men who had made the allegations. According to Lowry, Victor Mar, who was the commander of Post 755, was employed as plant foreman for the Earl Fruit Company in Loomis. Mar told Lowry that he had written to certain congressmen because of an incident at the Early Fruit Company on 30 June 1954. On that date two immigration officers, driving a government car bearing Texas license plates, had stopped to find out if any "wetbacks" were employed there. A Mr. Owens, who was the manager, told them that there were no "wetbacks" working there but that there was a young man of Mexican extraction who was a U.S. citizen employed there. The officers requested to speak to him, and Joe Vigil was called. When he appeared one of the officers "placed his hand against the man's shoulder in a forceful manner, placed his other hand on his gun, and spoke to him in Spanish in an abusive tone of voice."[49] Mar told Lowry that the officer asked Vigil for some identification. Vigil showed him a draft card and a social security card. The officer told Vigil, "that's no good, any damn wetback can get those cards. I want to see your birth certificate."[50]

Mar told Lowry that he intervened at this stage and told the officer that he had known Vigil for a long time and assured him that he was a citizen of the United States. The officer ignored Mar and continued to verbally abuse Vigil. Owens entered the discussion by suggesting that they go to Vigil's home and get his birth certificate. After agreeing to the suggestion the five men went to Vigil's house where he produced a birth certificate and certificate of baptism proving his citizenship.

Lowry said that Mar had no quarrel with the roundup. In fact he approved of it. Mar's only complaint was the manner in which the operation was being carried out. According to Mar, this was not the first such incident he had heard about, although it was the first he had actually witnessed. He believed that immigration officials should be more polite and considerate and less belligerent. When questioned further by Lowry, Mar said that the whole matter should be dropped because further investigation "would serve no useful purpose."[51]

Lowry did not drop the matter. Following his questioning of Mar, he contacted V.P. Owens and Joe Vigil. The chain of events they related to him was substantially the same as what Mar had told him. Owens said that Vigil was "incensed" at the officer who abused him and that they both argued vehemently. When Owens tried to intervene the second officer told him "that he was coming pretty close to impeding a government official in the performance of his duty." Owens told Lowry that the abusive officer was "a show-off from Texas."[52] When questioned, Joe Vigil said that he had been quite indignant at the way he had been treated.

Lowry next contacted Lawrence Wood, the man who had written about the incident to some congressmen. He readily admitted that what he had told them was based on what Mar had related to him and that such complaints of abusive treatment by immigration officials were not new.[53]

Lowry's report also related other incidents brought to his attention during his inquiry. One incident involved a Japanese employee who had been handcuffed and roughly treated during the raid on the Fowler Nursery located between Newcastle and Lincoln, California. Lowry said that the owner of the nursery was willing to testify. Another incident had occurred on 27 June, when John Ortega was shoved from a platform, placed on an immigration bus, and kept there for about two hours, despite the protests of several citizens who had witnessed the actions of the officers.[54]

These reports and others of abusive treatment of "aliens" and citizens by immigration officials were enough to bring about a meeting between Swing and four unnamed congressmen in mid-July. In addition to discussing the matter of the "discourteous attitudes [of officers] in their dealings, particularly with United States citizens of Mexican extraction," Swing and the congressmen also discussed allegations that immigration officials had bypassed some farms that employed "illegal aliens" because they were operated by friends. They also discussed charges that "officers were not questioning aliens sufficiently to discover those eligible for discretionary relief under the Immigration and Nationality Act; were picking up family groups inconsiderately; and were not giving due consideration to the rights of aliens under the law."[55]

After his meeting with the congressmen and after conferring with members of his staff, Swing took steps to begin dealing with the allegations raised concerning the misconduct of some officers. He ordered all of his District Directors to investigate all complaints and "to take immediate steps to correct any situation which would permit justified complaints to be made relating to these matters."[56]

In spite of planned publicity that was favorable to the efforts of the Immigration Service, the refusal of Clarence Porter to accept the suggestion of the Azusa Police Department concerning a raid on a theater patronized by Mexican "illegals" reflects that there existed strong opposition from different groups in California. It is interesting to note that whereas most of the opposition and bad press in California emanated from social welfare and reform groups, in Texas most of the adverse criticism to the roundup came from grower interests. Those individuals and groups who opposed the roundup did so on the basis that it violated the civil rights of undocumented workers and United States citizens of Mexican descent. They charged that the operation was discriminatory and un-American and that it represented a hypocritical approach in this nation's treatment of Mexicans.

This latter view was best reflected in the statements made by John Sheffield, an attorney who was extremely critical of conflicting INS policies regarding Mexican immigration. While Sheffield did not favor the large influx of "illegals," he did question this country's sudden reversal in its policies, which he believed had been largely responsible for encouraging illegal entry. As an example of this he cited an incident in early 1954 whereby immigration officials had "stood at the border and openly invited Mexicans to enter the United States in violation of their own laws."[57] To him it came as no surprise that the reaction of the Mexican populace, whatever its citizenship status, was one of consternation, anger, confusion, and resentment.

Others objected to the mass roundup of "illegals" because they believed that it was not really striking at the cause of the illegal influx from Mexico. Letters from civil rights groups and social reform groups, as well as private citizens, suggested that the United States aid Mexico in its economic development by increased loans and foreign aid. Such assistance, they claimed, would prove beneficial to both nations and help alleviate the mass exodus from Mexico because of economic underdevelopment, overpopulation, and high unemployment. They considered "Operation Wetback" a temporary stopgap measure that would prove largely unsuccessful.[58]

Some of the so-called more "radical" groups such as the Independent Progressive Party, the Los Angeles Committee for the Protection of the Foreign Born, and some locals from the International Longshoremen's and Warehousemen's Union (ILWU), were more vocal in their opposition of the drive against "illegals." They described it as "vicious" and "repressive." The Chairman of the Legislative Committee of Warehouse Union Local 6 of the ILWU said that his union viewed

"Operation Wetback" as "pure intimidation . . . against . . . a minority group," which went hand in hand with the anti-democratic activities which were "part and parcel of McCarthyism . . ."[59]

The Independent Progressive Party in Los Angeles asked people to join them in publicly protesting the ill-treatment of undocumented workers. It was "unalterably opposed to the use of the Elysian Park area—or any area—for concentration camps in which to imprison Mexican laborers," who were awaiting deportation.[60] The IPP, along with a number of other groups, accused the INS of totally disregarding the civil and human rights of Mexicans and demanded that immediate steps be taken to stop the mass deportations.

While groups such as the American Legion, the Fresno County Farm Bureau, and the Associated Farmers of Fresno County did not call for the cessation of the roundup, they too repeatedly asked that the INS take every precaution in ascertaining whether persons were citizens or not before deporting them. As one person wrote: "Better to allow a hundred 'wetbacks' access to our country, than to deport or even to imprison one Mexican-American unjustly accused of being a 'wetback.' "[61] Even though federal officials denied that they were violating anyone's civil rights and charged that stories of such violations emanated from radical groups who only wanted to stir up trouble, the fact that a number of groups who supported the drive found it necessary to caution authorities adds credence to the views set forth by the IPP and others.

Another organization expressing opposition was the Los Angeles Committee for the Protection of the Foreign Born. This committee had been organized in September of 1950 to work for the repeal of the Internal Security Act (the McCarran Act). They also fought against the passage of the McCarran-Walter Act of 1952, because they viewed it as a dangerous weapon that would be used against foreignborn minorities, including Mexicans and Mexican-American citizens. Their goals were to protect citizens and noncitizens from harrassment, to guarantee their civil rights and a due process of law, to defend those who would be victimized by the McCarran Act, and to bring an end to the use of police-state actions against people.[62]

When the drive began they undertook a concerted effort to force a speedy end to it. First of all, the committee called upon the people of Los Angeles to join them in protesting the illegal arrests and deportations of Mexicans. To muster support for the protest they circulated fliers throughout the community charging that Brownell's "concentration camp order" was "an insult to the 500,000 members of the Mexican-American Community."[63] Other groups in Los Angeles joined the committee in the protest, including members of the Jewish community who had witnessed some of the arrests. Members of the Japanese community also opposed the roundup and the detention of prisoners in the fenced in detention areas that had been set up.

Those opposed to the roundup recoiled at the thought that such raids were once again part of the American scene. They were angry and disturbed that people were being sought out by the color of their skin and that they were followed, approached, and picked up on the streets, in factories, and in their homes. They protested the "undemocratic herding and fencing of human beings."[64] They called for an end to such practices, stating that barbed wire and concentration camps had no place in America.[65] Others, while protesting the attack against the "wetbacks," took the opportunity to criticize the Attorney General's lack of action against the communists who should be deported, and not the "wetbacks."[66]

The raids caused terror and fear to spread throughout the Mexican American community in California and the Southwest. They reinforced the belief among Mexicans and Mexican Americans that they were unwelcome and once again demonstrated the precarious status of Mexicans in this country. "Operation Wetback" dredged up bitter memories about the indiscriminate mass deportations of the 1930s, when citizens and noncitizens of Mexican descent had been made scapegoats for the economic problems of the United States. It reminded people of Mexican descent about the injustices and injuries to life and property caused by the so-called Zoot-Suit Riots of 1943 in Los Angeles, when bands of service men had wandered the streets of the community terrorizing and attacking Mexicans. The riots, which had in part been caused by xenophobia, yellow press journalism, racism, by a tense, hostile environment engendered by wartime tensions and propaganda, had initially been blamed on the zoot-suiters or "pachuco" youth gangs.[67] Later investigations disproved this, charging that the riots had been triggered by unruly, drunken servicemen. The investigations also revealed that most of the physical injuries were inflicted on Mexicans by servicemen rather than vice versa, as had initially been reported by the media.[68] The Zoot-Suit Riots, just as the mass deportations of the 1930s, had once again caused American nativism to raise its ugly head—a nativism, which according to John Higham, "mirrored our national anxieties and marked out the bounds of our tolerance."[69]

The Mexican American community suffered another blow with the passage of the McCarran Act in 1950 and the McCarran-Walter Act in 1952. Although not specifically aimed at Mexican Americans, these laws had a great and negative impact on their organizations; they exposed their leaders to deportation and denaturalization if they were found guilty of subversive activities. Many activists were intimidated by the laws, as under their terms they were subject to charges of being subversives, and to arrest and deportation on purely technical violations of the laws.[70]

Under the McCarran-Walter Act some Mexican American activists were deported, which drove home the point to other leaders that they had better step lightly. Opponents of the law had argued that it enlarged upon and continued many existing discriminatory practices and that it introduced new and even more serious inequities. One critic called it an "affront to the conscience of the American people," while others described the penalties outlined for violations committed by "aliens" and naturalized citizens as relics of the feudal ages.[71] Men such as Secretary of State Dean Acheson and W. Averell Harriman, Director of Mutual Security, had pointed out that the immigration laws of this country were closely linked with our foreign objectives, and that "our immigration policy with respect to particular . . . racial groups [could] be taken as an indication of our general attitude toward them."[72] They had therefore urged that we examine our policies in this light. Yet these words of caution fell on deaf ears.

Proponents of the law who were concerned with safeguarding what they perceived to be the security of this nation were numerous and thus were able to put the law into effect by overriding Truman's veto. The passage of the McCarran-Walter Act once again served to reveal the fears, priorities, prejudices, and biases of this country by defining in very strict terms the types of persons who would be eligible for citizenship.[73] A committee opposed to the McCarran Act could muster only a meager 283 signatures, as opposed to the 10,000 which it had hoped to collect. Even more revealing was that only eight of these signatures were from persons who had a Spanish surname. While this small number may reflect that committee members did not seek signatures from the Spanish-speaking community, this seems rather unlikely. A more compelling reason for the lack of Spanish-surname signatures might be attributed to fear of reprisal, as the petition included a space for one's address. When one takes into consideration past events, such as the deportations of the 1930s, the Zoot-Suit Riots of 1943, the passage of the McCarran Acts, the lingering spectre of McCarthyism, and the events of the summer of 1954, it comes as little surprise that Mexicans and Mexican Americans were not vocal in their protestations concerning "Operation Wetback" and the climate of fear that it engendered.

Meanwhile, the drive against undocumented workers gathered a momentum of its own and no amount of protesting could stop it. In his report on the California operation, Bruce Barber wrote that there was no doubt the operation had had a telling effect upon the "wetback" situation. He stated that publicity in the area had been, for the most part, favorable. Barber reported that a total of 8,901 "wetbacks" had been apprehended and shipped out of the San Francisco District during the month of July. From 1 June to 2 August, a total of 19,620 "wetbacks" had been apprehended in the San Francisco area. Although apprehensions were becoming more difficult, the San Francisco District was still averaging about one hundred apprehensions per day.[74]

Reports from other districts in California with high concentrations of undocumented workers reported pretty much the same thing.[75] In all, the combined forces of the Border Patrol, local law-enforcement agencies and members of the United States Employment Service had apprehended some 21,000 "aliens" between 17 June and 30 June 1954. The addition of those apprehended between 1 June and 17 June brought the total number of apprehensions to 55,000 for the month of June alone.[76]

By the end of July most of the apprehensions were taking place along the international boundary between California and Mexico.[77] According to INS reports, a total of some 540,000 "illegal aliens" were either apprehended and deported or left California voluntarily as a result of the publicity accompanying the roundup.[78]

This figure appears inflated, since reports that the California roundup averaged about 2,000 apprehensions a day would bring the total number of apprehensions to 56,000, as the major sweep only lasted twenty-eight days, from 17 June to 15 July. After that, much of the manpower was transferred to Texas to begin operations there.[79] Another report stated that apprehensions from the California operation totalled 51,784.[80] When this number is subtracted from the total number of 540,000, we are still left with 488,216 "aliens" who supposedly fled the country voluntarily in order to escape apprehension. In light of reports by observers along the border that they could not keep any sort of count of those fleeing across the border, these figures pertaining to "voluntary" departures are highly questionable.

That the number of "aliens" who were deported and who left voluntarily was exaggerated is not too surprising, given the circumstances in which the INS found itself. The operation had been termed by Swing, Brownell, and others "a tremendous success." "Success" in this instance could only be judged in terms of numbers, and numbers is what these men gave to legislators, the press, and the public. Furthermore, the Immigration Service had received a boost in late June after Eisenhower had asked Congress to appropriate $3,000,000 for the INS to purchase twenty-four motor vehicles and three aircraft.[81] Eisenhower urged that Congress cooperate in helping the Border Patrol stem the influx of "illegals" by passing the appropriation measure. There were still a number of congressional members, especially from the border states, who opposed the appropriation and Brownell's proposed legislation.[82] However, Congress was sufficiently impressed by the results of the California operation to pass the supplementary appropriation bill.[83] Because of this, it became even more important for Swing and Brownell to "establish" the success of their plan if future increases in their budget were to be forthcoming.

The Arizona phase of the operation was not as intensive as that conducted in California because the harvest season there had pretty much come to an end when the drive began. With the end of the harvest season in Arizona legal and "illegal" workers usually moved on to California to seek employment there. At times this had created tension between the two states, as agencies in California resented having to bear the major financial burdens imposed on them by the influx from Arizona. Officials in California believed that their neighbor was not doing enough to keep "illegals" from entering their state. Officials from Arizona believed that California was being unrealistic in expecting them to patrol such a large area. They also thought that Californians were grossly mistaken in believing that a large number of "illegals" entered their state from Arizona.

The drive in Arizona was mainly concentrated in the Salt River Valley and in Yuma County.[84] A patrol unit stationed in Nogales was augmented in order to handle the increased number of deportees from the California-Arizona round-up who were awaiting transportation to interior points in Mexico.[85] Another reason for increasing the number of patrolmen in Nogales was to help prevent the return of "illegals" who had crossed into Mexico to avoid apprehension and to prevent reentry of those who had already been deported. The strategy proved effective for "only 23 of the 23,222 aliens deported through the area (during the month of June)" made an attempt to return to the United States.[86] Much of the credit for this low rate of reentry was attributed to the "excellent coopera- tion" of the Mexican government.[87]

Roadblock operations and inspection of trains were increased in Arizona as part of the "mopping-up" operations. New Border Patrol stations were also established in Somerton and Wellton, Arizona. Aware that these stations would not fully eradicate illegal entry at these two points, John P. Swanson nevertheless believed that they would be helpful to the senior patrol inspector in Yuma in assigning officers to these key areas.[88]

To further aid the INS in its efforts to reduce the number of illegal entries, Swanson reported that they had reached an agreement with the Native Ameri- cans who resided on a reservation north of Yuma, whereby they would receive rewards of from $2.50 to $3.00 for each Mexican apprehended on their lands. According to the agreement, which was consummated with Deputy Sheriff Ralph Rainbow of Winterhaven, California, rewards would only be paid for "il- legal aliens" captured on reservation property. Rainbow, a chief of the Yuma tribe, agreed to receive and hold apprehended "aliens" for the Border Patrol in his capacity as a deputy sheriff. After captured "illegals" had been delivered into the custody of INS officers, payment would be made in cash to members of the tribe.[89]

The daily arrival of such a large number of deported "illegals" into the border cities of Mexico for transportation to interior points caused Mexican officials a great deal of trouble. According to one eyewitness, the populations of San Luis and Mexicali had been swelled by the arrival of thousands of Mexicans who had either been apprehended and sent there or who had fled across the border to avoid capture. A great many of these people were without food and shelter, and little was being done to meet their needs.[90] Thus Mexico's fears that they would not be able to handle the number of "illegals" brought there by INS buses had been borne out. Because many of the staging areas lacked the train and rail facilities to handle such large numbers, Mexican officials had requested before the drive be- gan that shipments of "illegals" to border staging areas be limited to a thousand or less per day. However, INS officials had failed to take heed of this request, adding to the already overcrowded and depressed conditions of the border towns.

David Moore, who had been sufficiently disturbed by this situation to bring it to the attention of Governor Howard Pyle of Arizona, wrote that he hoped the governor could do something to help remedy the misery and suffering caused by the hunger and overcrowded conditions. He was upset by the fact that the United States had apparently overlooked the great contributions that the Mexican people had made to its development and growth. Nowhere was this contribution more apparent, he wrote, than in the Southwest. "These men had helped to clear and level the deserts of the great southwest and brought into being one of the most fruitful gardens man has ever created. Without their patient, willing labor, Arizona, California, New Mexico, and Texas could never have made the great strides they have made. made."[91] Moore called Brownell "reckless" and said that this sad condition had probably been brought about by the atmosphere engendered by the McCarthy hearings.[92]

Governor Pyle forwarded Moore's letter to Sherman Adams on 5 July. Adams replied on 12 July 1954 that the Immigration and Naturalization Service had made every effort to treat all "aliens" in a humanitarian way.[93] This was the last heard on the matter, for by mid-July the operation had shifted to Texas and New Mexico. In all, the Immigration Service reported that 107,000 "illegal aliens" had either departed voluntarily or had been apprehended and deported from Arizona.

NOTES

1. *New York Times* (10 June 1954), p. 2.
2. Report from Bruce G. Barber, District Director, San Francisco and Harlon B. Carter, El Centro, California, "Buslift Operation from Special Border Patrol Force" (11 June 1954), Special Border Patrol Task Force, Part 1, Volume 7, "Wetback, Operation: General, California Section," located in the Immigration and Naturalization Service Branch, Washington, D.C. (hereafter cited as Records, *S.B.P.F.* 1954, Part 1 Volume 7).
3. Memorandum, H. R. Landon to J. M. Swing (11 June 1954), pp. 1-2, Special Border Patrol Task Force, "Wetback, Operation," Volume 1, 1954, located in the Immigration and Naturalization Service Branch, Washington, D.C. (hereafter cited as Records, *S.B.P.F.*, 1954, Volume 1).
4. Julian Samora, *Los Majados: The Wetback Story* (South Bend, Ind.: University of Notre Dame Press, 1971), p. 50.
5. Memorandum, D.R. Kelly (7 June 1954), Records, *S.B.P.F.*, Volume 1.
6. Marcus T. Neelly to Harlon B. Carter (1 June 1954), Records, *S.B.P.F.*, 1954, Part 1, Volume 7.
7. Memorandum from Harlon B. Carter (1 June 1954), ibid.
8, Ibid.
9. Ibid.
10. H. B. Carter to commanding officers (10 June 1954), Records *S.B.P.F.*, 1954, Volume 1.
11. Harlon Carter to Joseph Swing (11 June 1954), ibid.
12. Report from Frank Partridge (29 July 1954), p. 2, Special Border Patrol Froce, "Wetback, Operation," Task Force, 1954, Volume 9, located in the Immigration and Naturalization Branch, Washington, D.C. (hereafter cited as Records, *S.B.P.F.*, 1954, Volume 9).
13. Fresno County Farm Bureau to Director, U.S. Immigration (16 June 1954), Records, *S.B.P.F.*, 1954, Volume 1.
14. E. G. Blayney to Director, U.S. Bureau of Immigration (16 June 1954), ibid.
15. Ellis W. Hawley, "The Politics of the Mexican Labor Issue, 1950-1965," *Agricultural History* 40, no. 3 (July 1966): 165.
16. Ernesto Galarza, *Merchants of Labor: The Mexican Bracero Story* (Charlotte: McNally & Loftin, 1964), p. 69.
17. Hawley, "The Politics," p. 162; John McBride, *Vanishing Bracero: Valley Revolution* (San Antonio: The Naylor Company, 1963), pp. 6-9.
18. U.S., Department of Justice, *Annual Report of the Immigration and Naturalization Service,* 1954 (Washington, D.C.: G.P.O., 1955), p. 31. J. Swanson was given command of Task Force "A" and C.B. Kirk was given command of Task Force "B." It should be

remembered that these two men, along with G. J. McBee, had created the task force design. Harlon B. Carter to all chiefs (16 June 1954), in Records, *S.B.P.F.*, 1954, Part 1, Volume 7. Operation," Part 1 Volume 7, located in the Immigration and Naturalization Service Office, Washington, D.C. (hereafter cited as Records, *S.B.P.F.*, 1954, Part 1, Volume 7).

19. U.S. Congress, House, *Reorganization of the Immigration and Naturalization Service*, Hearings before the Subcommittee on Legal and Monetary Affairs of the Committee on Government Operations, 84th Cong., 1st sess. (9 and 17 March 1955) (Washington, D.C.: G.P.O., 1955), p. 44 (hereafter cited as *Hearings, Reorganization*, 1955).

20. " 'Wetback' Tide Slowed," *New York Times* (28 June 1954), p. 3.

21. Gladwin Hill, " 'Wetback' Stream Stemmed in Part," *New York Times* (20 June 1954), p. 75.

22. Ibid.

23. Ibid.

24. Ibid.

25. Ibid.

26. C. R. Porter, Investigator, Special Detail, Los Angeles, to C. B. Kirk (29 July 1954), p. 1, Records, *S.B.P.F.*, 1954, Part 1, Volume 7.

27. Ibid.

28. Ibid., pp. 2-3.

29. Ibid., p. 3.

30. Ibid., p. 7.

31. Ibid., p. 5.

32. Ibid., p. 6.

33. Ibid., p. 7.

34. Ibid., pp. 7-8.

35. H. R. Landon to Joseph Swing, Memorandum: "Aliens Employed in Industry" (4 August 1954), pp. 1-2, Records, *S.B.P.F.*, 1954, Part 1, Volume 7.

36. Gladwin Hill, "Plan Gains to End Use of 'Wetbacks,' " *New York Times* (27 June 1954), p. 36.

37. Ibid.

38. "Drive Against Illegal Entrants Continues in Imperial Valley," *The San Diego Union* (15 July 1954), p. 10.

39. Report by Frank Partridge (29 July 1954), p. 1, Special Border Patrol Force, "Wetback, Operation," Volume 9, located in the Immigration and Naturalization Service Office, Washington, D.C. (hereafter cited as Records, *S.B.P.F.*, 1954, Volume 9).

40. Ibid.

41. Four-page report, untitled, n.d., ibid.

42. Report by Frank Partridge (29 July 1954), ibid.

43. Memorandum of Telephone call from Harlon B. Carter, 10:55 A.M. (EDT), 16 July 1954, pp. 1-2, found in Special Border Patrol Force, "Wetback, Operation," Volume 3, located in the Immigration and Naturalization Service Office, Washington, D.C. (hereafter cited as Records, *S.B.P.F.*, 1954, Volume 3).

44. "Note for Mr. [Harlon] Carter," no date, Records, *S.B.P.F.*, 1954, Part 1, Volume 7.

45. Ibid.

46. Joseph M. Swing to Senator Thomas H. Kuchel (19 July 1954), Records, *S.B.P.F.*, 1954, Part 1, Volume 7.

47. Not all farmers or ranchers supported the drive. Their sentiments were pretty much reflected in the statement by Charles H. Howard, a San Diego attorney and rancher, who accused Herbert Brownell of attempting to solve the "wetback problem" by carrying "on warfare, with the Immigration Service as his army, against farm and ranch owners of southern California." "S. D. Attorney Criticizes New Wetback Plan," *The San Diego Union* (15 July 1954), p. 10.

48. "State Officials Thanked for Cooperation in Handling Local Immigration Problem," *Loomis News* 41, no. 36 (16 July 1954), p. 2.

49. Memorandum: "Complaints Against Border Patrol Personnel" from Robert H. Lowry, Officer in Charge, Sacramento, California, to Bruce G. Barber (22 July 1954), p. 1, Records, *S.B.P.F.,* 1954, Volume 9.

50. Ibid.

51. Ibid., p. 2.

52. Ibid.

53. Ibid., p. 3.

54. Ibid., pp. 2-3.

55. Joseph Swing to Bruce Barber (13 July 1954), Records, *S.B.P.F.,* 1954, Volume 9.

56. Ibid.

57. John F. Sheffield to Herbert Brownell (29 June 1954), Special Border Patrol Force, "Wetback, Operation," Volume 1, located in the Immigration and Naturalization Service Office, Washington, D.C. (hereafter cited as Records, *S.B.P.F.,* 1954, Volume 1).

58. Letters and telegrams found in Records, *S.B.P.F.,* 1954, Volume 1; and in Files of the Justice Department, Attorney General's Office, Justice Department, Washington, D.C.

59. L. Kelley to Herbert Brownell (27 June 1954), in Department of Justice, Records Branch, Office of Legal Counsel, Justice Department, Washington, D.C.

60. Nan Blair to H. R. Landon (16 June 1954), Records, *S.B.P.F.,* 1954, Volume 1.

61. Anthony J. Ward to Herbert Brownell (25 July 1954), ibid.

62. Patricia Morgan, *Shame of a Nation: A Documented Story of Police-State Terror Against Mexican-Americans in the U.S.A.* (Los Angeles: Los Angeles Committee for the Protection of the Foreign Born, 1954), pp. 49-50.

63. "A Call to the People of Los Angeles," flier printed by the Los Angeles Committee for the Protection of the Foreign Born (Summer, 1954), Records, *S.B.P.F.,* 1954, Part 1, Volume 7.

64. Marion Grayson to Herbert Brownell (18 June 1954), Records, *S.B.P.F.,* 1954, Volume 1.

65. Lillian D. Emilio to Herbert Brownell (18 June 1954), ibid. These telegrams were typical of the many found in the files of the Immigration Service.

66. Earl Thomas to Herbert Brownell (18 June 1954), ibid.

67. Juan R. García, "The Causes of the Zoot-Suit Riots of 1943" (Unpublished paper, University of Notre Dame, 1973), pp. 14-15; Rudolfo Acuña, *Occupied America: The Chicano's Struggle Toward Liberation* (San Francisco: Canfield Press, 1972), pp. 200-02. "Pachucos" or "Zoot-Suiters" were youth gangs. Although mostly Mexican and Mexican-American in makeup, they also included black and Japanese youths. The term "Zoot-Suit" refers to the style of dress popular among these youths.

68. Ibid.

69. John Higham, *Strangers in the Land* (New York: Atheneum, 1972), p. i. Although Higham does not deal specifically with Mexican Americans in his study, his thesis concerning nativism in the United States is nonetheless quite applicable in partially explaining the plight of Mexican Americans in this country.

70. Report of the President's Commission on Immigration and Naturalization, *Whom We Shall Welcome* (Washington, D.C.: G.P.O., 1953), p. 196.

71. Ibid., p. 12.

72. Ibid., p. 47.

73. Lyle Saunders and Olen E. Leonard, "The Wetback in the Lower Rio Grande Valley of Texas," in *Inter-American Education,* Occasional papers 7 (Austin: University of Texas, 1951), p. 38.

74. Bruce G. Barber to Frank H. Partridge, Special Assistant to the Commissioner, Central Office (August 2, 1954), p. 1, Records, *S.B P.F.*, 1954, Volume 9.

75. "Wetback Situation," report from Robert Winston and John J. Mitchell (Investigation, Los Angeles, California) to District Director, Los Angeles (27 July 1954), pp. 1-7, ibid.

76. Gladwin Hill, "Wetback Purge to Shift to Texas," *New York Times* (5 July 1954), p. 11.

77. "Heat Fails to Slow Arrests of Aliens," *News of Imperial County* (20 July 1954), p. a-7. 1954), p. a-7.

78. Robert D. Tomasek, "The Political and Economic Implications of Mexican Labor in the United States under the Non-Quota System, Contract Labor Program, and Wetback Movement" (Ph.D. diss., University of Michigan, 1957), p. 194, citing Paul Crosby, Border Patrol, INS, Washington, D.C., Personal Interview.

79. Records, *S.B.P.F.*, 1954, Volume 9.

80. Four-page report, untitled, undated, p. 2, ibid.

81. "Legislators See No Action on Wetback Plan," *The San Diego Union* (22 June 1954), p. 10A.

82. Ibid.

83. *New York Times* (23 June 1954), p. 35.

84. Tomasek, "The Political and Economic Implications," pp. 194-95.

85. *Annual Report of the Immigration and Naturalization Service*, 1954.

86. Ibid.

87. Ibid.

88. John P. Swanson, Chief Police Inspector, El Centro, California, to District Director, Los Angeles (27 July 1954), Records, *S.B.P.F.*, 1954, Volume 9.

89. Ibid.

90. David H. Moore to Governor Howard Pyle (27 June 1954), pp. 1-2, in Central Files, Official Files, OF 124-A-1, Box 634, Folder 124-C (1), "Migratory Labor" located in the Dwight D. Eisenhower Library, Abilene, Kansas.

91. Ibid., pp. 3-4.

92. Ibid., p. 6.

93. Howard Pyle to Sherman Adams (5 July 1954); and Sherman Adams to Howard Pyle (12 July 1954), ibid.

8
The Texas Operation

AFTER JULY 2 the character of the operation in California and western Arizona changed. Instead of an intensive sweep of areas, border patrol officials concentrated on scattered mopping-up activities, the prevention of illegal crossings by setting up roadblocks, and the development of an intelligence system that would alert them to planned large-scale infiltration along the border.[1] By 19 July apprehension of undocumented workers had dropped dramatically because of the change in strategy and because of the shifting of the Mobile Task Forces into Texas and New Mexico. Thus between 10 July and 27 September, the Los Angeles Districts of Calexico, San Ysidro, Yuma, El Centro, and San Luis reported a sum total of only 548 apprehensions.[2] This led officials like Swing and Brownell to term the operation in California and Arizona an unqualified success. It also convinced them of the effectiveness of the task force approach in spite of the high cost. Finally, the success of the operation in California further buyoed their hopes of a successful operation in Texas.

In spite of such gratifying news and the promise of a successful campaign in Texas, Joseph Swing realized that resistance to the drive among growers and other employers in Texas, especially in the Lower Rio Grande Valley, would be strong. He therefore took extra care to prepare for his meetings with growers and other employers in Texas. For advice he turned to Harlon Carter, who was well acquainted with both the type of personality and the attitudes prevalent in the Valley.

The Rio Grande Valley of Texas had been described as a colonial empire by its critics, and in many ways it was. The lush fertile soil had made the large commercial growers prosperous. In turn they had used their wealth to consolidate their influence and power in the local politics of the area. For the most part the influential people in the Valley were highly individualistic and independent. Their wealth and status allowed them to exercise a power far out of proportion to their small numerical size. Left pretty much to themselves these men, along with many of the Valley residents, had developed their own identity and value system. Included in this scheme of values were contempt for authority exercised by outsiders, a strong resistance to any change that threatened their social and economic status, and the belief that white, English-speaking people were superior to others.[3] Nowhere were these beliefs better illustrated than in the widespread employment of "illegals" and in the continued defiance of border patrolmen during the performance of their duties.

The existence of a bracero program was largely ignored by employers in the Valley and their participation in the program was not great. They generally viewed the whole issue of contract requirements and guarantees with disdain and as one more example of bureaucratic bungling and interference. As far as they were concerned the bracero agreements took no cognizance of their needs, which included the need of a large but inexpensive supply of labor. They much preferred the more common practice of hiring "illegals" because they were available, worked for whatever wages were paid, and required no special care or consideration. In their view, this was the way things should operate, as "wetbacks" and employers both benefitted from it. Included in the elaborate social and economic rationalizations created by employers was the belief that "wetbacks" needed the jobs and were grateful for whatever they earned. In other words, the "wetbacks" never had it so good in Mexico and that is why they came to the Valley in search of work. So often had these rationalizations been heard by Valley residents that many had come to believe firmly in them.[4]

The widespread use of undocumented workers and the general acceptance of this practice as "legitimate" had forced the Border Patrol to adopt a modus operandi which would not offend or antagonize Valley growers. This mode of operation generally entailed the practice of limiting their apprehension of "illegals" to those captured while working along the side of the road. Border Patrol officials seldom picked up "illegals" working in the fields or on their way to an assigned job. Although this practice irritated and angered some Border Patrol officials, both superiors and "old-timers" warned them that deviation from this would only cause "trouble" for them. In this case "trouble" meant that they would be called before an investigating board that would look into charges levelled against them by influential growers concerning irregularities in the performance of their duties. Thus it was better to limit arrests to "aliens" on roadways, which would help them both meet their quotas and avoid doing anything which would antagonize the growers.[5]

When Border Patrol officials did choose to enforce the laws more strictly they became the object of derision and intensified media campaigns designed to embarrass them and to stir up local resistance to their efforts. Stirring up local resistance was easy to do, as Valley residents generally identified with and condoned the actions of the growers. Furthermore, they viewed border patrolmen as outsiders tampering with the status quo. They believed that every effort should be made to resist the officers when they were too zealous in the performance of their duties. Any effort to thwart the enforcement of immigration laws was viewed by most Valley residents as honorable and justified.[6]

Officials of the INS realized that there was little that they could do about such attitudes. They were helpless before the power of local interest groups supported by members of their local communities. Furthermore the Border Patrol was not without some blame in having encouraged this defiance toward immigration laws. They too had violated these laws when they had opened up the border to illegal entry during 1948 and 1954, after Mexico and the United States had failed to reach agreement on renewal of the bracero program. Of course, not all Border Patrol officials had condoned these actions. Those who had objected had done so because they knew that such incidents only served to undermine their enforcement efforts and their credibility in the eyes of "illegals" and employers alike. Men like Harlon Carter believed that the opening up of the border by those who were responsible for guarding it only served to encourage further violation of the laws.

Swing was aware of these issues as he prepared to meet with growers and grower organizations in Texas. He knew that it would be difficult to convince these men to go along with his suggestion that they use contract labor rather than "illegals" in light of their ingrained views concerning the Border Patrol and the bracero program. He could understand their individualism and their sense of independence. In many ways Swing was like these men—tough, demanding, and not easily intimidated by threats. He decided on a straightforward approach wherein he assured them that he was intent upon carrying out the roundup.

In a series of meetings with Texas growers, Swing asked for their cooperation in ridding the area of "wetbacks" by contracting braceros. He believed that if employers in both the rural and urban sectors used braceros that it would help to greatly reduce the influx of "illegals" from Mexico.[7] Swing's appeals had some impact on a few of the grower organizations. However, this was not sufficient, because grower organizations in Texas were not as influential with their members as they were in California. In fact, many growers did not belong to organizations because they believed that the benefits to be derived from membership were at best minimal.

Nonetheless a few organizations did attempt to persuade all growers to take heed of Swing's warnings. They published pamphlets informing employers of the advantages in hiring braceros and information on how to go about acquiring them. According to the American Agricultural Council, an organization which claimed to represent the Rio Grande Valley, the new contract agreement had eliminated much of the red tape and had reduced the costs involved in contracting braceros. It warned growers that they would be better off hiring braceros, especially as there was a big cotton crop to be harvested. It also cautioned growers about the impending roundup of "illegals" by the INS and asked them not to ignore their warnings.[8]

The warnings and the advice largely fell on deaf ears. Many Texas growers simply ignored Swing's words of caution and took little heed of what had occurred in California when the task forces had moved in. Many were still of the opinion that a similar drive in Texas could and would be blunted. They resented the planned roundup, and they made no effort to hide the fact that they would do everything in their power to foil it. As J. W. Holland, District Director in San Antonio reported after his meeting with members of the Valley Farm Bureau: "Officially they intend to destroy our effort at enforcement of the law here in the Valley."[9]

Swing's hopes for support and cooperation from Texas growers were quickly dashed. Reports from INS officials in the field were largely negative when it came to discussing the position of Valley growers.[10] Added confirmation to grower resistance came when Henry LeBlanc, head of the Texas Employment Office, reported that his office had not filled any requests for braceros from farmers in the McAllen-Brownsville area, as they were unwilling to pay the prevailing rate of $2.05 per hundred pounds of cotton picked. LeBlanc indicated that although a few growers had offered to contract braceros for $1.25 per hundred pounds, he had refused to contract them at that price.

To further complicate matters, officials at the Texas State Employment Office reported that there was an abundant supply of domestic labor available for those who would pay $2.05 per hundred pounds of cotton picked. Because of the availability of local labor, they could not certify a labor shortage, which would permit growers to contract braceros. However, Texas growers refused to pay the $2.05 rate to anyone and continued to hire "illegals."[11]

Swing and the INS did not receive a great deal of cooperation from officials at the state level either. When first informed about the upcoming roundup by immigration officials, Governor Allen Shivers made no immediate response.[12] Swing therefore found it necessary to dispatch J. W. Holland, District Director in San Antonio, to personally solicit the governor's aid. When Holland arrived at the capital he was informed that Governor Shivers was out of town soliciting support for his reelection campaign.[13]

Because of the upcoming elections and because of the strong influence Valley growers exercised it is not at all surprising to find that Shivers was reluctant to support the operation. He was well aware of the vocal opposition of many Valley residents to the planned "invasion," as many newspapers in that area had begun to term the mass roundup. Furthermore, both Shivers and members of his family had been known to employ "wetbacks" from time to time, which endeared him to local growers but placed enforcement officials in a difficult and embarrassing situation.[14]

When Shivers finally did respond to General Swing's letter, he did so in a cautious vein. After thanking the commissioner for having advised him of the upcoming roundup, the governor told Swing to let him know in what way his office might be of assistance. Unlike Governor Knight's reply, Shivers' response made no direct offer of assistance in terms of personnel or support from local law-enforcement officials.[15] Overall, the Border Patrol received little help from state or local officials in Texas during the roundup.

Although California contained a large Spanish-speaking population, there had been no attempt on the part of Swing and his staff to contact its leaders to marshal support for the drive. Their failure might have been due to the shortage of time and their lack of knowledge of Spanish-speaking organizations they might contact. There were also the intense feelings of alienation on the part of the Spanish-speaking community engendered by the enactment of the McCarran Acts, which might have led immigration officials to view chances of cooperation and support from them as minimal at best.

The Texas operation was to prove different in this respect. Because of the large concentrations of Mexican and Mexican American residents in Texas and because of the existence of influential and vocal groups such as the G. I. Forum, immigration officials decided that it would be a good idea to inform them about the mass roundup and to solicit their support and cooperation during the campaign. Officials also hoped to stave off some of the anticipated adverse publicity regarding alleged acts of brutality, abuse, and discrimination against citizens of Mexican descent during the drive.

In separate letters to the presiding officers of the American G.I. Forum and the League of United Latin American Citizens, the District Director in San Antonio notified them of the upcoming drive and made a special appeal for their help. The letters stated that such a drive was necessary and important and that it would benefit the Spanish-speaking community by eliminating one of the major causes of its economic distress—the "illegal alien." Holland wrote that it was important that officers of these organizations inform their membership about the drive and its purposes, particularly as there were some in Texas who would do everything possible to undermine the operation. According to Holland, these people would not hesitate to create incidents or foment trouble "for the purpose of embarrassing this Service, or injuring the good relations existing between employees of this Service and the Spanish speaking residents of this area."[16]

Both the G.I. Forum and the League of United Latin American Citizens responded positively to Holland's requests. Ed Idar, who was executive secretary of the G.I. Forum and who had earlier coauthored a blistering attack on the evils of "wetbackism" entitled *What Price Wetbacks?* sent a circular to local Forum officers informing them of the impending drive and urging them to cooperate with the Border Patrol. Idar also sent out press and radio releases in both English and Spanish to those areas where the drive would be most intense.[17] Holland was pleased at the show of support and indicated to Swing that the information being distributed by the Forum and other groups would greatly help in holding down complaints against the Border Patrol.[18]

The advance party of the Mobile Task Force arrived in McAllen, Texas, on 3 July 1954. As had been the case in California, their duty was to patrol railway lines, establish roadblock checkpoints, and to prevent "illegals" from moving further north to avoid apprehension.[19]

Harlon B. Carter, who was to oversee the operation in Texas, arrived with the advance group in order to set up a base of operations. When questioned by newsmen about the drive, Carter told them that they would witness the arrival of one of the most powerful immigration forces ever assembled for the purpose of rounding up

Five hundred "wetbacks" at the main assembly point near La Blanca, Hidalgo County, Texas. *Courtesy the Express-News Corporation.*

"illegals." When asked to elucidate on the specific size of the force, both Carter and Holland declined comment.[20] Later Carter recalled that he ordered his drivers to drive their vehicles through McAllen most of the night to give the impression to residents and "illegals" that a large force was indeed being transported in.

Both men proved evasive on the question of numbers, as they knew that the force would not be "the greatest ever assembled." Carter expected to have about 300 men at the beginning of the drive and anticipated that the force would never reach more than 750 men. Again, he and other immigration heads were relying on widespread publicity and scare tactics to drive a large number of "illegals" from the area.

Carter, Landon, and Partridge had decided beforehand that the best place for returning "illegals" to Mexico was through Presidio, Texas. This site was chosen because Ojinaja, Mexico, across the border from Presidio, had rail facilities. From there "illegals" would be taken to Durango, which was a considerable distance from the border.[21] On 9 July, Partridge informed Swing that the Mexican government had agreed to accept "illegals" through El Paso and Presidio. According to the memo the Mexican government could handle 500 "aliens" per day until 15 July. After that they could process about 1,000 per day.

On 6 July, immigration officials reported that railway checks and road block operations had netted 1,500 apprehensions for that day. These checkpoints continued to report steady or declining numbers of "illegals" captured until 14 July, when only 800 "illegals" were apprehended.

In Texas, 15 July marked the first full day of "Operation Wetback." On their first day mobile task forces rounded up a total of 4,800 men. The number of apprehensions decreased each day thereafter until 25 July, when apprehensions levelled off at 1,100 per day. On 29 July it was reported to Swing that the operation in the lower Rio Grande Valley of Texas had netted 41,951 apprehensions. As of that date 19,459 of those captured had been returned to Mexico through El Paso. The remaining number were either awaiting transportation or were being processed as braceros.[22]

Swing and other INS officials were pleased with the apparent success of the operation in Texas.[23] Not only were the mopping-up operations proving effective, but it also appeared that the intense publicity campaign had again paid great dividends. Daily reports from officers in the field indicated that large numbers of "illegals" were returning to Mexico in order to avoid apprehension by the Border Patrol. One official reported that as of 22 July, 45,933 "aliens" had fled across the border through the ports of Hidalgo, Brownsville, and Progresso. According to him, this number did not reflect the actual number of those fleeing into Mexico because many had either waded across the Rio Grande or had returned to Mexico via Eagle Pass and Laredo where a count had not been kept.[24]

The sudden rush of "illegal" workers from the area had forced many farmers to contract braceros to harvest their crops. The Labor Department confirmed this when it reported that its employees were processing 3,500 applications per day for the

A family of undocumented persons apprehended during the mass roundup in Texas. *Courtesy the Express-News Corporation.*

lower Rio Grande Valley alone, an area which traditionally had refused to hire braceros.[25] This information was particularly gratifying to Swing, who believed that the only way to end the illegal influx from Mexico was to convert employers to the use of legally contracted braceros. What Swing and those who had espoused this view failed to recognize was that the bracero program was itself a major cause of "illegal" immigration from Mexico.

Although a few of the small growers and farmers welcomed the roundup, the great majority of growers and processors opposed it.[26] At first, however, most people did not take the warnings of immigration officials about the upcoming drive seriously. They believed that the Border Patrol would find it an impossible task to drive out the "illegals" in spite of the highly touted success in California. As one grower put it: "California and Arizona had border fences and huge desert expanses between Mexico and their farms; we had only the muddy Rio Grande."[27] However, skepticism and mild concern turned to anger and consternation as the Texas operation continued.

Caught off guard at first by the unexpected effectiveness of the task forces, opponents of the drive began to feverishly marshal their forces to slow the operation down. The ensuing actions against the Border Patrol soon turned into "a war of nerves" between it and those determined to derail the operation.[28] As one correspondent reported, Valley residents were not going to accept their fate passively.

> They assert boldly that this 3,000-square-mile agricultural empire, with 300,000 inhabitants and an annual income of more than $300,000,000, was built on cheap "wetback" labor like the Southern slave owners of a century ago—it is a violation of their rights to take it away even if the "wetbacks" are lawbreakers.[29]

Gladwin Hill, who had favorably reported the operation in California, wrote, in a somewhat exaggerated sense, that feelings against the drive in Texas, "gave rise to a campaign of protest and villification of a sort rare in . . . the annals of law enforcement."[30] At the forefront of this campaign were newspapers such as the *McAllen Monitor,* the *Harlinger Star,* and the *Brownsville Herald,* all Valley newspapers owned and published by R. C. Hoiles, who had been a strident critic of the drive from the outset.

As Border Patrol officers arrived in their assigned areas, they were greeted by newspapers with banner headlines that described them as an "army of occupation" and as an "invading horde." In some communities, residents greeted officers with crudely lettered signs containing caustic remarks. One such sign read: "Welcome Comrades of the Border Patrol—Soon We Will Rule The World."[31] Editorials strongly criticized the militaristic approach of the Border Patrol to round up "illegals," depriving respectable citizens of much-needed labor. Some editorials embodied sarcasm, such as the one in the *San Benito News* which contained a suggestion from a local resident that the editor considered the best he had yet heard. It read: "How about putting the 700-800 invading Border Patrolmen into the cotton fields, picking?"[32] Others were more direct, and they troubled INS officials by bordering on direct threats to the Border Patrol.[33]

Carter and those patrolmen who had worked in Texas for some time were not especially surprised or concerned about the adverse publicity. In fact, Carter welcomed statements in the press which created the impression that the force involved in the roundup was a large one. Thus, ironically enough, those papers hostile to the Border Patrol aided the drive by helping to create the illusion of a large force of men by repeatedly using such superlatives as "hordes" and "battalions" when describing what was in reality a small number of officers.[34]

Along with the adverse newspaper publicity there arose a concerted whispering campaign about alleged "atrocities" committed by the Border Patrol during the roundup. One widely circulated story involved the refusal of a Border Patrol officer to take an arrested "illegal" who had been bitten by a rattlesnake to a doctor. According to the story the "illegal" had later died while being detained. An investigation of the incident did bear out the fact that an "illegal" had been bitten by a rattlesnake. The inquiry also showed that the officer involved had rushed the injured man to a hospital, where he was kept until he recovered. After his release, the man was sent back to Mexico by immigration authorities.[35]

Another incident involved the decapitation of a man by a low-flying Border Patrol search plane. The patrolman piloting the aircraft told investigators that he had lost momentary control of his craft after he had dropped down to take a closer look at a man riding a mule. He had tried to pull up before striking the man but failed in his attempt. One of the wings struck the man, shearing his head off. The pilot was brought to trial and was found not guilty. However, feelings ran so high over the death of the man that the pilot had to be transferred to a different region.[36]

Newspaper offices in the lower Rio Grande Valley received a number of phone calls from people who had seen border patrolmen taking money from "wetbacks" as they were loaded onto buses.[37] Harlon Carter informed Swing that this had brought a large outcry against the Service and asked that he be advised as to how the matter should be handled. The reason for Carter's concern was that Tom McCabe of United Press in Edinburg, Texas, and Brad Smith of radio station KRGV in Weslaco had threatened to blast him and the INS publicly if they did not receive some explanation regarding the collection of money from "wetbacks."[38]

The incidents occurred because Border Patrol officers had been instructed by Carter to collect money from apprehended "illegals" to help defray the cost of transporting them to staging areas. Officers were told to collect $10.00 from any "alien" who had at least $13.00 on his person. For those who had less than $10.00, officials were to collect only a proportionate amount. Border Patrolmen were ordered always to leave "illegals" with at least $3.00 in their pockets, if they had that much when apprehended.[39]

The problem with all of this was that neither Carter nor the INS possessed any legal authority to demand money from "illegals" to defray the cost of their transportation. The practice also appeared a little incongruous in that they were forcing men to pay for a ride that many of them did not wish to take.

Initially Carter had decided not to say anything about his idea to have "illegals" pay part of the cost, but he was forced to change his mind when the press corps began to inquire about the collection of money from "illegals" by Border Patrol officials. After some hurried communication with Swing he decided to tell the press the reasons for collecting the money.[40] It was decided that they would announce to members of the press that the INS had "statutory authority" to require "illegal aliens" to pay for their fares, especially as they were being "accorded the privilege of departing this country" without having criminal charges filed against them.[41]

The statement by Carter appears to have satisfied everyone, and no more questions arose about the practice of collecting money from "illegals." An interesting footnote to this is that Carter did not issue formal guidelines for the collection of fares to officers in the field until 16 July, the day that this practice was questioned by members of the press.[42] Furthermore, the Border Patrol had not collected fares from "illegals" apprehended during the California operation.

While the adverse publicity did little to end the drive in Texas, it did cause some concern in Mexico. In order to ascertain if Mexican "illegals" were being properly treated, Consul Bernardo Blanco and Vice Consul Dominguez visited the detention camp in McAllen, Texas. They told the director of the camp that Mexico City had asked them for a report. While at the barbed-wire enclosure, they questioned several "aliens" who showed them their receipts. The two Mexican officials appeared satisfied that not more than $10.00 was collected from any "alien" and that each was left with at least $3.00. Blanco did not inspect the sanitary facilities as he had seen them earlier and had judged them to be adequate.[43] Blanco told the press that he found no mistreatment of Mexicans and said that he would pass on his assurances to his Government.[44] Turner, the camp director at McAllen, reported to Fletcher Rawls that he did not know whether the two officials had purposely made an early and unexpected visit to make sure that the INS had not made special preparations or whether it just happened that they went out ahead of schedule. Nonetheless, INS officials believed the two Mexicans were satisfied over what they found and had no complaints.[45]

Records of the mass deportation drive do contain reports indicating that some patrol officers were guilty of mistreating "illegals" and of violating the civil rights of Mexican American citizens. As in the California-Arizona operation, officers at times failed to properly establish the status of Mexicans whom they apprehended and officials later admitted that it was quite likely that some U.S. citizens had been inadvertently deported.[46]

Because of the hostile press and the needed support of Spanish-speaking organizations, INS officials took extra care in investigating alleged instances of abuse and brutality against "illegals" and Mexican Americans by patrol officers. Generally

"Wetbacks" boarding deportation buses at McAllen detention center. *Courtesy of the Texas AFL-CIO Collection, The University of Texas at Arlington Library.*

such investigations came about as a result of complaints by individual citizens.

One such complaint was filed by J. L. Gavito of La Feria, Texas, who charged that a Patrol Inspector in Harlingen had "struck an American citizen of Mexican descent and hurt him rather severely." The officer had struck the man after the injured party had allegedly spoken an epithet to him. As a result of this a fellow officer had filed a complaint against the patrolman, who after a hearing before a Justice of the Peace had been fined a small amount.[47] According to Gavito the incident had not ended here. In another meeting between the officer and the injured party the former "had to be physically restrained by brother officers in order to prevent him from again assaulting the offended party."[48]

Carter reported the complaint to Frank Partridge and pointed out that Gavito had written letters to Senators Lyndon Johnson and Price Daniel and to Congressman Lloyd M. Bentsen in which he described "irregularities" on the part of Border Patrol officers. Carter called upon Gavito, who told him that the purpose of his letter to the legislators was to "obtain better training and supervision of Border Patrol officers who, he felt, sometimes went beyond the necessities of their job, especially in their conduct toward American citizens of Mexican extraction."[49]

Carter admitted to Partridge that the service was well aware of incidents such as the one described by Gavito and thus did not find Mr. Gavito's feelings or his conversation to be "controversial."[50] It is significant that on the day that Gavito met with Carter to file the complaint, the G.I. Forum retained Virgilio Roel and Robert P. Sanchez of McAllen as attorneys "to inquire into and protect the rights of American citizens of Mexican extraction who may get into difficulties with the Border Patrol . . ."[51]

The close scrutiny by INS officials of any incident involving border patrolmen and Mexicans or Mexican Americans, the willingness by Spanish-speaking groups to call any incidents to the attention of the proper authorities, and the close press coverage of Border Patrol activities all contributed to the reduction of brutality and abuse on the part of overzealous or prejudiced officers.

Mexicans and Mexican Americans were not alone in being victimized by discriminatory practices during the drive. Throughout the campaign in Texas immigration officials encountered difficulty in getting meals, places to sleep, and gasoline for their vehicles. In some areas merchants posted signs that read: "Price double to Border Patrol till cotton is picked." In most cases border patrolmen were not charged double, as the signs had been posted in an effort to be "humorous" rather than "spiteful."[52]

Some Valley residents were not in a humorous mood. A hotel operator refused to rent a room to Chief Patrol Inspector Parker after he learned that Parker was a member of the Border Patrol. The same person later ordered two more officers off his premises when they pulled up in a government car.[53] In a separate incident a border patrolman was ticketed and fined for making "an improper start from a parked position." The investigator concluded that the ticket was issued more out of malice than for due cause.[54]

Other border patrolmen were rudely treated when they went into banks or into local cafes and restaurants. One bank clerk told some officers that if he could he would charge them extra just for cashing their checks. At an Edinburg cafe two officers overheard several farmers remark that they were going to have another cup of coffee to "wash the dirty taste out of our mouth." The remark was made as the officers were preparing to leave the cafe.[55] In other towns restaurants posted signs which read: "Dogs and Border Patrolmen not allowed."[56]

The drive and the attendant hostility in the Valley proved even harder on officers who lived there. They complained to superiors that their wives had been ostracized and insulted by friends and neighbors. They also reported that their children were snubbed by playmates and picked on by teachers in school.[57] Although their superiors were sympathetic to these complaints, they told their men that there was little that they could do to stop this kind of discrimination and peer group pressure. They asked them to bear with it and to continue to conduct themselves in a professional manner.

By early to mid-August the number of complaints regarding brutality had dropped and the campaign against the Border Patrol on the part of what some called "a small, but vociferous, minority that did not think the government meant business"[58] had all but ended. The protest had been in vain, for the drive continued into September. Many growers, confronted by the fact that "illegals" would not be around to harvest their crops, made grudging applications for braceros at the contract centers. This led to the employment of braceros in an unprecedented degree.

The sudden rush by employers in Texas to contract braceros made it appear that Swing had accomplished one of his goals—that of "persuading" employers to use legal contract labor instead of "illegals." On the surface this was true, but the "persuasion" had come about only after many Texans realized that they must either contract braceros to harvest their crops or allow them to rot in the fields. Furthermore, the anger and hostility of many employers was assuaged when they realized that many of the braceros who were being contracted were in truth "dried-out" "illegals." To make the bitter pill more palatable Swing convinced Labor Department officials to make every effort to allow employers to retain their "specials." Swing also pledged to do everything in his power to convince federal officials responsible for the bracero program to streamline the procedures and to reduce the cost of contracting as much as possible. Swing kept his promise when he instituted a simple crossing-card system in August of 1955. Possession of the I-100 card allowed braceros to proceed immediately to contracting centers and to bypass procedures set up by the Mexican government. It also made it possible for employers to recontract braceros who had worked for them during previous seasons.

Mexican authorities objected to this unilateral policy change, claiming that the new procedure violated the bracero agreement and that it induced Mexican workers to evade the jurisdiction of the authorities of their own country. They regarded the use of the laminated cards for recruiting purposes as unsatisfactory and asked that their use be withdrawn immediately. Swing and Brownell responded that Mexican concerns were unfounded and that the crossing-card system would make the job of controlling the border easier for the INS and that it would help reduce infiltration by communist agents. In time, however, the INS was forced to discontinue issuing the cards.[59]

Every effort was made to accommodate those who had repeatedly hired "illegals" and who had paid little heed to the existence of a bracero program. Furthermore, the "drying-out" or legalizing of many of the "wetbacks" apprehended during the drive in Texas created the strange situation of the United States expending large amounts of money to oust "illegals" and then turning around and spending even more money to return many of them to this country as "legalized" braceros.

In many instances these "legalized" braceros accepted a contract only in order to gain entry back into the United States. Once here they struck out on their own in search of greater opportunities before their contracts had expired.[60] In breaking their contracts these braceros became classified as "illegals" who owed their presence here to the same government that had gone to a lot of time, effort, and expense to curtail the influx of undocumented workers from Mexico.

While the drive and buslift continued, officials of the INS made plans to add another wrinkle to their campaign against "illegal aliens." In early July, Swing assigned D. R. Kelley to locate a ship with either Mexican or United States registry to use in boatlifting "aliens" into the interior of Mexico. INS officials had become convinced of the practicality of removing "illegals" as far into the interior of Mexico as possible in order to discourage them from returning.

Kelley's search for a ship proved difficult. His initial choice, a Mexican ship named *Vera Cruz*, did not pass the Coast Guard safety inspection. According to Kelley the inspection had shown that the *Vera Cruz* lacked adequate firefighting and fire-detection equipment, and it needed more bunks and more lifesaving equipment before it could be pressed into service.[61] Kelley continued his search and eventually was able to locate two ships that were acquired for use in the boatlifting of undocumented workers to Mexico. One of the two ships was the refurbished *Vera Cruz*.

By early September the volume of apprehensions had dropped enough so that use of the ships could begin. The first deportation voyage took place on 3 September 1954, when the *S. S. Emanicpation* sailed from Port Isabel, Texas, to Veracruz, Mexico. From 3 September through the end of fiscal year 1955, the *Emancipation* and the *Vera Cruz* made twenty-six trips. Both ships carried a total of 800 "aliens" per trip and deposited them some 2,000 miles from the California border and more than 800 miles from the nearest point in Texas.[62] The United States paid $8.00 per head for transporting "illegals" by ship.[63] According to Swing those who were boatlifted were mainly repeaters, that is, "illegals" who had been expelled and had managed to reenter. Chronic repeaters were jailed by Mexican authorities in Veracruz in order to discourage them and others from crossing illegally again. Officials found that the sea voyage, which was unpleasant for many, and the threat of incarceration had a very salutory effect in cutting down the number of repeaters.[64]

By the end of 1955 the *Vera Cruz* and the *Emancipation* were replaced with two smaller vessels, the *Mercurio* and the *Frieda*. Boatlifting operations continued until September of 1956, when a mutiny on board the *Mercurio*, preceded by the drowning death of seven "illegals" who had jumped ship in order to escape, forced an investigation embarrassing to both countries. The investigation and the public outcry in Mexico against the boatlift forced the Mexican government to suspend operations.[65]

NOTES

1. Joseph M. Swing to Herman R. Landon, District Director, Los Angeles (2 July 1954), in Special Border Patrol Force, "Wetbacks, Operation," Volume 4, Part 2, located in the Immigration and Naturalization Service Office, Washington, D.C. (hereafter cited as Records, *S.B.P.F.*, 1954, Part 2, Volume 4).

2. Herman R. Landon to Frank Partridge (27 September 1954), Special Border Patrol Force, "Wetback, Operation," Volume 9, located in the Immigration and Naturalization Service Office, Washington, D.C. (hereafter cited as Records, *S.B.P.F.*, 1954, Volume 9).

3. Lyle Saunders and Olen E. Leonard, *The Wetback in the Lower Rio Grande Valley of Texas*, Occasional Papers VII (Austin: University of Texas, 1951), pp. 49, 65, 85.

4. Ibid., p. 65.

5. Ibid., pp. 79-80; Bruce S. Meador, " 'Wetback' Labor in the Lower Rio Grande Valley" (M.A. thesis, University of Texas, 1951), p. 70.

6. Edward Idar and Andrew McLellan, *What Price Wetbacks?* (Austin: American G.I. Forum and Texas State Federation of Labor-AFL, 1953), p. 14.

7. Gladwin Hill, "Plan Gains to End Use of 'Wetbacks,' " *New York Times* (27 June 1954), p. 36.

8. "Braceros vs. Wetbacks," issued by the American Agricultural Council of the Rio Grande Valley, Texas (June 1954), pp. 1-2, Special Border Patrol Force, "Wetback, Operation," 1954, Volume 5, located in Immigration and Naturalization Service Office, Washington, D.C. (hereafter cited as Records, *S.B.P.F.*, 1954, Volume 5).

9. Memo from J. W. Holland, District Director, San Antonio, Texas (14 July 1954), Special Border Patrol Force, "Wetback, Operation," Volume 3, Part 1, located in the Immigration and Naturalization Service Office, Washington, D.C. (hereafter cited as Records, *S.B.P.F.*, 1954), Part 1, Volume 3.

10. Frank Partridge to Joseph Swing (3 July 1954), Records, *S.B.P.F.*, 1954, Volume 5.

11. Ibid.

12. J. M. Swing to Allan Shivers (2 July 1954), Records, *S.B.P.F.*, 1954, Volume 5.

13. J. W. Holland to J. M. Swing (9 July 1954), in ibid.

14. "Rio Grande Drowns Many 'Wetbacks,' *New York Times* (12 August 1954), p. 9.

15. Allan Shivers to J. M. Swing (9 July 1954), Records, *S.B.P.F.*, 1954, Volume 5.

16. J. W. Holland to Chris Aldrete, President of the American G.I. Forum, Del Rio, Texas (7 July 1954), ibid.

17. Copy of circular sent to all State Officers, Directors, Forums, Auxiliaries, and Junior Forums in Texas, New Mexico, Arizona, and Colorado from Ed Idar, Jr. (8 July 1954), ibid.

18. J. W. Holland to J. M. Swing (13 July 1954), p. 2, Records, *S.B.P.F.*, 1954, Part 1, Volume 3.

19. "Texas Wetback Drive Planned," *San Antonio Express* (3 July 1954), p. 1.

20. "Top Immigration Heads Plan Big Wetback Drive," *San Antonio Express* (7 July 1954), p. 1.

21. Note to Swing from the Assistant Commissioner, Inspections and Examinations Division, Special Border Patrol Force (28 June 1954), Records, *S.B.P.F.*, 1954, Volume 5.

22. Four-page report of the Texas Operation (29 July 1954), p. 3, Records, *S.B.P.F.*, 1954, Volume 9.

23. Ibid.

24. Ibid., pp. 3-4.

25. Ibid., p. 4.

26. "Operation, Wetback: Impact on the Border States," *Employment Security Review* 22, no. 3 (March 1955): 17.

27. John McBride, *Vanishing Bracero: Valley Revolution* (San Antonio: The Naylor Company, 1963), p. 5.

28. Gladwin Hill, " 'Wetback' Drive Irks 'The Valley,' " *New York Times* (2 August 1954), p. 8.

29. Ibid.

30. Ibid.

31. Ibid.

32. *San Benito News* (8 July 1954), newspaper clipping found in Records, *S.B.P.F.*, 1954, Volume 5.

33. Frank Partridge to J. M. Swing (7 July 1954), in ibid.

34. U.S., Department of Justice, *Border Patrol Management* (Washington, D.C.: G.P.O., 1955), p. 53.

35. E. R. Decker to Harlon Carter (21 July 1954), Records, *S.B.P.F.*, 1954, Volume 5.

36. John M. Myers, *The Border Wardens* (Englewood Cliffs, New Jersey: Prentice Hall, 1971), p. 84.

37. " 'Wetbacks' Have to Pay," *New York Times* 19 July 1954), p. 21.

38. Memorandum for the Commissioner from D. R. Kelley, Acting Chief, Border Patrol Branch, Central Office (16 July 1954), Records, *S.B.P.F.*, 1954, Volume 5.

39. Ibid.

40. Memorandum of telephone call from Harlon B. Carter to J. M. Swing (16 July 1954), p. 2, Records, *S.B.P.F.*, 1954, Part 1, Volume 3.

41. Ibid.

42. Harlon B. Carter to all Officers Concerned, Re: Payment for Buslift transportation (16 July 1954), ibid.

43. Note from Turner to Fletcher Rawls, Chief Patrol Inspector, McAllen (19 July 1954), ibid.

44. "Alien Round-Up Approved," *New York Times* (21 July 1954), p. 17.

45. Turner to F. Rawls (19 July 1954), Records, *S.B.P.F.*, 1954, Part 1, Volume 3.

46. Leo Grebler, *Mexican Immigration to the United States: The Record and Its Implications*. Mexican American Study Project, Advance Report 2 (Los Angeles: University of California, 1966), p. 34.

47. File Memorandum (14 July 1954), Records, *S.B.P.F.*, 1954, Part 1, Volume 3.

48. Ibid.

49. Harlon B. Carter to Frank Partridge (14 July 1954), ibid.

50. Ibid.

51. File Memorandum (14 July 1954), ibid.

52. Memo: "Incidents Embarrassing to Our Officers," report from E. R. Decker (Investigator) to Harlon Carter (21 July 1954), Records, *S.B.P.F.*, 1954, Volume 5.

53. Ibid.

54. Ibid.

55. Ibid.

56. Myers, *The Border Wardens*, p. 83.

57. Ibid.

58. Hill, *New York Times* (2 August 1954), p. 8.

59. Charge d'Affaires of Mexico to Secretary of State, note No. 4499 (24 August 1955), pp. 1-4, in Central Files, Official Files, Box 634, Migratory Labor Folder-124-C(1), located in Dwight Eisenhower Library, Abilene, Kansas; Department of Justice Herbert Brownell to Henry F. Holland, Assistant Secretary of State (8 September 1955), in Department of Justice Records, File No. 12, located in Department of Justice, Washington, D.C.

60. "Bracero Skips," memo from Frank Partridge to District Directors in Los Angeles, California; San Francisco, California; San Antonio, Texas; and El Paso, Texas (14 July 1954), Records, *S.B.P.F.*, 1954, Volume 5.

61. Memo from D. R. Kelley to Frank Partridge (21 July 1954), ibid.

62. U.S., Department of Justice, *Annual Report of the Immigration and Naturalization Service* (Washington, D.C.: U.S. G.P.O., 1955), p. 19.

63. Ibid.

64. U.S., Congress, House, Hearings before the Subcommittee on Government Operations, *Reorganization of the Immigration and Naturalization Service*, 84th Cong., 1st sess. (Washington, D.C.: 1955), p. 33.

65. For details *see New York Times*, 24, 27, 29 August; 2 and 13 September 1956.

9
"Operation Wetback" Ends

BY MID-SEPTEMBER A number of factors combined to bring the campaign against undocumented persons in California, Arizona, and Texas to a close. The drive by then had pretty well exhausted INS funds. It had been an expensive undertaking, particularly in the per diem payments made to all the INS officials involved in the roundup. The depletion of funds also contributed to a reduction in the operation of the buslift. Another factor was that the growing season had almost come to an end. The reduction of employment opportunities, the drive, and the propaganda campaign discouraged illegal entry for the time being. As a result many of the officers detailed from other sections of the country were returned to their regular assignments by the end of September. That fall, Ed Castillo, a reporter for the San Antonio *Light*, wrote that the patrolmen who remained on the border region literally had to beat the bushes to capture any "illegals."

While some members of the task force moved north to begin operations in the Midwest, others remained in California and Texas to tighten their control of the border. It was at this time that the newly created intelligence agency was put into operation in order to collect, evaluate, and disseminate information concerning smuggling and other illegal activities. In addition, a new air-intelligence center was set up at El Centro, California. Its purpose was to collect and disseminate information relating to the illegal entry of aircraft from Mexico. Barricade fences were constructed or repaired near larger border cities where illegal traffic was particularly heavy. It was hoped that the fences, which totalled 18.8 miles, would serve to discourage illegal entry, especially by women and children. The fences were also designed to help divert the flow of "illegals" away from the city boundaries and toward sections where apprehensions would prove easier. In this way areas could be controlled with a minimum force, freeing officers for duty elsewhere.

When the operation moved north to the midwestern states, the INS instituted the Border Patrol Air Transport Arm. The inaugural flight took place on 18 September 1954, when fifty Mexican "illegals" were flown from Chicago, Illinois, to Brownsville, Texas. During its first year of operation the Air Transport Arm flew 11,459 "illegals" from interior points in the United States to staging areas on the Mexican border, where "aliens" were loaded onto waiting ships and transported to points as far south as Veracruz.

With the end of the drive in Texas the pestilential housing that had been inhabited by "illegals" now stood empty and abandoned. Near some of the mud huts, brush hutches, or hollows scooped out of a stream or canal bank stood makeshift crosses marking the final resting place of those victimized by hunger, disease, deprivation, and exploitation. Although the drives in California, Arizona, and Texas had been supported by some and opposed by others, and no one was completely satisfied when the drives were completed, they had not worked an extreme hardship on those involved on either side of the issue. The only ones who suffered the hardships of "Operation Wetback" were the undocumented workers.

In his annual report, Joseph Swing, Commissioner of Immigration and Naturalization, stated: "The so-called 'wetback' problem no longer exists. . . . The border has been secured."[1] In March of 1955 Swing told a House Government Operations subcommittee that the invasion of "wetbacks" had been stemmed for the first time since before World War II. He further stated that the number of "wetbacks" apprehended daily had been cut from 3,000 to 300 per day.[2] According to Swing and other top INS officials, "Operation Wetback" had had significant and beneficial effects on the social, economic, and political situation in the country and on the operation of the Border Patrol.

Swing's reorganization of the Border Patrol had created greater flexibility in its operation. It had also made for a more effective and coordinated approach in policing the border. This, along with an increased efficiency in carrying out mass roundups, served to rehabilitate the Border Patrol's self-image and its image in the public eye. By 1955 its prestige and reputation had noticeably improved, particularly in Texas.[3] An article in the San Antonio *Light* reported the change, not only in the renovated and newly-constructed buildings which housed the Border Patrol but also in the appearance of the officers themselves.

> Even the uniforms were different. Where, for years, patrolmen stationed in the Texas area had been accustomed to wearing casual khakis and soft-brimmed Stetsons, they were now garbed in snappy forest-green uniforms . . . , black shoes, and hard brimmed "patrol Stetsons." A Sam Browne belt and regulation pistol completed the outfit.[4]

The article also made reference to the esteem in which the corps was locally held, which the reporter termed a "novelty." The noticeable change led Swing to assert proudly that the Border Patrol now functioned with the precision and efficiency of a trained military or semimilitary body.[5]

All of this had its price, which some legislators believed to be high. The mobile task force approach was both effective and expensive, as it required the service to pay for travel and a per diem for officers who were moved from their regular patrol areas. In 1954 the cost had totalled $98,943, and estimates for 1955 and 1956 ran as high as $1,500,000 and $1,372,000, respectively. Yet Swing considered the benefits to be derived in control well worth the cost. Furthermore the new *modus operandi* made every effort to utilize the mobile task forces to the fullest extent, according to Swing. In 1955 he told a congressional subcommittee that task forces were moved to industrial areas when there was a lull in the agricultural sectors, which kept men from sitting around and getting paid for doing nothing. In his opinion, "If this system (the mobile task force) were not instituted, doubling the Border Patrol would not keep your border sealed. The expense of travel is negligible as compared to hiring 400 or 500 additional patrolmen to leave in stations at one place."[6]

Swing told the subcommittee that control of the border had already begun to pay other dividends that made the expense of mobile task forces negligible. For example, the mass roundup of "illegals" in California in 1954 had saved the California Unemployment Service $325,000 a week by opening up jobs for citizens previously held by "wetbacks." The Texas Employment Service had informed him that the drive by the Border Patrol had made it possible for citizens to obtain jobs at the decent wage levels after the unfair competition from "illegals" had been eliminated. Officials in the Texas Employment Service estimated that this had caused 25,000 to 30,000 citizens to remain in the Rio Grande Valley to work rather than to leave the area. This meant, he concluded, that money was now being earned and spent by citizens of this country rather than by "wetbacks."[7] Furthermore, as it proved almost as expensive to contract braceros, many employers had turned to hiring domestic laborers, which again redounded to the benefit of this country's citizens and its economy.[8]

Among other positive economic gains attributed to the roundup were reports that retail sales in areas of high concentrations of "illegals" had shown sharp increases after the "wetbacks" had been removed.[9] In addition to helping reduce demands for public welfare funds, the Service reported that many southwestern states had reported significant reductions in crime and disease rates as a result of the deportation of "illegals" begun in June.[10]

A major change brought about in part by "Operation Wetback" was the gradual substitution of legally imported labor for "wetbacks." According to government sources, figures following the mass roundup showed that the contracting of braceros had increased by 25 percent in California since September of 1953, representing an increase of 11,000 braceros.[11] In the lower Rio Grande Valley of Texas the contracting of braceros increased from 3,000 to 70,000 following the 1954 campaign.[12] After the 1954 campaign the number of braceros contracted nationwide continued to increase annually until the program ended in 1964.[13] (See tables 3 and 4.)

Swing and Brownell believed that the Border Patrol had proven its detractors wrong through its success in stemming the influx of "illegals" and that it merited an increase in staff size and in its operating budget. Swing warned legislators that any relaxation in enforcement efforts could again result in tens of thousands of "illegal aliens" crossing the border.[14] "The moment the defense is relaxed along the border, it immediately becomes known to the illegals, and they swarm right back in, and if he swarms back in this time, my successor will have a much more difficult time than I have had, because the rumor up and down the border is that this is just another flash in the pan. . . ."[15]

Some of Swing's predecessors had espoused similar views in arguing for increased appropriations, but they had had little success in convincing legislators to grant them increases. However, things were different this time, for Swing and the INS were appearing before Congress flushed with the "success" of "Operation Wetback." They could now argue from a position of strength and documented evidence that the border could be controlled if the Border Patrol were given the money and the personnel to do so. Traditional opponents to increased Border Patrol appropriations were not able to utilize the Patrol's ineffectiveness as a rationale for denying them the appropriation. The momentum favored the INS, and it was helped along by its own intense propaganda campaign, the highly touted and exaggerated success of "Operation Wetback," and a change in public and congressional attitudes concerning the Border Patrol, the "wetback," and the need to maintain control of the border.

Congress had already responded favorably by voting a supplementary appropriation of three million dollars during the roundup in 1954.[16] It continued to provide further increases until 1956, when the Border Patrol budget reflected a net increase of three million dollars.[17] The idea of a massive "wetback invasion" was used by Joseph Swing and Herbert Brownell to dramatize the need for a well-staffed, well-financed Border Patrol, and it provided them with the opportunity to at least silence, if not discredit, its critics and opponents for the moment.[18]

"OPERATION WETBACK": AN ANALYSIS

While a majority of people accepted many of the INS's claims concerning the "success" of "Operation Wetback," closer scrutiny of its "success" reveals inconsistencies and casts doubt upon its veracity. Furthermore, the campaign against "illegals," for all of its alleged dividends, had extremely undesirable and harmful outcomes that must be weighed and examined in gauging the overall effect and impact of "Operation Wetback."

One area in which there is a great deal of discrepency is in the number of reported departures. According to the INS, "Operation Wetback" resulted in the departure of some 1,300,000 "illegals" either through deportation, repatriation, or "voluntary" departure before formal operations began, in addition to those apprehended during the course of normal operations during fiscal year 1954.[19] However, the 1,300,000 figure appears exaggerated, as much of it is based on estimates of the number of "illegals" who left the country before the drive actually began. In fact, the actual number of apprehensions makes up only a small percentage of the figure reported by INS authorities following "Operation Wetback."

For example, the California operation yielded approximately 84,278 apprehensions. Most of these took place in the period between 10 June and 27 July 1954. After that, apprehensions decreased dramatically because of the sweeps and the removal of the task forces to Texas. Yet the INS reported that all told some 540,000 "illegals" had either been deported or forced to flee from California as a result of "Operation Wetback." Thus, after subtracting the recorded number of apprehensions, the INS claimed that the precampaign publicity and the operation had forced some 455,722 "illegals" to flee into Mexico in order to avoid apprehension. Nowhere in the records of the INS on the drive is there evidence to support this claim. If anything the statements by INS officials cast doubt on the validity of their estimate since they readily admit that the number of "aliens" who fled remained "uncounted"[20] and that "illegals" were fleeing so fast from the border area that "it was impossible to count them."[21]

In the San Antonio District, which includes all of Texas with the exception of the far western counties in the El Paso and Trans-Pecos area, a total of 80,127 apprehensions were reported for the campaign. Observers along ports of entry in Texas reported that they "counted some 60,456 aliens" who returned to Mexico before the drive began in order to avoid arrest.[22] Even if the latter figure is accepted and is added to the 80,127, there are still well over 700,000 "illegals" unaccounted for in the Texas operation.[23] INS officials claimed that precampaign publicity had caused somewhere between 500,000 and 700,000 "illegals" to flee into Mexico before the campaign began in order to avoid apprehension. This represents an extremely large contingent of people fleeing the country, and nowhere have reports from other sources been found which would corroborate this figure. Certainly an influx of this size to the border cities along the Texas-Mexican border would have been the subject of much communication between Mexico City and the United States, yet records do not contain correspondence concerning this matter. Nor was there evidence of newspaper publicity either in Mexico or the United States about this mass exodus. It is very unlikely that such a massive movement would have been overlooked by the press or viewed by it as unworthy of at least some coverage.

Officials in the INS had little or nothing to lose by presenting inflated figures. They realized that the more impressive the figures, the better congressional response might be to requests for increased budgetary support. They well knew that few if any would ever question their figures, particularly in light of the fact that they often used estimates in reporting deportation and repatriation figures.

Another crucial factor that brings into question the success of the operation is the large number of "illegals" who fled to points just south of the border before the roundup began. Although it is very unlikely that their number was as great as the INS claimed, they nonetheless represented a significant factor in terms of future illegal entry into the United States.

This was the view espoused by Milton Plumb, a labor representative who had visited the Mexican border region shortly after the campaign had ended. According to Plumb he had seen thousands of "illegals" along the border, and many of those he spoke to indicated that they were planning to cross as soon as the opportunity presented itself. Others told him that many of their compatriots had already effected illegal entry. Thus, wrote Plumb, "Wetbacks are still illegally entering the United States today—six months after the Justice Department's much-publicized roundup which was supposed to put an end to the 'open sieve' Mexican border."[24]

Like others before him, Plumb was critical of the way in which the INS had conducted its drive against "illegals." He described the campaign as "brutal" and accused it of having spawned new evils which were "potentially more dangerous than the 'wetback' traffic itself."[25] Among those evils listed by Plumb and others were: a growing anti-U.S. feeling among Mexicans and Mexican Americans; a widespread shakeup of the Border Patrol "which had already begun to militarize and dehumanize . . . the service"; "an increased illegal immigration of a new and more serious kind, involving misuse of tourist cards and entry permits, forged passports, and phony birth certificates"; and "virtually complete breakdown, particularly in the lower Rio Grande Valley, of enforcement of the 50 cent minimum wage and other protections for legal Mexican contract workers guaranteed by terms of the agreement between the United States and Mexico."[26]

The widespread abuse of braceros was not a new phenomenon. In fact, as already explained, the repeated violations on the part of contractors had created friction between the United States and Mexico, which had led Mexico to make repeated efforts to have the U.S. enforce contract guarantees more stringently. Although the United States agreed to do so, enforcement proved difficult and spotty. As a result, many braceros, feeling cheated and abused, "skipped" their contracts and struck out on their own. In so doing they became "illegals."

The growing number of "skips" in this country led Ernesto Galarza to accuse the Treasury Department of subsidizing "wetbacks." In Galarza's opinion public funds were spent in order to recruit and transport braceros into the United States. Once here thousands of braceros were either induced by private labor contractors to break their work contracts or were forced by unfavorable working and living conditions to leave their employers in search of better opportunities.[27]

In retrospect it is not difficult to understand why so many braceros decided to "skip" or why many later reentered illegally. The so-called end of the "wetback" era did not bring an end to the abuses of the bracero program, as many of the evils that had plagued the "wetback" system were merely transferred to the bracero program.

The Texas State Federation of Labor stated in one of its reports that the bracero program in the lower Rio Grande Valley of Texas had "assumed, in large measure, the trappings of 'legalized wetbackism.' "[28] This state of affairs was brought about because the solutions proposed by the INS and the United States government were only stopgap measures. Their efforts did little to change attitudes, particularly in those areas where exploiting "wetbacks" had become socially and morally accepted. Employers continued to deal with braceros in much the same way they had dealt with the "illegal alien," primarily because of their unchanged view concerning Mexicans and because many of the braceros were "dried out" "wetbacks." "The willingness to work at any assigned task regardless of the wages, the complacency toward the hazards of the job, the isolation of barracks life on the farms, the total absence of self-directed organization," and the lack of enforcement on the part of government agencies due to understaffing, graft, or both, "were carried over from one system to the other because the order had not changed and the men were the same ones."[29]

Yet little was done to alter or alleviate the situation, because pressure groups in the farm bloc remained powerful. The passage of Public Law 78 in 1951 misled people into believing that the bracero program afforded braceros insurance, housing, and transportation benefits not afforded to workers who were citizens of the United States.[30] In the eyes of the general public, the bracero "had it made."

Even after many of the abuses had been brought to light, little changed. The latter part of the decade witnessed a decline in Mexico's bargaining position, and employers found that they had little to fear in terms of government sanctions against them. The bracero situation was perhaps best summed up by a grower who stated: "We used to buy our slaves; now we rent them from the Government."[31]

In terms of actual gains the domestic migrants in the United States had little to cheer about. The supposed end of the "wetback era" did not bring about measurable change in the living and working conditions which many migrants endured. Legislation governing housing, wages, and transportation of migrants continued to be scuttled, and the nation at large remained largely oblivious to their suffering and misery. The migrant population of this country were truly the "forgotten people."

"Operation Wetback" had a significant impact on the people of Mexican descent in the United States. The mass repatriation and deportation of "illegals" once again attested to the fact that Mexicans were welcomed here only as long as there was a need for their labor.[32] This made their position in this country a tenuous one at best, for a downswing in the economic and labor markets did not usually bode well for them.

Mexican "illegals" usually fared worse since adverse economic conditions were usually attributed to their presence. Although this often represented a simplistic and erroneous explanation for economic problems, it was difficult to change prevailing attitudes. The "remedy" most often suggested and most readily administered was one of deporting or repatriating "illegals" who were in the country.

"Operation Wetback" further strained the relationship between the Mexican American community and the host society. The Mexican American community was affected because the campaign was aimed at only one racial group, which meant that the burden of proving one's citizenship fell totally upon people of Mexican descent. Those unable to present such proof were arrested and returned to Mexico. In some cases this involved long-time residents of this country. The result was that family and kinship ties were disrupted and an atmosphere of fear and hostility was engendered. This insult to people of Spanish-speaking descent only helped to strength-en feelings of alienation from U.S. society and to cause further mistrust of the gov-ernment.[33] However, there was little that the victimized people could do. The times were not conducive to protest and resistance. In fact it was a period of repression, fear, and witch-hunts brought about by the economic recession, the lingering specter of McCarthyism, and the existence of restrictive laws such as the McCarran-Walter Immigration Act of 1952. In essence " 'Operation Wetback' demonstrated the pre-carious status of Mexicans in the United States and their vulnerability to regulations and control," at the hands of a single government agency.[34]

Compounding the tragedy of "Operation Wetback" and the events that preceded it was the mistreatment and injustice suffered by many undocumented persons at the hands of the host society. They were accorded a *persona non grata* status, for many of the ills affecting the United States were either directly or indirectly at-tributed to their presence here. Much of the information concerning "illegals" was distorted, misleading, and not based on solid research data. The tendency was to focus on the perceived "evils" that "illegals" created, and they were described in terms that were stereotypic and negative. Rather than acknowledge them as human beings with dreams, hopes, aspirations, and needs, most people in this country chose to malign them and to shroud them with names and labels that reeked of derision, racism, and denigration.

The negative views toward "illegals" are indeed ironic in light of the predominant values espoused by American society such as hard work, frugality, the spirit of in-dividual initiative, and the desire for self-improvement. These values and character-istics are credited with having made the exploration, settlement, and progress of this country possible. In many ways undocumented persons have exhibited the character-istics that have been held up as examples. Like some of our revered predecessors, the "wetbacks" came to the United States in search of opportunity and a desire to make life better for themselves and their loved ones. They came to escape hunger and deprivation and in doing so many of them undertook great risks. Yet many undocumented persons were not to be denied or deterred; and in their determina-tion they exhibited qualities of courage, perseverance, and initiative. Once here many of them worked hard and long for what amounted to meager wages. For the most part "illegals" comported themselves well, setting their course on the path of hard work and frugality. Yet few people bothered to take cognizance of these things.

"Operation Wetback" did not bring an end to illegal immigration from Mexico. It did slow the influx for a short time but it brought no permanent solution to the problem. It was a stopgap measure, doomed to go the way of most stopgap measures.

Similarly, efforts to enact penalty legislation against employers also met with failure for a variety of reasons. Yet even if such legislation had been enacted, it is doubtful that it would have been an effective deterrent to illegal entry. Those who proposed such legislation failed to recognize that the needs of desperate men and women are often greater than their fear of the law. Furthermore, such legislation would not have been sufficient to discourage unscrupulous employers from hiring undocumented workers. In most cases prosecution and conviction of guilty parties would have been difficult, given the prevailing attitudes of the communities responsible for trying offenders. Even if convictions were handed down, the fines and penalties would not have imposed much hardship on the guilty parties. The fact that smugglers of "illegals" were seldom apprehended, much less convicted, leads one to believe that the chances of conviction for the "lesser" offense of hiring "illegals," would have been remote at best.

"Operation Wetback" and the accompanying propaganda served once again to shift attention away from the real problems in both Mexico and the United States that contributed to the influx of "illegals." The drive and the efforts to pass legislation to control illegal entry focused attention only on the symptom. Thus "illegal aliens" became the pawns of men who purposely cultivated an environment hostile to them in an effort to achieve their own personal ends. The image of the mysterious, sneaky, faceless "illegal" was once again stamped into the minds of many. Once this was accomplished, "illegals" became something less than human, with their arbitrary removal being that much easier to justify and accomplish.

NOTES

1. U.S., Department of Justice, *Annual Report of the Immigration and Naturalization Service,* 1955 (Washington, D.C., 1955), p. 15.

2. "Drive on Wetbacks Termed a Success," *New York Times* (10 March 1955), p. 29.

3. Jerry R. Holleman and A. C. McClellan, "Down in the Valley: A Supplementary Report on Developments in the Wetback and Bracero Situation of the Lower Rio Grande Valley Since Publication of 'What Price Wetbacks?' " (Texas State Federation of Labor, Austin, Tex., 1955), p. 2.

4. *San Antonio Light* (9 October 1955).

5. Holleman and McClellan, "Down in the Valley," p. 2.

6. U.S. Congress, House, Hearings before the Subcommittee on Legal and Monetary Affairs of the Committee on Government Operations, *Reorganization of the Immigration and Naturalization Service,* 84th Cong., 1st sess. (9 and 17 March 1955) (Washington, D.C., 1955), p. 61 (hereafter cited as *Hearings, Reorganization, 1955*).

7. Ibid., p. 33.

8. "Operation Wetback: Impact on the Border States," *Employment Security Review* 22, no. 3 (March 1955): p. 17. Not all of the effects were beneficial. One drawback was that it reduced the farm labor force by about 20,000 farm hands, who left the fields to take advantage of nonagricultural opportunities opened up by the removal of undocumented workers from city jobs. This was keenly felt in Imperial and San Diego Counties and in the interior and coastal districts of Northern California, ibid., p. 17.

9. Holleman and McClellan, "Down in the Valley," p. 2.

10. *Employment Security Review* (March 1955), pp. 1-26, *passim;* "Drive on 'Wetbacks' Cuts Crime in U.S." *New York Times* (11 April 1955), p. 25.

11. Ibid., p. 17.

12. Robert D. Tomasek, "The Political and Economic Implications of Mexican Labor in the United States under the Non Quota System, Contract Labor Program, and Wetback Movement" (Ph.D. diss., University of Michigan, 1957), p. 270.

13. After 1954 growers found it more difficult to claim innocence of their worker's citizenship status because new Social Security provisions made it mandatory for them to contribute to the old age and survivors insurance fund if their employees earned over $100 per year. The required forms provided a statement concerning the ethnic membership and country of the employee. This situation also helped to encourage employers to hire legally contracted workers. Nelson G. Copp, *Wetbacks and Braceros* (San Francisco: R and E Research Associates, 1971), p. 45.

14. *New York Times* (11 April 1955).

15. *Hearings, Reorganization, 1955,* p. 34.

16. Tomasek, "The Political and Economic Implications," p. 268.

17. *Hearings, Reorganization, 1955,* p. 3.

18. Richard Tait Jarnegin, "Effect of Increased Illegal Mexican Migration upon the Organization and Operations of the United States Immigration Border Patrol, Southwest Region" (M.A. thesis, University of Southern California, 1957), p. 197.

19. U.S. Department of Justice, *Annual Report of the Immigration and Naturalization Service, 1954* (Washington, D.C., 1954), p. 31; John Myers Myers, *The Border Wardens* (Englewood Cliffs, N.J.: Prentice-Hall, Inc., 1971), p. 92.

20. Department of Justice, *Annual Report, 1955,* p. 14.

21. U.S. Congress, House, Committee on Appropriations, *Hearings Before the Subcommittee of the Committee on Appropriations for the Departments of State and Justice, the Judiciary, and Related Agencies' Appropriations for 1956,* 84th Cong., 1st sess. (Washington, D.C., 1955), p. 224.

22. Department of Justice, *Annual Report, 1955,* p. 14.

23. The figure of 700,000 is an approximation and was arrived at by subtracting the California operation total of 540,000 from the 1,300,000 figure cited by the INS.

24. Milton Plumb, "The Border War—Wetbacks Fleeced by Texas Employers," CIO *News* (17 January 1955), first of two articles based on a tour of the border between the U.S. and Mexico, cited in U.S. Congress, House, Mexican Farm Labor Program, Hearings Before the Subcommittee on Equipment, Supplies, and Manpower of the Committee on Agriculture on H.R. 3822 (March 1955), 84th Cong., 1st sess. (Washington, D.C., 1955), p. 155.

25. Ibid.

26. Ibid.

27. U.S. Congress, Senate, *Hearings Before the Subcommittee on Labor and Labor-Management Relations of the Committee on Labor and Public Welfare on Migratory Labor* (February-March), 82d Cong., 2d sess., pt. 1 (Washington, D.C., 1952), p. 288.

28. Holleman and McClellan, "Down in the Valley," p. 1; "Flaws Are Noted in 'Wetback' Curb," *New York Times* (28 August 1955), p. 55.

29. Ernesto Galarza, *Merchants of Labor: The Mexican Bracero Story* (Charlotte: McNally and Loftin, Publishers, 1964), p. 71.

30. *New York Times* (28 August 1955), p. 55. The Department of Labor's files on the Migrant Labor Program and records located in the Eisenhower Library in Abilene, Kansas, are full of letters and resolutions criticizing the fact that alien workers received benefits not given to U.S. citizens. *See:* Department of Labor, Subject Files, Messages, Solicitor's Office of the Secretary, Record Group 174, Box No. 54, 1954, Migrant Labor Program File,

National Archives, Washington, D.C., and Records of the President's Committee on Migratory Labor, 1941-1963, Secretary of Agriculture, Boxes 1, 2, 3, 4, 78, 89, 94, and 102, located in the Dwight D. Eisenhower Library, Abilene, Kansas.

31. Address to Body of the Bishops on Bishop's Committee for the Spanish Speaking (16 November 1960), p. 1 in Lucey Papers, University of Notre Dame Archives, South Bend, Indiana.

32. Julian Samora, *Los Mojados: The Wetback Story* (South Bend, Ind.: University of Notre Dame Press, 1971), p. 50.

33. Leo Grebler, *Mexican Immigration to the United States: The Record and Its Implications.* Mexican-American Study Project, Advance Report 2 (Los Angeles: University of Califronia, 1966), p. 35.

34. Gilbert Cardanas, "United States Immigration Policy and Mexican Immigration" (South Bend, Ind.: Notre Dame, Centro de Estudios Chicanos y Investigaciones Sociales, 1974), p. 46.

Epilogue

"OPERATION WETBACK" MARKED the end of the "wetback decade." However, it did not mark the end of the "illegal." The mass deportation of undocumented workers was only a temporary stopgap measure, designed to quell critics and assuage an aroused public. For the moment employers had to content themselves with the contracting of braceros.

Between 1954 and 1960 there were dramatic increases in the number of braceros contracted, and a concomitant drop in the number of "illegals" apprehended.[1] (See tables 9 and 10.) This tended to add credence to probracero arguments that the program was indeed an effective deterrent to illegal immigration. Probraceroists argued that termination of the program would lead to increased illegal immigration and thus urged legislators to continue renewing the program. Agricultural interest groups succeeded in gaining renewal of the program until 1964, when the program was finally terminated after twenty-two years.

As if to underscore the warnings of probracero groups, illegal apprehensions began to reflect significant increases in 1963 and 1964. On the surface it seemed that the program had in fact been a deterrent to illegal entry. Yet appearances were deceiving, as other critical factors had been responsible for the apparent decline of illegal immigration from Mexico.

One factor was that after 1954 the Border Patrol returned to routine operations along the border region, which meant that the concentrated approach as implemented in 1954 was largely abandoned.[2] The Border Patrol also continued the legalization of apprehended "wetbacks," which meant that a good proportion of the braceros contracted were in reality apprehended "wetbacks" whose presence in this country was regularized. Another reason for the decline of illegal immigration was the reduction of employment opportunities caused by the introduction of increased laborsaving technology, which reduced needs in the unskilled agricultural labor market. Furthermore, employers were permitted regularly to contract their "specials," which guaranteed employers the services of Mexican workers whom they had trained in skilled or semiskilled jobs. Although the use of

TABLE 9
Number of
Undocumented Persons
Apprehended,
1951-1964

Year	Number
1951	500,628
1952	543,538
1953	875,318
1954	1,075,168
1955	242,608
1956	72,442
1957	44,451
1958	37,242
1959	30,196
1960	29,651
1961	29,877
1962	30,272
1963	39,124
1964	43,844

Source: U.S. Immigration and
Naturalization Service.

Mexican braceros as "specials" was in clear violation of contract agreements, the practice remained widespread.

After 1959 there was a rapid decline in the number of braceros contracted, in part because of laborsaving technology and the more rigid enforcement of wage guarantees. The government also began to tighten certification requirements for establishing the need to import and hire braceros. Thus prior to the end of the bracero program in 1964 many employers had again begun to resort to an increased use of undocumented workers.

Among those employed were large numbers of commuters who had effected entry into the United States by using a border crossing permit. The permits, which were fairly easy to acquire, permitted the holder to enter the United States for the purposes of entertainment, shopping, visiting, or business. Holders of this permit were prohibited from working while in this country or from travelling more than twenty-five miles from the border. Those holding the permit were allowed to enter the United States for periods not to exceed seventy-two hours.[3]

Obviously the temptation proved too great for many, who used the card to enter this country to seek employment. Once here they mailed the cards back to Mexico to avoid having them confiscated in case of apprehension by INS authorities. As no records were kept of the number of people entering or leaving the United

States on a daily basis, it proved almost impossible to determine the number of people who had entered legally and remained illegally. The unavailability of records in this area added to the numerical illusion that illegal entry, as shown by apprehensions, had declined.

Further adding to the incentive to enter illegally was the enactment of more stringent immigration restrictions by the United States. In 1965 and 1968 new restrictions made it even more difficult to enter this country legally. Under the new regulations applicants were given preference if they were blood relatives of citizens or legal residents already in the United States. Members of preferred professions such as engineering and medicine were also given higher priority. Preference was also shown to applicants who had employers who would sponsor them. People who did not fall into any of these categories were free to apply as well, although their chances for legal admission, given the long waiting lists, were almost nil. Many were unwilling to make application upon such slim chances, especially given the high costs and the complicated procedures.[4]

TABLE 10

Number of
Braceros Contracted,
1951-1964

Year	Contracted
1951	190,745[a]
1952	197,100
1953	201,380
1954	309,033
1955	398,650
1956	445,197
1957	436,049
1958	432,857
1959	437,643
1960	315,846
1961	291,420
1962	194,978
1963	186,865
1964	177,736
Total	4,215,499

[a]Includes 46,076 contracted under 1949 agreement prior to July 15.

Source: U.S., Department of Labor, "Summary of Migratory Station Activities."

In addition to the pull factors prevalent in the United States, there were the push factors extant in Mexico that encouraged many to emigrate to the United States.

Although Mexico's economy reflected substantial growth between 1950 and 1960, it nonetheless continued to fall short of ending the economic problems that plagued many of its people. Part of the reason for this was the tremendous growth in population that Mexico experienced after World War II. Between 1940 and 1963 Mexico's population grew from twenty-two million to forty-five million.[5]

The lack of economic opportunity in Mexico, a rapidly expanding population, high rates of underemployment or unemployment, and Mexico's economic over-dependence on the United States, coupled with economic opportunities and a largely unpatrolled common border, all served once again to attract the undocumented person from Mexico in increasing numbers.

By the late 1960s illegal immigration had increased significantly. Labor organizations and social reform groups once again called for measures to deal with what they saw as a problem of major proportion, yet their concern was not shared by important government officials or the general public. The boom economy of the 1960s appeared capable of absorbing and utilizing an enlarged labor force, regardless of what the source or sources. Furthermore the hostile environment toward undocumented persons had for the moment dissipated. Americans were more concerned with the domestic and foreign issues raised by the Vietnam War.

As the war ground to an end, as domestic tranquility returned, and as the country began to experience economic problems, the issue of illegal immigration once again became a topic of major public and governmental concern.[6] The press and the media once again focused their attention on it. Numerous studies were conducted, and various state and federal subcommittees held hearings on the issue. Measures to control illegal immigration reminiscent of the early and mid-1950s once again made their appearance in Congress, and the debate on how to deal with this problem once again intensified.

People without documents are still part of the American scene today, and their presence in increasing numbers has once again triggered concern. Words reminiscent of the early 1950s are once again seen and heard in the mass media. "Wetback invasion," the "silent invasion," and "a case of national crisis" are representative statements used to describe the influx of undocumented persons during the 1970s. A majority of the stories and features concerning this "invasion" are negative toward the influx, and they paint an uncomplimentary picture of many of the "evils" that allegedly are part and parcel of illegal entry. "Wetbacks" are still accused of lowering wage scales and of depriving citizens of the United States of jobs. They are blamed for increased welfare and educational costs in some areas, and increased crime rates and disease rates are attributed to their presence as well.

As for the undocumented persons, most of them are little different from their predecessors in terms of economic necessity and place of origin. Most of the illegal emigrants from Mexico come from rural areas, and most of them come to seek jobs and better economic opportunity. Most of them are relatively young, and a large percentage of these young people are single. A difference in this pattern is that the influx now contains growing numbers of women. Like their predecessors from previous decades they too continue to be victimized by unscrupulous employers. They continue to be the victims of stereotypes and misconceptions, although present-day researchers are attempting to rectify many mistaken views about their negative impact on American society.

Little change has occurred in the area of national policies regarding illegal immigration. Restrictive legislation has been promoted in Congress and mass deportations utilized in an effort to curb the numbers who enter illegally. Both the legislative efforts and the mass deportations have been justified with the argument that the presence of large numbers of undocumented workers has contributed to the growing rate of unemployment and that their uncontrolled entry has created serious social, political, and economic problems. While members of Congress have proven somewhat willing to underwrite the costs of mass roundups, they have not proven too cooperative in enacting penalty legislation against employers. Bills proposing penalty legislation have repeatedly failed.

President Jimmy Carter's administration has proposed a series of measures purposely designed to curb the influx of undocumented persons from Mexico. The proposed measures are similar to some of those espoused during the administrations of Truman and Eisenhower in that they call for increased personnel to patrol the border, legislation to penalize those who employ "illegals," and closer cooperation with countries from which these undocumented workers are coming. A fourth measure proposed by the Carter administration entails granting what has loosely been termed "amnesty" to "illegal aliens." According to U.S. officials, undocumented persons who entered before 1970 and resided in the U.S. continuously would be permitted to remain and to begin the process of becoming naturalized citizens of the United States. The plan also proposes that "aliens" who entered between 1970 and 1977 would be permitted to remain here and work, but only on a temporary basis. A more definite decision concerning their future status would be forthcoming after the federal government had studied the matter further and had determined the size of this population. Finally, undocumented persons who entered after 1977 would be subject to immediate deportation.[7] In some ways the part of this proposal that creates a new category of "temporary alien residents" is reminiscent of an earlier act that permitted the Secretary of Labor to legalize or regularize the presence of "illegals" when the need arose.

Carter's plan has been widely discussed and has received a wide variety of criticisms from different sectors, organizations, and interest groups.[8] The plan has been described as too amorphous, too stringent, or too lenient. While a discussion of the merits or demerits will not be undertaken here, let it suffice to say that approval of the proposed plan appears doubtful at the moment. Furthermore the plan is flawed in that it is largely premised on a unilateral approach to solving the problem—an approach that has doomed previous efforts to failure as well. Once again the United States is attempting to enact unilateral laws or measures without soliciting input or support from Mexico or other countries that are sources of illegal immigration.[9] As this study has shown mass deportations, restrictive measures, and contract labor programs have not proved effective deterrents to illegal immigration. Generally speaking, the United States has failed to attack the problem at its roots. It has not helped Mexico to remedy the lack of economic opportunities of its continually expanding population, and it seems unable and unwilling to deal with the seemingly insatiable appetite for cheap labor among certain groups of employers in this country.

NOTES

1. "The Migratory Farm Labor Problem in the United States," 87th Cong., 2d sess., Senate Report No. 1225 (Washington, D.C.: G.P.O., 1962), p. 10; U.S., Department of Labor, Bureau of Employment Security, "Farm Labor Market Developments," (Washington, D.C.: G.P.O., 1964 and 1965).

2. Julian Samora, *Los Mojados: The Wetback Story*. (South Bend, Ind.: University of Notre Dame Press, 1971), p. 55.

3. Ibid., p. 7.

4. Dick Reaves, *Without Documents* (New York: Condor Publishing Co., 1978), pp. 65-6.

5. Michael C. Meyer and William C. Sherman, *The Course of Mexican History* (New York: Oxford University Press, 1979), pp. 682-83.

6. U.S., Comptroller General, Report to the Congress, *More Needs To Be Done To Reduce the Number and Adverse Impact of Illegal Aliens in the United States* (Washington, D.C.: G.P.O., 1973).

7. Jimmy Carter, "President's Message: Regulation of Undocumented Aliens" (4 August 1977).

8. For a good sampling of diverse viewpoints *see*: Antonio José Rios-Bustamante, ed., *Immigration and Public Policy: Human Rights for Undocumented Workers and Their Families*, Chicano Studies Center Document no. 5 (Los Angeles: Chicano Studies Center, 1978).

9. Jorge A. Bustamante, "Undocumented Immigration from Mexico: Research Report," *International Migration Review* 2, no. 2 (Summer, 1977).

Appendix 1

AGREEMENT OF AUGUST 4, 1942
FOR THE TEMPORARY MIGRATION
OF MEXICAN AGRICULTURAL WORKERS TO THE UNITED STATES
AS REVISED ON APRIL 26, 1943,
BY AN EXCHANGE OF NOTES BETWEEN
THE AMERICAN EMBASSY AT MEXICO CITY
AND THE
MEXICAN MINISTRY FOR FOREIGN AFFAIRS* **

General Provisions

1) It is understood that Mexicans contracting to work in the United States shall not be engaged in any military service.

2) Mexicans entering the United States as a result of this understanding shall not suffer discriminatory acts of any kind in accordance with the Executive Order No. 8802 issued at the White House June 25, 1941.

3) Mexicans entering the United States under this understanding shall enjoy the guarantees of transportation, living expenses and repatriation established in Article 29 of the Mexican Federal Labor Law as follows:

Article 29. — All contracts entered into by Mexican workers for lending their services outside their country shall be made in writing, legalized by the municipal authorities of the locality where entered into and viased by the Consul of the country where their services are being used. Furthermore, such contract shall contain, as a requisite of validity of same, the following stipulations, without which the contract is invalid.

*Revised clauses are italicized
**Source: United States, Statutes at Large, vol. 56, pt. 2, 1942, pp. 1766-69.

I. Transportation and subsistence expenses for the worker, and his family, if such is the case, and all other expenses which originate from point of origin to border points and compliance of immigration requirements, or for any other similar concept, shall be paid exclusively by the employer or the contractual parties.

II. The worker shall be paid in full the salary agreed upon, from which no deduction shall be made in any amount for any of the concepts mentioned in the above sub-paragraph.

III. The employer or contractor shall issue a bond or constitute a deposit in cash in the Bank of Workers, or in the absence of same, in the Bank of Mexico, to the entire satisfaction of the respective labor authorities, for a sum equal to repatriation costs of the worker and his family, and those originated by transportation to point of origin.

IV. Once the employer establishes proof of having covered such expenses or the refusal of the worker to return to his country, and that he does not owe the worker any sum covering salary or indemnization to which he might have a right, the labor authorities shall authorize the return of the deposit or the cancellation of the bond issued.

It is specifically understood that the provisions of Section III of Article 29 above-mentioned shall not apply to the Government of the United States notwithstanding the inclusion of this section in the agreement, in view of the obligations assumed by the United States Government under Transportation (a) and (c) of this agreement.

4) Mexicans entering the United States under this understanding shall not be employed to displace other workers, or for the purpose of reducing rates of pay previously established.

In order to implement the application of the general principles mentioned above the following specific clauses are established:

(When the word 'employer' is used hereinafter it shall be understood to mean the Farm Security Administration of the Department of Agriculture of the United States of America; the word 'sub-employer' shall mean the owner or operator of the farm or farms in the United States on which the Mexican will be employed; the word 'worker' hereinafter used shall refer to the Mexican Farm laborer entering the United States under this understanding.)

Contracts

a) Contracts will be made between the employer and the worker under the supervision of the Mexican Government. (Contracts must be written in Spanish.)

b. The employer shall enter into a contract with the sub-employer, with a view to proper observance of the principles embodied in this understanding.

Admission

a. The Mexican health authorities will, at the place whence the worker comes, see that he meets the necessary physical conditions.

Transportation

a. All transportation and living expenses from the place of origin to destination, and return, as well as expenses incurred in the fulfillment of any requirements of a migratory nature shall be met by the Employer.

b. Personal belongings of the workers up to a maximum of 35 kilos per person shall be transported at the expense of the Employer.

c. In accord with the intent of Article 29 of the Mexican Federal Labor Law, quoted under General Provisions (3) above, it is expected that the employer will collect all or part of the cost accuring under (a) and (b) of Transportation from the sub-employer.

Wages and Employment

a. (1)*Wages to be paid the worker shall be the same as those paid for similar work to other agricultural laborers under the same conditions within the same area, in the respective regions of destination. Piece rates shall be so set as to enable the worker of average ability to earn the prevailing wage. In any case wages for piece work or hourly work will not be less than 30 cents per hour.*

b. (2) On the basis of prior authorization from the Mexican Government salaries lower than those established in the previous clause may be paid those emigrants admitted into the United States as members of the family of the worker under contract and who, when they are in the field, are able also to become agricultural laborers but who, by their condition of age or sex, cannot carry out the average amount of ordinary work.

c. The worker shall be exclusively employed as an agricultural laborer for which he has been engaged; any change from such type of employment *or any change of locality* shall be made with the express approval of the worker and with the authority of the Mexican Government.

d. There shall be considered illegal any collection by reason of commission or for any other concept demanded of the worker.

e. Work of minors under 14 years shall be strictly prohibited, and they shall have the same schooling opportunities as those enjoyed by children of other agricultural laborers.

f. Workers domiciled in the migratory labor camps or at any other place of employment under this understanding shall be free to obtain articles for their personal consumption, or that of their families, wherever it is most convenient for them.

g. *The Mexican workers will be furnished without cost to them with hygienic lodgings, adequate to the physical conditions of the region of a type used by a common laborer of the region and the medical and sanitary services enjoyed also without cost to them will be identical with those furnished to the other agricultural workers in the regions where they may lend their services.*

h. Workers admitted under this understanding shall enjoy as regards occupational diseases and accidents the same guarantees enjoyed by other agricultural workers under United States legislation.

i. Groups of workers admitted under this understanding shall elect their own representatives to deal with the Employer, but it is understood that all such representatives shall be working members of the group.

The Mexican Consuls, assisted by the Mexican Labor Inspectors, recognized as such by the Employer will take all possible measures of protection in the interests of the Mexican workers in all questions affecting them, within their corresponding jurisdiction, and will have free access to the places of work of the Mexican workers. The Employer will observe that the sub-employer grants all facilities to the Mexican Government for the compliance of all the clauses in this contract.

j. For such time as they are unemployed under a period equal to 75% of the period (exclusive of Sundays) for which the workers have been contracted they shall receive a subsistence allowance at the rate of $3.00 per day.

For the remaining 25% of the period for which the workers have been contracted during which the workers may be unemployed when such unemployment is not due to their unwillingness to work they shall receive lodging and subsistence without cost to them.

Should the cost of living rise this will be a matter for reconsideration.

The master contracts for workers submitted to the Mexican Government shall contain definite provisions for computation of subsistence and payments under the understanding.

k. The term of the contract shall be made in accordance with the authorities of the respective countries.

l. At the expiration of the contract under this understanding, and if the same is not renewed, the authorities of the United States shall consider illegal, from an immigration point of view, the continued stay of the worker in the territory of the United States, exception made of cases of physical impossibility.

Savings Fund

a. The respective agencies of the Government of the United States shall be responsible for the safekeeping of the sums contributed by the Mexican workers toward the formation of their Rural Savings Fund, until such sums are transferred to *the Wells Farbo Bank and Union Trust Company of San Francisco for the account of the Bank of Mexico, S.A., which will transfer such amounts to the Mexican Agricultural Credit Bank. This last shall assume responsibility for the deposit, for the safekeeping and for the application, or in the absence of these, for the return of such amounts.*

b. The Mexican Government through the Banco de Credito Agricola will take care of the security of the savings of the workers to be used for payment of the agricultural implements, which may be made available to the Banco de Credito Agricola in accordance with exportation permits for shipment to Mexico with the understanding that the Farm Security Administration will recommend priority treatment for such implements.

Numbers

As it is impossible to determine at this time the number of workers who may be needed in the United States for agricultural labor employment, the employer shall advise the Mexican Government from time to time as to the number needed. The Government of Mexico shall determine in each case the number of workers who may leave the country without detriment to its national economy.

General Considerations

It is understood that, with reference to the departure from Mexico of Mexican workers, who are not farm laborers, there shall govern in understandings reached by agencies of the respective Governments the same fundamental principles which have been applied here to the departure of farm labor.

It is understood that the employers will cooperate with such other agencies of the Government of the United States in carrying this understanding into effect whose authority under the laws of the United States are such as to contribute to the effectuation of the understandings.

Either Government shall have the right to renounce this understanding, given appropriate notification to the other Government 90 days in advance.

This understanding may be formalized by an exchange of notes between the Ministry of Foreign Affairs of the Republic of Mexico and the Embassy of the United States of America in Mexico.

Appendix 2

UNITED STATES DEPARTMENT OF AGRICULTURE
FARM SECURITY ADMINISTRATION
COOPERATIVE EMPLOYMENT AGREEMENT*

THIS COOPERATIVE EMPLOYMENT AGREEMENT, made this _____
day of _____ , 19 ____ , between the United States of America,
hereinafter called the "Government," and _____ of
_____ , State of _____ , hereinafter called
"Employer."

WITNESSETH:

WHEREAS the Government and the Employer wish to cooperate in making
agricultural workers available to alleviate the present shortage of agricultural
labor and to aid in the successful prosecution of the war:

NOW, THEREFORE, In consideration of the undertakings hereinafter stated,
the Government and the Employer agree as follows:

1. The Government shall use its best efforts to recruit and transport agricultural workers for employment by the Employer, from points of origin or intermediate points in the United States or Mexico to the destination point(s) hereinafter stated, and, upon completion of that employment, to the points of origin,
or to such intermediate points in the United States as the Government shall determine to be proper. The Government shall notify the Employer of the points of
recruitment, and the Employer may, if he desires, be represented during the recruiting process.

2. The Employer shall employ, upon the following terms, _____ such
agricultural workers if they are transported by the Government to the following

Source: U.S., Department of Labor, *Standard Work Contract* (Washington,
    D.C.: G. P. O., 1942), pp. iii-iv.

destination point (s) not later than _____ , 19 ____ , the number
to be transported to each destination point being as follows: _____ , to
_____ , State of _____ .

a. Each worker shall be employed, exclusively as an agricultural worker, for
at least seventy-five percent (75%) of the possible workdays (each day in the
week except Sunday to be considered a possible workday) between _____ ,
19____ , and ____ , 19____ , and for such further time as the Employer and the
workers, or any of them, may mutually agree, such entire time being hereinafter
called the "period of employment."

b. The Employer shall be required to furnish such employment to a worker
hereunder only so long as the worker is ready, willing, and able to work under
the supervision and direction of the Employer; but shall not require the worker
to work on Sundays.

c. The Employer shall pay each worker (except cotton workers paid on a piece
rate basis) a minimum subsistence allowance of $3.00 per day for each possible
workday within said minimum of seventy-five percent (75%) of the possible workdays that he is not so employed; provided, however, that no subsistence allowance shall be made for workdays in which the worker is unemployed as the result of his refusal to work or his illness or other physical incapacity. The amount
of such subsistence allowance shall be computed and payment therefor shall be
made at the end of each ninety (90) day period, if this contract is for a period in
excess of ninety (90) days.

d. A Workday shall contain not less than eight hours nor more than twelve hours;
provided, however, that to determine the amount of employment under paragraph 2 of this agreement, hours of work less than eight done on any day except
Sunday may be added to hours of work less than eight done on any other day
except Sunday, and for such purpose each ten hours of work shall be counted
as a workday.

e. Work shall be paid for in lawful money of the United States Government
at the end of each week of work, at not less than the prevailing piece work or
hourly wage rates within the particular area of employment; provided, however,
that the Government reserves the right to remove any worker who does not
average $3,00 a working day in any pay period. The prevailing wage rates shall
be determined by the Wage Boards appointed by the Secretary of Agriculture
for that purpose for the particular crops and areas involved.

f. It is mutually agreed that a worker of average ability is one who can, after
a three-day training period, at the prevailing piece work rate established by the
Government, earn at least three dollars ($3.00) per day.

g. The Employer shall pay all costs of transportation of the workers (and the
members of their families transported with them by the Government to the above-
specified point(s) of destination) between said destination point(s) and the place
or places at which the workers are to perform their work, and return to said
destination point(s).

h. No deduction from wages shall be made for commissions, fees, or any other purpose (except as may be required by law), which shall have the effect of reducing the workers' wages below those required by paragraph 2e of this agreement.

i. The Employer shall pay to the Government in trust for each such worker who has been transported by the Government from Mexico for employment in the United States, ten (10) percent of his wages and of the subsistence allowance provided for by paragraph 2c, which portion of his wages and subsistence allowance such worker will have assigned to the Government under the terms of its agreement with the worker. This payment shall be made to the Government upon request, and in no event more than 10 days after the termination of the period of employment of the worker.

j. The workers shall be entitled to the benefit and protection of all applicable child labor, compensation, and other laws and regulations of the Government and of the State or States in which the work is performed.

k. The workers shall not be required to purchase articles or services for consumption or use by them or their families at any source not of their choice.

l. The worker shall be entitled to freedom from discrimination in employment because of race, creed, color, or national origin, in accordance with the provisions of Executive Order No. 8802 of the President of the United States, dated June 25, 1941.

m. The Employer shall make available to the workers and their families, without charge, such shelter facilities as are owned by the Employer and are not otherwise occupied within the period of employment.

n. There shall be no strikes, lockouts, or stoppages of work during the period of employment. All disputes between the workers and the Employer shall be determined by mediation according to procedure prescribed by the Government.

3. The Government shall determine from time to time, and its determination shall be conclusive, whether the Employer has paid all sums to be paid by him hereunder, and shall have the right to pay (as subsistence allowances or otherwise) to the persons it determines to be entitled thereto, all or any part of any such sums which it determines have not been paid, in which case the Employer shall repay to the Government, upon demand by it, all sums so paid, together with interest thereupon at the rate of six percent (6%) per annum from the date or dates of such payments by the Government.

4. The Government shall transport under this Agreement both single men and families, but if families are transported the Government shall enter into work contracts only with the heads of the families and such other members of the families as are 18 years of age and over and able and willing to work full-time pursuant to the terms of the work contracts and this Agreement. Other members of the families transported may work for the Employer at the prevailing piece or hourly work rate, subject, however, to applicable school and child labor laws.

5. The Employer shall keep, upon forms to be supplied by the Government, full and complete records of the employment and wages of each worker under this Agreement. Such records shall be at all times open to inspection and examination by the Government, which shall be entitled to make copies thereof.

6. If the Government determines that the Employer has violated any of the terms or undertakings of this Agreement, it may, without waiving any other remedy or course of action, deprive the Employer of the further services of the workers under this Agreement.

7. All rights, privileges, and powers conferred herein upon the Government shall be exercised in its behalf by the Secretary of Agriculture, United States Department of Agriculture, or his duly authorized representative.

Bibliography

ARTICLES

"AFL vs. Wetback Labor." *New Republic,* no. 125 (24 September 1951), p. 7.

"Ants: Mexican Wetbacks." *Time* 61 (27 April 1953): 29.

Begemen, J. "Wetbacks, Slaves of Today. Report of Commission on Migratory Labor." *New Republic,* no. 126 (10 March 1952), pp. 15-16.

Bern, Bernard. "The Detention Facilities Along the Mexican Border." *Immigration and Naturalization Service Monthly Review* 9 (July 1951): 32.

Blaisdell, Donald C. "Pressure Groups, Foreign Policies, and International Politics." *Annals of the American Academy of Political and Social Science* 319 (September 1958): 149-57.

"Bulge of Braceros at the Border." *Life* 36 (15 February 1954): 26-29.

Busey, J. L. "The Political Geography of Mexican Migration." *Colorado Quarterly* 2 (Autumn, 1953): 181-90.

Bustamante, Jorge A. "Undocumented Immigration from Mexico: Research Report." *International Migration Review* 2, no. 2 (Summer, 1977), pp. 149-77.

Carter, Harlon B. "The Airlift." *Immigration and Naturalization Service Monthly Review* 9 (December 1951): 72.

Carusi, Ugo. "Border Patrol Use of Aircraft." *Immigration and Naturalization Service Monthly Review* 4 (May 1947): 137.

——. "The Federal Administrative Procedure Act and the Immigration and Naturalization Service." *Immigration and Naturalization Service Monthly Review* 4 (February 1947): 95-105.

Coalson, George O. "Mexican Contract Labor in American Agriculture." *Southwestern Social Science Quarterly* 33 (September 1952): 231.

"Constitutional Restraints on the Expulsion and Exclusion of Aliens." *Minnesota Law Review* 37 (May 1953): 440-58.

Corwin, Arthur F. "Mexican Emigration History, 1900-1970: Literature and Research." *Latin American Research Review* 8, no. 2 (Summer, 1973): 3-24.

——. "Mexican Emigration History, 1900-1970: Literature and Research." *Latin American Research Review* 8, no. 2 (Summer, 1973): 3-24.

——. "Causes of Mexican Emigration to the United States: A Summary Review." *Dislocation and Emigration: The Social Background of American Immigration.* Perspectives in American History, vol. 7. Edited by Donald Fleming and Bernard Bailyn. Cambridge: Harvard University, Charles Warren Center for Studies in American History, 1974.

Cregan, James F. "Public Law 78: A Tangle of Domestic and International Relations." *Journal of Inter-American Studies,* 7 (October 1965): 541-56.

Cumberland, Charles C. "The U.S.-Mexican Border: A Selective Guide to the Literature of the Region." *Rural Sociology,* Supplement to 25 (June 1960): 90-102.

Cutsumbis, Michael N. "The National Archives and Immigration Research." *The International Migration Review* 3, no. 2 (Summer, 1970): 90-99.

Davenport, Walter. "Border Patrol." *Collier's,* 14 December 1940, p. 66.

Del Guercio, Albert. "Some Mexican Border Problems." *Immigration and Naturalization Service Monthly Review* 3 (April 1946): 291.

Eckels, R. P. "Hungry Workers, Ripe Crops, and the Non-Existent Mexican Border." *Reporter,* 13 April 1954, pp. 28-32.

"Fresh Approach to the Wetbacks." *America,* no. 89 (29 August 1953), p. 510.

Galarza, Ernesto. "They Work for Pennies." *American Federationist* 59 (April 1952): 10-13, 29.

Gilmore, N. Ray, and Gladys W. Gilmore. "The Bracero in California." *Pacific Historical Review* 32 (August 1963): 265-82.

Greene, Sheldon L. "Immigration Law and Rural Poverty: The Problems of the Illegal Entrant." *Duke Law Journal* 1969, no. 3 (June 1969).

Hadley, Eleanor M. "A Critical Analysis of the Wetback Problem." *Law and Contemporary Problems* 21 (1956): 334-57.

Hager, Hoyt. "Antilabor Squeeze Group Discussed by Citrus Agency." Corpus Christi (Texas) *Caller-Times* (4 October 1951).

Hawley, Ellis W. "The Politics of the Mexican Labor Issue, 1950-1965." *Agricultural History* 40, no. 3 (July 1966): 157-76.

Hernandez, Jose. "A Demographic Profile of the Mexican Immigrant in the United States, 1910-1950." *Journal of Inter-American Studies* 8 (July 1966): 471-96.

Hill, Gladwyn. "Two Every Minute Across the Border." *New York Times Magazine* (31 January 1954): 13.

———. "Wetbacks: McCarran's Immigrants." *Nation,* no. 177 (22 August 1957), pp. 151-52.

Hispanic American Report, no. 6 (August 1953), p. 9.

Hispanic American Report, no. 7 (February 1954), p. 1.

Hispanic American Report, no. 10 (November 1957).

Hulsing, Harold E. "The Regional Concept." *I and N Reporter* 4 (January 1956): 29.

Jenkins, J. Craig. "Push/Pull in Recent Mexican Migration to the U.S." *International Migration Review* 2, no. 2 (Summer, 1977): 178-89.

Kelley, J. B. "The Deportation of Mexican Aliens and Its Impact on Family Life." *Catholic Charities Review* 37 (October 1954): 169-71.

Kelley, Willard F. "The Wetback Issue." *The I & N Reporter* 2, no. 3 (January 1954): 37-39.

Korcik, William. "Wetback Story." *Commonweal* 54 (13 June 1951): 327-29.

"Labor Month in Review: Agreement Between Mexico and the U.S." *Monthly Labor Review* 4, no. 77 (March 1954).

Le Berthon, Ted. "At the Prevailing Rate." *Commonweal* 67 (1 November 1957): 122-25.

Lee, John Franklin. "Statutory Provisions for Admission of Mexican Agricultural Workers: An Exception to the Immigration and Nationality Act of 1952." *George Washington Law Review* 24 (March 1956): 464-77.

Leibson, Art. "The Wetback Invasion." *Common Ground* 10, no. 1 (Autumn, 1949): 11-19.

Leroy, George P. "Contribution to the Study of the 'Wetback' Problem: Illegal Mexican Immigration to the United States." *Population* 7 (April-June 1952): 334-37.

"Long-Term Trends in Foreign-Worker Employment." *Farm Labor Developments* (February 1968): 10.

"Look at the Wetbacks." *New Republic,* no. 128 (28 August 1950), p. 8.

Lopez, Henry. "Here They Come Again." *Frontier* 6 (May 1955): 13-14.

Lopez, Malo Ernesto. "The Emigration of Mexican Laborers." *Ciencias Sociales* 5 (October 1954): 220-27.

Lucey, Robert E. "Migratory Workers." *Commonweal* 59 (15 January 1954): 370-73.

Mamer, John W. "The Use of Foreign Labor for Seasonal Farm Work in the United States: Issues Involved and Interest Groups in Conflict." *Journal of Farm Economics* 43 (December 1961): 1204-05.

McBee, Griffith J. "Air-Jeep Patrolling Operations in the El Paso Area." *I and N Monthly Review* 8 (October 1950): 43.

McDonagh, Edward C. "Attitudes Toward Ethnic Farm Workers in Coachella Valley." *Sociology and Social Research* 40 (September 1955): 10-18.

"Mexico Expects New Hiring Pact." *New York Times* (5 March 1954).

"Migratory Labor in American Agriculture." *Monthly Labor Review*, no. 72 (June 1951), pp. 691-93.

Mitchell, H. L. "Unions of Two Countries Act on Wetback Influx." *American Federationist* (January 1954): 28-30.

Morris, Manuel. "Battle to Rid Mexico of Corruption." *American Mercury* (July 1953): 85-89.

Myers, Frederic. "Employment and Relative Earnings of Spanish-Name Persons in Texas Industries." *Southern Economic Journal* 19 (April 1953): 494-507.

"Native Migrants. U.S. Democracy's Shame." *America*, no. 89 (26 September 1953), p. 613.

"New Procedures Planned to Eliminate 'Wetbacks.' " *Immigration and Naturalization Service Monthly Review* 4 (April 1947): 126.

"New Wetback Answers?" *Newsweek* 42 (31 August 1953): 26.

"Operation Wetback: Impact on the Border States." *Employment Security Review* 22, no. 3 (March 1955): 16-21.

Parker, James E. "Border Patrol Air Operations." *Immigration and Naturalization Reporter*, 4, no. 2 (November 1955): 17-18.

"Reorganization of the Service." *I & N Reporter* 3 (January 1955): 37.

Robinson, Robert H. "Importation of Mexican Agricultural Workers." *Monthly Labor Review* 5, no. 4 (October 1947): 41-42.

Romualdi, Serafino. "Hands Across the Border." *American Federalist* (June 1954): 20.

"Satisfactory Labor Importation Plan Would End Wetback Problem." McAllen (Texas) *Valley Evening Monitor* (30 September 1951).

Saunders, Lyle, and Leonard, Olen E. "The Wetback in the Lower Rio Grande Valley of Texas" in *Inter-American Education*, Occassional Papers 7, University of Texas, Austin, July 1951.

Scruggs, Otey M. "Evolution of Mexican Farm Labor Agreement of 1942." *Agricultural History* 34 (July 1960): 140-51.

——. "Texas and the Bracero Program." *Pacific Historical Review* (August 1963): 251-64.

——. "The United States, Mexico, and the Wetbacks, 1942-1947." *Pacific Historical Review* 30 (May 1961): 149-64.

Secretaria de Industria y Comercio, Direccion General de Estadistica. *Revista de Estadistica*. Vols. 19-23, March-April 1956 to February 1960.

Smith, T. L. "Farm Labor Trends in the United States, 1910-1969." *International Labor Review* 102 (August 1970): 149-69.

Spradlin, T. Richard. "The Mexican Farm Labor Importation Program: Review and Reform." Part I. *The George Washington Law Review* 30 (1961-1962): 84-122.

——. "The Mexican Farm Labor Importation Program: Review and Reform." Part II. *The George Washington Law Review* 30 (1961-1962): 311-27.

Steinberg, Albert. "United States Border Patrol." *New York Times Magazine* (8 October 1950), p. 77.

Sturmthal, Adolf. "Economic Policies in Mexico." *Journal of Political Economy* 63 (1955): 184-89.

Swing, J. M. "A Workable Labor Program." *The I and N Reporter* 4 (November 1955): 15.

Thompson, Albert H. "The Mexican Immigrant Worker in Southwestern Agriculture." *American Journal of Economics and Sociology*, no. 16 (October 1956), pp. 73-81.

Thunder, J. A. "Feature X: System of Mexican Contract Laborers." *America* 89 (September 1953): 599-600.

Todd, Henry C. "Labor's Viewpoint on Mexican Nationals and 'Wetbacks.' " *The Commonwealth* 29, no. 16 (20 April 1953).

Tomasek, Robert D. "The Migrant Problem and Pressure Group Problems." *Journal of Politics* 23, no. 2 (May 1961): 295-319.

Turner, William, and John Beecher. "Bracero Politics: A Special Report." *Ramparts* 4 (September 1965): 14-32.

"Valley C C Ponders Joining Labor Fight." *San Antonio* (Texas) *Express* (5 October 1951).

"Views of a Mexican Worker on His Return From the United States." *Inter-American* 3 (February 1944): 37.

"War With the Wetbacks." *Newsweek* 43 (28 June 1954): p. 22.

"Wetback Invasion." *Scholastic* 60 (20 February 1952): p. 12.

"Wetback Invasion in Texas." *Nation* 169 (20 August 1949): 168.

"The Wetbacks." *Time* (9 April 1951), p. 24.

"Wetbacks: Can the States Act to Curb Illegal Entry?" *Stanford Law Review* 6, no. 2 (March, 1954): 287-322.

"Wetbacks, Cotton, and Korea." *The Nation* 172, no. 18 (5 May 1951): 408.

"Wetbacks in Middle of Border War." *Business Week* (24 October 1953), pp. 62-64.

"Wetbacks Swarm In." *Life* 30 (21 May 1951): 33-37.

Whalen, William. "The Wetback Problem in Southwest Texas." *Immigration and Naturalization Service Review* 8 (Feburary 1951): 104.

Woodbridge, Hensley C. "Mexico and United States Racism." *Commonweal* 42 (22 June 1945): 234-36.

BOOKS AND PAMPHLETS

Acuña, Rodolfo. *Occupied America: The Chicano's Struggle Toward Liberation*, San Francisco: Canfield Press, 1972.

Anderson, Henry P. *The Bracero Program in California with Particular Reference to Health Status, Attitudes, and Practices*. Berkeley: School of Public Health, University of California, 1961.

Burma, John H. *Spanish-Speaking Groups in the United States*. Durham, North Carolina: Duke University Press, 1954.

California State Legislature. Assembly Committee on Agriculture. *The Bracero Program and Its Aftermath: An Historical Summary*. Sacramento: California Legislature, Assembly, Committee on Agriculture, 1965.

Cline, Howard F. *Mexico: Revolution to Evolution, 1940-1960*. New York: Oxford University Press, 1962.

——. *The United States and Mexico*. Cambridge: Harvard University Press, 1961.

Cohen, Bernard C. *The Influence of Non-Governmental Groups on Foreign Policy Making*. Princeton: Center for International Studies, 1959.

Copp, Nelson G. *Wetbacks and Braceros*. San Francisco: R and E Research Associates, 1971.

Craig, Richard B. *The Bracero Program. Interest Groups and Foreign Policy*. Austin: University of Texas Press, 1971.

County of San Diego. *A Study of the Socioeconomic Impact of Illegal Aliens on the County of San Diego*. San Diego: Human Resources Agency, 1977.

Direccion General de Estadistica. *Compendio Estadistico, 1953*. Mexico: Secretaria de Economica, 1954.

Folsom, Josiah C. *Migratory Agricultural Labor in the United States: An Annotated Bibliography of Selected References.* Washington, D.C.: Government Printing Office, 1953.

Galarza, Ernesto. *Merchants of Labor. The Mexican Bracero Story.* Charlotte: McNally and Loftin, 1964.

——. *Strangers in Our Fields.* Washington, D.C.: Joint U.S.-Mexico Trade Union Committee, U.S. Section, 1956.

Garner, Claude. *The Wetback.* New York: Coward-McCann, 1947.

Gil, Beatriz Massa. *Bibliografia Sobre Migracion de Trabajadores Mexicanos a los Estados Unidos.* Biblioteca del Banco de Mexico, S.A., Departamento de Estudios Economicos, Mexico, D.F., 1959.

Ginsberg, Eli, and Bray, Douglas W. *The Uneducated.* New York: Columbia University Press, 1952.

Grebler, Leo. *Mexican Immigration to the United States: The Record and Its Implications.* Mexican-American Study Project. Advance Report 2. Los Angeles: University of California, 1966.

Guzman, Ralph. *Rights Without Roots: A Study of the Loss of Citizenship by Native-Born Americans of Mexican Ancestry.* Los Angeles: Fund for the Republic, Inc., and Southern California Chapter, American Civil Liberties Union, 1955.

Hancock, Richard H. *The Role of the Bracero in the Economic and Cultural Dynamics of Mexico: A Case Study of Chihuahua.* Stanford, California: Hispanic American Society, 1959.

Harper, Elizabeth and J. Auerbach. *Immigration Laws of the United States.* Indianapolis: Bobbs-Merrill Company, 1971.

Heady, Earl O., Edwin O. Haroldren, Leo V. Mayer, and Luther G. Tweetin. *Roots of the The Farm Problem.* Ames, Iowa: The Iowa State University Press, 1965.

Heizer, Robert F., and Alan F. Almquist. *The Other Californians.* Berkeley: University of California Press, 1971.

Hidalgo, Ernesto. *La Proteccion de Mexicanos en los Estados Unidos.* Mexico City: Secretaria de Relaciones Exteriores, 1940.

Higham, John. *Strangers in the Land: Patterns of American Nativism, 1860-1925.* New York: Atheneum, 1972.

Hoffman, Abraham. *Unwanted Mexican Americans in the Great Depression: Repatriation Pressures, 1929-1939.* Tucson: University of Arizona Press, 1974.

Howland, Charles P., ed. *Survey of American Foreign Relations.* New Haven: Yale University Press, 1929.

Jerome, Harry. *Migration and Business Cycles.* New York: National Bureau of Economic Research, 1926.

Jones, Robert C. *Mexican War Workers in the United States: The Mexico-United States Manpower Recruiting Program, 1942-1944.* Washington, D.C.: Pan American Union, 1945.

Kibbe, Pauline R. "The Economic Plight of Mexicans." *Ethnic Relations in the United States.* Edited by Edward C. McDonagh and Eugene S. Richards. New York: Appleton-Century-Crofts, 1953.

Levenstein, Harvey A. *Labor Organizations in the United States and Mexico: A History of Their Relations.* Westport, Connecticut: Greenwood Press, 1971.

Lipschultz, Robert J. *American Attitudes Toward Mexican Immigration.* San Francisco: R and E Research Associates, 1971.

Lopez, Malo 'Ernesto. *Emigrantes. El Problema de los Trabajadores Mexicanos.* Mexico D. F.: Universidad de Mexico, 1954.

Martinez, John R. *Mexican Immigration to the United States, 1910-1930.* San Francisco: R and E Research Associates, 1971.

McBride, John. *Vanishing Bracero: Valley Revolution.* San Antonio, Texas: The Naylor Company, 1963.

McClellan, A. C. *Down in the Valley: A Supplementary Report on Developments in the Wetback and Bracero Situation of the Lower Rio Grande Valley of Texas Since Publication of "What Price Wetbacks?"* Austin, Texas: Texas State Federation of Labor, 1953.

McCune, Wesley. *The Farm Bloc.* New York: Doubleday, Doran and Company, 1943.

McConnell, Grant. *The Decline of Agrarian Democracy.* Berkeley: University of California Press, 1953.

McWilliams, Carey. *Factories in the Fields: The Story of Migratory Farm Labor in California.* Boston: Little Brown and Co., 1944.

———. *Ill Fares the Land: Migrants and Migratory Labor in the United States.* Boston: Little, Brown and Co., 1942.

Messessmith, James C. *Illegal Entrants and Illegal Aliens in the United States.* Carbondale: Southern Illinois University, 1958.

Mexico, Departamento de Informacion para el Extranjero. *Advice to the Mexican Laborers Who Go to the United States.* Contracted by the War Food Administration, Mexico, 1944.

Mexico. Secretaria de Relaciones Exteriores. Mexico. *La Proteccion de Mexicanos en Los Estados Unidos.* Mexico D.F.: Talleres Graficos de la Naction, 1940.

Moore, Truman. *The Slaves We Rent.* New York: Random House, 1965.

Morgan, Patricia. *Shame of a Nation: A Documented Story of Police-State Terror Against Mexican-Americans in the U.S.A.* Los Angeles: Los Angeles Committee for the Protection of the Foreign Born, 1954.

Myers, John Myers. *The Border Wardens.* Englewood Cliffs, New Jersey: Prentice-Hall, Inc., 1971.

Nelson, Eugene, comp. *Pablo Cruz and the American Dream: The Experiences of an Undocumented Immigrant from Mexico.* Peregrine Smith, 1975.

Newton, Horace E. *Mexican Illegal Immigration into California, Principally Since 1945.* San Francisco: R and E Research Associates, 1973.

Norquest, Carrol. *Rio Grande Wetbacks: Migrant Mexican Workers.* Albuquerque, New Mexico: University of New Mexico Press, 1971.

Parmet, Herbert S. *Eisenhower and the American Crusades.* New York: MacMillan, 1972.

Peon, Maximo (pseudonym). *Como Viven los Mexicanos en los Estados Unidos.* Mexico: 1966.

Perales, Alonso S., comp. *Are We Good Neighbors?* San Antonio, Texas: Artes Graficas, 1948.

Piño, Frank. *Mexican Americans: A Research Bibliography.* Vol. 1 and 2. East Lansing, Michigan: Latin American Studies Center, Michigan State University, 1974.

Radtke, T. J. *The Wetback Situation in the Rio Grande Valley.* Corpus Christi, Texas: Report of the Bishop's Committee for the Spanish-Speaking, August 1950.

Rasmussen, Wayne D. *A History of the Emergency Farm Labor Supply Program, 1943-1947.* Washington: United States Department of Agriculture, Bureau of Agricultural Economics, Government Printing Office, 1941.

Reisler, Mark. *By the Sweat of Their Brow: Mexican Immigration, 1900-1940.* Westport, Connecticut: Greenwood Press, 1975.

Rios-Bustamante, Antonio Jose. *Immigration and Public Policy: Human Rights for Undocumented Workers and Their Families.* Chicano Studies Center Document No. 5. Berkeley: Chicano Studies Center-Publications, 1978.

Robinson, Cecil. *With the Ears of Strangers.* Tucson: University of Arizona Press, 1963.

Salinas, Jose Lazaro. *La Emigracion de Braceros: Vision Objetica de un Problema Mexicano.* Mexico D.F.: Cuauhtemoc, 1955.

Samora, Julian. *Los Mojados: The Wetback Story*. South Bend, Ind.: University of Notre Dame, 1971.

——, ed. *La Raza: Forgotten Americans*. South Bend: University of Notre Dame, 1966.

Schwartz, Harry. *Seasonal Farm Labor in the United States*. New York: Columbia University Press, 1945.

Scott, Robert E. *Mexican Government in Transition*. Rev. ed. Urbana: University of Illinois Press, 1964.

Stein, Walter J. *California and the Dust Bowl Migration*. Westport, Connecticut: Greenwood Press, 1973.

Steiner, Stan. *La Raza: The Mexican Americans*. New York: Harper and Row, 1969.

Tannenbaum, Frank. *The Struggle for Peace and Bread*. New York: Alfred A. Knopf, 1950.

Tweeten, Luther. *Foundations of Farm Policy*. Lincoln: University of Nebraska Press, 1970.

U.S. Bureau of Employment Security. Farm Placement Service. *Information Concerning Entry of Mexican Agricultural Workers into the United States*. Washington, D.C., 1952.

Wylie, Kathryn H. *Mexico as a Market and Competition for the United States Agricultural Products*. New York: Alfred A. Knopf, 1960.

THESES AND DISSERTATIONS

Campbell, Howard L. "Bracero Migration and the Mexican Economy, 1951-1964." Ph.D. dissertation, American University, 1972.

Carney, John P. "Postwar Mexican Migration, 1945-1955: With Particular Reference to the Policies and Practices of the United States Concerning Its Control." Master's thesis, University of Southern California, 1956-1957.

Coalson, George O. "The Development of the Migratory Farm Labor System in Texas, 1900-1954." Ph.D. dissertation, University of Oklahoma, 1955.

Elac, John C. "The Employment of Mexican Workers in United States Agriculture, 1900-1960: A Binational Economic Analysis." Ph.D. dissertation, University of California, Los Angeles, May 1961.

Graves, Ruth Parker. "A History of the Interrelationships between Imported Mexican Labor, Domestic Migrants, and the Texas Agricultural Economy." Master's thesis, The University of Texas at Austin, 1960.

Jarnagin, Richard Tait. "The Effect of Increased Illegal Mexican Migration upon the Organization and Operations of the United States Immigration Border Patrol, Southwest Region." Master's thesis, University of Southern California, January 1957.

Kirstein, Peter N. "Anglo over Bracero: A History of the Mexican Worker in the United States from Roosevelt to Nixon." Ph.D. dissertation, Washington University, St. Louis, Missouri, 1973.

Lipschultz, Robert J. "American Attitudes Toward Mexican Immigration, 1924-1952." Ph.D. dissertation, University of Chicago, 1961-1962.

Lyon, Richard M. "The Legal Status of American and Mexican Migratory Farm Labor: An Analysis of United States Farm Labor Legislation, Policy and Administration." Ph.D. dissertation, Cornell University, 1954.

Massey, Ellis Leonard. "Migration of the Spanish-Speaking People of Hidalgo County." Master's thesis, University of Texas, 1953.

Meador, Bruce S. "Wetback Labor in the Lower Rio Grande Valley." Master's thesis, University of Texas, 1951.

Moore, Woodrow. "El problema de la emigracion de los braceros." Master's thesis, Universidad Nacional Autonoma de Mexico, 1961.

McBride, Sister Mary Ann Patrick. "A History of the Bracero Program in California." Ph.D. dissertation, University of Notre Dame, 1975.

McCain, John. "Contract Labor as a Factor in U.S.-Mexican Relations, 1942-1947." Ph.D. dissertation, University of Texas, 1970.

Pheiffer, David G. "The Mexican Farm Labor Supply Program: Its Friends and Foes." Master's thesis, The University of Texas at Austin, 1963.

Scruggs, Otey M. "A History of Mexican Agricultural Labor in the United States, 1942-1954." Ph.D. dissertation, Harvard University, 1959.

Thomas, Sister Mary E. "A Study of the Causes and Consequences of the Economic Status of Migratory Farm Workers in Illinois, Indiana, Michigan, and Wisconsin, 1940-1958." Ph.D. dissertation, University of Notre Dame, 1959-1960.

Tomasek, Robert D. "The Political and Economic Implications of Mexican Labor in the United States under the Non-Quota System, Contract Labor Program, and Wetback Movement." Ph.D. dissertation, University of Michigan, 1957.

Vargas y Campos, Gloria R. "El problema del bracero mexicano." Ph.D. dissertation, Universidad Nacional Autonoma de Mexico, 1964.

PUBLIC DOCUMENTS AND
GOVERNMENT PUBLICATIONS

Direccion General de Estadistica. *Compendido Estadistico, 1951.* Mexico City: Secretaria de Economia, 1952.

——. *Compendido Estadistico, 1952.* Mexico City: Secretaria de Economia, 1953.

Jones, Robert C. *Los braceros mexicanos en los estados unidos durante el periodo belico.* Washington, D.C.: Union Panamericana, 1946.

President's Commission on Migratory Labor. *Migratory Labor in American Agriculture.* Washington, D.C.: U.S. Government Printing Office, 1951.

President's Commission on Migratory Labor. Stenographic Report of the Phoenix, Arizona, *Hearings on Migratory Labor.* Washington, D.C.: Ward and Paul Official Reporters, 1950.

Report of the President's Commission on Immigration and Naturalization. *Whom We Shall Welcome.* Washington, D.C.: Government Printing Office, January 1, 1953.

U.S. Bureau of Employment Security. *Information Concerning Entry of Mexican Agricultural Workers into the United States.* Washington, D.C.: Bureau of Employment Security, Farm Placement Bureau, 1952.

U.S. Congress, House, Committee on Agriculture. *Extension of Mexican Farm Labor Program: Hearings on H.R. 3480.* 83d Congress, 1st session, 24, 25, and 26 March 1953. Washington, D.C.: Government Printing Office, 1953.

——. *Farm Labor: Hearings on H.R. 2955, H.R. 3048.* 82d Congress, 1st session, 8-14 March 1951. Washington, D.C.: Government Printing Office, 1951.

——. *Mexican Farm Labor: Hearings on H.J. Res. 355.* 83d Congress, 2d session, 3, 5, 8, 9, 10 and 11 February 1954. Washington, D.C.: Government Printing Office, 1954.

——. *Mexican Farm Labor Program: Hearings before Subcommittee on H.R. 3822.* 84th Congress, 1st session, 16-22 March 1955. Washington, D.C.: Government Printing Office, 1955.

——. Report No. 1199, "Mexican Agricultural Workers." 83d Congress, 2d session, 12 February 1954. Washington, D.C.: Government Printing Office, 1954.

U.S. Congress. House. Committee on Appropriations. *Hearings* before the Subcommittee of the Committee on Appropriation for Departments of State and Justice, the Judiciary, and Related Agencies' Appropriations for 1956. 84th Congress, 1st session, 1955.

U.S. Congress. House. Committee on Appropriations. *Mexican Farm Labor Program, 1954.* *Hearings* before subcommittees of the Committee on Appropriations, House of Representatives, on H.R. 355. 83d Congress, 2d session, 1954.

U.S. Congress. House. Committee on the Judiciary. *Hearings Before the President's Commission on Immigration and Naturalization,* September and October 1952. 82d Congress, 2d session. Washington, D.C.: Government Printing Office, 1952.

U.S. Congress. House. *Improper Use of Government Equipment and Government Personnel* (Immigration and Naturalization Service). Twenty-Sixth Intermediate Report of the Committee on Government Operations. 84th Congress, 2d session. House Report No. 2948. Washington, D.C.: Government Printing Office, 1956.

U.S. Congress. House. *Mexican Agricultural Workers,* House Report No. 1199. 83d Congress, 2d session, 1954.

U.S. Congress. House. *Mexican Farm Labor Program. Hearings* before subcommittee on Equipment, Supplies, and Manpower of Committee on Agriculture. 84th Congress, 1st session, 1955.

U.S. Congress. House. *Reorganization of the Immigration and Naturalization Service.* Hearings before the subcommittee on Legal and Monetary Affairs of the Committee on Government Operations. 84th Congress, 1st session, 9 and 17 March 1955. Washington, D.C.: Government Printing Office, 1955.

U.S. Congress. House. Subcommittee on Legal and Monetary Affairs of the Committee on Government Operations. *Hearings, Reorganization of the Immigration and Naturalization Service.* 84th Congress, 1st session, 1955.

U.S. Congress. Senate. *Importation of Foreign Agricultural Workers,* Senate Report No. 214. 82d Congress, 1st session, 1951.

U.S. Congress, Senate, Committee on Agriculture and Forestry. *Extension of the Mexican Farm Labor Program: Hearings on S. 1207.* 83d Congress, 1st session, 23 and 24 March 1953. Washington, D.C.: Government Printing Office, 1953.

——. *Farm Labor: Hearings on S. 949, S. 984, and S. 1106.* 82d Congress, 1st session, 13-16 March 1951. Washington, D.C.: Government Printing Office, 1951.

——. Report No. 214, "Importation of Foreign Agricultural Workers." 82d Congress, 1st session, 11 April 1951. Washington, D.C.: Government Printing Office, 1951.

U.S. Congress. Senate. Committee on the Judiciary. *Report. The Immigration and Naturalization Systems of the United States.* Washington, D.C.: Government Printing Office, 1950.

U.S. Senate. Committee on the Judiciary. *To Control Illegal Immigration.* Hearings before the subcommittee on Immigration and Naturalization of the Committee on the Judiciary. Senate Documents 3660 and 3661. 83d Congress, 2d session, 12-14 July 1954.

U.S. Congress. Senate. Committee on Labor and Labor-Management Relations. *Migratory Labor, Part I.* Hearings before Subcommittee, 82d Congress, 2d session. 5, 6, 7, 11, 14, 15, 27, 28, 29 February and 27, 28 March 1952. Washington, D.C.: Government Printing Office, 1952.

U.S. Congress. Senate. *Migratory Labor.* Hearings before the subcommittee on Labor and Labor Management Relations of the Committee on Labor and Public Welfare. 82d Congress, 2d session, Part I, February-March 1952.

U.S. Congress. Senate. *Report. Admission of Foreign Agricultural Workers.* 81st Congress, 1st session, 1949.

U.S., *Congressional Record,* 1948-1956.

U.S. Department of Justice. *Annual Reports of the Commissioner General of Immigration.* 1946-1956. Washington, D.C.: Government Printing Office.

U.S. Department of Justice. Immigration and Naturalization Service. *Annual Report of the Commissioner of Immigration and Naturalization, 1946.* Washington, D.C.: Government Printing Office, 1946.

U.S. Department of Justice. *Annual Report of the Immigration and Naturalization Service, 1954.* Washington, D.C.: 1954.

U.S. Department of Justice. *Annual Report of the Immigration and Naturalization Service, 1955.* Washington, D.C.: 1955.

U.S. Department of Justice. *The Immigration Border Patrol.* Washington, D.C.: Government Printing Office, 1952.

U.S. Department of Justice. Immigration and Naturalization Service. *Border Patrol Management.* Washington, D.C.: Government Printing Office, 1955.

U.S. Department of Justice. Immigration and Naturalization Service. *Mexican Agricultural Laborers Admitted and Mexican Aliens Located in Illegal Status, Years Ended June 30, 1949-1967.* Washington, D.C.: Government Printing Office, 1968.

U.S. Department of Labor. *Selected References on Domestic Migratory Agricultural Workers, Their Families, Problems, and Programs, 1955-1960.* Washington, D.C.: Government Printing Office, 1961.

U.S. Department of State. "United States and Mexico Reach Agreement on Agricultural Workers." United States Department of State Bulletin 24 (19 February 1951).

U.S. Federal Interagency Committee on Migrant Labor. *Migrant Labor: A Human Problem: Report and Recommendations.* Washington, D.C.: Department of Labor, 1947.

U.S. House Committee on Agriculture. *Mexican Farm Labor.* Washington, D.C.: Government Printing Office, 1952.

U.S. House. Committee on the Judiciary. *Illegal Alien's Hearings.* 92d Congress, 1st and 2d sessions (1971-1972), five parts. Washington, D.C.: Government Printing Office, 1971-1972.

NEWSPAPERS

Caller-Times (Corpus Christi, Texas), 1953-1954.
El Universal (Mexico), 1951-1954.
Excelsior (Mexico), 1953-1954.
Novedades (Mexico), 1951-1954.
New York Times, 1952-1956.
Reporter, 1953-1954.
San Antonio Express, 1953-1954.
San Antonio Light, 1953-1954.
San Diego Union, 1953-1954.
San Francisco Chronicle, 1953-1954.
Valley Evening Monitor (McAllen, Texas), 1953-1954.

UNPUBLISHED MATERIALS

Cardenas, Gilbert. "United States Immigration Policy and Mexican Immigration." South Bend, Ind.: Notre Dame, Centros de Estudios Chicanos y Investigaciones, September, 1974.

Central Files of the White House. Migratory Labor File, Box 634, Folder 124-C. Dwight D. Eisenhower Library, Abilene, Kansas.

Central Files of the White House. Migratory Labor File, Box 968, Folder 126-J. Dwight D. Eisenhower Library, Abilene, Kansas.

Columbia University Oral History Project. Oral History Interview with Herbert Brownell, Volume 3 (5 May 1967). Dwight D. Eisenhower Library, Abilene, Kansas.

Columbia University Oral History Project. Oral History Interview with Arthur Watkins (4 January 1968). Dwight D. Eisenhower Library, Abilene, Kansas.

Dwight D. Eisenhower. Central Files of the White House. General File, Box 968. Dwight D. Eisenhower Library, Abilene, Kansas.

Dwight D. Eisenhower. Central Files of the White House. Official File, Boxes 127, 151, 152, 153, 165, and 334. Dwight D. Eisenhower Library, Abilene, Kansas.

Dwight D. Eisenhower. White House Records Office. Bill File. Reports to the President on Pending Legislation (9 March through 26 March 1954), Box 16. Dwight D. Eisenhower Library, Abilene, Kansas.

Dwight D. Eisenhower. White House Records Office. Bill File. Reports to the President on Pending Legislation (6 August through 9 August 1955), Box 60. Dwight D. Eisenhower Library, Abilene, Kansas.

Elac, John C. "The Employment of Mexican Workers in U.S. Agriculture, 1900-1960: A Binational Economic Analysis." Los Angeles: University of California, May 1961.

Harry W. Frantz Papers, 1954-1961. Box 1. Dwight D. Eisenhower Library, Abilene, Kansas.

James P. Mitchell Papers, Secretary of Labor, 1953-1961. Box 46. Dwight D. Eisenhower, Abilene, Kansas.

Joseph Dodge Papers, Bureau of Budget, 1953-1954. Dwight D. Eisenhower Library, Abilene, Kansas.

National Agricultural Workers Union. *Proceedings: Seventh National Convention of the National Farm Labor Union*. Memphis, Tennessee: 1951.

Sanchez, George I., and Lyle Saunders. "Wetback. A Preliminary Report to the Advisory Committees Study of the Spanish-Speaking People." Xerox copy. The University of Texas, 1949. From the Private Library of Dr. J. Samora

Saunders, Lyle. "Sociological Study of the Wetbacks in the Lower Rio Grande Valley." Proceedings of the Fifth Annual Conference on the Education of the Spanish-Speaking People. Mimeographed. Los Angeles: George Pepperdine College, 1951.

Secretary of Agriculture. Records of the President's Committee on Migratory Labor, 1941-1963. Boxes 1, 2, 3, 4, 78, 89, 94, and 102. Dwight D. Eisenhower Library, Abilene, Kansas.

Special Border Patrol Force. "Wetback, Operation." Vol. 1, General Task Force Information, 1954. Immigration and Naturalization Service Branch, Washington, D.C.

Special Border Patrol Force. "Wetback, Operation." Vol. 3, General Task Force Information, McAllen Section, 1954. Immigration and Naturalization Service Branch, Washington, D.C.

Special Border Patrol Force. "Wetback, Operation." Vol. 4, Part 2, General Task Force Information, California Section 1954. Immigration and Naturalization Service Branch, Washington, D.C.

Special Border Patrol Force. "Wetback, Operation." Vol. 5, General Task Force Information, San Antonio Section, 1954. Immigration and Naturalization Service Branch, Washington, D.C.

Special Border Patrol Force. "Wetback, Operation." Vol. 7, Part 1, General Task Force Information, California Section, 1954. Immigration and Naturalization Service Branch, Washington, D.C.

Special Border Patrol Force. "Wetback, Operation." Vol. 9, General Task Force Information, 1954. Immigration and Naturalization Service Branch. Washington, D.C.

U.S. Department of Justice. Files of the Attorney General and the Commissioner of Immigration and Naturalization. Located in Justice Department, Washington, D.C.

U.S. Department of Labor. Office of the Secretary. Departmental Subject Files, 1953, Mexican Labor Program (July-December), Record Group 174, Box 6. National Archives, Washington, D.C.

U.S. Department of Labor. Office of the Secretary. Departmental Subject Files, 1955, Messages-Public Relations Material, Record Group 174, Box 94. National Archives, Washington, D.C.

U.S. Department of Labor. Office of the Secretary. Departmental Subject Files, 1956, Mexican Labor Right-to-Work File, Record Group 174, Box 140. National Archives, Washington, D.C.

U.S. Department of Labor. Office of the Secretary. Messages-Solicitor's Office, 1954, Migrant Labor Program File, Record Group 174, Box 54. National Archives, Washington, D.C.

U.S. Department of Labor. Office of the Secretary. Organization Subject Files, 1954, Committees (Labor Department and Interdepartmental Correspondence) File, Record Group 174, Box 68. National Archives, Washington, D.C.

U.S. Department of Labor. Office of the Secretary. Organization Subject Files, 1954, Committees (Labor Department) File, Record Group 174, Box 18, National Archives, Washington, D.C.

U.S., Office of Labor. Record Group 224, 1947, Box 114. National Archives, Washington, D.C.

"Wetbacks and Mexican National Agreements." San Francisco: 1953. *The Commonwealth* 29, no. 16, pt. 2, Commonwealth Club of California, Hotel St. Francis.

William P. Rogers Papers, Attorney General, 1938-1962. Boxes 9, 10, and 30. Dwight D. Eisenhower Library, Abilene, Kansas.

Index

ABOUT THE AUTHOR

JUAN RAMON GARCÍA is Associate Professor of History and Director of the Chicano Studies program at the University of Michigan-Flint. He has written several studies and articles on Mexican-American history.